Political Science

Political Science
An Introduction

Seventh Edition

Michael G. Roskin
Lycoming College

Robert L. Cord
Northeastern University

James A. Medeiros

Walter S. Jones

Prentice Hall, Upper Saddle River, New Jersey 07458

Library of Congress Cataloging-in-Publication Data

Political science: an introduction/Michael G. Roskin ... [et al.].
  —7th ed.
     p.   cm.
    Includes bibliographical references and index.
    ISBN 0-13-020872-8
    1. Political science.   I. Roskin, Michael.
JA71.P623   1999
320—dc21   99-15765
                            CIP

Editorial director: Charlyce Jones Owen
Editor in chief: Nancy Roberts
Senior acquisitions editor: Beth Gillett Mejia
Associate editor: Nicole Conforti
Editorial assistant: Brian Prybella
Marketing manager: Christopher DeJohn
Editorial/production supervision: Kari Callaghan Mazzola
Electronic page makeup: Kari Callaghan Mazzola and John P. Mazzola
Interior design: John P. Mazzola
Cover director: Jayne Conte
Cover design: Bruce Kenselaar
Cover photo: Robert Stanton/Tony Stone Images
Buyer: Ben Smith

This book was set in 10/12 Meridien by Big Sky Composition
and was printed and bound by Courier Companies, Inc.
The cover was printed by Phoenix Color Corp.

Printed in the United States of America
10 9 8 7 6 5 4 3 2 1

ISBN 0-13-020872-8

PRENTICE-HALL INTERNATIONAL (UK) LIMITED, *London*
PRENTICE-HALL OF AUSTRALIA PTY. LIMITED, *Sydney*
PRENTICE-HALL CANADA INC., *Toronto*
PRENTICE-HALL HISPANOAMERICANA, S.A., *Mexico*
PRENTICE-HALL OF INDIA PRIVATE LIMITED, *New Delhi*
PRENTICE-HALL OF JAPAN, INC., *Tokyo*
PEARSON EDUCATION ASIA PTE. LTD., *Singapore*
EDITORA PRENTICE-HALL DO BRASIL, LTDA., *Rio de Janeiro*

Contents

8   Public Opinion   128

Part III   Political Interactions

9   Political Communication and the Media   149

10 Interest Groups 169

11 Political Parties and Party Systems 189

15   Executives   266

16   Administration and Bureaucracy   286

17   Legal Systems and the Courts   304

Part V   What Political Systems Do

21   The Global System   374

Index   390

Preface

It is indeed gratifying to see a book one has worked on reach a seventh edition; it means one is doing something right. It also means that the editors at Prentice Hall recognize that the basic approach used in the first edition, published in 1974, was sound and should not be greatly altered. The success of this book owes something to the fact that it is neither a U.S. government text nor a comparative politics text. Instead, it draws from both U.S. and comparative examples to introduce the whole field of political science to new students.

The seventh edition continues with an eclectic approach that avoids selling any single theory, conceptual framework, or paradigm as the key to political science. Attempts to impose a methodological grand design are unwarranted by the nature of the discipline and are not conducive to the broadening of students' intellectual horizons. Instructors with a wide variety of viewpoints will have no trouble using this text. Above all, the seventh edition still views politics as exciting and tries to communicate that feeling to young people approaching the discipline for the first time.

New to This Edition

Although the basic structure of the text has remained the same, the seventh edition is the most extensive revision of the text since it first appeared in 1974, due in part to the suggestions of Prentice Hall political science editor Beth Gillett Mejia, who keeps close track of shifting interests in the field. Heeding her recommendations and the comments of outside reviewers, I have expanded the treatment of political theories, political economy, and international relations. Chapters have been recast to reflect the many changes of the past few years, and many new instructional devices have been added to help the student read and review the material.

Content and Organization

Every chapter has been edited to include new material and to take out repetitive and outdated material. Students and professors will note that this edition of the book has not increased in length, and that the material presented is more concise. In addition, the following changes in content and organization have been made:

- The Chapter 1 of previous editions has been split into a new Chapter 1, which is a general introduction to the field, and a new Chapter 2, which expands the coverage of political theories.
- Chapter 5 has been totally recast to discuss democratization.
- Chapter 18, which focused on "Public Policy" in previous editions, has been refocused to "Political Economy."
- A new Chapter 21 concentrates on "The Global System" and what globalization means for U.S. foreign policy.

Instructional Features

A series of boxed features throughout the text help emphasize concepts and definitions as well as provide interesting information about countries, cultures, and personalities:

- Key Concepts boxes: These features help students understand important concepts in political science.
- Classic Works boxes: These features give students some background in classic theories about political science.
- Case Studies boxes: These brief studies help students put concepts into context by providing specific examples.
- Other boxes: Other boxed material highlights personalities and cultural information for students as they read and review the text.

Also, in response to reviewer feedback, marginal definition boxes—Key Terms boxes—have been added to build vocabulary and further reinforce key terms and definitions throughout the text. *Note*: The definitions provided are in the context under discussion; change that context and you may need another definition. There is a difference, for example, between the governing elites discussed in Chapter 5 (a tiny fraction of 1 percent of a population) and public-opinion elites discussed in Chapter 8 (probably several percent).

End-of-Chapter Materials

The end-of-chapter materials have been revised and expanded as follows for the seventh edition:

- Key Terms: For further review, a list of key terms has been added to the end of each chapter. (The page number that follows each listed key term indicates the page upon which the corresponding marginal definition box appears.)
- Key Websites: An annotated list of key website addresses has been added to the end of each chapter to help students with further research.

■ Further Reference: Each chapter now ends with a brief section listing materials for further reference instead of endnotes.

Companion Website

www.prenhall.com/roskin   This brand new website brings an online study guide to students, absolutely free. When students log on they will find a wealth of study and research resources. Chapter outline and summary information, true/false tests, fill-in-the-blank tests, and multiple-choice tests, all with immediate feedback and chapter page numbers, give students ample opportunity to review the information. Also, each chapter has links to additional resources for further research, information on writing in political science, and resources for resume, job, and internship information.

Acknowledgments

Several people reviewed this and earlier editions, and I sincerely considered most of their comments. For this edition, I wish to thank David Rapoport, UCLA; Michael Curtis, Rutgers; Don Tanenbaum, Gettysburg College; Shari L. Lyes, Palm Beach Community College; David C. Saffell, Ohio Northern University; Thomas P. Dolan, Georgia State University; Henry P. French, Jr., SUNY–Monroe; Robert A. Wood, North Dakota State University; Kay M. Knickrehm, James Madison University; Rekha Datta, Monmouth University; Daniel W. O'Connell, Palm Beach Community College; and Bonita A. Sessing-Matcha, Hudson Valley Community College.

Instructors' input on changes to the text—or indeed on anything else related to the text or supplementary materials—is highly valued. Instructors may contact me directly at Lycoming College, Williamsport, Pennsylvania 17701, or by e-mail, roskin@lycoming.edu.

Michael G. Roskin

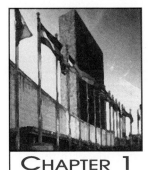

CHAPTER 1

A Science of Politics?

Interest in politics in the United States has slumped. Not only students but also attentive and educated citizens have turned away from politics. People are more likely to talk about sports and the stock market than about politics. The mass media find the strongest viewer and reader interest in health and business news, lifestyles, and famous personalities. National and international political news is less interesting; many don't care at all.

This itself should be a major topic of investigation by political scientists. Is it a general disgust with politicians and their constant, empty struggle for partisan advantage? Is it a feeling of helplessness, that individual citizens don't matter? Is it the perception that Washington is the playground of rich and powerful interest groups who simply buy whatever they want, including politicians? Or is it a healthy sign that in relatively good times people naturally turn to other concerns? If the economy is doing well and the Cold War is over, why follow politics? Perhaps threats and worries are needed to generate interest in politics.

QUESTIONS TO CONSIDER
1. Why is politics now out of favor?
2. What does it mean to "never get angry at a fact"?
3. What did Aristotle mean in calling politics "the master science"?
4. What did Machiavelli bring to the study of politics?
5. How are legitimacy, sovereignty, and authority different but similar?
6. Is politics largely biological, psychological, cultural, rational, or irrational?
7. How can something as messy as politics be a science?
8. What is a "provable thesis"?

It is the thesis of this book that politics still matters. If you do not take an interest and participate, others will, and they will influence the decisions that govern your life. Will they take us to war in a distant part of the globe? Who might have to fight in that war? You. Will they alter the tax code to favor one group of citizens? Who will have to pay in taxes what others avoid paying? You. Will they set up federal programs with costs escalating far beyond what anyone had foreseen? Who then will have to pay those costs? You. One of the objectives of this book is to make you aware of what politics is, how it works, and why it matters, so that you may look after yourself and prevent others from misusing you.

Note: The chapter-opener photo (here and throughout) is from the United Nations: UN Photo 185522/A. Brizzi (January 1995).

Many find politics distasteful, and perhaps they are right. Politics may be inherently immoral, or at any rate amoral. Misuse of power, influence peddling, and outright corruption are prominent features of politics. But you don't have to like the thing you study. A biologist may behold a disease-causing bacterium under a microscope. He or she doesn't "like" the bacterium but is interested in how it grows, how it does its damage, and how it may be eradicated. Neither does the biologist get angry at the bacterium and smash the glass slide with a hammer. The biologist first understands the forces of nature and then works with them to try to improve humankind's existence. Political scientists try to do the same with politics.

The Master Science

Aristotle, the founder of the **discipline** of political science, called politics "the master science." He meant that almost everything happens in a political context, that the decisions of the *polis* (the Greek city-state) governed most other things. Politics, in the words of Yale's Harold Lasswell, is the study of "who gets what." But doesn't the economic system determine who gets what in countries with free markets? Yes, but who determines if we shall have a free-market system? Who tells Bill Gates that he may or may not

Key Concepts — NEVER GET ANGRY AT A FACT

Never get angry at a fact. This basic point of all serious study sounds like common sense but is often ignored, even in college courses. It actually traces back to the extremely complex thought of the German philosopher Hegel, who argued that things happen not by caprice or accident but for good and sufficient reasons: "Whatever is real is rational." That means that we should be able, by the application of our reason, to figure out why things are so. We study politics in a "naturalistic" mode, not getting angry at what we see but trying to understand how it came to be.

For example, we hear of a politician who took money from an interest group. As political scientists, we push our anger to the side and ask questions like: Do most politicians in that country take money? Is it an old tradition? Does the culture of this country accept and even expect politicians to take money? How big are campaign expenses? Can the politician possibly run for office without taking money? In short, we see if extralegal exchanges of cash are part and parcel of the political system. If they are, it makes no sense to get angry at an individual politician. If we don't like it, we may then consider how the system might be changed to discourage the taking of money on the side. And reforms may not work. Notice how reforms in Japan's electoral laws did not stamp out its traditional "money politics." Like bacteria, some things in politics have lives of their own.

bundle his Internet access with his latest Windows, a decision worth billions of dollars? Politics is intimately connected to economics.

Suppose something utterly natural occurs, like a flood. It is the political system that decides whether and where to build dikes and whether and which of the flood victims to aid. Yes, the flood is natural, but its impact on society is controlled in large part by politics. How about science, our bacteriologist squinting through a microscope? That isn't political. But who funds the scientists' education and their research institutes? It could be private charity (the donors of which get tax breaks), but chances are the government plays a major role. When the U.S. government decided that AIDS research deserved top priority, funding for other programs was cut. Bacteria and viruses may be natural, but studying them is often quite political. In this case, it pitted gays against women concerned with breast cancer. Who gets what: funding to find a cure for AIDS or for breast cancer? The choice is political.

Because almost everything is political, studying politics means studying nearly everything. Some students select "interdisciplinary majors." Political science already is one, borrowing from and overlapping with all of the other social sciences. At times, it is hard to tell where history, human geography, economics, sociology, anthropology, and psychology leave off and political science begins. Here, briefly, is how political science relates to the other social sciences.

History

History is one of the chief sources of data for political scientists. When we discuss the politics of the Third French Republic (1871–1940), the growth of presidential power under Franklin Roosevelt, and even something as recent as the Cold War, we are studying history. But historians and political scientists look for different things and handle data differently. Typically, historians study one episode in careful detail, digging up all the documents, archives, and diaries they can find on the topic. With masses of data focused on just one point, they offer few or no generalizations. Political scientists, on the other hand, begin by looking for generalizations. We often take the findings of historians and compare and contrast them. A historian might do a detailed study of Weimar Germany (1919–1933); a political scientist might put that study alongside studies of France, Italy, and Russia of the same period to see what similarities and dissimilarities can be found. To be sure, some historians do comparative studies; we promote them to the rank of political scientist.

Human Geography

Human geography (as distinct from physical geography) has in recent decades been neglected by political scientists, although it influences their work more than many realize. The territorial component of human behavior—such as borders, ethnic areas, trade flows, centralization of power, and regions—have great political ramifications. Strife in Northern Ireland, Chechnya, and Kosovo are heavily geographical problems, as is Canada's unsettled federalism, from which Quebec may someday depart. French political scientist André Siegfried pioneered the use of maps to explain regional political variations, a technique of today's electoral studies.

Economics

Economics, proclaim some economists, is the subject matter of politics. (Political scientists are apt to claim the opposite.) True, many political quarrels are indeed economic: who gets what. Sufficient economic development may be the basis for democracy; few poor countries are democratic. A declining economy may doom democracy, as in the case of the Weimar Republic (and possibly that of present-day Russia). What policies promote economic development? How big a role should government have? What will the new *euro* currency do to European union? When economists get into questions of policy, they become "political economists." A relatively new school of political science, "rational-choice theory," borrows the economic perspective that humans do what is in their own interest.

Sociology

Sociology and political science sometimes merge. Sociologist Seymour Martin Lipset is equally renowned as a political scientist. It was he who first demonstrated the close connection between democracy and level of wealth. As we shall consider in the next chapter, political science conventionally starts by looking at society to see "who thinks what" about politics. In demonstrating how political views vary among social classes, regions, religions, genders, and age groups, sociology gives an empirical basis to political-culture, public-opinion, and electoral studies.

Anthropology

Anthropology, which traditionally focused on primitive societies, at first may not seem relevant to political science. But the descriptive and interviewing techniques of anthropology have been heavily adopted by political scientists. The subfield of political culture could be viewed as a branch of anthropology. Japanese deference patterns, which we still see today, were laid down more than a millennium ago. Some current political systems still reserve political power for traditionally influential families or clans. In Central Asia, the families of *emirs* who ruled under the Persians did so under the tsars, the Communists, and now the newly independent states. In Africa, voting and violence follow tribal lines.

Psychology

Psychology, particularly social psychology, contributes much to political science's understanding of which personalities are attracted to politics, why and under what circumstances people obey authority figures, and how people form national, group, and voting attachments. Studies of Hitler, Stalin, or Mao Zedong are almost by definition psychological. Psychologists are among the best **methodologists** of the social sciences; that is, they devise ways to study things objectively and teach us to doubt claims that have holes in them. Asking questions in a "blind" manner and "controlling" for certain factors are techniques developed from psychology.

KEY TERM
methodology The techniques for studying questions objectively.

Political Power

Political science often uses the findings of other social sciences, but one feature distinguishes it from the others—its focus on power. Our second founding father (after Aristotle) is the renaissance Florentine philosopher Niccolò Machiavelli, who emphasized the role of power in politics. You can take all the factors and approaches mentioned, but if you are not using them to study power—which is a very broad subject—you are probably not doing political science.

Some people don't like the concept of **political power**. It smacks of coercion, inequality, occasionally of brutality. Some speakers denounce "power politics," suggesting governance without power, a happy band of brothers and sisters regulating themselves on the basis of love and sharing. Communities formed on such a basis do not last; or if they do last, they transform themselves into conventional structures of leaders and the led, buttressed by obedience patterns that look suspiciously like nasty old power. Political power seems to be built into the human condition. But why do some people hold political power over others? There is no definitive explanation of political power. Biological, psychological, cultural, rational, and irrational explanations have been put forward.

KEY TERMS
political power Ability of one person to get another to do something.
legitimacy Mass feeling that the government's rule is rightful and should therefore be obeyed. (See pp. 6–7.)
sovereignty A national government being boss on its own turf, the last word in law in a given country. (See pp. 6–7.)
authority Political leaders' ability to command respect and exercise power. (See pp. 6–7.)

Biological

Aristotle said it first and perhaps best: "Man is by nature a political animal." (Aristotle's words were *politikon zoon*, which can be translated as either "political animal" or "social animal." The Greeks lived in city-states in which the social system was the same as the political system.) Aristotle meant that humans live naturally in herds, like dolphins or deer. They biologically need each other for sustenance and survival. It is also natural that they array themselves into ranks of leaders and led, like all herd animals. Taking a cue from Aristotle, a modern biological explanation would say that forming a political system and obeying its leaders is innate human behavior, passed on to future generations with one's genes. Some thinkers argue that human politics shows the same "dominance hierarchies" manifested among other mammals.

The advantage of the biological approach is its simplicity, but it raises a number of questions. If we grant that humankind is naturally political, how do we explain the instances when political groups fall apart and people disobey authority? Perhaps we could improve the theory by modifying it: Humans are imperfectly political (or social) animals. Most of the time people form groups and obey authority, but sometimes, under certain circumstances, they don't. This invites the following question: "Which circumstances promote or do not promote the formation of political groups?"

Key Concepts   LEGITIMACY, SOVEREIGNTY, AND AUTHORITY

The three related concepts of **legitimacy**, **sovereignty**, and **authority** are basic to political science. Legitimacy originally meant that the rightful king or queen was on the throne by reason of "legitimate" birth. Since the Middle Ages, the term has broadened to mean not only the "legal right to govern" but also the "psychological right to govern." Legitimacy now refers to people's attitude that the government's rule is rightful. Therefore, even if we do not particularly like our government, we generally obey it. We even pay taxes. One quick test of legitimacy is how many police there are. Few police, as in Sweden and Norway, is a sign that no coercion is needed; legitimacy is high. Many police, as in Franco's Spain or Ceausescu's Romania, is a sign that much coercion is needed; legitimacy is low.

When legitimacy erodes, people feel less obliged to pay their taxes and obey the law because the government itself is perceived as dirty and dishonest. Eventually, massive civil disobedience can break out. As President Mobutu of Zaire (now Congo), President Suharto of Indonesia, and President Ceausescu of Romania discovered, once a regime's legitimacy has disappeared, no amount of coercion can get people to obey.

A government achieves legitimacy by existing a long time. Long-established governments are generally respected by their citizens. The fact that the Constitution is two centuries old confers a great deal of legitimacy on the U.S. government. New governments, on the other hand, have shaky legitimacy; many of their citizens are not quite sure whether or not to respect them.

Second, a government gains legitimacy by governing well. Ensuring economic growth and jobs and dispensing equal justice builds legitimacy. The government of West Germany, founded in 1949 after defeat in World War II, had little legitimacy at first, but level-headed political leadership with sound economic policies gradually earned the Bonn government a good deal of legitimacy. On the other hand, the German Weimar Republic that followed World War I  faced a series of economic and political catastrophes that severely undermined its legitimacy and paved the way for Hitler's rise to power.

Third, the structure of government can also contribute to its legitimacy. If people feel they are fairly represented and have a say in the selection of their officials, they are more likely to obey. Finally, governments shore up their legitimacy by national symbols. The flag, historic monuments, patriotic parades, and ringing speeches aim at convincing people the government is legitimate and should be obeyed. When the other elements of legitimacy have fallen away, however, the manipulation of national symbols may appear to be a hollow joke. A gigantic statue of dictator Marcos of the Philippines became an object of ridicule and a symbol of what was wrong with his regime. Symbols by themselves don't create legitimacy.

Sovereignty (from the Old French "to rule over") originally meant the power of a monarch to rule over his or her kingdom. Later, the term broadened to mean national control over the country's territory, being boss of one's own turf. Nations are very jealous of their sovereignty, and governments take great care to safeguard it. They maintain armies to deter foreign invasion, they control their borders with passports and visas, and they hunt down terrorists.

Disputes over sovereignty get quite nasty: Palestine, Northern Ireland, and Bosnia are a few recent examples. Sovereignty and legitimacy are connected. With a decline of legitimacy may come a decline of sovereignty. Lebanon, for example, was ruled for decades by Christians, even though they were a minority. In the eyes of many Lebanese Muslims, the government lacked

LEGITIMACY, SOVEREIGNTY, AND AUTHORITY (CONTINUED)

legitimacy because it listened mostly to Christian demands and ignored Muslims. In 1975, civil strife broke out as a dozen politico-religious militias battled to assume a leading role. Syria occupied eastern Lebanon in 1976, and Israel occupied southern Lebanon in 1982. Essentially, Lebanon lost its sovereignty (which it is now slowly trying to regain). It could neither control its own territory nor repel foreign invaders. A loss of legitimacy led to a loss of sovereignty.

Authority is the psychological ability of leaders to get others to obey them. It relies on a sense of obligation based on the legitimate power of office. A private obeys a captain; a motorist obeys a state trooper; a student obeys a professor. But not all people obey authority. Some privates are insubordinate, some motorists are speeders, and some students neglect the assigned reading. Still, most people obey what they perceive as legitimate authority most of the time.

Some authority comes with the office, but it must also be cultivated. An American president gets some authority just because he is the president. Gerald Ford was respected even though he was not elected, either as president or vice-president. (Minority leader of the House of Representatives, he became vice-president when Spiro T. Agnew resigned and president when Richard Nixon resigned.) But his elected predecessor, Richard Nixon, implicated in the Watergate scandal of 1972, suffered an erosion of executive authority so acute that he could not effectively govern, so he resigned in 1974 just before a House panel could vote on his impeachment. A president needs the willing consent of Congress, the courts, the civil service, and important interest groups. When Nixon lost this consent, he was finished.

In short, legitimacy means respect for a government, sovereignty respect for a country, and authority respect for a leader. None are automatic; all must be earned. Where you find one, you find the others. Where one erodes, so usually do the others.

The Berlin Wall crumbled in 1989 because the East German regime had totally lost legitimacy. (Michael Roskin)

Psychological

Psychological explanations of politics and obedience are closely allied with biological theories. Both posit needs derived from centuries of evolution in the formation of political groups. The psychologists have refined their views with empirical research. One is the famous Milgram study, in which unwitting subjects were instructed by a professor to administer progressively larger electric shocks to a victim. The "victim," strapped in a chair, was actually an actor who only pretended to suffer. Most of the subjects were willing to administer potentially lethal doses of electricity simply because the "professor"—an authority figure in a white lab smock—told them to do so. Most of the subjects didn't like hurting the victim, but they rationalized that they were just following orders and that any harm done to the victim was really the professor's responsibility. They surrendered their independence of thought and action because an authority figure told them to do so. The Milgram study has been replicated and confirmed in other settings.

Psychological studies also show that most people are naturally conformist. Most members of a group see things a certain way. Psychologist Irving Janis found many of the great mistakes of U.S. foreign and defense policy were made in a climate of "groupthink," a situation in which a leadership group tells itself that all is well and that the present policy is working. Groups tend to ignore nonconformist critics who tell them, for instance, that the Japanese will attack Pearl Harbor in 1941 or that the 1961 Bay of Pigs landing of Cuban exiles will fail. Obedience to authority and groupthink suggest that humans have deep-seated needs—possibly innate—to fit into groups and go along with their norms. Perhaps this is what makes human society possible, but it also makes possible horrors such as the Nazi Holocaust and the more recent Balkan massacres.

Cultural

How much of human behavior is learned as opposed to biologically inherited? This is a very old debate. For much of the twentieth century, the *cultural theorists*—those who believe behavior is learned—dominated. Anthropologists concluded that all differences in behavior were learned. If some societies are cooperative and peaceful, it is because their children have been raised that way. Political communities are formed and hold together on the basis of cultural values transmitted by parents, schools, churches, and the mass media. Political science developed an interesting subfield called *political culture*, and researchers in this field often found that a country's political **culture** was formed by many long-term factors: child rearing, land tenure, economic development, religion, and so forth.

> **KEY TERM**
>
> **culture** Human behavior that is learned as opposed to biologically inherited.

The cultural school maintains that trouble comes when the political system is out of touch with the cultural system, as when the shah of Iran attempted to modernize an Islamic society that did not like Western values and lifestyles. The Iranians threw the shah out and celebrated the return of a medieval-style religious leader, the Ayatollah Khomeini, who voiced the values favored by traditional Iranians. Cultural theories can also be applied to U.S. politics. Ronald Reagan won the presidency twice by articulating the values of religion, family, and self-reliance, which are deeply ingrained into American culture.

The cultural approach to political life contains an optimistic streak. If all human behavior is learned, bad behavior can be unlearned and society improved. Educating young people to be tolerant, cooperative, and just will gradually change a society's culture for the better, according to this view.

Although most thinkers agree that culture contributes a lot to political behavior, the theory has some difficulties. First, where does culture come from? History? Economics? Psychology? Second, if all behavior is cultural, various political systems should be as different from each other as their cultures. But especially in the realm of politics, we see similar political attitudes and patterns in lands with very different cultures. Politicians everywhere, for example, take illegal money.

Rational

Another school of thought approaches politics as largely the application of human **rationality**; that is, people know what they want most of the time, and they have good reasons for doing what they do. Classic political theorists, such as Hobbes and Locke, as we shall see in the next chapter, held that humans form "civil society" because their powers of reason tell them that it is much better than anarchy. To safeguard life and property, people form governments. If those governments become abusive,

KEY TERM
rational Based on the ability to reason.

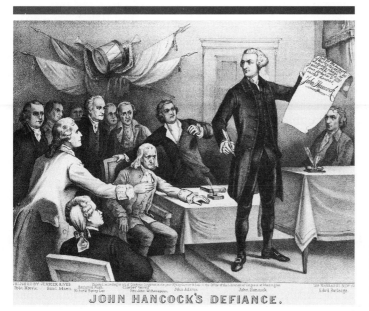

JOHN HANCOCK'S DEFIANCE.

The Declaration of Independence, here being signed in large bold letters by John Hancock, embodied a rational view of politics. (Library of Congress)

the people have the right to dissolve them and start anew. This Lockean notion greatly influenced the U.S. Founding Fathers.

The biological, psychological, and cultural schools downplay human reason, arguing that people are either born or conditioned to do certain things, and individuals seldom think rationally. But then how can we explain those cases in which people break away from group conformity and argue independently? How can we explain a change of mind? "Well, I was for Jones until he came out with his terrible economic policy, so now I'm voting for Smith." People make judgments like that all the time, based at least in part on their ability to reason. A political system based on the presumption of human reason stands a lot better chance of governing justly and humanely. If leaders believe that people obey out of biological inheritance or cultural conditioning, they will think they can get away with all manner of corruption and misrule. If, on the other hand, they believe people are rational, rulers will respect the public's ability to discern wrongdoing. Accordingly, even if people are not completely rational, it is good that rulers fear their possible rationality and their ability to protest misrule.

Irrational

KEY TERM
irrational Based on the power of fears and myths to cloud reason.

Late in the nineteenth century a group of thinkers founded a new school of thought, **irrationalism**, to explain political power. Taking the psychological view that people are basically emotional, dominated by myths and stereotypes, some argue that politics is really the manipulation of symbols. A crowd is like a wild beast that can be whipped up by charismatic leaders to do their bidding. What people regard as rational is really just myth; all you have to do is keep feeding them myths to control them. The first practitioner of this school was Mussolini, founder of fascism in Italy, followed by Hitler in Germany and Perón in Argentina. Stalin also used the techniques of the irrationalists; he transformed himself into a demigod that most Russians worshiped. Both Hitler's friends and enemies portrayed him as a genius at understanding and manipulating the innermost fears and feelings of Germans.

There may be a good deal of truth to the irrational view of human political behavior, but it has catastrophic consequences. Leaders who use irrationalist techniques start believing their own propaganda and eventually lead their nations to devastating war, economic ruin, or slavery. Some detect irrationalism even in the most advanced societies, where much of so-called "reality" is filtered through myths.

Power as a Composite

We can see elements of truth in all these explanations of political power. At different times in different situations, any one of them seems to explain power. The drafters of both the U.S. Declaration of Independence and the Constitution were deeply imbued with the rationalism of their age. Following the philosophers then

popular, they framed their arguments as if human political activity were as logical as Newtonian physics. The late historian Henry Steele Commager referred to
the Constitution as "the crown jewel of the enlightenment," the culmination of
an age of reason.

But how truly rational were they? By the late eighteenth century, the thirteen American colonies had grown culturally separate from Britain. People
thought of themselves as Americans rather than as English colonists. They
increasingly read American newspapers and communicated among themselves
rather than with Britain. Perhaps the separation was more cultural than rational.

Nor can we forget the psychological and irrational factors. Samuel Adams was
a gifted firebrand, Thomas Jefferson a powerful writer, and George Washington a
charismatic general. Did Tom Paine's pamphlet *Common Sense* press rational or
psychological buttons in his readers? It's hard to tell. And that is the point of this
example. The American break with Britain and the founding of a new order is a
complex mixture of all these factors. The same complex mixture of factors goes
into any political system you can mention. To be sure, at times one factor seems
more important than others, but we cannot exactly determine the weight to give
any one factor. And notice how the various factors blend into one another. The
biological factors lead to the psychological, which in turn lead to the cultural, the
rational, and the irrational, forming a seamless web.

One common mistake about political power is to view it as a finite, measur-
able quantity. Power is a connection between people, the ability of one person to
get another to do his or her bidding. Political power does not come in jars or
megawatts. Revolutionaries in some lands speak of "seizing power," as if power
were kept in the national treasury and they could sneak in and grab it at night.
Afghan Communists "seized power" in 1978, but they were a small minority of
the Afghan population. Most Afghanis hated them and refused to cooperate with
them. Some revolutionaries think that they automatically get legitimacy and
authority when they "seize power"; they do not. Power is earned, not seized.

Is power identical to politics? Some power-mad people (including more than
a few politicians) see the two as the same, but this is an oversimplification. We
might see politics as a combination of goals or policies and the power necessary
to achieve them. Power, in this view, is a prime *ingredient* of politics. It would be
difficult to imagine a political system without political power. Even a religious figure who ruled on the basis of love would be exercising power over followers. It
might be "nice power," but it would still be power. Power, then, is a sort of
enabling device to carry out or implement policies and decisions. You can have
praiseworthy goals, but unless you have the power to implement them, they
remain wishful thoughts.

Others see the essence of politics as a *struggle for power*, a sort of gigantic
game in which power is the goal. What, for example, are elections all about?
The getting of power. There is a danger here, however. If power becomes the
goal of politics, devoid of other purposes, it becomes cynical, brutal, and even
self-destructive. The Hitler regime destroyed itself in the worship of power.
Obsessed with retaining presidential power, President Nixon ruined his own

administration. As nineteenth-century British historian and philosopher Lord Acton put it, "Power tends to corrupt; absolute power corrupts absolutely."

Is Politics a Science?

If we cannot pinpoint which factors weigh most heavily in politics, how can politics be a science? Part of the problem here is the definition of *science*. The original meaning of science, from the French, is simply "knowledge." Later, the natural sciences, which rely on precise measurement and mathematical calculation, took over the term. Now most people think of science as precise and factual, supported by experiments and data. Some political scientists (as we will consider later) have in fact attempted to become like natural scientists; they collect **quantified** data and manipulate them statistically to validate **hypotheses.** The quantifiers make some good contributions, but usually they focus on small questions of detail rather than on large questions of meaning. This is because they generally have to stick to areas that can be quantified—public opinion, election returns, and congressional voting.

> ### KEY TERMS
>
> **quantify**   To measure with numbers.
>
> **hypothesis**   An initial theory a researcher starts with, to be proved by evidence.
>
> **empirical**   Based on observable evidence.

But large areas of politics are not quantifiable. How and why do leaders make the decisions they do? Many decisions are made in secret, even in democracies. We don't know exactly how decisions are made in the White House in Washington, the Elysée in Paris, or the Kremlin in Moscow. When a member of Congress votes on an issue, can we be certain why he or she voted that way? Was it constituents' desires, the good of the nation, or the campaign contributions of interest groups? What did the Supreme Court have in mind when it ruled that laying off schoolteachers based on race is unconstitutional but hiring them based on race is not? Try quantifying that. A lot of politics—especially with regard to how and why decisions are made—is just too complex to be quantified.

Does that mean that politics can never be like a natural science? Political science is an **empirical** science that accumulates both quantitative and qualitative data. With such data, we can find persistent patterns, just like in biology. Gradually, one begins to generalize. When the generalizations become firmer, we may call them theories. In a few cases, the theories become so firmly established that we may even call them "laws." In this way, the study of politics accumulates knowledge—and "knowledge" is the original meaning of science.

The Struggle to See Clearly

Political science does resemble a natural science when its researchers, if they are professional, study things as they are and not as they wish them to be. This is more difficult in the study of politics than in the study of stars and molecules. Most political scientists have viewpoints on current issues, and it is very easy to let these views contaminate the analysis of politics. Indeed, precisely because a given question interests us enough to study it indicates that we bring a certain passion with us. Can you imagine setting to work on a study of a topic you cared absolutely nothing about? Some concern is therefore to be expected. There is a certain point, however, at which too much concern renders the study biased; it becomes a partisan outcry rather than a scholarly search for the truth. How can you tell when this happens? The traditional hallmarks of **scholarship** give some guidance. A scholarly work should be *reasoned, balanced*, and supported with *evidence*.

> **KEY TERM**
>
> **scholarship** Balanced intellectual inquiry supported by reason and evidence.

Reasoned   You must spell out your reasoning, and it should make sense. If your perspective is colored by an underlying assumption, you should say so. You might say, "For the purpose of this study, we assume that people are rational" or "This is a study of the psychology of voters in a small town." Your basic assumptions influence what you study and how you study it, but you can minimize bias by honestly stating your assumptions. Early in the twentieth century, German sociologist Max Weber, who contributed so much to all the social sciences, held that any of your findings that come out in support of your own political views must be discarded as biased. Few attempt to be that pure, but Weber's point is well taken: Beware of structuring the study so that it comes out to support a given view.

Balanced   You can also minimize bias by acknowledging that there are other ways of looking at your topic. You should mention the various approaches to your topic and what they have led to. Instructors are impressed that you are familiar with the literature in a given area. They are even more impressed when you can then criticize the various studies and explain why you think they are incomplete or faulty: "The Jones study of voters found them largely apathetic, but this was an off-year election in which turnout is always lower." By putting several approaches and studies side-by-side and stating what you think of them and why, you present a much more objective and convincing case. Do not totally commit yourself to a particular viewpoint or theory, but admit that your view is one among several.

Evidence   All scholarly studies require evidence, ranging from the quantified evidence of the natural sciences to the qualitative evidence of the humanities. Political science utilizes both. Ideally, any statement open to interpretation or controversy should be supported with evidence. Common knowledge does not have to be supported; you need not cite the U.S. Constitution to "prove" the president is inaugurated the January after the election.

But if you say presidents have gained more and more power over the decades, you need to have some evidence. At a minimum, you would cite a leading scholar who has amassed evidence to demonstrate this point. That is called a "secondary source," evidence that has passed through the mind of someone else.

How to Write a Political Science Paper

When writing a political science paper, begin with a clear, punchy thesis: a first sentence giving your main argument, which must be *provable*. It could be something like, "U.S. television advertising makes viewers cynical and indifferent and leads to low voter turnout." If your thesis cannot be proved, it is a bad thesis. Your thesis is more definite than what the paper is "about." This, for example, is no thesis: "This paper is about U.S. policy toward Iran." This is a thesis: "U.S. policy toward Iran was doomed by overreliance on the shah." Your thesis paragraph should be about as long as this one.

Supporting Elements

"Well, that's what I think" isn't good enough. You must bring in evidence to back up your thesis, say, three to five supporting elements. Use *subheads* like the one just above to separate them. This helps you structure your ideas and makes the paper easier to read and understand. If you can't support your thesis with facts, numbers, quotes, or just plain reasoning, abandon or change it: "Back it up or back off."

Accordingly, you will probably not come up with a thesis until you've done some reading and thinking on the subject. When you've done enough reading to develop a thesis, make an outline of the main points your paper will make, like this:

Thesis: Bush's environmental policies created a backlash.

I. What Bush *said* about the environment
   a. 1988 campaign statements
   b. statements after coming to the White House
II. What Bush *did* about the environment
   a. budget cuts for EPA?
   b. people appointed to head EPA
   c. scandals and criticism of EPA
III. Backlash
   a. quotes from environmentalist groups
   b. moves on Capitol Hill to help environment—did they vote any more money for EPA?
   c. public-opinion polls on environment
IV. How did Democrats use this?
   a. statements in 1988 and 1992 elections
   b. Dems play issue big or not so big?
   c. Did it work for them?

Each Roman numeral is a supporting element that then becomes a subhead. If your paper is five pages, make your thesis not more than half a page long, each supporting element one to two pages long, and finish with a half-page evaluation.

Sources

Sources—where you get your facts, data, quotes, and ideas—are very important, one of the first things an instructor checks. Good sources are from specialized books, scholarly articles,

---

HOW TO WRITE A POLITICAL SCIENCE PAPER (CONTINUED)

or respected periodicals. Bad sources are ones that appear commonplace or dubious, such as textbooks (never use your current text as a source), encyclopedias, dictionaries, and the popular press (such as your hometown newspaper). Be careful with Web sites; many are advertising or propaganda.

Scholars divide sources into two types, *primary* and *secondary*. A primary source is direct material unfiltered through the mind of another. In the example, it might be a 1992 quote from President Bush (Jones, 1992). A secondary source is another's synthesis and views. In this case, it might be an article in a magazine of opinion about Bush's environmental policy (Smith, 1989). To use a football analogy, which is better—your personal observation of the game (primary source) or the sportscaster's description of it (secondary source)? Instructors usually like primary sources. An article may include as a primary source numbers from official documents, such as EPA budget cuts under Bush (Williams, 1992)

Instructors are impressed if you have lots of good sources, say ten in a five-page paper. Just noting the same source twice doesn't make it two sources (Thompson, 1991, p. 247). Where needed, note page number. A source means a *different* book or article. In the library's reference section there are ways to get started fast, most on computer.

New York Times Index
Reader's Guide to Periodical Literature
Social Sciences Index
Public Affairs Information Service
Facts on File

For anything to do with executive-legislative relations (Congress, the White House, new laws, budgets) there's something so good it's almost like cheating, the *Congressional Quarterly*, which puts out a weekly, an annual, and best of all, a *Congress and the Nation* for each presidential term. For foreign countries, there's the magazine *Current History* and the *Country Study* series of books published by the Library of Congress.

Conclusion

Now, physically, your paper should look about like this. By the end you should have *proved* your thesis with evidence to the satisfaction of the instructor. Thesis is to evidence as head is to body; you can't have one without the other. Below is how you do sources from a newspaper, a magazine article, a book, and a scholarly article. Sources are alphabetical, by author's last name. Your paper, of course, will be longer and have more sources. For more information, consult the student writing center at www.prenhall.com/polisci.com.

Sources

Jones, Robert. March 4, 1992. Bush Announces Environment Program. *New York Times*.

Smith, Paul. June 20, 1989. Bush Against the Environment. *New Republic*.

Thompson, Earl. 1991. *George Bush and the Environment*. New York: Simon & Schuster.

Williams, Charles. The EPA Budget Under Bush. 1992. *Ecology Quarterly*, 17: 417. [last numbers are volume and pages]

Most student papers use only secondary sources, but instructors are mightily impressed when you use a "primary source," the original gathering of data, as in your own count of what counties in your state showed the strongest Perot vote. Anyone reading a study must be able to review its evidence and judge if it is valid. You can't keep your evidence or sources secret.

What Good Is Political Science?

Some students come to political science supposing it is just opinions; they write exams or turn in papers that ignore all or some of the preceding points. Yes, we all have political views, but if we let them dominate our study we get invalid results, junk political science. A professional political scientist pushes his or her personal views well to one side while engaged in study and research. A first-rate thinker is able to come up with results that actually refute his or her previously-held opinion. When that happens, we have real intellectual growth, an exciting experience that should be your aim.

Something else comes with such an experience: You start to conclude that you shouldn't have been so partisan in the first place. You may back away from the strong views you had earlier and take them with a grain of salt. Accordingly, political science is not necessarily training to become a practicing politician. Political science is training in the calm, dispassionate analysis of politics, whereas the practice of politics often requires fixed, popular, and simplified opinions.

Key Concepts | POLITICS VERSUS POLITICAL SCIENCE

Political science is not necessarily training to become a practicing politician. Political science is training in the analysis of politics, which may or may not aid working politicians. Side-by-side, the two professions compare like this:

Politicians	Political Scientists
love power	are skeptical about power
seek popularity	seek accuracy
think in practical terms	think in abstract terms
give firm viewpoints	give tentative conclusions
give single-cause explanations	give multi-cause explanations
see short-term payoff	see long-term consequences
work toward next election	work for the long-term
respond to groups	seek good of whole
have name recognition	have quiet prestige

The two professions bear approximately the same relation to each other as bacteria and bacteriologists.

Political science can contribute to good government, mainly by warning those in office that all is not well, "speaking truth to power," as the Quakers say. Sometimes this advice is useful to working politicians. Public-opinion polls, for example, showed a slow erosion of government legitimacy in the United States from the mid-1960s to the early 1980s. The causes were Vietnam, Watergate, and inflation. Candidates for office, knowing public opinion, could tailor their campaigns and policies to try to counteract this decline. Ronald Reagan, with his sunny disposition and upbeat views, utilized the discontent to win two presidential terms.

As far back as 1950, the American Political Science Association had warned about the weaknesses of U.S. political parties; they were too decentralized and uncontrolled. Political parties in the United States cannot even define what they stand for or who can be regarded as a member. In 1989, David Duke, a former leader of the Ku Klux Klan with ties to Nazis, won a seat as a Republican in the Louisiana state legislature. The Republican National Committee tried to distance itself from Duke, but he continued to call himself a Republican, and there was no legal way to stop him from doing so. Parties in the United States are too weak to even control who uses their names.

Some political scientists warned for years of the weak basis of the shah's regime in Iran. Unfortunately, such warnings were unheeded. Washington's policy was to support the shah; only two months before the end of his reign did the U.S. Embassy in Tehran start reporting accurately how unstable Iran had become. State Department officials had let their political analyses become contaminated by politics; they could not see clearly. Journalists were not much better; few covered Iran until violence broke out. Well in advance, American political scientists specializing in Iran saw trouble coming. Political science can be useful.

Key Terms

authority (p. 5)	irrational (p. 10)	rational (p. 9)
culture (p. 8)	legitimacy (p. 5)	scholarship (p. 13)
discipline (p. 2)	methodology (p. 4)	sovereignty (p. 5)
empirical (p. 12)	political power (p. 5)	
hypothesis (p. 12)	quantify (p. 12)	

Key Websites

The American Political Science Association is the major society for individuals engaged in the study of politics and government.
http://www.apsanet.org/
The John F. Kennedy School of Government has an excellent online introduction to all aspects of political science.
http://ksgwww.harvard.edu/ksgpress/opin/index.html

One of the best places to start researching political science is Yahoo's political science section.
http://dir.yahoo.com/Social_Science/Political_Science/

Adam Smith Institute has a website that is keeping Adam Smith's work and philosophy alive and in use today. The site covers developing policy privatization, regulatory reform, and government restructuring.
http://www.adamsmith.org.uk/

Further Reference

Boulding, Kenneth E. *Three Faces of Power*. Newbury Park, CA: Sage, 1989.

Friedrich, Carl J., ed. *Authority*. Cambridge, MA: Harvard University Press, 1958.

Janis, Irving L. *Victims of Groupthink: A Psychological Study of Foreign-Policy Decisions and Fiascoes*. Boston, MA: Houghton Mifflin, 1972.

Kagan, Jerome. *Galen's Prophecy: Temperament and Human Nature*. New York: Basic Books, 1994.

Lasswell, Harold. *Politics: Who Gets What, When, How*. New York: McGraw-Hill, 1936.

Milgram, Stanley. *Obedience to Authority: An Experimental View*. New York: Harper & Row, 1974.

Minogue, Kenneth. *Politics: A Very Short Introduction*. New York: Oxford University Press, 1995.

Wilson Edward O. *Sociobiology: The New Synthesis*. Cambridge, MA: Harvard University Press, 1975.

CHAPTER 2

Theories:
Classic and Modern

W hy bother with theories at all, wonder many students new to political science. Why not just accumulate a lot of facts and let the facts structure themselves into a coherent whole? Because they won't. Gathering facts without a guiding principle leads only to large collections of meaningless facts. To be sure, theories can grow too abstract and depart from the real world, but without at least some theoretical perspective, we don't even know what questions to ask. Even if you say you have no theories, you probably have some unspoken ones. Just the kind of questions you ask and which questions you ask first are the beginning of theorizing.

Take, for example, the structure of this book. We have adopted the view—which has been widespread in political science for decades—that the proper starting point of political analysis is society. That is, we assume that politics grows out of society. You start with people's values, attitudes, and opinions and see how they influence government. The subtitle of one widely read and highly influential book by a leading sociologist was *The Social Bases of Politics*. Its message: You start with society and see how it influences politics.

But doesn't that stack the deck? If you assume that society is the basis of politics and that values and opinions are the important facts, you will gather a great deal of material on values and opinions and relatively little material on the history, structure, and policies of government. Everything else will appear secondary to citizens' values and opinions. And, indeed, political science went through a period in which it was essentially sociology, and many political scientists did survey research. This was part of the behavioral tide; survey research was seen as the only way to be "scientific" because it generated quantifiable data.

> **QUESTIONS TO CONSIDER**
>
> 1. Who founded political science?
> 2. What did Machiavelli, Confucius, Kautilya, and Ibn Khaldun have in common?
> 3. How did Hobbes, Locke, and Rousseau differ?
> 4. What is the crux of Marx's theory?
> 5. What is "positivism" and how does it underlay much of social science?
> 6. What is Easton's theory of the political system?
> 7. How does modernization theory borrow from Marx?
> 8. What is rational-choice theory based on?

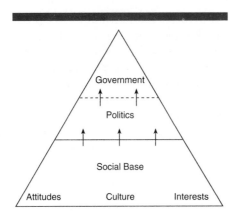

Figure 2.1   *Pyramid with Social Base and Political Superstructure*
(Flow is from bottom to top.)

Most textbooks offered a "percolation up" model of politics. The first major bloc of most studies was concerned with the society and covered such things as how political views were distributed, how interest groups were formed, who supported which political parties, and how people voted. That was the basis, the bottom part of the pyramid. The second major bloc was usually the institutions of government. They were assumed to be a reflection of the underlying social base. Legislatures and executives reacted to public opinion, interest groups, and political parties. The study of politics looked like Figure 2.1, above.

But just using the term *social base* assumes that society is the underlying element in the study of politics. Could it be the other way around? To use a coffee-making metaphor, instead of "percolating up," could politics "drip down"? If there were a book entitled *The Political Basis of Society*, such a book would posit society as largely the result of political institutions formed and decisions made over the decades. Maybe politics really does lead society, in which case our model would look like Figure 2.2, below.

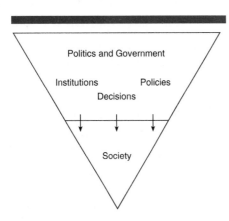

Figure 2.2   *Pyramid with Political Institutions Forming the Social Base*
(Flow is from top to bottom.)

How can you prove which model is more nearly correct? It is possible (and very likely) that the flow is going both ways simultaneously and that both models are partly correct. Why, then, emphasize one model over the other? There is no good reason; it is simply the current fashion in political study, which began as a reaction against the emphasis on institutions that dominated political science before World War II. A seemingly simple matter of which topics to study first has theoretical implications. You can't escape theory. We can only whet your appetite for political theories in our very brief discussion here. Consider further study of political theory; you will find that nothing is so practical as theory.

Classic Theories

Some say Plato founded political science. His *Republic*, among other things, described an ideal political system, but his reasoning was largely speculative, and his ideal system ended up looking a bit like modern fascism or communism. Plato's student, Aristotle, on the other hand, was the first *empirical* political scientist. As noted in the previous chapter, he regarded politics as the "master science" and sent out his students to gather data from the dozens of Greek city-states. With these data, he constructed his great *Politics*. Both Plato and Aristotle saw Athens in decline; they attempted to understand why and to suggest how it could be avoided. They thus began a tradition that is still at the heart of political science: a search for the sources of political peace and stability. Aristotle was not shy about defining what was politically "best," as in this passage:

> [T]he best political community is formed by citizens of the middle class, and those states are likely to be well administered in which the middle class is large … in which the citizens have moderate and sufficient property; for where some possess much and others nothing there may arise an extreme democracy or a pure oligarchy, or a tyranny may develop out of either extreme.… [D]emocracies are safer and more permanent than oligarchies, because they have a middle class which is more numerous and has a greater share in government, for when there is no middle class, and the poor greatly exceed in number, troubles arise, and the state soon comes to an end.

Even though the passage above was written in the fourth century B.C., Aristotle could be describing why democracy succeeds or fails today: Much depends on the size of the middle class, a point confirmed by modern research. Aristotle was both **descriptive** and **normative**: He used the facts he and his students had collected to prescribe the most desirable political institutions. Political scientists have been doing the same ever since, both describing and prescribing.

Most European medieval and Renaissance political thinkers took a religious approach to the study of government and politics.

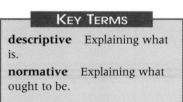

KEY TERMS

descriptive   Explaining what is.

normative   Explaining what ought to be.

They were almost strictly normative, seeking to discover the "ought" or "should" and were often rather casual about the "is," the real-world situation. Informed by religious, legal, and philosophical values, they tried to ascertain which system of government would bring humankind closest to what they believed God wished.

With Niccolò Machiavelli in the early sixteenth century emerged what some

---

Classic Works — Not Just Europeans

China, India, and North Africa produced brilliant political thinkers long before their European counterparts. Unknown in the West until relatively recently, it is unlikely that their ideas influenced the development of Western political theory. It does suggest that the political nature of humans is basically the same no matter what the cultural differences and that great minds come to similar conclusions on how to deal with politics.

In China, Confucius, a sixth-century B.C. advisor to rulers, propounded his vision of good, stable government based on two things, the family and correct, moral behavior instilled in rulers and ruled alike. At the apex, the emperor sets a moral example by purifying his spirit and perfecting his manners. He must think good thoughts in utter sincerity; if he doesn't, his empire crumbles. The subjects, arrayed hierarchically below the emperor, copy him, down to the father of a family, who is like a miniature emperor, to whom wives and children are subservient. The Confucian system bears some resemblance to Plato's ideal Republic; the difference is that the Chinese actually practiced Confucianism, which lasted two and a half millennia and through a dozen dynasties. Some observers claim it formed the cultural basis for East Asia's remarkable economic growth in the late twentieth century.

Two millennia before Machiavelli and Hobbes, the Indian writer Kautilya, in the fourth century B.C., arrived at the same conclusions. Kautilya, a prime minister and adviser to an Indian monarch, wrote in *Arthasastra* (translated as *The Principles of Material Well-Being*) that well-being comes from living in a well-run kingdom. Like Hobbes, Kautilya posited a state of nature that meant anarchy. Monarchs arose to protect the land and people against anarchy and ensure their prosperity. Like Machiavelli, Kautilya advised his prince to operate on the basis of pure expediency, doing whatever it takes to secure his kingdom domestically and against other kingdoms. Kautilya thus could be said to have founded both political economy and the realist school of statecraft.

In fourteenth century A.D. North Africa, Ibn Khaldun was a secretary, executive, and ambassador for several rulers. Sometimes out of favor and in jail, he reflected on what had gone wrong with the great Arab empires. He concluded, in his *Universal History*, that the character of the Arabs and their social cohesiveness was determined by climate and occupation. Ibn Khaldun was almost modern in his linking of underlying economic conditions to social and political change. Economic decline in North Africa, he found, had led to political instability and lawlessness. Anticipating Marx, Toynbee, and many other Western writers, Ibn Khaldun saw that civilizations pass through cycles of growth and decline.

Notice what all three of these thinkers had in common with Machiavelli: All were princely political advisors who turned their insights into general prescriptions for correct governance. Practice led to theory.

believe is the crux of modern political science, the focus on power. His great work *The Prince* was about the getting and using of political power. Many philosophers peg Machiavelli as the first modern philosopher because his motivations and explanations had nothing to do with religion. Machiavelli wasn't as wicked as some people say. He was a **realist** who

> **KEY TERM**
>
> **realism** Working with the world as it is and not as we wish it to be; often focused on power.

argued that to accomplish anything good—such as the unification of Italy and expulsion of the foreigners who ruined it—the Prince had to be rational and tough in the exercise of power.

Although long depreciated by American political thinkers, who sometimes shied away from "power" as inherently dirty, the approach took root in Europe and contributed to the elitist analyses of Mosca, Pareto, and Michels. Americans became acquainted with the power approach through the writings of the refugee German scholar of international relations, Hans J. Morgenthau, who emphasized that "all politics is a struggle for power."

The Contractualists

Not long after Machiavelli, the "contractualists," Hobbes, Locke, and Rousseau, analyzed why political systems should exist at all. They differed in many points but agreed that humans, at least in principle, had joined in what Rousseau called a **social contract** that everyone now had to observe.

Thomas Hobbes lived through the upheavals of the English Civil War in the seventeenth century and opposed them for making individuals frightened and insecure. Hobbes imagined that life in the **state of nature**, before **civil society** was founded, must have been terrible. Every man would have been the enemy of every other man, a "war of each against all." Humans would live in savage squalor with "no arts; no letters; no society; and which is worst of all, continual fear, and danger of violent death; and the life of man, solitary, poor, nasty, brutish, and short." To get out of this horror, people would—out of their profound self-interest—rationally join together to

> **KEY TERMS**
>
> **social contract** Theory that individuals join and stay in civil society as if they had signed a contract.
> **state of nature** Humans before civilization.
> **civil society** Humans after becoming civilized. Modern usage: associations in between family and government.

form civil society. Society thus arises naturally out of fear. People would also gladly submit to a king, even a bad one, for a monarch prevents anarchy. Notice how Hobbes's theory, that society is based on rational self-interest, is at odds with Aristotle's theory that humans are born "political animals." Which theory is right? (Hint: Have humans ever lived as solitary animals?) But also notice that Hobbesian situations appear from time to time, as in Somalia in the early 1990s.

Another Englishman, John Locke, also saw the seventeenth-century upheavals but came to less-harsh conclusions. Locke theorized that the original state of nature was not so bad; people lived in equality and tolerance with one another. But they could not secure their property: There was no money, title deeds, or courts of law, so their property was uncertain. To remedy this, they contractually formed civil society and thus secured "life, liberty, and property." Locke is to property rights as Hobbes is to fear of violent death. Some philosophers argue that Americans are the children of Locke. Notice the American emphasis on "the natural right to property."

Jean Jacques Rousseau lived in eighteenth-century France and, some say, laid the philosophical groundwork for the French Revolution. He accepted the theories of Hobbes and Locke but gave them a twist. Life in the state of nature, Rousseau theorized, was downright good; people lived as "noble savages" without artifice or jealousy. (All the contractualists were influenced by not-very-accurate descriptions of American Indians.) What corrupted humans, said Rousseau, was society itself. The famous words at the beginning of his *Social Contract*: "Man is born free but everywhere is in chains."

> **KEY TERM**
>
> **general will**   Rousseau's theory of what everybody in the community wants.

But society can be drastically improved, argued Rousseau, leading to human freedom. A just society would be a voluntary community with a will of its own, the **general will**, what everyone wants over and above the particular wills of individuals and interest groups. In such communities humans gain dignity and freedom. Societies make people, not the other way around. If people are bad, it is because society made them that way (a view still held by many today). A good society, on the other hand, can "force men to be free" if they misbehave. Many see the roots of totalitarianism in Rousseau: the imagined perfect society; the general will, which the dictator claims to know; and the breaking of those who do not cooperate. Happily, the U.S. Founding Fathers were uninfluenced by Rousseau, but the architects of the French Revolution believed passionately in Rousseau, which perhaps explains why it ended badly.

Most of the U.S. Founding Fathers had studied the contractualists, whose influence is obvious. What is the Constitution but a social contract? Much of the Declaration of Independence reads as if it had been cribbed from Locke, which it had, by Jefferson. Please don't say political theories have no influence.

Marxist Theories

Another political theory that made a big difference was Marxism. A German living in London, Karl Marx, who was trained in Hegelian philosophy, produced an exceedingly complex theory consisting of at least three interrelated elements: a theory of economics, a theory of social class, and a theory of history. Like Hegel, Marx argued that things happen not by accident; everything has a cause. Hegel posited the underlying cause that moves history forward as spiritual, specifically the **Zeitgeist**, the spirit of the times. Marx found the great underlying cause in economics.

> **KEY TERM**
>
> **Zeitgeist**   German for "spirit of the times"; Hegel's theory that each epoch has a distinctive spirit, which moves history along.

Economics   In economics, Marx concentrated on the "surplus value"—what we would call profit. Workers produce things but get paid only a fraction of the value of what they produce. The capitalist owners skim off the rest, the surplus value. The workers, paid only for a fraction of what they produce, cannot go out on the market and buy all the products. The capitalist system pumps out an abundance of goods onto the market, but the bulk of the population—what

> **KEY TERMS**
>
> **proletariat**   Marx's name for the industrial working class.
> **bourgeois**   Adjective, originally French for city dweller; later and currently, middle class in general. Noun: *bourgeoisie*.

Marx called the **proletariat** (industrial working class)—can't afford to buy them. The result is repeated overproduction, which, when products can't be sold, leads to depressions. Eventually, argued Marx, there will be a depression so big it will doom the capitalist system.

Social Class   Every society divides into two classes: a small class of those who own the means of production and a large class of those who work for the small class. Society is run according to the dictates of the upper class, which sets up the laws, arts, and styles needed to maintain itself in power. (The theory of elites, discussed in Chapter 5, was influenced by Marx.) Most laws concern property rights, noted Marx, because the **bourgeoisie** (the capitalists) are obsessed with hanging on to their property, which, according to Marx, is nothing but skimmed-off surplus value anyway. If the country goes to war, said Marx, it is not because of the wishes of the common people but because the ruling bourgeoisie needs a war for economic gain. The proletariat, in fact, has no country; proletarians are international, all suffering under the heel of the capitalists.

History   Putting together his economic theory and his social-class theory, Marx explained historical changes. When the underlying economic basis of society gets out of kilter with the structure that the dominant class has established (its laws, institutions, ways of doing business, and so on), the system collapses. This, said Marx, is what happened in the French Revolution. Prior to the revolution, the ruling class was the feudal nobility. Their system was from the Middle Ages, based on hereditary ownership of great estates worked by peasants, on laws stressing the inheritance of these estates and the titles that went with them, and on chivalry and honor. All were part and parcel of a feudal society. But the economic basis changed. Ownership of land and feudal values eroded with the rise of manufacturing. A new class rose, the urban capitalists (or bourgeoisie), whose way of life and economy were quite different. By the late eighteenth century, France had an economy based on manufacturing but was still dominated by feudal aristocrats with their minds in the past. The system was out of kilter: The economic basis had moved ahead, but the class "**superstructure**" had stayed behind. In 1789, the superstructure came down with a crash, and the bourgeoisie took over with its new capitalist and liberal values of a free market, individual gain, and legal (but not material) equality.

> **KEY TERM**
>
> **superstructure**   Marx's term for everything that is built on top of the economy (laws, art, politics, etc.).

The capitalists did a good job, Marx had to admit. They industrialized and modernized much of the globe. They put out incredible new products and inventions. But they too are doomed, Marx wrote, because the faster they transform the economy, the more it gets out of step with the capitalist superstructure, just as the previous feudal society was left behind by a changing economy. This leads us back to Marx's theory of surplus value and recurring economic depressions. Eventually, reasoned Marx, the economy will be so far out of kilter from the bourgeois setup that it too will come crashing down. Socialism, predicted Marx, will come next, and we should aid in its coming. Marx was partly a theorist and partly an ideologist. We will consider Marxism as ideology in Chapter 6.

Marxism, as applied in the Soviet Union and other Communist countries, led to tyranny and failure, but as a system of analysis, Marxism is still interesting and useful. Social class is important in structuring political views, but never uniformly. For example, many working-class people are conservative, and many middle-class intellectuals are liberals or **leftists**. Economic interest groups still ride high and, by means of freely spending on election campaigns, often get their way in Washington. They seldom get all they want all of the time, however, as they are opposed by other interest groups. Marx's enduring contributions are (1) his understanding that societies are never fully unified and peaceful but always riven with conflict and (2) that we must ask "Who benefits?" in any political controversy.

KEY TERMS

leftist   In favor of radical change to level social classes.

institution   A formal structure of government, such as the U.S. Congress.

Institutional Theories

From the nineteenth century through the middle of the twentieth century, American thinkers focused on **institutions**, the formal structures of government. This showed the influence of law on the development of political science in the United States. Woodrow Wilson, for example, was a lawyer (albeit unsuccessful) before he became a political scientist; he concentrated on perfecting the institutions of government. Constitutions were a favorite subject for political scientists of this period, for they assumed that what was on paper was how the institutions worked in practice. The rise of the Soviet, Italian, and German dictatorships shook this belief. The constitution of Germany's Weimar Republic (1919–1933) looked fine on paper; it had been drafted by experts. Under stress it collapsed, for Germans of that time did not have the necessary experience with or commitment to democracy. Likewise, the Stalin constitution of 1936 made the Soviet Union look like a perfect democracy, but obviously it didn't work that way.

Contemporary Theories

Some thinkers of a classic bent dismiss contemporary theories as trivial, obvious, superficial, or simply restatements of classic ideas. One such scholar sniffed that everything he learned from modern theories could be written on the inside of a matchbook cover. We need not be so harsh. Contemporary—meaning post-World War II—theories have made some contributions. Even when they ultimately fail and are abandoned, they leave a residue of interesting questions. True, compared to classic theories, most are pretty thin stuff.

Behavioral Theory

The Communist and Fascist dictatorships and World War II forced political scientists to rethink their institutional focus, and many set to work to discover how politics really worked, not how it was supposed to work. Postwar American political scientists here followed in the tradition of the early nineteenth-century French philosopher Auguste Comte, who developed the doctrine of **positivism**, the application of natural-science methods to the study of society. Comtean positivism was an optimistic philosophy, holding that as we accumulate valid data by means of scientific observation—without speculation or intuition—we will perfect a science of society and with it improve society. Psychologists were perhaps the most deeply imbued with this approach (and still are); many took the name **behavioralists** for their concentration on actual human behavior as opposed to thoughts or feelings.

> **KEY TERMS**
>
> **positivism**   Theory that society can be studied scientifically and incrementally improved with the knowledge gained.
>
> **behavioralism**   The empirical study of actual human behavior rather than abstract theories.

Beginning in the 1950s, behaviorally inclined political scientists borrowed the natural scientists' approach and accumulated statistics from elections, public opinion surveys, votes in legislatures, and anything else they could hang a number on. Behavioralists made some remarkable contributions to political science, shooting down some long-held but unexamined assumptions and giving political theory an empirical basis from which to work. Behavioral studies were especially good in examining the "social bases" of politics, the attitudes and values of average citizens, which go a long way in making the system work the way it does. Their best work has been on voting patterns, for it is here they can get lots of valid data.

During the 1960s, the behavioral school established itself and won over much of the field. In the late 1960s, however, behavioralism came under heavy attack, and not just by rear-guard traditionalists. Many younger political scientists, some of them influenced by the radicalism of the anti-Vietnam war movement, complained that the behavioral approach was static, conservative, loaded with its practitioners' values, and irrelevant to the urgent tasks at hand. Far from being "scientific" and "value-free," behavioralists often defined the current situation in the United States as the norm and anything different as deviant. Almond and Verba found that Americans embody all the good, "participant" virtues of the civic culture. By examining only what exists at a given moment, behavioralists neglected the possibility of change; their studies may be time-bound. Behavioralists have an unstated preference for the status quo; they like to examine settled, established systems, for that is where their methodological tools work best.

Perhaps the most damaging criticism, though, was that the behavioralists focused on relatively minor topics and steered clear of the big questions of politics. Behavioralists can tell us, for example, what percentage of Detroit blue-collar Catholics vote Democratic, but they can't tell us much about what this means in terms of the quality of Detroit's governance or the kinds of decisions elected officials will make. There is no necessary connection between how citizens vote and what comes out of government. Critics charged that behavioral studies were often irrelevant.

KEY TERM
postbehavioral Synthesis of traditional, behavioral, and other techniques in the study of politics.

By 1969, even a top political theorist like David Easton had to admit that there was something to the criticism of what had earlier been called the "behavioral revolution." Some call the new movement **postbehavioral**, a synthesis of traditional and behavioral approaches. Postbehavioralists recognize that facts and values are tied together; they are willing to use both the qualitative data of the traditionalists and the quantitative data of the behavioralists. They are willing to look at history and institutions as well as public opinion and rational-choice theory. They are not afraid of numbers and happily use correlations, graphs, and percentages to make their cases. If you inquire around your political science department, you are apt to find traditional, behavioral, and postbehavioral viewpoints among the professors—or even within the same professor.

Systems Theory

One of the major postwar inventions was the "political systems" model devised by David Easton, which contributed to our understanding of politics by simplifying reality but in some cases departed from reality. The idea of looking at complex entities as systems originated in biology. Living entities are complex and highly integrated. The heart, lungs, blood, digestive tract, and brain perform their functions in such a way as to keep the animal alive. Take away one organ and the animal dies. Damage one organ and the other components of the system alter the way they work in an effort to compensate and keep the animal alive. The crux of systems thinking is this: You can't change just one component, because a change in one component changes all the others.

In the political systems model, many argued that the politics of a given country worked the same way as a biological system. According to the Easton model (see Figure 2.3), citizens' demands, "inputs," are felt by the government decision makers, who process them into authoritative decisions and actions, "outputs." These outputs make an impact on the social, economic, and political environment that the citizens may or may not like. The citizens express their demands anew—this is the crucial "feedback" link of the system, which may modify the earlier decision. Precisely what goes on in the "conversion process" was left opaque, a "black box."

In some cases, the political systems approach fits reality: A weak economy in the United States increasingly worried citizens. The winning presidential candidate,

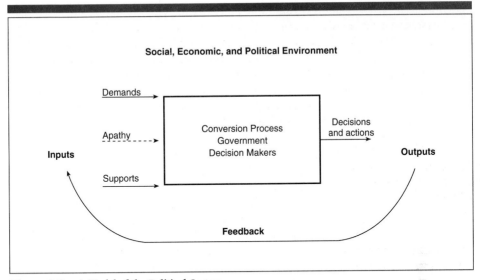

Figure 2.3   *A Model of the Political System*

Source: Adapted from David Easton, *A Systems Analysis of Political Life*. Chicago, IL: University of Chicago Press, 1965, p. 32.

Bill Clinton, vowed to speed economic growth and create more jobs. Clinton enjoyed several years of a good economy, and the feedback was positive, supporting him even amid scandal and impeachment. During the Vietnam war, feedback on the military draft was very negative. The Nixon administration defused much youthful anger by ending the draft in 1971 and changing to an all-volunteer army. In yet another example, the socialist economics of French President François Mitterrand produced inflation and unemployment. The French people, especially the business community, complained loudly, and Mitterrand altered his policy away from socialism and back to capitalism. The feedback loop worked.

But in other cases, the systems model falls flat. Would Hitler's Germany or Stalin's Russia really fit the systems model? How much attention do dictatorships pay to citizens' demands? To be sure, there is always some citizen input and feedback. Hitler's generals tried to assassinate him—a type of feedback. Workers in Communist systems made an impact on government policy by not working much. They expected more consumer goods, and by not exerting themselves they communicated this desire to the regime. Sooner or later the regime had to respond. In the USSR such a response came from the Gorbachev regime. All over the Soviet bloc, workers used to chuckle: "They pretend to pay us and we pretend to work."

How could the systems model explain the Vietnam war? Did the citizens of the United States demand that the administration send half a million troops to fight there? No, nearly the opposite: Lyndon Johnson won overwhelmingly in

Key Concepts	MODELS: SIMPLIFYING REALITY

A model is a simplified picture of reality that social scientists develop to order data, to theorize, and to predict. A good model fits reality but simplifies it, because a model that is as complex as the real world would be no help. In simplifying reality, however, models run the risk of oversimplifying. The real problem is the finite capacity of the human mind. We cannot factor in all the information available at once; we must select which points are important and ignore the rest. But when we do this, we may drain the blood out of the study of politics and overlook many key points. Accordingly, as we encounter models of politics—and perhaps as we devise our own—we must pause a moment to ask if the model departs too much from reality. If it does, we should discard or alter the model. Attempts to disregard reality because it doesn't fit the model end in catastrophe.

1964 on an antiwar platform. The systems model does show how discontent with the war hurt Johnson's popularity and led him to not seek reelection in 1968. The feedback loop did go into effect but only long after the decision to send troops to Vietnam had been made. By the same token, how could the systems model explain the Watergate scandal? Did U.S. citizens demand that members of President Nixon's staff order the Democratic headquarters bugged? No, but once details started leaking out in 1973 about the cover-up, the feedback loop went into effect, putting pressure on the House of Representatives to form an impeachment panel.

Plainly, there are some problems with the systems model, and they seem to be in the "black box" of the conversion process. A lot of things are happening in the mechanism of government that are not initiated by and have little to do with the wishes of citizens. The American people were little concerned about the health effects of smoking. Only the analyses of medical statisticians, which revealed a strong link between smoking and lung cancer, prodded Congress into requiring warning labels on cigarette packs and ending television advertising of cigarettes. It was a handful of specialists in the federal bureaucracy that got the anticigarette campaign going, not the masses of citizens.

The systems model is essentially static, biased toward the status quo, and unable to handle upheaval. This is one reason political scientists were caught by surprise at the collapse of the Soviet Union; "systems" aren't supposed to collapse; they are supposed to be continually self-correcting.

We can modify the systems model to better reflect reality. By diagramming it as in Figure 2.4, we logically change nothing. We have the same feedback loop: outputs turning into inputs. But by putting the "conversion process" of government first, we suggested that it—rather than the citizenry—originates most decisions. The public reacts only later.

Next, we add something that Easton himself later suggested. Inside the "black

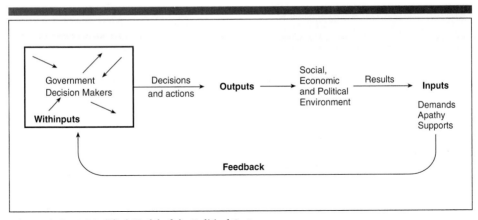

Figure 2.4 *A Modified Model of the Political System*

box" a lot more is happening than simply the processing of outside demands. Pressures from the various parts of government—government talking mostly to itself and short-circuiting the feedback loop—are what Easton called "within-puts." These two alterations, of course, make our model more complicated, but this also reflects the complicated nature of reality. The systems model, like all models in political science, must be taken with a grain of salt.

Modernization Theory

Modernization theory, a broad-brush term, is rooted in Hegel, who argued two centuries ago that all facets of society—the economic, cultural, and political—hang together as a package, which changes and moves all societies in the same direction. Hegel thought the underlying cause of this process was spiritual, but Marx argued that it was economic: Society changes in response to industrialization ("Steam engines and dynamos bring their own philosophy with them"). You can't have a feudal society with a modern economy, at least not for long. At the beginning of the twentieth century, Max Weber argued the cause was cultural, specifically, the rise of Protestantism. Others have emphasized the growth of education, communications, and the middle class, but all agree it happens as a package deal. Today's modernization theorists see the process as complex, multicausal, and little amenable to outside guidance. We don't develop countries; they develop themselves.

Most now agree on the importance of industrialization. When a country industrializes, its economy, culture, and politics also change, although it is hard to pinpoint any one underlying cause. Giving new life to this theory was the remarkable Chapter 2 of Seymour Martin Lipset's 1960 *Political Man*. Lipset classified countries as either "stable democracies" (such as Canada and Norway) or "unstable democracies and dictatorships" (such as Spain and Yugoslavia). With

Key Concepts	THE RISE AND FALL OF STRUCTURAL-FUNCTIONALISM

An extreme form of systems theory, borrowed from the complex (some say impenetrable) theories of sociologist Talcott Parsons, had great influence on political science during the 1960s. It held that to survive all societies must perform the same functions: interest articulation, interest aggregation, rule initiation, rule application, rule adjudication, and a few others. In the United States, which was their norm and model, these functions were carried out by, respectively, public opinion, parties, legislatures, executives, and judiciaries. Other countries might have different structures, but they had to be performing the requisite functions, otherwise they wouldn't survive. Or so went the theory.

Unsupported by evidence, this theory led to serious mistakes in analyzing other political systems. Structural-functionalists argued that since a given country, say, the Soviet Union, is surviving, it must be carrying out the stated functions, although the structures for doing so are quite different. Ergo, the Soviet Union is a durable, functioning system with the ability to self-correct when it gets into difficulties. This theory is one reason political scientists were taken by surprise at the collapse of the Soviet Union; according to structural-functional theory, it wasn't supposed to happen. Examined more closely, the structural-functionalists were extrapolating a simplified version of the U.S. political system onto the rest of the world. New students of political science should be grateful they do not need to learn this complex and mistaken theory; it died unmourned decades ago.

few exceptions, the stable democracies had more wealth, industry, radios, doctors, cars, education, and urban dwellers than the unstable democracies and dictatorships. In a word, they were more industrialized. And Lipset supplied an explanation: Industrialized countries have large middle classes, and they are the bases of democracy. Lipset, in effect, combined Marx with Aristotle (see the quote from Aristotle earlier in this chapter).

More recent research tends to confirm the connection between level of economic development and democracy. Some have found a sort of dividing line between poor and middle-income countries. Lands with a per capita **Gross Domestic Product (GDP)** of less than $5,000 are rarely democracies. If they attempt to found a democracy, it often fails, usually by military coup. Countries with a per capita GDP of more than $6,000, however, are mostly democracies. When they found a democracy, it usually lasts. South Korea and Taiwan are good examples. When they were poor, they were dictatorships. As they industrialized, their middle classes and education levels grew, and by the 1990s both had turned into democracies. Much U.S. thinking on China is based on these hopeful examples. China's rapid economic growth suggests it will become a

KEY TERM
Gross Domestic Product (GDP)   Sum total of goods and services produced in a given country in one year, often expressed per capita by dividing population into GDP.

middle-income country in the first half of the twenty-first century and hence be ripe for democracy. (Be a little skeptical here. Economic growth is rarely smooth, and China is a huge, complex nation; South Korea and Taiwan are small and relatively easy to govern.) Notice how Russia at the same time was growing poorer, and many doubted that its new democracy would survive. There is one interesting exception to this wealth-democracy connection: India, with a per capita GDP of only about $1,500, was founded and stayed democratic. (Any ideas why?)

Modernization theory also has some insights into the turmoil and instability that afflict many developing countries. It is because they modernize just one or two facets—often their economy and military—and leave the rest—such as religion and social structure—traditional. The two do not happily coexist; the traditional sectors resent and oppose the modern sectors. This helps explain the upsurge of Islamic fundamentalism in Iran, Egypt, Algeria, and Turkey. One must also note the serious economic difficulties of these lands as well. If modernization theory is correct, though, if and when they reach middle-income levels they should stabilize and democratize.

Developmentalist Theories

A Cold War offshoot of modernization theory flourished for a time among American social scientists, who in the late 1950s started believing that we were engaged not merely in discovery for its own sake but to beat or outlast the Communists. Federal and private-foundation funding encouraged social scientists to devise ways to develop Third World countries—Asia, Africa, and Latin America—before the Communists could. It was like a race: Either we get there first with plans and models of economic and political development, or wide areas of the world will slide into revolution and communism. Many top political scientists embraced this view, which led to "developmentalism" as a major, often commanding, topic. As is often the case, when politics becomes entwined with political science, the results are not impressive or durable.

The developmentalists of the 1960s sought a kind of alchemy to make countries modern. Like the alchemists of old, they tried everything: communications, bureaucracy, education, political culture, political parties, and other approaches. The books and articles almost followed a formula: "The crux of development is _____. With the proper _____, Third World lands can rapidly develop in a non-Communist and democratic direction. This article seeks to explain how _____ can make this happen." Just fill in the blanks with one of the above topics. Their mistake was in supposing that any one facet of modernity could be a **causal** factor in making countries modern. Developmentalist theory departed from modernization theory by supposing that we could pick out one factor to hasten the process along. Modernization theory is very much alive; developmentalist theories have been discarded.

KEY TERM
causality   One thing causes another; hard to prove in the social sciences.

One example of developmentalism is "communications," which became prominent in the 1960s thanks in great part to the fertile imagination of Yale (and later Harvard) political scientist Karl Deutsch. His 1953 *Nationalism and Social Communication* was a pathbreaking book. Nationalism (for an explanation, see Chapter 6) is not a mystical or spiritual thing, as many nationalists claim, but an offshoot of "social communication." The more people communicate with each other, the more it heightens their self-awareness as a people. This is why there was little nationalism before mass communications but lots of it with the growth of mass media in the nineteenth and twentieth centuries. In some cases, you could actually quantify the flow of communications in the circulation of newspapers and letters. For example, as more Finns communicated with each other in Finnish (instead of Swedish, the language of Finland's colonial masters), the more they became aware of themselves as a distinct people who ought to have their own nation. The crux of a nation is intense communication among its citizens, argued Deutsch and his followers.

The problem here, as with all the social sciences, is causality, proving that one thing causes another. Communications indeed grow with nationalism, but does the former cause the later? Could it be reversed? Could there be a third cause that underlies both? If you can't determine the causal flow, you can commit major blunders if you prescribe communications to hasten development. And we did. A section of the U.S. Agency for International Development (AID) promoted newspapers, radio, and television to develop lands like Iran and South Vietnam, both of which turned into catastrophes. (Ayatollah Khomeini's Islamic revolution was spread by cheap cassette recorders, which bypassed the shah's official communications system. This was sort of a backhanded confirmation of communications theory.) Communications theorists pushed the hardware of communications and neglected its content. What exactly would be communicated? Were the messages ones that most Iranians and South Vietnamese accepted? The communications approach, which was riding high in the 1960s, is now a fading and embarrassing memory in the minds of some older political scientists. It illustrates what goes wrong when a dubious theory is first exaggerated and then applied to a real-world situation in order to gain research dollars. The point (borrowed from Max Weber, p. 13): Be very skeptical when government hires a political scientist.

Rational-Choice Theory

In the 1970s a new approach, borrowed from economics, rapidly grew in political science—rational-choice theory. Little interested in culture or development, rational-choice theorists argued that one could generally predict political behavior by knowing the interests of the actors involved. They would rationally choose to maximize their interests. As U.S. Congresspersons take positions on issues, they calculate what will give them the best payoff. They might think,

"This business group gives me a lot of money, but this block of voters gets me reelected." The position taken will likely partially satisfy the business group but not offend the block of voters. Politicians waffle not out of weakness but out of calculation, argue rational-choice theorists.

Rational-choice theorists have sometimes enraged other political scientists. One study of Japanese bureaucrats claimed you didn't have to study Japan's language, culture, or history. All you needed to know was what their career advantages were and you could predict how they would decide things. A noted U.S. specialist on Japan blew his stack at such glib, superficial shortcuts and denounced rational-choice theory. More modest rational-choice theorists immersed themselves in Hungary's language and culture but still concluded that Hungarian political parties, in cobbling together an extremely complex voting system, were making rational choices to give themselves a presumed edge in parliamentary seats. (They may have also been influenced by Hungary's past voting system and by French, German, and Swedish voting systems.)

Rational-choice theorists have begun to back down from some of their more know-it-all positions. A few have even called themselves "neo-institutionalists" (see following section) because all their rational choices are made within one or another institutional contexts: the U.S. Congress, for example. Even if rational-choice theory does not establish itself as the dominant paradigm—and, to judge by the fate of other modern theories, it very probably will not—it has contributed a lot by reminding us that politicians are consummate opportunists, a point many other theories forgot.

Key Concepts   POLITICS AS A GAME

Some rational-choice thinkers developed game theory, setting up political decisions as if they were table games. A Cuban missile crisis "game" might have several people play President Kennedy, who must weigh the probable payoffs of bombing or not bombing Cuba. Others might play Khrushchev, who has to weigh toughing it out or backing down. Seeing how the players interact gives us insights and warnings of what can go wrong in crisis decision making. If you "game out" the 1962 Cuban missile crisis and find that three games out of ten end in World War III, you have the makings of an article of great interest to decision makers.

Game theorists argue that constructing the proper game teaches how decision makers think. We learn how their choices are never easy or simple. The great weakness of game theory is that it depends on correctly estimating the "payoffs" decision makers can expect, and these are only approximations arrived at by examining the historical record. We know how the Cuban missile crisis came out; therefore we adjust our game so it comes out the same way. In effect, game theory is only another way to systematize and clarify history (not a bad thing).

New Institutionalism

In the 1970s political science began to rediscover institutions and, with help from sociological theory, in the 1980s proclaimed the "New Institutionalism." Its crux is the recognition that government structures—legislatures, parties, bureaucracies, and so on—take on lives of their own and powerfully shape the behavior and attitudes of the people who live under and work in them. Institutions are not simply the reflections of social forces. (Our discussion of the importance of structures, on pp. 19–20, is a neoinstitutionalist argument.) Politicians behave as they do in large measure because of various "institutional constraints" (laws, customs, expectations), which they internalize and uphold. The preservation and enhancement of the institution becomes one of their major goals. Thus, institutions, even if outmoded or ineffective, tend to rumble on. The Communist parties of the Soviet bloc kept going not because true believers supported them, but because they guaranteed the jobs and perquisites of their members.

The new institutionalism is a sound approach—and popular in current research—and with it political science comes full circle, back to where it was before World War II, with some interesting and important insights and borrowings from other disciplines. It is, however, likely not the last model we shall see, for we will never have a model that can consistently explain and predict political actions. Roughly every couple of decades political science comes up with a new model—usually one borrowed from another discipline—that attracts much excitement and attention. Its proponents exaggerate its abilities to explain or predict. Upon examination and criticism, the model usually fades and is replaced by another hot trend. Political science tends to get caught up in trends, hot one decade and fading the next. After a few iterations of this cycle, we come to expect no breakthrough theories. Politics is slippery; it isn't easily confined to our mental constructs. By acknowledging this, we open our minds to the richness, complexity, and drama of political life.

Key Terms

behavioralism (p. 27)	general will (p. 24)	proletariat (p. 25)
bourgeois (p. 25)	institution (p. 26)	realism (p. 23)
causality (p. 33)	leftist (p. 26)	social contract (p. 23)
civil society (p. 23)	normative (p. 21)	state of nature (p. 23)
descriptive (p. 21)	positivism (p. 27)	superstructure (p. 25)
GDP (p. 32)	postbehavioral (p. 28)	Zeitgeist (p. 24)

Key Websites

This site provides a variety of information on Confucius, his teachings, and his cultural impact.
   http://www.albany.net/~geenius/kongfuzi/index.html

Machiavelli Online provides biography, links, critiques, reviews, and essays.
   http://www.sas.upenn.edu/~pgrose/mach/

This site contains a biography of Thomas Hobbes.
   http://www.rjgeib.com/thoughts/nature/hobbes-bio.html

This site takes a look at Plato and his many works.
   http://www.rit.edu/~flwstv/plato.html

The Political Philosophy home page is a site that provides links of interest to students of political theory and political philosophy.
   http://www-personal.ksu.edu/~lauriej/index.html

Further Reference

Almond, Gabriel A., and James S. Coleman. *Politics of Developing Areas*. Princeton, NJ: Princeton University Press, 1960.

Almond, Gabriel A., and G. Bingham Powell, Jr. *Comparative Politics: System, Process, and Policy*, 2nd ed. Boston, MA: Little, Brown, 1978.

Apter, David E. *The Politics of Modernization*. Chicago, IL: University of Chicago Press, 1965.

Curtis, Michael, ed. *The Great Political Theories*, 2 vols. New York: Avon, 1962.

Dahl, Robert A. *Modern Political Analysis*, 5th ed. Englewood Cliffs, NJ: Prentice Hall, 1991.

Deutsch, Karl. *Nationalism and Social Communication: An Inquiry into the Foundations of Nationality*. New York: Wiley, 1953.

Easton, David. *A Framework for Political Analysis*. Englewood Cliffs, NJ: Prentice Hall, 1965.

Lane, Ruth. *Political Science in Theory and Practice: The "Politics" Model*. Armonk, NY: M. E. Sharpe, 1997.

Laver, Michael. *Private Desires, Political Action: An Invitation to the Politics of Rational Choice*. Thousand Oaks, CA: Sage, 1997.

Lipset, Seymour Martin. *Political Man: The Social Bases of Politics*, rev. ed. Baltimore, MD: Johns Hopkins University Press, 1981.

Morgenthau, Hans J., and Kenneth W. Thompson. *Politics Among Nations: The Struggle for Power and Peace*, 6th ed. New York: Knopf, 1985.

Tannenbaum, Donald, and David Schultz. *Inventors of Ideas: An Introduction to Western Political Philosophy*. New York: St. Martin's, 1998.

Nations, States, and Governments

Which came first, states or nations? A **nation** is a population with a certain sense of itself, a cohesiveness, a commonality of attitudes and ideals, and often (but not always) a common language. A **state** is a government structure, usually sovereign and powerful enough to enforce its writ. (Notice that here we use *state* in its original sense; the fifty U.S. states are not states in this sense of the word.) Many argue that nations must have developed before states. States are rather artificial creations; they come and go and change form through the centuries. Surely nations must be the underlying element: Groups of people with kindred feelings must antedate government structures.

Historical research tends to refute this commonsense view. In most cases, it was states—government structures—that created

QUESTIONS TO CONSIDER

1. What is the difference between a nation and a state?
2. What is nationalism and where did it originate?
3. Describe the "crises" of nation-building.
4. What is the difference between socialism and statism?
5. Are American attitudes about the role of government widely held?
6. What were Aristotle's six types of government?
7. What is "symbolic politics"?

their nations around them. The Zulus of South Africa, for example, are not a tribe but an artificially created nation, one put together from many clans and tribes less than two centuries ago by a powerful and brutal warrior, Shaka. Present-day people think of themselves as Zulus only because Shaka united them by conquest, forced them to speak his language, and made them great warriors.

France often comes to mind as a "natural" nation, a neat hexagon with a common history, language, and culture. But present-day France consists of several regions with very different languages and histories that were united—mostly by the sword—over the course of centuries. Paris inculcated a sense of Frenchness by means of education, language, and centralized administration. The French nation is an artificial creation developed by the French state for its own convenience.

For many countries, the process of creation is not yet complete. The Spanish state coincides imperfectly with the Spanish nation. The kings of Toledo and Madrid tried to copy the French methods of centralization, but these Castilians

KEY TERMS

nation A population with a historic sense of self.

state The government structures of a nation.

were never able to impose a uniform sense of Spanishness on Catalans, Basques, Galicians, Andalucians, Navarese, and others. **Regionalism** bedevils Spanish politics to this day. In another example, India scarcely existed as a concept before the British conquered the Indian subcontinent and turned it into the Raj. The English language, the railroad, and the telegraph stitched India together. It, too, is plagued by breakaway ethnic movements such as the independence movement of the Sikhs in the Punjab.

KEY TERMS

regionalism   A feeling of difference sometimes found among populations of a nation's regions.

nationalism   A people's heightened sense of cultural, historical, and territorial identity, unity, and sometimes greatness.

Key Concepts   THE NOTION OF NATION

What are we to call this entity that dominates our lives, structures our politics, and calls forth our patriotism? Many terms are used, sometimes interchangeably. The terms have somewhat different meanings, though.

The common colloquial expression is *country*, as in "Have you ever visited another country?" *Country*, of course, can also mean a rural or farming area, and centuries ago the two meanings were one. When people spoke of their "country" (French *pays*, Spanish *país*, Italian *paese*, German *Land*) they meant their native locality, perhaps not much bigger than a large U.S. county, where people shared the same traditions and dialect. Later, the term broadened to mean a big, sovereign political entity, a nation.

The term *nation* has also been around for centuries, but not necessarily in its present sense. Far back in history, human groups called themselves nations, but originally this meant something like a big tribe, such as the "nation of Israel" or "Sioux nation." The Latin root of *nation* means "birth," so the word connoted the group you were born into and had some blood linkage with. The term *ethnic group*, from the Greek *ethnos*, meaning "nation," in turn is from the Greek for custom, *ethos*, indicating people with shared customs.

In the seventeenth century, the definition of nation changed to mean these large, powerful political entities that currently govern us. State power was merged with the notion of a people with much in common (history, culture, language) occupying a territory. This was the *nation-state*, a combination of people (nation) and government structure (state). It is usually just called *nation*.

The rise of the modern nation changed the face of the globe. Citizens—an old Roman concept that originated with the Latin for "city" and that revived with the idea of nation-states—transferred their ultimate loyalties from kings, churches, and localities to this new entity, the nation. Starting with the French Revolution in 1789 came the new force of **nationalism**. This new force quickly spread over Europe and then over the globe, unleashing the desire for peoples to govern themselves as independent nations. Vast empires, such as those of Austria-Hungary and Britain, fell apart as subject peoples demanded their independence. As a result, many new countries were created, especially in Eastern Europe, the Americas, Asia, and Africa. Today there are some 185 entities calling themselves nations.

The most artificial nation of all could well be the United States—put together through deliberate design by a group of men meeting in Philadelphia from thirteen different colonies. While assimilating tens of millions of immigrants with different languages and cultures, the United States developed a sense of nationhood over the years based largely on the ideals articulated in its founding documents. Nations do not fall from heaven; they are created by human craftsmanship of varying degrees of quality.

The Elements of Nationhood

Nations are commonly said to have several defining characteristics, such as territory, population, independence, and government. By each point, however, we could place a little question mark, for the characteristics are sometimes strong and clear and sometimes weak or absent.

Territory

In general, every nation occupies a specific geographical area. It's hard to have a nation without territory. But what about peoples without territory who carry the idea of their "nation" around with them in their heads? Jews lost their territorial nation to Greek and Roman conquest some two millennia ago, but because many of them had a firm ideal of their peoplehood, they were able to establish the modern state of Israel in 1948. Ironically, the people they displaced, the Palestinian Arabs, now also have a rather firm ideal of their peoplehood and strive to establish their own state. Should we count dispersed peoples, such as Jews or Palestinians, as a "nation"? Perhaps they are a potential nation, a people waiting or struggling to establish themselves on a territory.

And what occurs when territorial claims overlap? Wars often result. As stated earlier, most states and nations are rather artificial things; few have natural boundaries. Germany has fought France over Alsace; the United States has fought Mexico over Texas; and Argentina still claims what it calls the Malvinas Islands from Britain, which calls them the Falklands. Which claim is rightful? What criteria should be used to decide?

History is a poor guide, for there was almost always someone else there first. Israelis and Arabs quarrel endlessly about this. (If you go back far enough, neither of them was there first.) Language and ethnicity may also be poor guides in deciding which territory belongs to which state. The peoples of the earth, unfortunately, are not neatly arrayed into nations; rather there is a lot of spillover into neighboring states. Most Alsatians, for example, are or were originally German in language, culture, and family names. Most, however, also speak perfect French and think of themselves as French. To whom, then, does Alsace rightfully belong, Germany or France?

Population

Every nation has people within its borders. Ideally, it should be a population with a sense of cohesion, of being a distinct nationality. Having a common language is a real help but is often not the case. For example, there has long been conflict between French-speaking and Flemish-speaking Belgians. Still, enough of both language groups "feel" Belgian to hold the country together. States with populations diverse in language, culture, or identification are called *multinational states*. Only half of the Soviet population was Russian; many other Soviet nationalities did not like being ruled by Moscow and broke away, producing fifteen countries where there used to be one.

What if part of a nation's population doesn't want to belong to that particular nation? Some Basques in Spain would like to form an independent nation; some Québécois in Canada and Sikhs in India would like to do the same. If a substantial portion of the population is unhappy, the nation could fall apart. Many Slovaks resented being governed by Czechs and in 1993 set up a separate Slovakia. Slovenes and Croats resented being governed by Serbs, and in 1991 they declared their independence from Yugoslavia. Eritreans fought a long guerrilla war with Ethiopia and won their independence in 1993. Just because people are living in a particular state does not necessarily mean they like it; the state may be ready to explode.

Independence

The nation should also be independent, meaning that it governs itself as a "sovereign" entity (see Chapter 2). Colonies, such as Algeria under the French, become nations only when they get formal independence, as Algeria did in 1962. Subdivisions of a nation, such as Quebec or Nevada, are also not considered nations since they lack sovereignty. Many Québécois, of course, mean to change this situation.

There are some problems with the concept of independence, too. When a large, powerful country dominates a smaller, weaker country, is the latter fully independent and sovereign? Stalin set up obedient puppet governments in Eastern Europe—which is why these countries were known as Soviet "satellites"—and Soviet tanks crushed anti-Communist uprisings in Central Europe. Were these countries truly independent? For that matter, doesn't the United States supervise things in its own backyard, in the Caribbean and Central America? Is Haiti, which was briefly occupied by U.S. forces in 1994, truly sovereign? By definition, all nations are sovereign and independent, but some are more sovereign and independent than others.

Bolstering sovereign independence is **diplomatic recognition** by other countries, especially by the major powers. This may be followed by exchanges of ambassadors and the setting up of embassies. If most

KEY TERM
diplomatic recognition   The official announcement by one state that it is prepared to have dealings with another state.

of the important nations recognize a new country, it automatically confers a certain legitimacy on it. If no one recognizes the country, its claim to exist is dubious. South Africa created nominally independent puppet states out of some of its "black homelands," but no one else recognized them; the fake little republics were re-merged into South Africa as soon as Nelson Mandela became president.

Government

KEY TERMS
anarchy   The absence of government.
protogovernment   A beginning or trial-basis government.
cohesive   Holding together.

A nation must obviously have some organizing hold over its population. The absence of such organization is **anarchy**, and it probably means that the territory will soon split apart or be conquered and absorbed by other nations. No government, no nation. Somalia is a recent example of the horrors of anarchy.

Government, however, can in certain circumstances exist independently of the nation. Underground governments or "governments-in-exile" struggle to expel occupiers or puppet governments. The Continental Congress was a **protogovernment** that preceded, conceived of, and fought for an independent United States. In 1940, General Charles de Gaulle declared a "Free French" government in London to expel the Germans, and many major powers recognized it as the government of France. With the liberation of Paris in 1944, it turned into a government with territory, population, and independence.

The existence of a legal government does not necessarily mean it is an effective government that controls its territory and population (discussed later). Where weak, governments may have trouble even staying alive in the face of domestic and foreign opposition. Colombia, for example, has difficulty controlling powerful drug cartels that defy the Colombian state.

Older political theorists, influenced by legal abstractions, tended to take these characteristics of nations as givens. Wherever there was a nation, they reasoned, it must automatically have territory, population, independence, government, and sometimes other qualities. Modern political scientists tend to discard purely legalistic notions and search for the empirical reality. Theoretically, country X is a nation, but does it really have a **cohesive** population and an effective independent government that allows it to control its territory? Nations are not necessarily perfected, finished products. Many—perhaps all—are continually building and rebuilding themselves.

The Crises of Nation Building

Some social scientists hold that the process of constructing nations—if the process is to be successful—requires that countries go through the same five stages in approximately the same sequence. Each opportunity for further growth represents a "crisis" in the life of the nation, which the state structure must resolve with greater or lesser success.

Identity

The "identity crisis" is the first hurdle in building a nation. People who previously identified with a tribe, region, or other subnational group must come to think of themselves as first and foremost citizens of the nation. This does not happen easily, quickly, or automatically. The American Civil War was fought over this point. France and Britain still contain regional groups that don't think of themselves as French or British but rather as Breton and Corsican (in France) or Scottish, Welsh, and Irish (in Britain). Swiss, except when traveling abroad, will identify themselves as members of a canton (Bern, Geneva, Basel). Yugoslavia never established a national identity for its Serbs, Croats, Slovenes, Bosnians, Macedonians, and others. In this, Yugoslavia resembles many Third Word countries, which have not yet solved their identity crisis. In Africa, people still think of themselves as members of a tribe rather than as Ugandans or Nigerians.

Legitimacy

Legitimacy does not fall from heaven. As discussed in Chapter 1, a government must cultivate the respect and willing obedience of its citizens, the widespread feeling among the people that the regime's rule is rightful. Regimes with legitimacy problems are prone to overthrow (often by military coup, as in Latin America and Africa) or revolution (as in Iran and Burma). Ultimately, as in the case of Yugoslavia, no legitimacy means no nation.

Penetration

Related to both identity and legitimacy, the "crisis of penetration" means that the nation must get substantially all the population, even in outlying or culturally distinct regions, to obey the government's writ. One quick check of penetration: Do all areas pay taxes? If not, there is a penetration problem. Typically, the regime establishes its rule first in the capital, then slowly extends its rule over the country, often encountering resistance that requires military strength to overcome. Lack of penetration means that a government can have a law on its books—against cocaine trafficking, for example—but much of the country, including some officials, disregard the law.

Participation

As people become more aware that they are being governed, they demand to have a say in their governance. This feeling typically starts with the educated, better-off, and prominent people. The knights and wealthy burghers in effect tell the king or queen, "If you want taxes and military service from us, we demand a say in policy." The monarch, usually desperate for taxes, sets up a representative body to gain their compliance, such as the Parliament in England or Riksdag in Sweden. At first, only the elite of society are thus represented, but gradually, the desire for participation reaches all sectors of society—the common men and women—and they demand the right to vote. At a minimum, people need to *feel* they can participate in order for nationhood to evolve.

Regimes are often fearful of the consequences of expanding voting rights. Women got the right to vote in the United States only with the Nineteenth Amendment in 1920; Swiss women, only in 1971. The danger is that unrepresented people will oppose the government, and regime legitimacy will erode. Eventually, the regime usually decides that expanding participation is better than breeding revolution. Said one British parliamentarian in the nineteenth century, "We count ballots rather than crack skulls." The white minority regime of South Africa was slow to realize this basic point.

The best way to solve the participation crisis is through slow and incremental steps, as Britain succeeded in doing in the nineteenth century. A series of Reform Acts in Britain expanded the electoral franchise one step at a time, gradually giving more people the right to vote. This allowed both institutions and people time to adjust. Voting was meaningful and participation genuine. When suffrage is suddenly thrust on an unprepared people, however, the result is seldom democracy. On paper, Spain got universal male suffrage in 1874, well ahead of Britain, but in practice, election results were controlled by local bosses and the interior ministry. Voting in much of the Third World—where largely uneducated people got the franchise all at once—is often problematic because local political bosses or tribal leaders tell people how to vote.

Distribution

In a sense, the "crisis of distribution" is never permanently resolved. It concerns the classic question of "who gets what." Once the broad masses of citizens are participating in elections, it usually occurs to them that the economic rewards of the nation are unfairly apportioned, and they want to change the distribution of the nation's income in their favor. Much of the working class throws its votes to the party that promises higher wages, increased educational opportunities, and more welfare benefits. This is how the Labor parties of Britain and Norway and the Social Democratic parties of Germany and Sweden grew until they won power and established extensive welfare states funded by taxes that fall more heavily on the rich. To a lesser degree, the American working class gave much of its vote to the Democrats under Franklin D. Roosevelt and Lyndon Johnson in order to carry out a redistribution of national income.

The distribution question is never settled, however, because the poorer sectors of society always want more welfare, whereas the better-off, represented by the more conservative parties, argue that the welfare state has gotten out of hand, that taxes are too high and benefits too generous. When conservatives win elections—as Margaret Thatcher did in Britain in 1979 and Ronald Reagan did in the United States in 1980—they try to cut welfare programs. This raises a hue and cry from some voters who fear their benefits will be cut, and they try to preserve the benefits of the welfare state. That is the story of most elections in advanced, industrialized democracies.

Key Concepts   WAR AND NATION BUILDING

War clearly plays a role in the growth of states. Most nations were established and consolidated by conquest. Heresies, rebellions, and breakaway movements were put down with great bloodshed. In some lands, this is still happening.

For any ruler, state survival is the top priority. Monarchs and presidents alike will do whatever they must to avoid foreign conquest or internal dismemberment. In the interest of survival they build their military power to counter any combination of threats. This means that they must also enlarge and modernize their political systems.

First, they must constantly increase taxes to provide for armies and equipment. Peter the Great of Russia ordered his officials "to collect money, as much as possible, for money is the artery of war." The French monarchs instituted the mercantilist economic system, with its protected industries, to raise revenues for defense. It was to raise money needed for war that kings and queens began sharing power with parliaments. The power to tax is the preeminent power of legislatures. James I and Charles I precipitated the English Civil War, when they tried to bypass Parliament by decreeing their own taxes in order to pay for their wars in Europe. After winning the English Civil War the Parliamentarians beheaded Charles I in 1649 and laid the groundwork for establishing the eventual predominance of the House of Commons.

The need for a larger and better military establishment forced monarchs to improve the organization and administration of their kingdoms. They needed to raise both taxes and manpower. Prior to gunpowder and cannon in the fifteenth century, feudal lords in their castles could defy monarchs. Because kings could afford more cannons, they were able to crack castle walls and subdue lords. This power was a blow to the feudal state and a boost to the absolutism of monarchs. Failure to modernize one's administration and army could lead to loss of power. The map of Europe became much simpler as small states succumbed to military conquest and were absorbed by larger states. War was the great engine of modernization and consolidation.

When French revolutionaries in 1792 faced an invading army of professional soldiers, they mobilized the entire population, "the nation in arms," and beat the invaders. Harnessing this new nationalism and using the new idea of drafting all young males, Napoleon built the largest army in Europe and proceeded to conquer the entire continent. To resist Napoleon's legions, other European lands turned to nationalism and conscription as well.

By either the power or example of its arms, European nations spread their organization, technology, and nationalism into what we call the Third World. In Asia, Africa, and the Middle East, one country after another fell to Europeans and soon adopted their ways. Those who were not conquered, the Turks and the Japanese, modernized sufficiently to stave off the Europeans. Warfare gave countries little choice: Modernize or die.

Reflecting on U.S. history, we may ask which contributed more to modernization: the modest welfare measures of Roosevelt's New Deal or the gigantic industrial and manpower mobilization of World War II? Indeed, many welfare measures flowed as a result of the war. The G.I. Bill educated millions of ex-soldiers who wouldn't have gone to college without it. The National Defense Education Act of 1958, triggered by the 1957 launch of the Soviet Sputnik, pumped millions of dollars into U.S. higher education. One of the largest federal "welfare" programs is the Department of Veterans Affairs, a department that even conservatives support. War plays a major role in the foundation and growth of governmental powers.

Few nations have had the luxury of being able to deal with these crises one at a time and with sufficient pauses in between each crisis. These circumstances would allow a country's institutions—its parties, parliament, executive departments, and so on—to become stronger each time they surmount a new crisis. But what if all five crises hit at the same time? This has especially been the situation in the Third World. Newly independent countries, many of them with serious identity and legitimacy problems, are expected to implement complex laws, to give all citizens the right to vote, and to provide rising and equitable living standards. It's too much for their weak institutions to bear all at once, and they collapse into revolution or military rule. The first item to go is usually participation, hence the many Third World dictatorships. Unfortunately, the Third World does not have the luxury of spreading out its crises in this world of rapid change.

Government: What It Is and What It Does

All but the most primitive societies have had well-defined government structures. As noted, Locke, from whom our Founding Fathers borrowed heavily, viewed government as a device to protect rights and property. "The great and chief end," wrote Locke in *Two Treatises of Civil Government*, "of men uniting … under government, is the preservation of their property [and so, their natural rights]." To Locke, government represented an agreement between the rulers and the ruled, who would support those in power as long as the government served in their interests.

A society without a government would be like a baseball game without umpires. The players would argue forever about whether the pitch was a ball or a strike or whether the runner was safe or out. Each game would turn into a brawl (which sometimes happens anyway). Government performs the same tasks as the umpires: It sets down the basic rules that everyone must abide by. In part, a government is able to enforce its rules (or laws) because it controls the supreme penalty of death and has a monopoly on the legal use of force. Yet to stay in power, a government must enjoy the support of its people. One way of maintaining legitimacy is to fulfill successfully the goals of nationhood.

Classifying Governments

Most theorists agree that the task of government should be to provide for the lives, stability, and economic and social well-being of citizens. This does not necessarily mean that government directly runs or supervises the economy or society. Nor does it mean that all governments pursue these tasks; corrupt governments do not pursue them, but they risk being overthrown.

First, a nation must preserve itself as a state and ensure its national survival. It helps if the world community recognizes the nation's independence and the integrity of its boundaries, in a word, its sovereignty. Also important is a country's stability. A politically stable nation has an established system with the orderly transfer of power from one party or leader to another. It preserves domestic peace by maintaining law and order and by protecting property. A government can also enlist popular support by ensuring there are jobs, education, and health for all of its citizens, who are then likely to see the regime as legitimate.

How can government best advance the economic and social well-being of its citizens? States face two questions: (1) How much of the economy should the state own or supervise? (2) How much of the nation's wealth should be redistributed to help the poorer sectors of society? The answers produce four general approaches to promoting the general welfare: laissez-faire, statism, socialism, and the welfare state. These array themselves into a fourfold table, much beloved of political scientists (see Figure 3.1).

A **laissez-faire** system owns little or no industry and redistributes relatively little in the form of welfare programs. As we shall explore in Chapter 6 on ideologies, these countries are the followers of Adam Smith, who argued that any government interference in the economy slows growth and ultimately decreases prosperity. Thomas Jefferson summed up this approach with his famous dictum, "That government is best that governs least." The theory here is that people will prosper or fail on the basis of their abilities and drive and that government has no right to intervene in this natural process.

KEY TERMS

laissez-faire   French for "let it be"; economic system of minimal government interference and supervision; capitalism.

welfarism   Economic system of major government redistribution of income to help less-fortunate citizens.

A **welfare state** owns little or no industry but does redistribute wealth to aid the less well-off. Sometimes also known as "social democracies," the welfare states of northwest Europe offer "cradle-to-grave" benefits in the form of health insurance, child care, job training, and retirement funds. To pay for this, they charge the world's highest taxes—in Sweden and Denmark, for example, more than 50 percent of the country's gross domestic product (GDP). Industry,

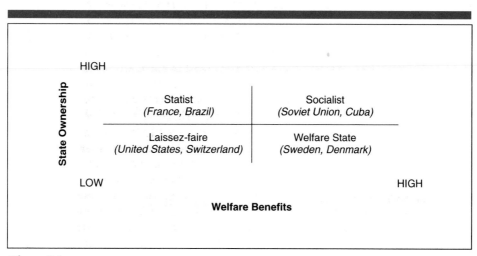

Figure 3.1

though, is almost strictly private and oriented to capitalist
moneymaking.

Statism is an old system that predates laissez-faire. A statist system is one in which the state (meaning the national
government) is the number-one capitalist, owning and running much major industry. It is little interested, however, in
providing welfare benefits. Statism began when the French
kings founded a powerful, centralized state that supervised
industry for the sake of French wealth and power. Sometimes
called by its French name *étatisme*, it typically includes state
ownership of railroads, steel mills, banks, oil, and other big
enterprises. Small and medium business is left in private
hands. Statism caught on in much of Europe, but especially found a home in
Latin America; Brazil and Mexico were statist systems (now reforming). The
bureaucratic supervision of Japan's economy has led some to call it statist, even
though there is little government ownership. Many developing countries have
followed statist models with the argument that only the government has the
money, ideas, and talent to start up new industries. The economic results suggest
state-owned firms are inefficient because they are run by bureaucrats and face no
competition; often they operate at a loss and have to be subsidized by the national treasury. Statist systems such as Argentina and Chile grew more prosperous
after they privatized their state-owned firms.

A **socialist** system practices both state ownership and extensive welfare benefits. Exemplified by the former Soviet Union, government owns most of the
means of production, claiming it runs the economy in the interests of the society
as a whole. However, the collapse of Communist regimes (which called themselves "socialist"; we called them "Communist") throughout Europe indicates
those governments ran things poorly. Today, only China, Vietnam, North Korea,
and Cuba remain as (negative) examples of socialism, and their systems seem ripe
for change.

In actual practice, governments tend to combine elements of these four systems. Even the basically laissez-faire United States has some government supervision of the economy and welfare measures. Communist China and Vietnam
have private, capitalistic sectors of their economy. The questions are never settled,
and countries often change their combinations. In our day, we have seen a massive shift away from state-owned industry in the ex-Soviet Union, France, and
Latin America. Extensive welfare states like Sweden have felt the pinch of too-
generous benefits and too-high taxes.

The State as Agent of Modernization

A basic American attitude is that government—known in other countries as "the
state"—be kept small. In much of the rest of the world, however, state power is
accepted as natural and good. In France, for example, a strong state was started
by Louis XI in the fifteenth century, expanded under Louis XIII and Cardinal

Richelieu in the seventeenth century, implanted itself into French consciousness, and later spread through most of Europe. It was taken for granted that the state should supervise the economy and education, collect taxes, build highways and canals, and field standing armies. A bureaucratic elite, trained in special schools, ran the country.

These attitudes lasted well into our century and are still present. Defeated by Germany in 1870–1871, the French elite used the state as an agent of modernization. The government in Paris tried to build a unified and cohesive population, to turn "peasants into Frenchmen." A centralized school system stamped out local dialects, broke stagnant rural traditions, and recruited the best talent for universities. State-owned industries turned France into an industrial power. Beaten by Germany again in World War II, the French elite again used state power to modernize France.

Did it work? France did modernize greatly, but was this the fastest or most efficient way to do so? Britain and the United States historically advanced farther with minimal government supervision; the competitive spirit of the free-market economy did the job faster and cheaper. (The comparison is not quite fair; Britain and the United States didn't face a powerful, expansionist Germany on their borders. If they had, the role of government probably would have been much bigger.)

Another example of state-led modernization is Japan. With the Meiji Restoration of 1868, Tokyo assigned various branches of industry to samurai clans, provided funds, and told them to copy the best of the West. In one generation, Japan went from the bamboo age to the steel age under the slogan "Rich nation, strong army!" After World War II, the Ministry of Finance and Ministry of International Trade and Industry (MITI) supervised Japan's economic leap by aiming bank loans to growth industries, keeping out foreign products, and penetrating the world market with Japanese products. Before we say government supervision of the economy doesn't work, we had better explain why it worked in Japan. (The Japanese, of course, have an entirely different and more cooperative culture. An American MITI might not work in our economic and attitudinal context.)

Does—or should—the state serve as an agent of modernization? Should government attempt to supervise the economy by providing plans, suggestions, industrywide cooperation, and loans? The traditional American answer is "No, it'll just mess things up." Looking more closely, though, we notice that the federal government has repeatedly goaded American society forward by acquiring large territories, letting settlers homestead them, and giving railroads rights of way. Earlier in our century, the Tennessee Valley Authority brought electricity and flood control to a backward part of America. Faced with murderous competition in computers, the U.S. government, under conservative Ronald Reagan, set up a consortium of private firms to plan and build the next generation of computers before our friends across the Pacific could. America, too, has used the state as an agent of modernization and still use federal programs to promote industry. One of the great questions of modern politics is how much state intervention do we want?

Classic Works — ARISTOTLE'S SIX TYPES OF GOVERNMENT

The earliest and most famous classification of governments was Aristotle's in the fourth century B.C. Aristotle distinguished among three legitimate kinds of government—where the ruling authority acts in the interests of all—and three corrupt counterparts—where government acts only in the interests of self.

A monarchy, according to Aristotle, is one person ruling in the interest of all. But monarchy can degenerate into tyranny, the corrupt form, under which the single ruler exercises power for the benefit of self. Aristocracy, Greek for rule of the best (*aristos*), is several persons ruling in the interest of all. But this legitimate rule by an elite can decay into oligarchy, the corrupt form, in which several persons rule in the interest of themselves.

Aristotle saw the *polity* (what we might call constitutional democracy) as the rule of many in the interests of all and the best form of government. All citizens have a voice in selecting leaders and framing laws, but formal constitutional procedures protect rights. But Aristotle warned that polity can decay into the corrupt form, democracy, the rule of many in the interests of themselves, the worst form of government. Deluded into thinking that one person is as good as another, the masses in a democracy follow the lead of corrupt and selfish demagogues and plunder the property of the hardworking and the capable. Aristotle's classification, which reigned for nearly twenty-five centuries, is still useful and can be summarized as shown below:

Who Governs	Legitimate Forms: Rule in the Interest of All	Corrupt Forms: Rule in the Interest of Selves
One	Monarchy	Tyranny
A few	Aristocracy	Oligarchy
Many	Polity	Democracy

The Autonomy of Associations   One more recent approach identifies the extent of *subsystem autonomy* or *pluralism* as a key feature that distinguishes one type of government from another. Every modern society contains many institutions and organizations that can be thought of as subsystems of society: religious denominations, colleges, labor unions, industrial corporations, civic associations, political parties, and the mass media. We can classify governments according to how much **autonomy** they allow these subsystems. In a pluralistic system, associations are largely free to run their own internal affairs and even try to influence government.

Totalitarian governments, such as Nazi Germany and the Soviet Union, permit little or no subsystem autonomy. As Carl J. Friedrich and Zbigniew Brzezinski pointed out, such societies have official and dogmatic ideologies to which all social institutions must adhere. Everything is organized—even churches and sports—and supervised by the state. What is called **civil society** is either crushed or controlled. The reestablishment of civil society in ex-Communist countries is a difficult but crucial task if democracy is to flourish.

Democratic or constitutional governments, on the other hand, give great autonomy to subsystems. Civil society is firmly established. Private associations may govern themselves and do as they wish, provided it does not harm the general well-being of the society. In a pluralistic system, groups are free to voice their demands, support candidates, and influence government.

Centralization of Political Power within the State Governments may also be classified into unitary and federal states by their territorial distribution of power. Great Britain, France, Italy, Israel, and the vast majority of the world's nations are **unitary states**. A single national or central government drafts and administers most laws and allows little local autonomy. The national government in London and Paris writes the rules for Lincolnshire or Bordeaux. In the twenty or so **federal nations**, such as the United States, Germany, Australia, and Canada, power is divided between the national government and the state or provincial governments. Usually, the national government controls foreign affairs, defense, and currency, whereas state authorities handle education, welfare, and policing.

> ### KEY TERMS
>
> **civil society** In modern usage, all associations bigger than the family but smaller than the state, such as churches, firms, clubs.
>
> **unitary systems** The concentration of power in the nation's capital with little autonomy accorded to subdivisions.
>
> **federalism** The territorial balancing of power between a nation's capital and autonomous subdivisions, such as U.S. states.

Making Public Policy

All modern governments are involved in the complex business of making public policy. Backward or corrupt governments are less involved in such matters. President Mobutu of Zaire was chiefly interested in enriching himself, a demonstration that Aristotle's classification is still applicable. In legitimate systems, public policies are created to meet perceived national needs. Policies include legislation, judicial rulings, executive decrees, and administrative decisions. Policies are implemented through programs, which are specific measures aimed at influencing the direction of government activity and public life.

Although governments claim to pursue policies and programs consistent with the good of the nation, the programs are often steered to favor influential interest groups. Since money is always limited, everyone cannot get everything they want. Is it more important for the United States to send rockets into space or to rebuild our cities? Should we use public funds to clean up polluted rivers or to put additional police officers on our streets? Decision makers must make such choices amid debate, lobbying, partisan bickering, and sometimes outright bribery. With almost every choice, someone gets helped while others are hurt. Out of sight, money often changes hands. Conflict over public-policy choices constitute what is conventionally called "politics." It can never be totally clean because it is tightly bound up with power and money. "Politics," as one politician said, "is like a delicate flower. It needs a little dirt to grow in."

Public Policies: Material and Symbolic

Material public-policy decisions require the expenditure of public funds, which are scarce in every country. Most acts of Congress have dollar signs attached. Symbolic public policies, on the other hand, involve little money or personnel and often are not even passed as laws. They create sentimental attachments (patriotism, loyalty, deference, or national pride) or confer social status on certain groups. The proclamation of a new public holiday, such as for slain black civil rights leader Martin Luther King, Jr., is a symbolic policy that does nothing in a material way to help African Americans. As Murray Edelman pointed out in *The Symbolic Uses of Politics*, governments often use **symbolic policies** to deflect public concern. Material, or **tangible**, policies can be expensive and may anger the groups that have to bear the burden. Thus it is easier to proclaim "National Clean Air Day" with televised publicity than to enforce emission standards that cost industry money. Notice how much of current politics, especially that which is covered in the mass media, are symbolic rather than material.

KEY TERMS
symbolic Acts and things calculated to make people feel satisfied and arouse patriotism, national pride, and obedience.
tangible Real benefits to complaining groups, usually dollars.

All governments are careful to support and foster symbols of national unity. Symbols are created and popularized to give people something they can identify with. When Americans think of the United States, they may get an image of the Statue of Liberty, "Old Glory," or the Liberty Bell. Occasionally, such symbols can become a source of controversy: In Canada a bitter debate over a proposal for a new national flag contributed to the defeat of the Conservative party in 1963. (The maple leaf won, and is now accepted by most Canadians.) South Africa adopted a totally different flag with the advent of a black government in 1994, one that pleases the newly enfranchised black majority.

Moral symbols are often invoked by public officials to build support. In America, most candidates for public office like to be photographed in church, because religious worship is a powerful moral symbol linked with family values and stability. Few high public officials are seen smoking or drinking in public, and for many years it was taboo for elected officials to be divorced. (Conservative Ronald Reagan, ironically, was the first divorced person to win the presidency.) Symbolic issues can become politically divisive, as in the question of prayer in public schools.

Symbols can even lead to war. When Croatia declared its independence from Yugoslavia in 1991, it restored the use of medieval Croatian currency, uniforms, and coat of arms. These old symbols made many Croats feel good, but they

Polish Symbol: Three giant steel crosses at the Gdansk shipyard mark the spot where forty-five workers were gunned down as they demonstrated against the regime in December 1970. This powerful symbol helped launch the Solidarity movement and bring down the Communist regime in 1989. (Michael Roskin)

alarmed the Serbian minority of Croatia, for they were exactly the names and symbols used by the Croatian fascist regime of World War II, a regime that murdered some 350,000 Serbs. As a result, the Serbs of Croatia broke away with their mini-republic of Krajina, which the Croats finally retook in 1995. If the Croatian regime had been more sensitive with its symbols in 1991, it might have avoided much tragedy. Symbols can be dynamite.

Key Terms

anarchy (p. 42)	laissez-faire (p. 47)	state (p. 38)
autonomy (p. 50)	nation (p. 38)	statism (p. 48)
civil society (p. 51)	nationalism (p. 39)	symbolic (p. 52)
cohesive (p. 42)	protogovernment (p. 42)	tangible (p. 52)
diplomatic recognition (p. 41)	regionalism (p. 39)	unitary systems (p. 51)
federalism (p. 51)	socialism (p. 48)	welfarism (p. 47)

Key Websites

This website has links illustrating the structures of nationalism: globalism, macro-cultural, nation state nationalism, ethno-nationalism, and localism.
http://web.inter.nl.net/users/Paul.Treanor/nationalism.links.2.html# national

This site lists all sorts of links to online nationalism resources.
http://kennedy.soc.surrey.ac.uk/socresonline/2/1/natlinks.html

Popular theory of nationalism is Bullets and Borders, from the New Internationalist.
http://www.oneworld.org/ni/issue277/keynote.html

The International Affairs WWW Virtual Library links to many sites.
http://www.etown.edu/home/selchewa/international_studies/ firstpag.htm

A clickable map that lists all of the wars currently in progress around the world. Click on an area and be connected to weblinks related to that conflict.
http://www.cfcsc.dnd.ca/links/wars/index.html

Further Reference

Bebler, Anton, and Jim Seroka, eds. *Contemporary Political Systems: Classifications and Typologies*. Boulder, CO: Lynne Rienner, 1990.

Edelman, Murray. *The Symbolic Uses of Politics*. Urbana, IL: University of Illinois Press, 1964.

Emerson, Rupert. *From Empire to Nation: The Rise to Self-Assertion of Asian and African Peoples*. Cambridge, MA: Harvard University Press, 1960.

Finer, S. E. *The History of Government from the Earliest Times*, Vols. I–III. New York: Oxford University Press, 1997.

Kohn, Hans. *Nationalism: Its Meaning and History*. New York: Crowell-Collier and Macmillan, 1955.

Lipset, Seymour Martin. *The First New Nation: The United States in Historical and Comparative Perspective*. Garden City, NY: Doubleday, 1967.

Miller, David. *On Nationality*. New York: Oxford University Press, 1995.

Palmer, Monte. *Political Development: Dilemmas and Challenges*. Itasca, IL: F. E. Peacock, 1997.

Porter, Bruce D. *War and the Rise of the State: The Military Foundations of Modern Politics*. New York: Free Press, 1994.

Tilly, Charles, ed. *The Formation of National States in Western Europe*. Princeton, NJ: Princeton University Press, 1975.

Weber, Eugen. *Peasants into Frenchmen: The Modernization of Rural France, 1870–1914*. Stanford, CA: Stanford University Press, 1976.

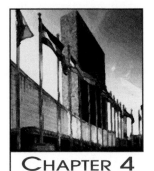

Individuals and Constitutions

The problem of establishing and limiting power exists in every political system. Government and the people must both have certain powers and rights, but their activities must also be limited to keep them from encroaching on the rights of others. Choices such as a fair balance between government powers and civil liberties and between the welfare of the majority and the rights of the minority are not easy ones. For example, do air traffic controllers, who are federal employees, have the right to strike and inconvenience thousands of people? If Congress votes "legislative vetoes" into bills as a way to supervise the executive branch, can the Supreme Court declare them unconstitutional? If religious parents believe that children should pray in public schools, does this conflict with the separation of church and state?

> ### QUESTIONS TO CONSIDER
>
> 1. What is a constitution?
> 2. What is constitutionalism?
> 3. What is wrong with constitutions specifying social and economic rights in detail?
> 4. How can the very short U.S. Constitution still work in the modern age?
> 5. Do most constitutions specify "checks and balances"?
> 6. How has the U.S. Constitution changed over time?
> 7. What, if any, limits can be placed on free speech?

These questions raise problems of rights and political power, and some of these problems are admittedly more difficult than others. Most of us would probably agree that a Supreme Court decision is law even if Congress doesn't like it. We will probably disagree, though, on the right of air traffic controllers to strike. It can be argued that the controllers should not be denied the right to ask for higher wages simply because they perform a public service. Yet a case can also be made that no one, including overworked air traffic controllers, has the right to deny people such an important element of public safety. The question of whether children should pray in public school is also difficult. Which prayers would suit all religions? What about children who do not wish to pray at all? How does society determine how to limit political power and how to balance the needs of the majority with the rights of individuals and **minorities**? Governments need some guidelines in determining where this balance should fall. These guidelines are provided by

> ### KEY TERM
>
> **minority** Subgroup distinct by language, ethnicity, race, or religion within the larger society.

traditions, by **statutes**, and above all by national constitutions, which lay down
the basic ground rules for governing society.

Constitutions in the Modern World

In common usage, a **constitution** is a written document that
sets forth the fundamental rules by which a political system is
governed. Political scientists define the word as that set of
rules and customs, either written or unwritten, legally established or extralegal, by which a government conducts its
affairs. By this definition, almost all nations have constitutions since they operate according to some set of rules. In
chaotic, corrupt, or dictatorial systems, constitutions may not
count for much. Afghanistan, torn between rival Islamic militants, does not yet have a stable constitution. In Congo (formerly Zaire),
Mobutu allowed nothing to limit his stealing of the country's wealth. And Stalin
in 1936—precisely when he began his bloody purges—set up a Soviet constitution that looked fine on paper. The Stalin constitution was just a trick to fool the
gullible. A few countries like Britain and Israel may have no single written document but still have constitutions. British customs, statues, precedents, and traditions are so strong that the British government considers itself bound by practices
developed over the centuries. Thus, Britain is governed by a constitution.

In the modern world, nearly every nation has a written constitution, and it
is supposed to establish the forms, institutions, and limits of government and set
guidelines for balancing minority and majority interests. Not all function that
way. Political scientists learn to ask not only what is written but what is actually
practiced as the true functioning of a constitution. The Constitution of the United
States, for example, is very short and leaves much unsaid. Its seven articles mostly define the powers of each branch of government; the subsequent twenty-six
amendments broadly define civil rights but leave much open for interpretation.

In contrast, most of the nations that have won independence since World
War II have adopted constitutions of remarkable detail. The post-war Japanese
constitution, which was drafted by the U.S. military government after World
War II, contains no less than forty separate articles outlining the rights and
duties of the people alone. Among the individual rights enumerated are the
rights to productive employment, a decent standard of living, and social welfare
benefits—a sharp contrast to the general values of "justice … domestic tranquillity … common defense … general welfare … liberty" outlined in the American
Preamble. Article I of the German constitution (the Basic Law) also enumerates
a long list of rights. These include not only fundamental rights, such as legal and
political freedoms, but also a number of social and economic safeguards, including state supervision of the educational system and public control of the economy. The 1988 Brazilian constitution enumerates so many rights—a forty-hour
work week, medical and retirement plans, minimum wages, maximum interest

---

THE DANGERS OF CHANGING CONSTITUTIONS

Beware the country that keeps changing its constitution; it is a sign of instability and indicates that no constitution has rooted itself into the hearts and minds of the people. France, since the Revolution, has had fifteen constitutions, not all of them put into practice. Brazil has had seven since independence in 1822. Yugoslavia under Tito came out with a new constitution every decade, each more dubious than the one before. The 1963 Yugoslav constitution provided for a legislature of *five* chambers. Such constant experimentation with the highest law of the land meant that no constitution was really established and legitimate. It is one reason Yugoslavia fell apart in bloodshed in 1991. Constitutions are too important to experiment with.

---

rates, environmental protection, you name it—that Brazil's struggling economy cannot afford them; these are rights that also block economic reform. Many now believe that detailed social and economic rights should never have been put into the constitution; they belong to statutes (the ordinary laws that parliaments pass) or to the workings of the market. Such detailed enumerations of rights that cannot be fulfilled are common in post-World War II constitutions, whose drafters liked to think they can mandate fixes to social and economic evils.

Britain may be able to get by with no written constitution, although an increasing number of Britons think it is high time they too had a written constitution, complete with a charter of rights and freedoms on the U.S. model. The somewhat newer United States manages to function with a very general constitution. In both Britain and the United States, the details are filled in by usage over time. But most recently established nations commit themselves to long written constitutions that try to spell out everything in detail.

The Highest Law of the Land

Nations adopt constitutions for the same reason that the ancient Mesopotamian lawgiver Hammurabi codified the laws of Babylon: to establish a supreme law of the land. Constitutions state the fundamental laws of society and are not meant to be easily revised. They stand as a yardstick by which any activities of the government or the people are to be measured. A legislature can pass a law one year and repeal it the next, but basic constitutional provisions cannot be amended so easily. In Sweden, constitutional amendments must be passed by two successive legislatures with a general election in between. In the United States, amending the Constitution is even more difficult. The most common procedure is to secure the approval of two-thirds of both the Senate and the House of Representatives, then obtain ratification by three-fourths of the state legislatures. The fact that our Constitution has been amended only seventeen times since the adoption of the Bill of Rights in 1791 illustrates how difficult the amendment procedure is. The

Equal Rights Amendment failed to pass in 1983, for example, because fewer than three-fourths of the state legislatures voted to ratify it.

The General Nature of Constitutional Law   Since constitutions, no matter how detailed, cannot provide specifically for every legal or administrative problem that may arise, many provide for a constitutional court to interpret the highest law in specific cases. This concept of judicial interpretation of a constitution is a fairly new thing worldwide; it was pioneered by the United States and has spread only in recent decades. Accordingly, many of our examples are American.

The U.S. Constitution says that "Congress shall make no law respecting an establishment of religion, or prohibiting the free exercise thereof" in Amendment I of the Bill of Rights. This is a very general statement. The way it will be interpreted in a specific case (such as the question of prayer in school or perhaps a satanic cult that believes in animal sacrifice or illegal drugs) must depend on the decision makers in power at the time the case arises. Does it mean that children must not pray in public schools, because that breaches the separation of church and state? Or that they may pray in schools as part of their free exercise of religion? Or that they must pray in schools because that is what most people in a given school district want?

Constitutional law must be interpreted to be applied to specific incidents. Who is given the immense authority to decide what the general wording of a constitution means? In over thirty nations, including the United States, this responsibility belongs to the highest national court. The procedure by which the court rules on the constitutionality of a government act and declares null and void those acts it considers unconstitutional is known as **judicial review**. The power of judicial review is a controversial one. Many critics have accused the Supreme Court (most notably when Earl Warren was chief justice from 1953 to 1969) of imposing a personal philosophy as the law of the land. To a large extent, a constitution is indeed what its interpreters say it is, but the possibility of too subjective an interpretation seems to be a necessary risk taken by any nation that has one.

KEY TERMS

judicial review Ability of courts to decide if laws are constitutional; not present in all countries.

judicial activism Willingness of some judges to override legislatures by declaring certain statutes unconstitutional.

judicial restraint
Unwillingness of some judges to overturn statutes passed by legislatures.

The courts do not always interpret a constitution in a consistent fashion. In the United States, the Warren Court best exemplified the type of judicial philosophy generally known as **judicial activism**. This does not necessarily mean "liberal." It refers to a judge's willingness to strike down certain laws and practices in order to guarantee citizens' rights. The opposite philosophy is that of **judicial restraint**—a generalization that describes a Supreme Court that sees its job not as legislating but as following the lead of Congress. Justices Oliver Wendell Holmes and Felix Frankfurter, who counseled the Court on judicial restraint, were regarded by many as great liberals.

Likewise, Germany's Federal Constitutional Court is no stranger to controversy. Modeled after the U.S. Supreme Court—except that it has sixteen justices—the German court is mandated to make sure all laws conform to the **Basic Law**. In 1975, the German court found that a law permitting abortions conflicted with the strong right-to-life provisions of the Basic Law—which had been put in to repudiate the horrors of the Nazi era—

> **KEY TERM**
>
> **Basic Law** German *Grundgesetz*. Germany's constitution since 1949.

and declared abortion unconstitutional. After German unification in 1990, the court allowed some abortions in East Germany, because that had been the established law and usage there. In 1979, the Federal Constitutional Court found there was nothing unconstitutional about "worker codetermination"—that is, employees having nearly the same rights as owners and managers in determining the long-term future of businesses.

Not all nations give their highest court the power to rule on the constitutionality of laws. In nations that do not have a clearly established procedure of judicial review, this responsibility is often given to the legislature. In Great Britain, Parliament itself makes the final determination of what is constitutional.

Constitutions and Constitutional Government The meaning of a constitution depends largely on the way it is interpreted. Two separate nations could adopt very similar constitutions but have them work quite differently. What is written does not necessarily occur in practice. The Soviet constitution set a government framework—a federal system with a bicameral legislature, with executive and administrative powers given to the cabinetlike Council of Ministers—and accorded to its citizens a long list of democratic rights. Yet in actuality, the government was controlled by the top command of the Communist party, and individual rights were tightly circumscribed.

The governments of Canada, Great Britain, and the United States are constitutional governments; the government of the Soviet Union was not. **Constitutionalism** refers to the degree to which the power of government is limited and individual rights are respected. In a constitutionally governed nation,

> **KEY TERM**
>
> **constitutionalism** Degree to which government limits its powers.

government is limited by laws and institutions to make sure that the fundamental rights of citizens—such as freedom of speech and religion and freedom from arbitrary imprisonment—are not violated. In contrast, an authoritarian government is not limited by its constitution; individuals and minority groups have little protection against arbitrary acts of government, in spite of what the constitution may say. In the 1970s, the military regimes of Argentina and Chile "disappeared" (meaning tortured and killed) thousands of suspected leftists even though their written constitutions promised human rights.

The Purpose of a Constitution

If some nations pay little heed to what is written in their constitutions, why do they bother to write a constitution at all? Constitutions fulfill a variety of roles: They provide the symbolic function of putting in writing a statement of national ideals, they formalize the structure of government, and they attempt to justify the government's right to govern.

A Statement of National Ideals   According to the Preamble of the U.S. Constitution, our nation is dedicated to six goals: to form a more perfect union, to establish justice, to ensure domestic tranquillity, to provide for the common defense, to promote the general welfare, and to secure the blessings of liberty. The 1977 Soviet constitution proclaimed the Soviet Union to be a "developed socialist society" dedicated to building a classless utopia. The constitution of the Federal Republic of Germany, seeking to erase any traces of Nazi rule, states its determination to "serve the peace of the world" and expressly proclaims that no group of people can be stripped of their German citizenship—a reaction to Hitler's Nuremburg Laws, which declared hundreds of thousands of citizens to be non-citizens.

Preambles and lists of rights are symbolic statements: They indicate the values, ideals, and goals of those who draft the documents. Preambles are by nature very general and have dubious legal force. How are they interpreted? What does the U.S. Constitution mean by a "more perfect union," for example? There is considerable disagreement over this question; in fact, debate over the meaning of this term led to the Civil War a century ago. What does the Constitution mean by "establishing justice"? What is justice, and is it the same for all citizens? If American blacks have been denied equal rights for two centuries, does this mean that it is just for them to be given an advantage now in admission to colleges or getting jobs and housing? Or, again, what does the Preamble mean by "promoting the general welfare"? The questions of what the general welfare is and how it is to be balanced against the rights of the individual or of a minority group are almost certain to produce different answers from everyone. Are children who wish to pray formally in school setting a precedent disruptive to the general welfare? Does the ability to purchase handguns like the "Saturday-night special," which are not accurate enough for any use but robbery, harm the general welfare, even though the Bill of Rights seems to give citizens the right to bear arms? Although constitutions provide a statement of national ideals, the interpretation of these goals and values necessitates an active choice by the decision makers of government.

Formalizes the Structure of Government   A constitution is also a blueprint, a written description of who does what in government, defining the authority and limiting the powers of each branch and providing for regularized channels through which conflict may be resolved. Articles I through III of the U.S. Constitution outline the duties of Congress, the president, and the judiciary. Congress may collect taxes and customs duties but is prohibited from taxing exports. The president is named commander in chief of the armed forces but must have the "advice and consent" of the Senate to conclude treaties. In a system in which there is **separation of powers**, the constitution divides authority and responsibilities among the various branches of government; it also limits the power of each branch.

> **KEY TERM**
>
> **separation of powers**   U.S. doctrine that branches of government should be distinct, a doctrine found in few other governments.

No other constitution uses "checks and balances" like the American one in an elaborate attempt to limit power; most, in fact, specify the unification of power, a point we will study in Chapter 14. Few constituent assemblies view the concentration of power with the

KEY TERM

State Duma   Russia's national legislature.

same abhorrence shown by the U.S. Founding Fathers. By our lights, the new Russian constitution gives the president far too much power and the parliament, the **State Duma**, too little, an imbalance that bothers few Russians, most of whom prefer a strong hand at the top to "get things done."

A constitution also outlines the division of power between central and regional or local governments. In a federal system of government, powers and responsibilities are divided between one national government and several provincial or state governments. Germany and Australia, like the United States, are federal states. Their constitutions give their central governments control over certain areas, such as foreign policy, foreign commerce, and coinage. Thus, the *Land* of Bavaria in the Federal Republic of Germany may not practice its own foreign policy; neither may the state of Texas mint its own currency. Certain powers are delegated to the central government and others left to the states. In the U.S. Constitution, this division is a general one; any powers not accorded to the central government are reserved for the states and for the people. Thus, the states traditionally control education, police protection, health and welfare services, and local commerce. Of course, this division of power has become less clear-cut, especially in recent years, as the federal government has taken on a greater share of financing the operations of education, health, welfare, housing, and scores of other services.

As we shall explore in Chapter 13, most nations are unitary systems; that is, they do not divide power territorially but concentrate it in the nation's capital. The constitutions of unitary systems, such as France's, specify some powers of regions and localities to raise taxes, engage in urban and economic planning, and hold elections for regional assemblies. Unitary systems do not seek to "balance" powers between central and provincial, but they may give a little autonomy to

---

Case Studies   CANADA'S NEW CONSTITUTION

Canada was in a curious situation. Canada got its independence in 1867 with the British North America Act passed by the British Parliament. As the British Dominion of Canada, it could amend its constitution only by approval of the House of Commons in London. Increasingly, this rankled Canadians, who demanded "patriation" of their constitution, that is, bringing it back to Canada. They got this only in 1982 along with something they had never had before, a Charter of Rights and Freedoms modeled on the U.S. Bill of Rights.

local bodies. They may also remake and even erase existing states and localities; this is not true with federal systems, which cannot erase or alter their component states, each of which has a guaranteed legal existence.

Establishes the Legitimacy of Government   A third role of a constitution is to give a government the stamp of legitimacy. Although this function is undeniably symbolic, its practicality cannot be denied. Many nations in the world community will not even recognize a new state until it has adopted a written constitution; it is a sign of permanence and responsibility.

Most constitutions were written shortly after major changes in regime, and their purpose was to help establish the new regime's right to rule. Typically, **constituent assembly** is the name a legislature gives itself when it meets for the first time after the overthrow of one regime to write a new constitution. The Spanish parliament elected in 1977 turned itself into a constituent assembly to repudiate the Franco system with the new 1978

> **KEY TERM**
>
> **constituent assembly**
> Legislature convened to draft new constitution.

Case Studies — THE RIGHT TO BEAR ARMS

In 1789, the United States was a sparsely settled frontier nation where guns were necessary for survival, and the Constitution reflected this. Amendment II of the Bill of Rights (adopted in 1791) guarantees the right of the citizens to "keep and bear arms." Today, the United States is urbanized, and guns are rarely necessary for survival; instead, they are often used in crime. Recent decades have seen the assassinations of President John F. Kennedy, Dr. Martin Luther King, Jr., and Senator Robert F. Kennedy. President Ronald Reagan and Alabama Governor George Wallace were seriously wounded. Armed robberies and killings by drug dealers are common. Many now argue that it is time to restrict lethal weapons. Yet opponents of gun-control legislation argue that the Constitution ensures the right of every citizen to purchase and own firearms. Hunters, shopkeepers who have been robbed, and those who feel that police cannot protect them argue that their constitutional right to pursue a hobby or to protect their lives will be jeopardized by gun-control legislation.

The "right to bear arms" case illustrates that a two-century-old constitution—at least in its traditional interpretation—may not provide the right answer for all of the needs of modern society. If gun controls are necessary to limit violence in America (and there is no consensus on the issue), can the Constitution be interpreted to allow such legislation to be passed? Amendment II reads, "A well regulated Militia, being necessary to the security of a free State, the right of the people to keep and bear Arms, shall not be infringed." Does this mean that the citizens can own guns privately or that they can own guns for the purpose of maintaining a militia, what we now call the National Guard? Due in large part to handguns, the U.S. murder rate is four to five times higher than European murder rates and three times higher than the Canadian rate.

Case Studies

THE SHIFT IN THE FEDERAL
BALANCE OF POWER

The role of the central government has grown markedly in relation to the powers of the state governments since the era of the New Deal in the 1930s. The Great Depression resulted in around 20 percent of the workforce being unemployed; they needed assistance, and the states could not afford to provide it. In response, the federal government took on a broader range of employment, welfare, health, and housing services than ever before, and this responsibility has grown. Even recent budget-balancing cutbacks in federal spending have still left us with a large federal government, one that states still turn to for help.

The writers of the American Constitution probably never envisioned that the federal government would someday take on the tasks of feeding the poor, licensing TV networks, cleaning up chemical wastes, or building highways. They assumed that the states would provide practically all services. How has the document they wrote been able to adapt to the modern American federalism? The so-called "elastic clause" gives Congress the power to enact all legislation necessary to carry out its enumerated powers. For example, feeding poor children and helping schools can be seen as promoting the general welfare. High-tech research helps to provide for the common defense. Licensing communications networks falls under the powers granted to the Congress to lay and collect taxes and to regulate commerce. The elastic clause was put there for a reason, so the Constitution could change and adapt over time.

constitution. That job done, it turned itself back into the Cortes, the regular parliament. In 1990, Bulgaria elected a 400-member Grand National Assembly to write a new, post-Communist constitution. That done, in 1991 Bulgaria elected a regular parliament, the 240-member National Assembly. The U.S. Articles of Confederation and, subsequently, the U.S. Constitution symbolized American independence. The French constitution of 1791 (which never went into effect) tried to replace the divine right of Louis XVI with the sovereign right of the people. And the first Soviet constitution of 1918 established a "dictatorship of the people" to replace tsarist rule. As a symbolic statement of intentions with a practical outline of structure, a constitution helps to set the stamp of legitimacy on a new regime.

The Adaptability of the U.S. Constitution

Constitutions are modified by countless traditions, customs, and laws. For instance, the U.S. Constitutions does not mention political parties, yet our party system is an established part of the American political process. Judicial precedents and government traditions, too, make up the fundamental laws of society.

Constitutions need some flexibility to adapt over time. A look at the way in which the Constitution has adapted over two centuries and in two areas—the "right to bear arms" and the growth of "big government" in the twentieth century—demonstrate this.

Can the Constitution Ensure Rights?

Civil Liberties and Civil Rights   During World War II, Nazi Germany set up concentration camps to exterminate millions, and the Japanese army raped and pillaged through China. In reaction, the world community took steps to try to prevent such horrors in the future. In 1948, the General Assembly of the United Nations adopted the Universal Declaration on Human Rights, a symbolic statement (with no real power of sanction), which establishes fundamental precepts and norms which most nations are reluctant to violate openly. Countries that do—Mao had tens of millions of Chinese killed; Saddam Hussein used poison gas against fellow Iraqis; Laurent Kabila condoned and covered up tribal massacres in the Congo—risk being isolated from world aid and trade. Human-rights violations may persuade the United Nations to engage in peacekeeping operations, as in Bosnia. Although not directly enforceable, the setting of norms for human rights helps a little.

The Universal Declaration, patterned on the French Declaration of the Rights of Man and Citizen and on the American Declaration of Independence and the Bill of Rights, affirms the basic **civil and human rights** that government may not arbitrarily take away. These include the rights to life and freedom of assembly, expression, movement, religion, and political participation. The Universal Declaration also provides for many economic and cultural needs: the rights to work; to an education; to marry, raise a family, and provide for that family; the right to live according to one's culture. These rights are almost impossible to enforce and few have tried. The fact is that rights and liberties are difficult to define, and all nations restrict civil liberties in some way. The problem of minority groups occurs almost everywhere, certainly in the United States.

> ### KEY TERMS
>
> **civil rights**   Ability to participate in politics and society, such as voting, free speech, and equal opportunity; sometimes confused with but at a higher level than human rights.
>
> **human rights**   Freedom from government mistreatment such as arrest, torture, jail, and death without due process.

Minority Groups and Civil Liberties   Few nations are homogeneous; most have citizens with a variety of racial, ethnic, religious, cultural, or linguistic backgrounds, and their civil or cultural liberties are often compromised. Haitians living in Florida or Chicanos in New Mexico are at a disadvantage unless they speak what to them is a foreign language. Indians and Pakistanis in Great Britain, Algerians in France, and Turks in Germany must conform to the ways of the dominant culture. But the Universal Declaration states that minorities have the right to preserve their cultural uniqueness. Can it—or should it—be enforced in these situations? The major U.S. debate over "multiculturalism" hinges on this question. Should the United States abandon *e pluribus unum* and instead cultivate

Case Studies   THE HORROR OF INTERNMENT

One of the biggest U.S. violations of minority rights happened in 1942, when some 120,000 Japanese-Americans on the West Coast were interned under the infamous Executive Order 9066 in the mistaken belief that they were enemy aliens (most were born in the United States). Robbed of their homes, businesses, and liberty without due process of law, they were sent to ramshackle, dusty camps surrounded by barbed wire and guard towers—in some ways similar to Nazi concentration camps. Not one case of disloyalty was ever demonstrated against a Japanese-American; they were victims of racism and wartime hysteria.

Even Secretary of War Henry L. Stimson, who signed the order, feared it "would make a tremendous hole in our Constitution." It did, but not until 1983 did a federal court overturn the legality of internment. The incident shows that even a well-established democracy can throw its civil liberties out the window in a moment of exaggerated and groundless panic. The 442nd Regimental Combat Team, recruited from Japanese-Americans, covered itself with glory and was the most decorated U.S. unit of World War II.

and preserve the distinctiveness of each ethnic group? Do the children of each group have the right to be schooled in their parents' language? In 1998 California voters—including a majority of Latinos—approved Proposition 227, ending bilingual education and making English the only and standard language of instruction. Were somebody's rights being violated? Or were they being improved? Most Spanish-speakers want their children to master English *para ganar más dinero.*

Freedom of Expression in the United States

"Congress shall make no law ... abridging the freedom of speech, or of the press; or the right of the people peaceably to assemble, and to petition the government for a redress of grievances." So says Amendment I of the U.S. Bill of Rights. We think of freedom of expression as one of the hallmarks of any nation calling itself democratic. Citizens who think the government is bad or wrong may say publicly. A surrealist antigovernment or antireligion artwork should draw no interference or investigation from any government agency.

It sounds easy but is not that simple. Does freedom of speech give a campus bigot the right to incite hatred of African-American students? Does a newspaper have a right to publish information that might damage the security of the nation? We may all believe in the right of free expression, but most of us would agree that there are limits. In the example used by Justice Oliver Wendell Holmes, nobody should be permitted to yell "Fire!" in a crowded theater unless there really is a fire. Free speech does not include the right to spread dangerous or malicious falsehoods, for example, telling police there are drugs in a certain apartment when there are not.

According to Justice Holmes, freedom of expression must also be restricted in cases in which statements or publications present a "clear and present danger" of bringing about "substantive evils," which Congress has a right to prevent. The Supreme Court, in its 1925 *Gitlow v. New York* decision, upheld the conviction of a radical who had called for the violent overthrow of the government on the grounds that his words had represented a "bad tendency," which could "corrupt morals, incite crime, and disturb the public peace." That decision, during a time of "red scare," would likely come out different today.

Controversies relating to free speech are neverending. In 1994, in another First Amendment case, the Supreme Court struck down the ordinance of a posh suburb prohibiting homeowners from posting political signs on their property. Recently, some have argued that free speech has gone too far, especially if it deals in racism and pornography or throttles others' speech in the name of "political correctness." Congress in 1998 was unable to pass a campaign-reform law to curb the influence of big money partly because campaign contributions are seen by many (including the Supreme Court) as a form of free speech. Dollars, they argue, are like words; both should flow without restriction to support candidates and causes. The Internet has opened whole new areas to this debate. Can anyone say anything to anyone else at any time? No matter what the consequences?

Free Speech and Sedition

KEY TERM
sedition   Incitement to public disorder or to overthrow the state.

Sedition is defined in the common law as any criticism of the government or government officials designed to produce discontent or rebellion. It has been used by the U.S. government to suppress some forms of radical expression during several periods of our history since the adoption of the Bill of Rights. Congress passed the first Sedition Act in 1798, after the XYZ affair. It was aimed at the "Jacobins," as American defenders of the French Revolution were called, at a time when the United States was in an undeclared naval war with France. The Sedition Act was supposed to expire the day that President John Adams left office (which indicates that its true purpose may have been to influence the election). The act aroused controversy, but it lapsed without any test of constitutionality in the Supreme Court. The next Sedition Act went into effect during the Civil War, when President Lincoln acted under his war powers to suppress Northern opponents of the Union effort. The president's action was brought to the Supreme Court, which declined to judge on the legality of his actions. Lincoln's action went untested, but all "political prisoners" were pardoned at the end of the war.

Twentieth-Century Sedition Acts   It was World War I and the Espionage Act of 1917 that gave rise to Justice Holmes's "clear and present danger" doctrine. At a time when socialists and pacifists were urging people to resist U.S. involvement

Bizarre but legal, this peace vigil, in Lafayette Park across from the White House since 1981, urges people to turn from war to God. In a democracy, even slightly eccentric demonstrations are tolerated.
(Michael Roskin)

in the war by refusing to serve in the army and to disrupt the war effort in other ways, this act prohibited any attempts to interfere with the military recruitment policies of the U.S. government. The Espionage Act resulted in several court cases in 1919. In one case, the Supreme Court upheld the law on the grounds that free speech could be restricted if it created a "clear and present danger" to national security. And so several hundred people, including Socialist party leader Eugene Debs, were imprisoned under the act, but most were pardoned as soon as the war ended.

More recent sedition acts have been directed primarily against Communists. The Smith Act of 1940, the most comprehensive sedition act ever passed by Congress, made it a crime to advocate the violent overthrow of the government, to distribute literature urging such an overthrow, or to knowingly join any organization or group that advocated such actions. The Smith Act aroused much controversy but was not put to a constitutional test until 1951, when the Supreme Court upheld the convictions of the leaders of the American Communist party even though they had not been charged with any overt acts of force against the government. "It is the existence of the conspiracy which constitutes the danger," ruled Chief Justice Vinson, "not the presence or absence of overt action." Since then, there have been other court rulings on the constitutionality of the Smith Act, and they have fluctuated. In *Yates v. the United States* in 1957, the Warren Court reversed the conviction of the American Communist party leaders on the grounds that there was no overt action, only abstract advocacy of rebellion. Four years later, in *Scales v. the United States*, the Court upheld the section of the Smith Act that makes membership in the Communist party illegal—but this ruling also specified that it is active membership, involving the direct intent to bring about

Case Studies   THE PENTAGON PAPERS

In 1971 a multivolume, secret Defense Department study of the decisions that went into the Vietnam war was leaked to the *New York Times* and the *Washington Post*, which started publishing a series of sensational articles based on them. The Nixon administration immediately got a court order blocking further publication on national-security grounds. In what became known as the *Pentagon Papers* case, the Supreme Court quickly and unanimously rejected the government's claim that official secrets had been compromised. By that time, most Americans were fed up with the war. The reasoning of Justice Hugo Black was as follows:

Only a free and unrestrained press can effectively expose deception in government. And paramount among the responsibilities of a free press is the duty to prevent any part of the Government from deceiving the people and sending them off to distant lands to die of foreign fevers and foreign shot and shell.... [T]he newspapers nobly did precisely that which the founders hoped and trusted they would do.

the violent overthrow of the government, that is criminal. The Court was careful to point out that membership per se was not made illegal by the Smith Act.

Probably the most stringent legislation ever enacted in our history to counter the threat of Communist subversion was passed during the McCarthy era after World War II, another red scare. The McCarran Act of 1950 (the Internal Security Act) barred Communists from working for the federal government or in defense-related industries, established a Subversive Activities Control Board (SACB) to enforce the act, and required organizations declared by the SACB to be Communist-influenced to register with the attorney general. The McCarran Act aroused a great deal of controversy. Its critics charged that the law not only encroached on the rights of free speech and free assembly but also violated the self-incrimination clause of the Fifth Amendment. Although the Internal Security Act in its entirety has never been declared unconstitutional, every action by the SACB demanding specific organizational or individual registration with the attorney general's office has been declared unconstitutional. Finally, with the realization on all sides that the SACB was accomplishing nothing, it was abolished in 1973. Interestingly, the U.S. government did essentially nothing to stop criticism of the Vietnam war; opposition was too widespread, and there was no declaration of war.

The history of government action against sedition in the United States indicates that the guarantees of the First Amendment have been interpreted to mean different things at different times. When Congress, the president, and the courts perceive danger and threat, they tend to be more restrictive, in other times more permissive. Free speech is highly context-dependent. We should remember this when we see legal restrictions on human and civil rights in other lands. Some regimes really are under siege; opponents want to overthrow them (often with good reason). And since elections are routinely rigged, the only way to overthrow such regimes is by extralegal means, which may include violence. In such situations, free speech may lead quickly to violent overthrow, which may be richly deserved. Governments of whatever stripe clamp down when they are scared, and they are scared because they know they may be overthrown. Myanmar (formerly Burma), South Korea, Indonesia, Egypt, South Africa, Argentina, and other lands have imprisoned political opponents for speaking out. "Free speech" is not just a nice thing; it can be dynamite. Freedom of expression thrives best under long-established, legitimate governments in tranquil times. It is, in short, political.

Key Terms

Basic Law (p. 59)   human rights (p. 64)   sedition (p. 66)

civil rights (p. 64)   judicial activism (p. 58)   separation of powers (p. 60)

constituent assembly (p. 62)   judicial restraint (p. 58) State Duma (p. 61)

constitution (p. 56)   judicial review (p. 58)   statute (p. 56)

constitutionalism (p. 59)   minority (p. 55)

Key Websites

Constitution of the United States of America: From the U.S. Senate, this site has an annotated version that helps to explain the context and background of different parts of the U.S. Constitution.
http://www.law.emory.edu/FEDERAL/usconst.html

The purpose of The Federalist Papers was to gain popular support for the proposed U.S. Constitution. In effect, The Federalist Papers were a public-relations campaign to convince people that the U.S. Constitution was an effective document.
http://www.law.ou.edu/hist/federalist/

The Constitution Society is a private, non-profit organization dedicated to research and public education on the principles of constitutional republican government. It has a very conservative bent, but it also has links to many Constitution-related sites,
http://www.constitution.org/
including the constitutions to many other countries
http://www.constitution.org/cons/natlcons.htm

Manifesto of the Communist Party
http://www.anu.edu.au/polsci/marx/classics/manifesto.html

The Magna Carta (The Great Charter)
http://www.constitution.org/eng/magnacar.htm

Further Reference

Bagehot, Walter. *The English Constitution*. New York: Oxford University Press, 1936.

Cord, Robert L. *Protest, Dissent and the Supreme Court*. Cambridge, MA: Winthrop, 1971.

Dworkin, Ronald. *Freedom's Law: The Moral Reading of the American Constitution*. Cambridge, MA: Harvard University Press, 1996.

Giglio, Ernest. *Rights, Liberties and Public Policy*. Brookfield, VT: Avebury, 1995.

Greenawalt, Kent. *Fighting Words: Individuals, Communities, and Liberties of Speech*. Princeton, NJ: Princeton University Press, 1996.

Irons, Peter. *Justice at War*. New York: Oxford University Press, 1983.

Levy, Leonard W. *Seasoned Judgments: The American Constitution, Rights, and History*. New Brunswick, NJ: Transaction, 1994.

Lewis, Anthony. *Make No Law: The Sullivan Case and the First Amendment*. New York: Random House, 1991.

McIlwain, Charles H. *Constitutionalism Ancient and Modern*. Ithaca, NY: Cornell University Press, 1940.

Maddex, Robert L., Jr. *Constitutions of the World*. Washington, D.C.: CQ Books, 1995.

Spiro, Herbert J. *Government by Constitution*. New York: Random House, 1959.

Tribe, Laurence A., and Michael C. Dorf. *On Reading the Constitution*. Cambridge, MA: Harvard University Press, 1991.

Democracy, Totalitarianism, and Authoritarianism

CHAPTER 5

In 1949, after many years of reflection on totalitarianism, George Orwell startled the public with his publication of *1984*, a thinly disguised portrayal of life in the Soviet Union in particular and of totalitarian societies in general. In this nightmare, individuals have no rights; they are creatures of the state. The government brainwashes them, spies on them, controls every aspect of their lives, and breaks doubters psychologically. The media systematically lie.

At the extreme opposite is Athens in the fifth century B.C. All adult male citizens were treated as equals and had the right and duty to attend the General Assembly, which met ten times a year, to enact laws, elect executives (who were accountable for their actions), all by simple majority votes. Thousands turned out for the General Assembly, for participation in politics was highly valued and gave Athenians dignity and human worth.

QUESTIONS TO CONSIDER

1. Why does modern democracy mean representative democracy?
2. Which are the most crucial elements of democracy?
3. What is the elite theory of politics?
4. What is the pluralist theory of politics?
5. Is totalitarianism a twentieth-century phenomenon?
6. What is the difference between totalitarian and authoritarian?
7. Why have many countries turned democratic in our time?

George Orwell's picture of totalitarianism and the Athenian ideal of democracy are at opposite ends of the spectrum of government; in between are many variations. Table 5.1 (on p. 73) shows the principal gradations from perfect democracy to perfect totalitarianism and lists some characteristics of each of the systems. Democratic governments have limited powers; totalitarian ones have more or less unlimited power over citizens.

Like all generalizations, this one has problems. There is no "average" democratic state or "average" nondemocratic state, much less "perfect" ones. There is much variation in how things work in practice. Athens's democracy fell far short of perfect democracy, for most of the population—women, resident aliens, and slaves—were excluded from participation in the political process, and effective control actually belonged to an elite. The Soviet Union held elections and reported that 99 percent of eligible voters turned out for them. These were, however, elections without choices. Similarly, democracies claim to protect civil liberties, but often these are accorded unevenly—in high degree to middle-class whites and grudgingly to impoverished nonwhites. Political science looks to see how things actually work, not just what's written on paper.

Modern Democracy

There is probably no single word that has been given more meanings than *democracy*. In the twentieth century, the word has been seriously misused by dictators to persuade subjects that they lived in a just system. The Soviet Union used to claim it was the most democratic system in the world, and the government of mainland China still calls itself the "People's Republic."

Democracy (from the Greek *demokratía; demos* = "people" and *kratía* = "government") carried a negative connotation until the nineteenth century, as thinkers accepted the ancient Greeks' criticism of direct democracy as unrestrained mob rule. A "true" democracy, a system in which all citizens meet periodically to elect state officials and personally enact laws, has been extremely rare. The few examples are Athens's General Assembly, New England town meetings, and Swiss *Landsgemeinde*. This model of democracy is extremely difficult to carry out because of the size factor. As Madison noted in arguing for representative democracy: "The room will not hold all." A national government that had to submit each decision to millions of voters would be too unwieldy to function. Therefore, **representative democracy** has evolved as the only workable alternative.

Representative Democracy

Modern democracy is not policy by the people. Instead, the people play a more general role. Democracy today is, in Lipset's words, "a political system which supplies regular constitutional opportunities for changing the governing officials, and a social mechanism which permits the largest possible part of the population to influence major decisions by choosing among contenders for political office." *Constitutional* means that the government is limited and can wield its authority only in specific ways. Representative democracy has several essential characteristics. Notice that it is not a simple system or one that falls into place automatically.

Popular Accountability of Government In a democracy, the policymakers must obtain the support of a majority or a plurality of votes cast. Leaders are accountable to citizens. Elected leaders who govern badly can be ousted. No one has an inherent right to occupy a position of political power; he or she must be freely, fairly, and periodically elected by fellow citizens, either at regular intervals (as in the United States) or at certain maximum time spans (as in Britain). Most systems permit reelection, although some specify term limits, as the U.S. Twenty-second Amendment limits each president to two full terms. Reelection is the peo-

Table 5.1 The Spectrum of Government Power

Democratic Government			Nondemocratic Government		
Perfect Democracy (Power in Hands of the People)	Democracy (USA, Great Britain, France)	Limited Democracy (Mexico, Egypt, Yugoslavia)	Authoritarianism (Syria, Iraq, Burma)	Totalitarianism (Communist China, Fascist Italy, Nazi Germany)	Perfect Totalitarianism (All Power Held by Government)
Nonpartisan politics	Two-party or multiparty politics	Dominant-party politics	Single-party or no-party politics	Single-party politics	Single-party politics
Full individual participation in government	Popular elections with universal franchise	Popular elections with limited slate	Self-determined or party-determined leadership	Self-determined or party-determined leadership	Absence of voting franchise
Virtually unlimited individual liberties	Carefully protected individual liberties	Limited individual liberties	Elections without choices	Voting franchise varies in scope, limited to approval of party candidates	Absence of individual liberties
Absolute social and economic equality	Vertical mobility with progress toward social and economic equality	Approximate freedom of the press	Irregular tolerance of individual liberties	Absence of constitutionalism	Government control of press
Free access to administrative office	Detailed constitutional restraints on government	Some social and economic equality	Little or no constitutional restraint on government	Extremely narrow political liberties	Enforced economic and social stratification
Absolute freedom of the press	Freedom of the press	Limited constitutional restraint on government	Intermittent martial law	Social structure determined by state	Total economic control by government
	Broad access to public office	Some access to public office	Direct military influence on government	Substantial economic control by government	Thought control and obliteration of individual conscience
	Unrestricted formation of political groups	Formation of some political groups	Government determination of economic system and structure	Government control of mass media	
			Government control of press		

ple's means both of expressing support and of controlling the general direction of government policy.

Political Competition   Voters must have a choice, either of candidates or parties. That means a minimum of two distinct alternatives; one-party or one-candidate elections are fake. Americans typically have a choice of two candidates, one for each major party, but some congresspersons run unopposed, as the costs of a campaign dissuade challengers from even trying. When this happens, the United States becomes a little less democratic. In most of Europe, voters have a choice among several parties, each of which tries to distinguish its ideology and policies. One unstated but important role of political competition is control of corruption. An opposition party that hammers incumbents for corruption is a powerful corrective to the human tendency to misuse public office. Systems without competition are almost always corrupt.

Alternation in Power   The reins of power must occasionally alternate. The "ins" become the "outs," and they do it in a peaceful, legitimate way. No party or individual can get a lock on power. A system in which the ruling party stays in power many decades cannot really be democratic. Such parties claim that they are so popular that they are voted in every time. More likely is that they rig elections by disrupting the opposition and miscounting ballots. Mexico, whose Institutional Revolutionary Party (PRI) has ruled since the 1920s, looked less and less democratic as the decades went by. In 1988, the Mexican computers counting the vote "broke down"; when they were "fixed," PRI won. By allowing opposition parties to win the 1997 elections for the National Congress for the first time in seven decades, PRI showed a more democratic attitude. The real democratic test will be when PRI allows itself to be voted out of office, as did India's Congress Party in 1989 and 1998.

Popular Representation   In representative democracies, the voters elect representatives to act as legislators and, as such, to voice and protect their general interest. Each legislator usually acts for a given district or group of people. But

THE "TWO-TURNOVER TEST"

Harvard political scientist Samuel Huntington proposes a "two-turnover test" to mark a stable democracy. That is, two electoral alternations of government indicate that democracy is firmly rooted. Poland, for example, overthrew its Communist regime in 1989 and held free and fair elections (called "founding elections"), won by the Solidarity coalition of Lech Walesa. Some Poles, hurt by rapid economic change, however, in 1995 voted in a president from the Socialists, a party formed out of the old Communist party. But after a while they did not like the Socialists either and in 1997 voted in a right-of-center party. Poland has thus had two turnovers and has established its democratic credentials. Russia under President Yeltsin has not yet had its first turnover.

how should he or she act? Some theorists claim that a
system is not democratic unless legislators treat elections as **mandates** to carry out constituents' wishes.
What the voters want is what they should get, says
this theory. Other theorists disagree; constituents
often have no opinion on issues. Therefore, the representative must act as a **trustee**, carrying out the wishes of constituents when feasible but acting for what he
or she feels are the best interests of the community as

> ### KEY TERMS
>
> **mandate**   An order or com-
> mission to carry out some
> policy.
> **trustee**   Someone in a posi-
> tion of power deciding what is
> best without a direct mandate.

a whole. Joseph Schumpeter puts the argument against the mandate theory as
follows: "Our chief problems about the classical (democratic) theory centered in
the proposition that 'the people' hold a definite and rational opinion about every
individual question and that they give effect to this opinion—in a democracy—
by choosing 'representatives' who will see to it that the opinion is carried out."

Of course, the people as a whole do not hold definite opinions on each subject. If they were asked to vote on every question of truck tonnage restrictions,
parliamentary rules of order, or the staff organization of the Weather Bureau, few
would bother voting. Representative democracy, therefore, does not mean that
the representative must become a cipher for constituents; rather, it means that
the people as a body must be able to control the *general* direction of government
policy. For example, if the people have made the general policy decision that
equal economic opportunity belongs to everyone, they will leave the administrative details of achieving this goal to their legislators. It is this partnership between
the people and the lawmakers that is the essence of modern democracy. E. E.
Schattschneider summarizes the case succinctly:

> The beginning of wisdom in democratic theory is to distinguish between the
> things that the people can do and the things the people cannot do. The worst pos-
> sible disservice that can be done to the democratic cause is to attribute to the peo-
> ple a mystical, magical omnipotence which takes no cognizance of what very
> large numbers of people cannot do by the sheer weight of numbers. At this point
> the common definition of democracy has invited us to make fools of ourselves.

Majority Decision   In any important government decision there is rarely
agreement. Usually one faction favors an issue and another group opposes it.
How then shall the popular will be determined? The simple answer is that the
majority should decide: In any controversy, the policy that has the support of the
greatest number should generally become the policy of government. This is the
procedure that was used in the democracies of ancient Greece. However, our
more modern and practical concept of democracy is that the majority decides but
with respect for minority rights.

Minority views are important. It is safe to say that every view that is now
widely held was once a minority view. Most of what is now public policy became
law as a result of conflict between majority and minority groups. Furthermore,
just as it is true that a minority view may grow over time until it is widely accepted, so may a majority view eventually prove to be unwise, unworkable, or

unwanted. Just as minorities may be right, so, too, may majorities be wrong. If minority views are silenced, the will of the majority becomes the "tyranny of the majority," which is just as foreboding as executive tyranny.

Right of Dissent and Disobedience   Related to minority rights, the people must have the right to resist the commands of government if those commands no longer serve the public will. This right was invoked in 1776 by Thomas Jefferson in the Declaration of Independence. Henry Thoreau, in his opposition to the war with Mexico, made probably the most profound American defense of **civil disobedience** when he declared, "All men recognize the right of revolution; that is, the right to refuse allegiance to, and to resist, the government, when its tyranny or its inefficiency are great and unendurable." The most celebrated advocate of civil disobedience was the Indian philosopher Mahatma Gandhi, who was strongly influenced by Thoreau. Gandhi considered his method of resistance to be "civil"; that is, it was disobedience but it was nonviolent and did not exceed the general legal structure of the state. It was an attention-getting device that forced the authorities to rethink. Ultimately, Gandhi and his followers forced the British to leave India.

KEY TERM
civil disobedience   Breaking what is perceived as an unjust law in the service of a higher law.

Thoreau and Gandhi looked on civil disobedience as an individual act of conscience, but others have sought to organize it and mobilize it. The most prominent American organizer was Reverend Martin Luther King, Jr., whose nonviolent resistance campaigns of the 1960s in the name of civil rights brought him into controversy. The many sit-ins and marches that he planned, directed, and often led kept him face to face with the law for nearly a decade, and he and other members of his Southern Christian Leadership Conference were often imprisoned. The long-range consequence of their actions, however, was a minor revolution in judicial decisions concerning peaceful protest. Without civil disobedience, minority claims would have gone unheard.

Political Equality   In a democracy, all adults (usually now age eighteen and over) are equally able to participate in politics: "one person, one vote." In theory, all are able to run for public office, but critics point out that it takes a great deal of money—and often specific racial and religious ties—to really enter public life. Under the pressure of minority claims and civil disobedience, however, systems tend to open up over time and become less elite in nature.

Popular Consultation   Most leaders realize that to govern effectively they must know what the people want and must be responsive to these needs and demands. Are citizens disturbed—and, if so, *how* disturbed—about foreign policy, taxes, unemployment, the cost of living? Intelligent leaders realize that they must not get too far ahead of—nor fall too far behind—public opinion. Therefore, a range of techniques has evolved to test opinion. Public opinion polls are taken on specific issues. The media, by thoughtful probing, can create a dialogue between the people and their leaders. At press conferences and news interviews with elected officials, reporters will ask those questions that they believe the people want answered. Editorials and letters to the editor are also indicators of citizens' moods and feelings.

> **KEY TERM**
>
> **mass media**   The means of communication that quickly reaches large audiences.

In recent years, several critics have noted that U.S. officials often rely heavily on the opinions of small segments of their constituencies because they are well organized and highly vocal. On the issue of gun control, for example, polls have consistently shown the public at large to be in favor of stronger regulation of firearms. But the National Rifle Association, a strong and outspoken lobby, sometimes blocks efforts to strengthen legislation in this area.

Free Press   Dictatorships cannot tolerate free and critical **mass media**; democracies cannot do without them. One of the clearest ways to determine the degree of democracy in a country is to see how free its press is. The mass media provide citizens with facts, raise public awareness, and keep rulers responsive to mass demands. Without a free and critical press, rulers can disguise wrongdoing and corruption and lull the population into passive support. As China permitted a "democracy movement" in the late 1980s, the Chinese media became freer, more honest, and more critical. As part of the crushing of this movement in 1989, outspoken journalists were fired or arrested.

Some Americans argue that the U.S. media go too far, that they take an automatic adversarial stance that undermines government authority and weakens the nation. In some cases this may be true, but in a democracy there is no mechanism to decide what "too far" is. The checks on reckless reporting are competing journals and channels that can criticize and refute unfair commentary. Then citizens, with no government supervision, can decide for themselves if charges are accurate. Only half in jest has the U.S. press been called "the fourth branch of government."

Democracy in Practice: Elitism or Pluralism?

Even if all these democratic criteria are met—no easy feat—political power will still not be evenly distributed; few will have a lot, and many will have little. Political scientists have generally concluded that this unevenness of power is normal and unavoidable: **Elites** make the actual decisions, and ordinary citizens, the *masses*, generally go along with these decisions. The key dispute is how much elites are accountable to masses. Those who argue that elites are little accountable are *elite theorists*; those who argue that elites are ultimately accountable are **pluralists**.

> **KEY TERMS**
>
> **elites**   The "top" or most influential people in a political system, often the ones who govern.
> **pluralism**   Theory that politics is the interaction of many groups.

One of the early thinkers on elites, Italian political scientist Gaetano Mosca, argued that government always falls into the hands of a few:

> In all societies—from societies that are very undeveloped and have largely attained the dawnings of civilization, down to the most advanced and powerful

societies—two classes of people appear—a class that rules and a class that is ruled. The first class, always the less numerous, performs all of the political functions, monopolizes power, and enjoys the advantages that power brings, whereas the second, the more numerous class, is directed and controlled by the first, in a manner that is now more or less legal, now more or less arbitrary and violent.

The German thinker Robert Michels argued that any organization, no matter how democratic its intent, ends up run by a small elite; he called this the "Iron Law of Oligarchy." More recently, Yale political scientist Robert Dahl held that "participatory democracy is not possible in large modern societies; government is too big and the issues are too complex.... The key political, economic, and social decisions ... are made by tiny minorities.... It is difficult—nay, impossible—to see how it could be otherwise in large political systems." These three agree on the inevitability of elites, but Mosca and Michels, elite theorists, see elites as unaccountable, whereas Dahl, a pluralist, sees them as accountable.

Contrary to what one might suppose, modern elite theorists are generally not conservatives but radicals; they decry rule by elites as unfair and undemocratic. Columbia sociologist C. Wright Mills denounced the "Power Elite" in which big business gave money to politicians, politicians voted massive defense spending, and top generals gave the contracts to big business. This interlocking conspiracy was driving the United States to war, Mills predicted. Money and connections give elites access to the political system, which they use to favor themselves. Laws, subsidies, and tax breaks all favor the rich, argue elite theorists. Elections count for little, as elites and their money control both major parties. Massive campaign contributions make sure no important industry gets seriously harmed; witness the tobacco companies' ability to block laws and lawsuits.

Look again, argue pluralists. The Cold War, not a power elite, drove defense spending, which has declined sharply after the Soviet threat disappeared. Most politicians are of modest origins; few are from wealthy families (exceptions: both Roosevelts, JFK, and Bush). Politicians may take big contributions, but they are usually attuned to what wins votes. Big companies do get leaned on. The entire asbestos industry was closed down as a health hazard. Tobacco firms have had to pay millions in lawsuits and face continual government pressure.

Politics really works, say pluralists, through **interest groups**, which we will explore more fully in Chapter 9. Just about any group of citizens can organize a group to protest or demand something, and politicians generally listen. To be sure, if the group is wealthy and well-placed, it gets listened to more, but nobody has a hammerlock on the political system. U.S. oil companies are among the richest firms in the world, and they are pro-Arab. Why then does U.S. policy permanently tilt toward Israel? Because most American Jews and many fundamentalist Christians demand pro-Israel policies, and politicians listen to them more than to the oil companies. According to pluralists, interest groups are the great avenues of democracy,

KEY TERM
interest groups Associations that pressure government for policies they favor.

Interest groups such as these trade unionists are a key element in the pluralistic make-up of this country. (Laima E. Druskis)

making sure government listens to the people. Many argue that only a pluralist society can be democratic. Efforts to found democracies in societies without traditions of pluralism are like trying to plant trees without soil, as we have seen in Russia, where the long Communist rule erased most naturally occurring interest groups.

The pure elite theorist views society as a single pyramid, with a tiny elite at the top. The pure pluralist views society as a collection of billiard balls colliding with each other and with government to produce policy. Both views are overdrawn. A synthesis that more accurately reflects reality might be a series of small pyramids, each capped by an elite. There is interaction of many units, as the pluralists would have it, but there is also stratification of leaders and followers, as elitist thinkers would have it. (See Figure 5.1, on p. 80.) Robert Dahl called this a "polyarchy," the rule of the leaders of several groups who have reached stable understandings with each other. Arend Lijphart called it "consociational democracy." The elites of each important group strike a bargain to play by the rules of a constitutional game and to restrain their followers from violence. In return, each group gets something; no one gets everything. Lijphart's example of where this has worked successfully is the Netherlands, where the elites of the Catholic, Calvinist, and secular blocs have reached an "elite accommodation" among each other. In Lebanon, by contrast, elite accommodation broke down, resulting in a horrible civil war. Most stable countries have "conflict management" by elites. The United States shows an interplay of business, labor, ethnic, regional, and other elites, each delivering enough to keep their people in line, each cooperating to varying degrees with other elites. When elite consensus broke down, the United States, too, experienced a bloody civil war.

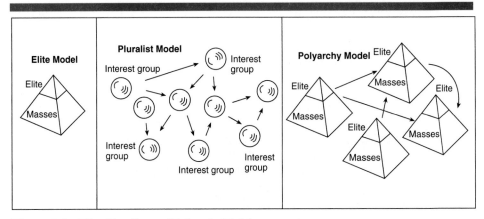

Figure 5.1   *Elite, Pluralist, and Polyarchy Models*

Totalitarian Government

In **totalitarian** systems, elites are almost completely unaccountable; they lock themselves into power and are very difficult to oust, short of regime collapse, which we saw recently
in Eastern Europe and the former Soviet Union.
Totalitarianism is becoming an endangered species, perhaps on
the brink of extinction. Its emphasis on total control, brain-
washing, and worship of the state and its leaders has proven
mistaken and inefficient. Few people are now attracted to such political models.
Now, only North Korea remains as a pristine example of totalitarianism, while
China, Vietnam, and Cuba have opened up economically if not politically. Earlier
in the twentieth century, though, with the regimes of Stalin, Mussolini, and
Hitler, it looked like totalitarianism was riding high and might even be the wave
of the future. Now it is more likely that it will prove to be a disease of the twentieth century. In any case, most of our examples are historical, not current.

What Is Totalitarianism?

The twentieth-century phenomenon of totalitarianism is far removed from the
autocracies of the past. Peter the Great and Louis XIV were powerful despots, but
the scope and extent of their power and authority were severely limited by the
relatively primitive means of communication and transportation of the time.
Until the twentieth century, communications were so slow and difficult that it
was impossible for the most autocratic rulers to control effectively or completely
all the territory in their domain. Even Louis XIV, a kind of royal dictator, did not
try to control everything in France; average citizens lived their private lives. In
contrast, totalitarian states of the twentieth century attempted to remold and

transform the people under their control and to regulate every aspect of human life and activity.

Totalitarianism, then, is a unique development dating only from the post-World War I period and made possible by modern technology. It is essentially a system of government in which one party holds all political, economic, military, and judicial power. This party attempts to restructure society in accordance with party values and interferes massively in the personal lives of individual citizens. Freedom disappears. The old autocratic rulers kept their subjects out of political participation, but the totalitarian state insists on mass participation and tries to generate enthusiasm. With modern electronic devices, the state is able to control communications and private activities and to coordinate and centralize economic life.

Carl J. Friedrich and Zbigniew Brzezinski identified six basic features common to all totalitarian states. Four of them would have been impossible to achieve in preindustrial societies and are central to the system.

An All-Encompassing Ideology   Totalitarian ideology is an official body of doctrine that includes theories of history, economics, and future political and social development. It is the philosophical framework within which decisions are made. The ideology portrays the world in terms of black and white, with very little gray in between. Citizens are judged to be either for the state or against it. The ideology usually points toward a perfect society, which humankind will attain in the future (such as Marx's prediction that the classless society would lead to an eventual withering away of the state). All citizens are supposed to adhere to the official ideology, and they usually devote time to its study. Courses on Marxist-Leninist thought were required in the schools of all Communist states.

Dictator's fantasy: The "People's Palace" in Bucharest, huge, outrageously expensive, and unfinished, was to be the personal palace of Romanian dictator Nicolae Ceausescu, who was deposed and shot in late 1989. With no checks or controls, dictators can launch insane projects. (Michael Roskin)

Before the breakup of the Soviet Union, long lines waited to file past Lenin's tomb in Red Square. (Charles Gatewood)

A Single Party   Only one party legally exists, usually led by one man who establishes a cult of personality around himself. Mussolini, Hitler, Stalin, and Mao had themselves worshiped. Entrance into the party is controlled (official membership is usually less than 10 percent of the population) and is considered an honor. Certain privileges accompany membership, and in return the members give their dedication and support to the party. **Hierarchically** organized and oligarchically controlled, the party is either superior to or tied in with the formal institutions of government. The party leader wields considerable power in the government, and party functionaries hold all important posts in the bureaucracy. The party's cadres are responsible for imposing at least outward conformity at all levels of society.

KEY TERM

hierarchy   Organized in a ranking of power from top to bottom, as if on a ladder.

Organized Terror   A security police, using both physical and psychological methods, ensures that citizens stay cowed. The Nazi Gestapo, the Soviet NKVD under Stalin, and Mussolini's OVRA were immune from judicial restraints. Constitutional guarantees either did not exist or were ignored in these societies, thus making possible secret arrests, jailings, and torture. The security forces—sometimes called "secret police"—are often directed against whole classes of people, such as Jews, landlords, capitalists, socialists, or clergy. The threat of the "knock at the door" terrorizes large segments of the population into acquiescence. The mass extermination of entire groups of people under Hitler and Stalin demonstrates the state's enormous power and the individual's corresponding helplessness. Systematic terror doesn't work over the long run, however, and the Soviet Union abandoned the more ruthless tactics of Stalin. The purges and mass executions were replaced by more subtle forms of control and intimidation, such as loss of job or exile to a remote city.

Monopoly of Communications   The primary function of the mass media in totalitarian states is to indoctrinate the people with the official ideology. Enlightenment and entertainment are subordinated to political propaganda.

Now, hardly anyone waits in line to see Lenin, whose ideas and system became irrelevant with the collapse of communism. (Michael Roskin)

Monopoly of Weapons Governments of totalitarian nations have a complete monopoly on weapons, thus eliminating armed resistance.

Controlled Economy Totalitarian regimes control the economy, Stalin directly by means of state ownership and Hitler indirectly by means of party "coordination" of private industry. Either way, it makes the state powerful, for resources can be allocated to heavy industry, weapons production, or whatever the party wishes. Workers can be moved wherever labor is needed, and incentives can stimulate production. The needs or wants of the consumer are unimportant. The Soviet Union was the first to send men to outer space, for example, but non-Communist countries always had vastly more and better consumer products. Economic backwardness proved to be the great weakness of the Soviet Union.

Starting in late 1989, as one Communist country in Eastern Europe after another cast off its system, we beheld how weak the system was. In ideology, most citizens, even former party members, detested communism. The single ruling parties collapsed and handed power over to non-Communists. Organized terror lost its punch. The official mass media, widely ignored for years, was simply discarded in favor of a free press. The controlled economies were turned, with much pain, into market economies. We now realize that these Communist regimes had never exercised total control. In addition, we must be aware that there is more than one type of totalitarianism.

Right-Wing Totalitarianism Right-wing totalitarianism, as exemplified in Italian Fascism and German National Socialism, developed in industrialized nations that were plagued by economic depression, social upheaval, and political confusion and weakness, and in which democratic roots and traditions were shallow and weak. Germany in the late 1920s and early 1930s was in turmoil. The nation was saddled with an enormous reparations debt following World War I; unemployment was widespread; labor disputes were frequent and violent; and a runaway inflation had wiped out the savings of the lower-middle and middle classes—the shopkeepers,

Case Studies   IMAGE AND REALITY OF TOTAL CONTROL

Just as there is no perfect democracy, so also is there no perfect totalitarian dictatorship. Often outsiders are overly influenced by the image of total control projected by these states. Visitors to fascist Italy were impressed by the seeming law, order, cleanliness, and purposefulness of what they thought was one-man rule. We know now that many Italians disliked Mussolini, that his organizations and economic plans were mostly for show, and that he wasn't even in firm command of the country. In 1943, as the British and Americans overran the southern part of Italy, Mussolini's own generals—who had been disobeying and lying to him for years—overthrew him in a coup. Then the king of Italy—Italy was technically a kingdom until 1946—fired Mussolini as prime minister. Now what kind of total control is that?

Since Stalin's death, every Soviet party chief denounced the bureaucracy, the deadening hand of routine, and the economic irregularities that impeded Soviet growth. But neither Khrushchev, Brezhnev, nor Gorbachev touched the problem. Much of Soviet economic life ran by means of under-the-table deals and influence that defied centralized planning. Soviet workers stole everything from radios to locomotives and often showed up to work drunk or not at all. Where was the total control? The pages of *Pravda* and *Izvestia* thundered against these problems, but the government seemed unable to do anything about them.

We should bear in mind that the model of totalitarianism presented above never precisely matched reality. The model describes an *attempt* to impose total control, not the achievement of it.

the petty bureaucrats, and the skilled workers. In his rise to power, Hitler promised to discipline the labor unions, to restore order, to renounce the humiliating Versailles Treaty, and to protect private property from the Communist menace to the east. His program appealed to industrialists, militarists, and middle-class people, who typically constitute the backbone of a fascist state's support.

Right-wing totalitarianism does not seek to revolutionize society completely; rather it aims to strengthen the existing social order and to glorify the state. It attempts to get rid of those deemed foreign or inferior, as Hitler strove to annihilate Jews and Gypsies. Economic policies are also directed toward national glory and war. Private ownership is generally permitted, but obedient cartels and national trade associations carry out party wishes.

KEY TERM

authoritarian Nondemocratic government but not necessarily totalitarian.

Authoritarianism

The terms *authoritarianism* and *totalitarianism* are often confused, but the two words have different meanings. **Authoritarian** regimes are governed by a small group—a party, a dictator, or the army—with minimum popular input. They do not attempt to control everything. Many economic, social, religious, cultural, and familial matters are left up to individuals. Most of the six points of totalitarianism discussed earlier are diluted or absent. Authoritarian regimes, for example, rarely have a firm ideology to sell.

This is not to say that authoritarian regimes promote individual freedoms. Authoritarians view society as a hierarchical organization with a chain of command under the leadership of one ruler or group. Command, obedience, and order are higher values than freedom, consent, and involvement. Therefore, the citizen is expected to obey laws and pay taxes that he or she has no voice in establishing. The trappings of democracy may exist in an authoritarian state but have little function. The legislature is usually little more than a "rubber stamp" to approve the dictator's laws. Likewise, puppet prime ministers and cabinets carry out the dictator's wishes. Louis XIV of France showed his authoritarian rule with his famous phrase: *"L'état c'est moi"* (The state—that's me).

Spain under Franco (1939–1975) was "traditional authoritarian" rather than totalitarian, as the *caudillo* (leader) sought political passivity and obedience rather than enthusiastic participation and mobilization. Franco and his supporters had no single ideology to promote, and the economy and press were pluralistic within limits. Jeane J. Kirkpatrick, a political scientist and President Reagan's ambassador to the United Nations, argued that there is a clear difference between authoritarian and totalitarian regimes. The former (such as Argentina, Chile, Brazil) can reform, but once a totalitarian system (such as communism) takes over, the system cannot reform itself. Argentina, Chile, and Brazil did return to democracy in the 1980s. Kirkpatrick's thesis was to some extent borne out in the fact that the Communist regimes of the Soviet bloc never did reform themselves; they collapsed while trying reform. In contrast, China illustrated the nature of totalitarian regimes by bloodily crushing its democracy movement in 1989.

Authoritarianism and the Developing Nations

One of the great political movements since the end of World War II has been the breaking up of colonial empires into independent nations. For the most part, the ideological struggle for national independence in these states followed the "self-determination" argument of the American Declaration of Independence and the French Declaration of the Rights of Man and Citizen. Yet once national independence was won, democracy did not last long. A political culture in which self-rule and self-determination were never integral values does not adapt well to political democracy. Democracy in the Western tradition is characterized by an individualism that grew out of a competitive market economy. The developing societies have preindustrial, traditional peasant economies that stress families and tribes. Levels of education and income are often low, and most people are absorbed in the struggle to survive. The leadership often believes that political and economic survival and growth need centralized power to make what is really needed rather than according to what people want. The leaders think they know what is really needed.

In this way, much of the Third World fell into authoritarianism with single-party dominance. Zimbabwe started with a two-party system in 1980 but found that the parties encouraged tribal animosities and guerrilla terror. The leader of the largest party, Robert Mugabe, cracked down harshly with soldiers of his dominant tribe and created a single-party system, arguing that this was the only way to build unity and a socialist economy. Often the results of such systems are terrible. Government officials devise wasteful, unrealistic projects, stifle individual initiative by regulations and taxes, and crush critical viewpoints. Corruption becomes massive. In this way have such countries as Tanzania and Myanmar (Burma) impoverished themselves, ending up with neither democracy nor economic growth.

The Democratization of Authoritarian Regimes

Since 1974, dozens of countries have abandoned authoritarian or totalitarian systems in favor of democratic systems. Now, over half of the world's nations are at least approximately democratic. The expansion of democracy from the previous two dozen countries—mostly in Western Europe and North America, where it had earlier taken root—became a major scholarly topic. An excellent new quarterly appeared in 1989, *Journal of Democracy*, devoted to explaining and encouraging the spread of democracy.

There seem to be two types of regimes contributing to the trend toward democracy: authoritarian regimes that enjoyed strong economic growth and collapsed Communist regimes whose economic growth lagged. The fast-growth authoritarian systems—such as Chile, South Korea, and Taiwan—were politically authoritarian but developed a market economy largely in private hands. It was as if the dictator said, "I'll take care of politics; you just work on your various businesses." The pro-business regimes set macroeconomic policy (sound currency, low inflation, sufficient capital for loans) and plugged into the world market. After a time, the growing economy starts transforming the whole society in the direction of democracy. As countries improve from poor to middle-income, they become ready for stable democracy. (See "modernization theory" in Chapter 2.) Democracy seldom lasts in poor countries—India is the massive exception—but it almost always works in middle-income and higher countries.

Why should this happen? First, economic growth creates a large middle class, one of the bases for democracy. Middle classes are inherently democratic. They have a stake in the system; they may wish to modify it but not overthrow it. Second, and related to the size of the middle class, education levels have risen. Most people are high-school graduates, and many are college graduates. They are no longer ignorant and do not fall for demagogues or extremist ideas. Third, and related to both the previous two points, people increasingly recognize their interests and express them: pluralism. They have business, professional, regional, and religious points of view that they want considered. They

---

Case Studies · UNPREPARED POLITICAL SCIENTISTS

Most political scientists, including top specialists, were taken by surprise at the collapse of the Soviet Union. Political science deserves to be taken to task, for it failed to provide early warning of the greatest political change of the late twentieth century. Some economists charted the slowing of the Soviet economy since the 1970s and concluded that at a certain point something drastic would happen; and a few historians of conservative bent sensed that the Soviet system couldn't go on as before. But very few political scientists heeded the warning signs.

One suspects that the main culprit leading to this error was "systems theory," discussed in Chapter 2. Political scientists have tended to reify systems, to see them not as theories and suggestions but as reality. Systems thinking depicts political systems as stable, durable, and self-correcting feedback loops that never break down. At a minimum, systems theory must be enlarged to include the possibility of system collapse; perhaps the theory should be abandoned altogether. It never adequately explained totalitarian systems.

---

can spot cruel, corrupt, or inefficient governments and do not like being treated like small children. Finally, the market itself teaches citizens about self-reliance, pluralism, tolerance, and not expecting too much, all attitudes that help sustain a democracy. Gradually, the regime eases up, permitting a critical press, the formation of political parties, and finally free elections. Taiwan is an excellent example of this transition.

How about the other trend that has led to newly democratic systems, the collapse of Communist regimes? Here, too, the economy has a great deal to do with the process, but in a negative sense. It was poor economic performance and slow growth, especially in comparison with the West and with the rapid-growth countries, that persuaded relatively liberal Communists, such as Mikhail Gorbachev, to attempt to reform the system. They knew they were falling behind, especially in crucial high-tech areas, and thought they could energize the system by bringing elements of the free market into an otherwise socialist economy. But communism, like other brands of totalitarianism, doesn't tolerate reform. By attempting to control everything, as in the six points outlined earlier by Friedrich and Brzezinski, they have created a brittle system that can break but not bend. Once they started admitting that the system needs to be fixed, they are admitting that they were wrong. The ideology was wrong; single-party control was wrong; the centralized economy was wrong; and so on. The attempt at reform turns into system collapse.

Will the countries that emerged from the wreckage of communism be able to establish lasting democracies? So far, Poland, the Czech Republic, and Hungary have done so. As you go farther east and south, however, democracy is still incomplete. Market systems are strange and rather frightening to

Boris Yeltsin toughed out the 1991 coup attempt and emerged stronger than ever. Yeltsin represented sweeping change in favor of democracy and a market economy, which old-guard Russian Communists hated. (AP/Wide World Photos)

Russians, Ukrainians, Bulgarians and others, and indeed the transition from a controlled to a market economy inflicts terrible hardships. Some voters, never having known democracy, turn to Communist or authoritarian parties, who promise to restore stability and paychecks. Boris Yeltsin constructed a system in Russia that falls short of democracy. The president is extremely powerful and can rule by decree; the State Duma (parliament) is weak and fragmented; privatization has favored a few who have made themselves tremendously rich while others starve; and the mass media is controlled by these few. One close observer called Russia a "procedural democracy" because it has reasonably free and fair elections but not yet a "substantive democracy" because it is weak in most of the attributes of democracy we discussed earlier. Some call the Russian system a **kleptocracy**, and similar systems are found in many ex-Soviet republics, especially in Central Asia, and in the Balkans.

Democracy is not easy. It is a complex, finely balanced system that depends on a set of attitudes that grow best under a market economy with a large, educated middle class and a tradition of pluralism. Centuries of religious and philosophical evolution prepare democratic attitudes. Perhaps the greatest task of democracy in our day is to foster the transformation of collapsed totalitarian societies into democracies. If they don't make the transition, the world's democracies may have to face new and even uglier forms of totalitarianism and authoritarianism.

KEY TERM
kleptocracy   Rule by thieves; used in derision and jest.

Key Terms

authoritarian (p. 84)   interest groups (p. 78)   pluralism (p. 77)

civil disobedience (p. 76)   kleptocracy (p. 88)   representative democracy (p. 72)

elites (p. 77)   mandate (p. 75)   totalitarian (p. 80)

hierarchy (p. 82)   mass media (p. 77)   trustee (p. 75)

Key Websites

This site lists many political parties around the world and classifies them by orientation, which includes authoritarian, dictatorial, regional, religious, and separatist, to name a few.
http://www.agora.stm.it/elections/parties.htm

The Journal of Democracy monitors and analyzes democratic regimes and movements around the world. It features analysis, reports from democratic activists, updates on news and elections, and reviews of important recent books.
http://www.press.jhu.edu/journals/jod/

From Out There News: This site examines Iraq with an interactive Iraq political map—a who's who in the Iraqi government.
http://www.megastories.com/iraq/

The History Place website contains a complete biography of Adolf Hitler and the Nazi movement.
http://www.historyplace.com/worldwar2/riseofhitler/index.htm

The World Factbook is prepared by the Central Intelligence Agency for use by U.S. Government officials, and the style, format, coverage, and content are designed to meet their specific requirements (but there is a lot here for anyone to use).
http://www.odci.gov/cia/publications/factbook/index.html

Further Reference

Bachrach, Peter. *The Theory of Democratic Elitism*. Boston, MA: Little, Brown, 1967.

Bentley, Arthur F. *The Process of Government*. San Antonio, TX: Principia Press, 1949. Originally published in 1908.

Dahl, Robert A. *Polyarchy: Participation and Opposition*. New Haven, CT: Yale University Press, 1971.

Downs, Anthony. *An Economic Theory of Democracy*. New York: Harper & Row, 1957.

Dye, Thomas R. *Who's Running America? The Clinton Years*, 6th ed. Englewood Cliffs, NJ: Prentice Hall, 1994.

Friedrich, Carl J., and Zbigniew Brzezinski. *Totalitarian Dictatorship and Autocracy*. Cambridge, MA: Harvard University Press, 1965.

Huntington, Samuel P. *The Third Wave: Democratization in the Late Twentieth Century*. Norman, OK: University of Oklahoma Press, 1991.

Lijphart, Arend. *Democracy in Plural Societies: A Comparative Exploration*. New Haven, CT: Yale University Press, 1977.

Lipset, Seymour Martin, ed. *The Encyclopedia of Democracy*, four vols. Washington, D.C.: Congressional Quarterly, 1995.

Parenti, Michael. *Democracy for the Few*, 6th ed. New York: St. Martin's, 1995.

Schattschneider, E. E. *The Semisovereign People: A Realist's View of Democracy in America*. New York: Holt, Rinehart & Winston, 1960.

Schumpeter, Joseph. *Capitalism, Socialism, and Democracy*, 3rd ed. New York: Harper & Row, 1950.

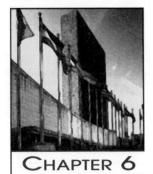

CHAPTER 6

Political Ideologies

The Republican takeover of Capitol Hill in the 1994 elections reminded us that political **ideology** is still alive in the United States. These Republicans were distinctly ideological, prescribing what they called conservatism to solve problems from the economy to welfare. Probably few of them knew it, but they were actually classic *liberals*, harkening back to Adam Smith's two-century-old admonition to get government out of the economy. Their ideas on individual initiative, a deregulated economy, and the self-correcting power of the marketplace were pure Adam Smith.

The people that the Republicans put on the defensive, the so-called liberals, also had a history of which they were probably unaware. Their liberalism was actually a greatly changed one dating from the late nineteenth century; it was very different from Adam Smith's. The point here is that Americans, who usually think of themselves as pragmatic rather than ideological, are heirs to centuries of ideological thought and often subscribe (if unwittingly) to one or another doctrine that was penned generations ago.

> **QUESTIONS TO CONSIDER**
>
> 1. Is it possible to be totally pragmatic, with no ideology?
> 2. How did classic liberalism turn into U.S. conservatism?
> 3. How closely related are modern liberalism and social democracy?
> 4. What changes did Lenin make to Marxism?
> 5. Why is nationalism perhaps the strongest ideology?
> 6. What are the main elements of fascism?
> 7. Do any of the recent ideologies attract today's students?
> 8. Could ideological politics really die out?

What Is Ideology?

An ideology begins with the belief that things can be better than they are; it is basically a plan to improve society. As Anthony Downs put it, ideology is "a verbal image of the good society, and of the chief means of constructing such a society." Political ideologies are not the same as political science; that is, they are not

> **KEY TERM**
>
> **ideology** Belief system that society can be improved by following certain doctrines; usually ends in "-ism."

calm, rational attempts to understand political systems. They are, rather, commitments to *change* political systems. (One exception here might be classical conservatism, which aims at keeping things from changing too much.) Ideologues are apt to make poor political scientists, for they confuse the "should" or "ought" of ideology with the "is" of political science.

Classic Works	THE ORIGINS OF IDEOLOGIES

Many ideologies stem from the political theories discussed in Chapter 2. Classical liberalism traces back to the seventeenth-century English philosopher John Locke, who emphasized individual rights, property, and reason. Communism traces back to the late eighteenth-century German philosopher G. W. F. Hegel, who emphasized that all facets of a society—art, music, architecture, statecraft, law, and so on—hang together as a package, the expression of an underlying cause.

The philosophers' ideas, however, become simplified and popularized. Ideologists want plans for action, not abstract ideas. Marx, for example, "stood Hegel on his head" to make economics the great underlying cause for everything else in society. Most ideologies have a large economic component, for it is economics that will provide the basis for social improvement. Lenin later stood Marx on *his* head to make his ideas apply to a backward country where Marx doubted they should. Mao Zedong then applied Lenin's ideas to an even more backward country, where they didn't fit at all. In this way, one ideology gives rise to others (Figure 6.1).

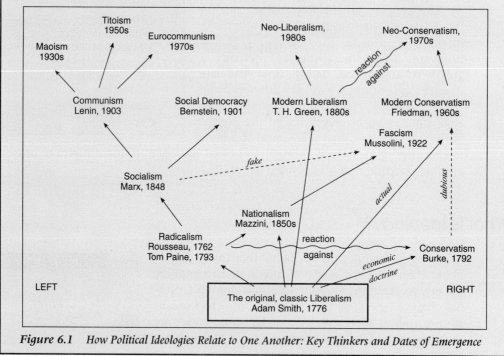

Figure 6.1   *How Political Ideologies Relate to One Another: Key Thinkers and Dates of Emergence*

CLASSIFYING IDEOLOGIES

Ideologies can be classified—with some oversimplification—on a left-to-right spectrum that dates back to the meeting of the French National Assembly in 1789. To allow delegates of similar views to caucus and to keep apart strong partisans who might fight, members were seated as follows, in a semicircular chamber: Conservatives (who favored continuation of the monarchy) were on the speaker's right; radicals (who favored sweeping away the old system altogether in favor of a republic of freedom and equality) were seated to his left; and moderates (who wanted some change) were seated in the center.

We have been calling their ideological descendants the left, the right, and the center ever since, even though the content of their views has changed. The left now favors equality, welfare programs, and sometimes government intervention in the economy. The right stresses individual initiative and private economic activity. Centrists try to synthesize and moderate the views of both. People a little to one side or the other are said to be center-left or center-right. Sweden's political parties form a rather neat left-to-right spectrum: a small Communist party; a large Social Democratic party; and medium-sized Center (formerly Farmers'), Liberal, and Conservative parties.

In politics, ideology becomes an important cement, holding together movements, parties, or revolutionary groups. To fight well and endure sacrifices, people need ideological motivation, something to believe in. Americans have sometimes been unable to grasp this point. With their emphasis on moderation and **pragmatism**—"if it works, use it"—they fail to understand the energizing effect of ideology in the world today. "Our" Vietnamese, the South Vietnamese, were physically no different from the Vietcong and North Vietnamese, and they were better armed. But in the crunch, the Vietnamese who had a

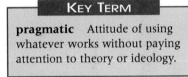

KEY TERM

pragmatic Attitude of using whatever works without paying attention to theory or ideology.

doctrine to believe in—a mixture of Marx, Lenin, and Mao with heavy doses of nationalism and anticolonialism—won against the Vietnamese who didn't have much to believe in. We tend to forget that more than two centuries ago Americans were quite ideological, too, and—imbued with a passion for freedom and self-rule, via the pens of John Locke and Thomas Paine—beat a larger and better equipped army of Englishmen and Hessians who had no good reason to fight. Have we forgotten the power of ideas?

Ideologies never work precisely the way their advocates claim. Some are hideous failures. All ideologies contain a certain amount of wishful thinking, which frequently collapses in the face of reality. Ideologies imagine a perfect world; reality is highly imperfect. The classic liberalism of Adam Smith did contribute to the nineteenth century's economic growth, but it also led to great inequalities of wealth and recurring depressions; it had to be modified into modern liberalism. Communism led to brutal tyrannies, economic failures, and collapse. All ideologies, when measured against their actual performance, are to greater or lesser degrees defective. They should all be taken with a grain of salt.

The Major Ideologies

Classic Liberalism

According to the late Frederick Watkins of Yale, 1776 could be called "the Year One of the Age of Ideology," and not just for the American Revolution. In that same year, Scottish economist Adam Smith published *The Wealth of Nations*, thereby founding classic laissez-faire economics. The true wealth of nations, Smith argued, is not in the amount of gold and silver they amass but in the amount of goods and services their people produce. Smith was refuting an earlier notion, called *mercantilism*, that the bullion in a nation's treasury determined whether it was a rich country. Spain had followed this view in looting the New World but actually grew poorer. The French, too, since at least Louis XIV in the previous century, had followed mercantilist policies by means of government supervision of the economy with plans, grants of monopoly, subsidies, tariffs, and other restraints on trade.

Smith reasoned that this was not the way to produce maximum economic growth. Government interference always retards growth. If you give one firm a monopoly to manufacture something, you banish competition and with it efforts to produce new products at better prices. The economy stagnates. If you protect domestic industry by tariffs, you take away incentives for domestic producers to make better or cheaper products. By getting the government out of the economy, by letting the economy alone (*laissez-faire*, in French), you will actually have the best system.

But what about the chaos that will come with free competition unsupervised by government? Not to worry, said Smith; the market itself will regulate the economy. Efficient producers will prosper and inefficient ones will go under. The public will get the best products for the lowest prices. Supply and demand determine prices better than any government official can. In the free marketplace, an "unseen hand" regulates and self-corrects the economy. If people want more of a given item, manufacturers increase production, new manufacturers enter the field, foreign producers bring in their wares, or there is a combination of all three. The unseen hand—actually, the rational calculations of myriad individuals all pursuing their self-interest—micro-adjusts the economy with no government help.

This ideology took the name **liberalism** from the Latin word for "free," *liber*: Society should be as free as possible from government interference. As aptly summarized by Thomas Jefferson, "That government is best that governs least." Americans took to classic liberalism like a duck takes to water. It seemed perfectly suited to the needs of a vigorous, freedom-loving population with plenty of room to expand. The noneconomic elements also suited Americans. Government should also not supervise religion, the press, or free speech.

> **KEY TERM**
>
> **liberalism** Ideology founded by Adam Smith to keep government out of the economy; became conservatism in the United States.

But, you say, what you're calling liberalism here is actually what Americans today call conservatism. True. In the late nineteenth century, liberalism changed and split into modern liberalism and what we now call conservatism, which we will discuss next. To keep our terminology straight, we should call the original ideas of Adam Smith "classic liberalism" to distinguish it from the modern variety.

Classic Conservatism

By the same token, we should call the ideas of Edmund Burke, published in the late eighteenth century, "classic conservatism," for his conservatism diverges in many ways from modern conservatism. Burke knew Adam Smith and agreed that a free market was the best economic system. Burke also opposed sending troops to crush the rebellious American colonists; after all, they were only trying to regain the ancient freedoms of Englishmen, said Burke. So far, Burke sounds like a liberal.

But what Burke strongly objected to was the way liberal ideas were being applied in France by revolutionists. There, liberalism turned into radicalism, influenced by philosopher Jean-Jacques Rousseau and, fresh from the U.S. revolution, Thomas Paine. As is often the case, an ideology devised in one place becomes warped when applied to different circumstances. To apply liberalism in America was easy; once the English and their Tory sympathizers cleared out, it fell into place without resistance. But in France, a large aristocratic class and a state-supported Roman Catholic church had a lot to lose. The revolutionaries tried to solve the problem with the guillotine; they swept away all established institutions.

This, warned Burke, was a terrible mistake. Liberals place too much confidence in human reason. People are only partly rational; they also have wildly irrational passions. To contain them, society over the years has evolved traditions, institutions, and standards of morality, such as the monarchy and an established church. Sweep these aside, said Burke, and man's irrational impulses will lead to chaos, which in turn will end in tyranny far worse than that which the revolutionaries overthrew. Burke, in his 1792 *Reflexions on the Revolution in France*, actually predicted that France would fall under the rule of a military dictator. In 1799, Napoleon took over.

Institutions and traditions that currently exist can't be all bad, Burke reasoned, for they are the products of hundreds of years of trial and error. People have become used to them. The best should be preserved or "conserved" (hence the name **conservatism**). Never mind if they aren't perfect; they work. This is not to say that things should never change. Of course they should change, wrote Burke, but only gradually, giving people time to adjust. "A state without the means of some change is without the means of its conservation," wrote Burke.

> **KEY TERM**
>
> **conservatism** Ideology of keeping the system largely unchanged.

Burke was an important thinker for several reasons. He helped discover the *irrational* in human behavior. He saw that institutions are like living things; they grow and adapt over time. And most important, he saw that revolutions tend to end badly, for society cannot be instantly remade according to human reason. Although Burke's ideas have been called an *anti-ideology*—for they aimed to shoot down the radicalism that was then engulfing France—they have considerable staying power. Burke's emphasis on religion, traditions, and morality strikes a responsive chord in many a modern conservative's heart. His doubts about applying reason to solve social problems were echoed by Jeane Kirkpatrick, President Reagan's UN ambassador and a political scientist, who found that leftists are always imagining that things can be much better than they are when in point of fact violent upheaval always makes things worse. In these ways, classic conservatism is still alive in modern thought.

Modern Liberalism

What happened to the original, classic liberalism of Adam Smith? By the late nineteenth century, it had become apparent that the free market was not as self-regulating as Smith had thought. Competition was not perfect. Manufacturers tended to rig the market—a point that Smith himself had warned about. There was a drift to bigness and fewness: monopoly. The system produced a large underclass of the terribly poor. Class positions were largely inherited; children of better-off families got a good education and the right connections to speed them on their way. Worst of all, there were recurring economic depressions in which the poor and the working class suffered greatly. The laissez-faire society created some problems.

The Englishman Thomas Hill Green rethought liberalism in the 1880s. The goal of liberalism, reasoned Green, was a free society. But what happens when economic developments take away freedom? The classic liberals placed great store in contracts (agreements between consenting parties with no government supervision): If you don't like the deal, don't take it. But what if the bargaining power of the two parties is greatly unequal, as between a rich employer and a poor person desperate for a job? Does the latter really have a free choice in accepting or rejecting a job with very low wages? Classic liberalism said let it be; wages will find their own level. But what if the wage is below starvation level? Here, Green said, it was time for government to step in. In such a case it would not be a question of government infringing on freedoms but of government protecting them. Instead of the purely negative "freedom from," there had to be a certain amount of the positive "freedom to." Green called this *positive freedom*. Government was to step in to guarantee the freedom to live at an adequate level.

Classic liberalism had expelled government from the marketplace; **modern liberalism** brought it back in, this time to protect people from a sometimes unfair economic system. Modern liberals championed wage and hour laws, the right to form unions, unemployment and health insurance, and improved educational opportunities for all. To do this, they were willing to place heavier taxes on the rich than on the

> **KEY TERM**
>
> **modern liberalism** Ideology that moderate government intervention can correct economic and social ills; the sort of liberalism practiced in United States.

working class. This is the liberalism we speak of in the twentieth-century United States, the liberalism of Woodrow Wilson, Franklin D. Roosevelt, and Ted Kennedy. One strand of the old liberalism remains in the new, however: the emphasis on freedom of speech and press.

Modern Conservatism

What happened to the other branch of liberalism, the people who stayed true to Adam Smith's original doctrine of minimal government? They are very much around, only we call them conservatives. (In Europe, they still call them liberals or neo-liberals, a source of confusion between Americans and Europeans.) American conservatives got a big boost from Milton Friedman, the Nobel Prize-winning economist. Friedman argued forcefully that the free market is still the best, that Adam Smith was right, that wherever government intervenes it messes things up. Margaret Thatcher in Britain and Ronald Reagan in the United States applied this revival of classic liberalism in the 1980s with mixed but generally positive results.

Modern conservatism also borrows from Edmund Burke a concern for tradition, especially in religion. American conservatives would get prayer into public schools, outlaw abortion, and support private and church-related schools. Modern conservatives are also traditional in opposing special rights for women and homosexuals. Modern conservatism is thus a blend of the economic ideas of Adam Smith and the traditionalist ideas of Edmund Burke.

Marxist Socialism

Although liberalism (classic variety) dominated the nineteenth century, a strand of critical opinion arose in reaction to the obvious excesses of the capitalist system. Unlike T. H. Green, some critics didn't believe that a few reforms would suffice; they wanted the overthrow of the capitalist system. They were the socialists, and their leading thinker was Karl Marx, whose complex theory we discussed in Chapter 2. Marx wrote not to promote truth but to promote revolution. He hated the "bourgeoisie" long before he developed his elaborate theories that they were doomed. The initial outline of his ideas, the 1848 *Communist Manifesto*, appeared in a pamphlet ending with the ringing words: "The proletarians have nothing to lose but their chains. They have a world to win. Workers of all countries, unite!" Marx participated in organizing Europe's first socialist parties.

Marx's great work *Capital* was a gigantic analysis of why capitalism would be overthrown by the proletariat. Then would come socialism, a just, productive society without class distinctions. Later, at a certain stage when industrial production was very high, this socialist society will turn into communism, a perfect society that won't need police, money, or even government. Goods will be in such plenty that people will just take what they need. There won't be private property, so there will be no need for police. Since government is simply an instrument of class domination, with the abolition of distinct classes there won't

Karl Marx glares down at the citizens of Tashkent, Uzbekistan, now an independent ex-Soviet republic. The communists built such statues—more of Lenin than of Marx—all over the Soviet Union. (Michael Roskin)

need to be government; it will "wither away." Communism, then, was the predicted utopia beyond socialism.

Marx focused on the ills and malfunctions of capitalism and never specified what socialism would be like, only that it would be much better than capitalism; its precise workings he left vague. This has enabled a wide variety of socialist thinkers to put forward their own vision of socialism and say it is what Marx really meant. This has ranged from the mild "welfarism" of social-democratic parties, to anarcho-syndicalism (unions running everything), to Lenin's and Stalin's hypercentralized tyranny, to Trotsky's denunciation of same, to Mao's self-destructive permanent revolution, to Tito's experimental decentralized system. All, and a few more, claim to espouse "real" socialism. These different interpretations of socialism caused first the Socialist and then the Communist movement to splinter.

Social Democracy

By the beginning of the twentieth century the German Social Democrats (SPD), espousing Marxism, had become Germany's biggest party. Marx hadn't thought much of conventional parties and labor unions; bourgeois governments would simply crush them, he believed. At most, they could be training grounds for more serious revolutionary action. But the German Social Democrats started having success. Their members got elected to the Reichstag and local offices; their unions

Case Studies — WHY DIDN'T CAPITALISM COLLAPSE?

One of the enduring problems and weaknesses with Marx is that capitalism, contrary to his prediction, has not collapsed. Marx thought the Paris Commune of 1870–1871 was the first proletarian uprising. (It wasn't.) True, capitalism has gone through some major depressions, in the 1890s and 1930s, but it has always bounced back. Now it is stronger than ever.

Marx erred in at least a couple of ways. First, he failed to understand the flexible, adaptive nature of capitalism. Old industries fade, and new ones rise. Imagine trying to explain Bill Gates and the computer software industry to someone a quarter century ago. They wouldn't believe you. Capitalism rarely gets stuck at one stage; it is the system of constant change. Second, Marx failed to understand that capitalism is not just one system; it is many. U.S., French, Singaporean, and Japanese capitalisms are all distinct from each other. Marx's simplified notions of capitalism illustrate what happens when theory is placed in the service of ideology: Unquestioning followers believe it too literally.

won higher wages and better working conditions. Some began to think that the working class could accomplish its aims without revolution. Why use bullets when there are ballots?

Eduard Bernstein developed this viewpoint. In his *Evolutionary Socialism* (1901), he pointed out the very real gains the working class was making and concluded that Marx had been wrong about the necessity for collapse of the system and revolution. Reforms that won concrete benefits for the working class could also lead to socialism, he argued. In revising Marxism, Bernstein earned the name **revisionist**, originally a pejorative hurled at him by orthodox Marxists. By the time of the ill-fated Weimar Republic in Germany (1919–1933), the Social Democrats had greatly toned down their militancy and worked together with Liberals and Catholics to try to save democracy. Persecuted by the Nazis, the SPD revived after World War II, and in 1959 they dropped Marxism altogether, as did virtually all **social democratic** parties. As social democrats in many countries moderated their positions, they got elected more and more. They transformed themselves into center-left parties with no trace of revolution.

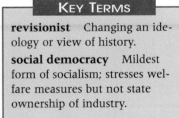

KEY TERMS

revisionist Changing an ideology or view of history.

social democracy Mildest form of socialism; stresses welfare measures but not state ownership of industry.

What, then, do social democrats stand for? They have abandoned their plans to nationalize industry. Sweden, for example, has only about 10 percent of its industry nationalized, and much of that was done a long time ago by conservatives to keep firms from going under and creating unemployment. Said the late Olof Palme, Sweden's Social Democratic prime minister, "If industry's primary purpose is to expand its production, to succeed in new markets, to provide good jobs for their employees, they need have no fears. Swedish industry has never expanded so rapidly as during these years of Social Democratic rule." Instead of nationalization of industry, social democrats have used *welfare* measures to improve living conditions: unemployment insurance, national medical plans, generous pensions, and subsidized food and housing. Social democracies have become welfare states: *Welfarism* would be a more accurate term than *socialism*.

There's one catch—there's always at least one catch—and that is that welfare states are terribly expensive. To pay for these welfare measures, taxes climb. In Denmark and Sweden, taxes consume a majority of the gross domestic product, exactly the kind of thing conservative economist Milton Friedman warned about. With those kinds of taxes, soon you are not free to choose how you live. U.S. liberalism is tinged with social-democratic ideas on welfare. The left wing of our Democratic party resembles ideologically the moderate wings of European social democratic parties.

Communism

While the social democrats evolved into reformists and welfarists, a smaller wing of the original socialists stayed Marxist and became the Communists. The key figure in this transformation was a Russian intellectual, Vladimir I. Lenin. He made several changes in Marxism, producing Marxism-Leninism, another name for **communism**.

Imperialism   Many of Russian intellectuals of the late nineteenth century hated the tsarist system and embraced Marxism as a way to overthrow tsarism. Ironically, Marx meant his theory to apply in the most *advanced* capitalist countries, not in backward Russia, where capitalism was just beginning. Lenin, mostly in exile in Zurich, Switzerland, remade Marxism to fit backward Russia. He offered a theory of economic **imperialism**, one borrowed from German Communist Rosa Luxemburg and English economist J. A. Hobson. These thinkers had all wondered why the proletarian revolutions Marx had foreseen had not broken out in the advanced industrialized lands. They concluded that capitalism had succeeded in transforming itself, expanding overseas into colonies to exploit their raw materials, cheap labor, and new markets. Capitalism had won a temporary new lease on life by turning into imperialism. The domestic market couldn't absorb what the capitalist system was producing, so it found overseas markets. Making enormous profits from its colonies, the mother imperialist country could also pay off its working class a bit to render it reformist rather than revolutionary.

While imperialism was expanding, Lenin noted, it was growing unevenly. Some countries, such as Britain and Germany, were highly developed, but where capitalism was just starting, as in Spain and Russia, it was weak. The latter sort of countries were exploited as a whole by the international capitalist system. It was

> ### KEY TERMS
>
> **communism** Marxist theory merged with Leninist organization into a totalitarian party.
>
> **imperialism** Amassing of colonial empires, mostly by European powers; pejorative in Marxist terms.

in them that revolutionary fever burned brightest; they were imperialism's "weakest link." Accordingly, a revolution could break out in a backward country, reasoned Lenin, and then spread into advanced countries. The imperialist countries were highly dependent on their empires; once cut off from exploiting them, the imperialists would fall. World War I, wrote Lenin, was the collision of imperialist powers trying to dominate the globe. Lenin shifted the Marxian focus from the situation *within* capitalist countries to the situation *among* countries. The focus went from Marx's proletariat rising up against the bourgeoisie to exploited nations rising up against imperialist powers. Marx would probably not have approved of such a shift.

Organization   Lenin's real contribution lay in his attention to *organization*. With the tsarist secret police always on their trail, Lenin argued, the Russian socialist party could not be like other parties—large, open, and trying to win votes. Instead, it had to be small, secretive, made up of professional revolutionaries, and tightly organized under central command. In 1903 the Russian Social Democratic Labor party split over this issue. Lenin had enough of his supporters at their party's Brussels meeting to win the votes of thirty-three of the fifty-one delegates present. Lenin called his faction *bolshevik* (Russian for "majority"). The losers, who advocated a more moderate line and a more open party, took the name *menshevik* ("minority"). In 1918, the Bolsheviks changed the party name to Communist.

Lenin's attention to organization paid off. Russia was in chaos from World War I. In March 1917, a group of moderates had seized power from the tsar, but they were unable to govern the country. In November, the Bolsheviks, shrewdly manipulating councils (*soviets* in Russian) that had sprung up in the leading cities, seized control from the moderates. After consolidating power in a desperate civil war, Lenin called on all true socialists around the world to join in a new international movement under Moscow's direct control. It was called the Communist International, or Comintern. Almost all socialist parties in the world split; their left wings went into the Comintern and became Communist parties in 1920–1921. The resultant social democratic and Communist parties were more or less natural enemies ever since.

How much Marxism-Leninism did the rulers of the Soviet Union really believe? They constantly used Marxist rhetoric, but many observers argued they were actually indifferent or even cynical about ideology and just used it as window dressing. The Soviets never defined their society as Communist—that was yet to come; it was what they were working on. It is we in the West who called these countries "Communist." In 1961, party chief Nikita Khrushchev was rash enough to promise "communism in our generation," indicating that utopia would be reached by 1980. Instead, it declined, and in late 1991 the system collapsed.

Maoism and Titoism   In the 1930s, Mao Zedong concluded that the Chinese Communist Party (CCP) had to be based on poor peasants and guerrilla warfare. This was a break with Stalin's leadership, and after decades of fighting, the CCP took over mainland China in 1949. Mao pursued a radical course that included a failed attempt at overnight industrialization (the Great Leap Forward in 1958), the destruction of bureaucratic authority (the Proletarian Cultural Revolution in 1966), and even border fighting with the Soviet Union in 1969. After Mao's death in 1976, calmer heads moved China away from Mao's extremism, which had severely damaged China's economic progress. A few revolutionary groups stayed Maoist: Pol Pot's murderous Khmer Rouge and Peru's Shining Path. **Maoism** is a form of ultraradical communism.

Yugoslav party chief Josip Tito went the other way, developing a more moderate and liberal form of communism. Even though Tito's partisans fought the Germans in Stalin's name, Stalin felt he didn't fully control Tito, and in 1948 had Yugoslavia kicked out of the Communist camp. During the 1950s, the Yugoslav Communists radically reformed their system, basing it on decentralization, debureaucratization, and worker self-management. Trying to find a middle ground between a market and a controlled economy, Yugoslavia suffered severe economic problems in the 1980s. **Titoism** might have served as a warning to Communist rulers who wanted to experiment with "middle ways" between capitalism and socialism. The combination is unstable and worked only because Tito ran it; when he died in 1980, Yugoslavia started coming apart until by the early 1990s it was a bloodbath.

Nationalism

The real winner among ideologies—and the one that's still dominant today—is nationalism, the exaggerated belief in the greatness and unity of one's country. Nationalism is often born out of occupation and repression by foreigners. "We won't be pushed around by foreigners any more!" shout Irish, Cuban, Palestinian, Israeli, Vietnamese, and many other nationalists. Nationalism has triumphed over all other ideologies and influenced all the others, so that in the United States classic liberalism is combined with American nationalism, and in China communism became intertwined with Chinese nationalism.

Some scholars trace the beginning of nationalism back to the Renaissance monarchs who proclaimed their absolute power and unity and greatness of their kingdoms. *Nationality* was born out of sovereignty. *Nationalism*, however, didn't appear until the French Revolution, which was based on the "people" and heightened French feelings about themselves as a special, leading people destined to free the rest of Europe. When conservatives tried to invade France in 1792, the "nation in arms" stopped them at Valmy; enthusiastic volunteers beat professional soldiers. The stirring "Marseillaise," France's national anthem, appeared that same year. Napoleon's legions were ostensibly spreading the radical liberalism of the French Revolution, but were really spreading nationalism. The conquered nations of Europe quickly grew to hate the arrogant French occupiers. Spaniards, Germans, and Russians soon became nationalistic themselves as they struggled to expel the French. Basic to nationalism is resentment of foreign domination, be it by British redcoats, Napoleon's legions, or European colonialists. Nationalism awoke in Europe in the nineteenth century and by the twentieth century had spread to Europe's colonies throughout the world. It is in the Third World that nationalism is now most intense.

By the mid-nineteenth century, thinkers all over Europe—especially in Germany and Italy—were defining the nation as the ultimate human value. Some began to worship the nation, seeing in it the source of all things good. Italian writer Giuseppe Mazzini espoused freedom not for individuals—that was mere liberalism—but for nations instead. One achieved true freedom by subordinating oneself to the nation. Education, for example, had to inculcate a sense of nationalism that blotted out individualism, argued Mazzini.

Nationalism generally arises when a population, invariably led by intellectuals, perceives an enemy or "other" to despise and struggle against. In the twentieth century, this has often been a colonial power such as Britain, France, or the Netherlands, against whom, respectively, Indians, Algerians, and Indonesians could rally in their fight for independence. At bottom, nationalism is the feeling that it is terribly wrong to be ruled by others. Thus, Bosnian Serbs do not consent to be ruled by Bosnian Muslims, Palestinians do not consent to be ruled by Israelis, and Chechens do not consent to be ruled by Russians. Some Chinese and Iranians, feeling they have been repressed and controlled by outside powers, lash out with highly nationalistic military and diplomatic policies. Even some Canadians, fearful of U.S. economic and cultural dominance, turn nationalistic.

The big problem of nationalism is that it tends to economic isolation. "We won't let foreigners take over our economy!" say nationalists, but rapid economic growth depends heavily on foreign investment and world trade. More than any of the previous ideologies, nationalism depends on emotional appeals. The feeling of belonging to a nation seems to go to our psychological center. What other human organization would we fight and kill for?

Regional Nationalism   In recent decades the world has seen the rise of another kind of nationalism: regional nationalism, which aims at breaking up existing nations into what its proponents argue are the true nations. Militant Québécois want to separate from Canada, Basques from Spain, Corsicans from France, and Kosovari from Serbia. It too is based on hatred of being ruled by unlike peoples.

Fascism

In Italy and Germany nationalism grew into **fascism**, one of the great catastrophes of the twentieth century. One tipoff of a fascist movement: Its members tend to wear uniforms. Before World War I, Italian journalist Benito Mussolini was a fire-breathing socialist; military service changed him into an ardent nationalist. Italy was full of discontented people after World War I.

> ### KEY TERM
>
> **fascism** An extreme form of nationalism with elements of socialism and militarism.

Maximalist socialists threatened revolution. In those chaotic times, Mussolini gathered around him a strange collection of people in black shirts who dreamed of getting rid of democracy and political parties and imposing stern central authority and discipline. These Fascists—a word taken from the ancient Roman symbol of authority, a bundle of sticks bound around an ax (the *fasces*)—hated disorder and wanted strong leadership to end it.

Amid growing disorder in 1922, the king of Italy handed power to Mussolini, and by 1924 he had turned Italy into a one-party state with himself as *Duce* (leader). The Fascists ran the economy by having their men in all key positions. Italy looked impressive: There was little crime, much monumental construction, stable prices, and as they used to say, "The trains ran on time." Behind the scenes, however, fascism was a mess, with hidden unemployment, poor economic performance, and corruption.

With the collapse of the world economy in 1929, however, some thought fascism was the wave of the future. Adolf Hitler in Germany copied Mussolini's fascism but had his followers wear brown shirts and added racism. For Hitler, it wasn't just Germans as a nation who were rising up against the punitive and unfair Versailles Treaty and chaos of the Weimar Republic; it was Germans as a distinct and superior race. Hitler didn't invent German racism, which went back generations, but he hyped it. The racist line held that a special branch of the white race, the Aryans, were the bearers of all civilization. A subbranch, the Nordics, which included Germans, were even better. (Actually, Germans are of very mixed genealogy.) Hitler argued that the superior Nordics were being subjugated to the sinister forces of Judaism, communism, world capitalism, and even Roman Catholicism. This doctrine was the basis for the death camps.

Hitler was named chancellor (prime minister) in 1933 in a situation of turmoil and, like Mussolini, within two years had perfected a dictatorship. Probably

Work makes you free, proclaims the sign over the gate at the notorious concentration camp of Auschwitz. The Nazis' aim was to make prisoners think they were headed for work rather than for the gas chambers. (Michael Roskin)

a majority of Germans supported Hitler. With Nazis "coordinating" the economy, unemployment lessened and many working people felt they were getting a good deal with the jobs, vacations, and welfare the regime provided. The Nazis' full name was the National Socialist German Workers Party, but the socialism was fake. Hitler's true aim was war, and his economic policies were designed for war. For a few years Hitler dominated Europe and started turning the Slavic lands of Eastern Europe into colonies for Germans—*Lebensraum* (living space). Jews and many Slavic peoples were simply exterminated. Nazi death camps killed some 6 million Jews and a similar number of Christians who were in the way. Was Hitler mad? Many of his views were widely held among Germans, and he had millions of enthusiastic helpers. Rather than insanity, the Nazis demonstrate the danger of nationalism run amok.

The word *fascist* has been overused and misused. Some leftists hurl it at every-thing they don't like. Spanish dictator Francisco Franco, for example, was long considered a fascist, but he was actually a "traditional authoritarian," for he tried to minimize mass political involvement rather than stir it up the way Mussolini and Hitler did. Brazilian President Getúlio Vargas decreed a fascist-sounding "New State" in 1937, but he was merely borrowing some fascist rhetoric at a time when the movement was having its heyday in Europe. The Ku Klux Klan in the United States is sometimes called fascist, and its members wear uniforms. The Klan's populist racism is similar to the Nazis', but the Klan strongly opposes the power of the national government, whereas the Nazis and Fascists worshiped it.

In our day a kind of neofascism has appeared in the anti-immigrant parties in Britain, France, and Germany. The possibility of fascism catching on in Russia should not be discounted; all the ingredients—despair, confusion, unemploy-ment, extreme nationalism, and the longing for strong leadership—are present.

Ideology in Our Day

The Collapse of Communism

By the 1980s, communism the world over was showing signs of ideological exhaustion. Exceedingly few people in China, Eastern Europe, and even the Soviet Union believed in it any longer. In the non-Communist world, leftists deserted Marxism in droves. Several West European Communist parties embraced "Euro-communism," a greatly watered-down ideology that renounced dictatorship and nationalization of industry. Capitalism was supposed to have col-lapsed; instead, it was thriving in the United States, Western Europe, and East Asia. Many Communist leaders admitted that their economies were too rigid and centralized and that the cure lay in cutting back state controls and letting free enterprise take on a bigger role. Reform-minded Soviet President Mikhail Gorbachev (1985–1991) offered a three-pronged approach to revitalizing Soviet communism: *glasnost* (openness, or publicizing problems), *perestroika* (economic restructuring), and *demokratizatzia* (democratization). Applied haltingly and halfheartedly, the reforms actually heightened discontent, for now Soviets could voice their complaints. Starting in Eastern Europe in 1989, non-Communist parties took over. In the Soviet Union, a partially free parliament was elected and began debating change. Non-Communist parties and movements appeared. Gorbachev still couldn't make up his mind how far and fast reforms should go, and the economy, barely reformed, turned wildly inflationary. A 1991 coup failed, and by the end of the year the Soviet Union had ceased to exist.

The speed and sweep of the change showed, among other things, that the Soviet Union was not nearly as strong as we had thought, that communism is an inherently defective system, and that few Soviets had believed in it as a serious ideology. The danger now is, what do they have to believe in? Many observers fear that Western concepts of pluralism, tolerance, and democracy have no roots in Russian soil. What, then, will fill the ideological vacuum? Let us hope that a Western-type free democracy and economy can before something else does.

Neoconservatism

KEY TERM

neoconservatism U.S. ideology of the 1970s and 1980s of former liberals turning away from ineffective programs and relativism.

In the 1970s, a new ideology emerged in the United States: **neoconservatism**. It was much like modern conservatism but came from disillusioned liberals and leftists. As neoconservative writer Irving Kristol put it, "A neo-conservative is a liberal who's been mugged by reality." Neoconservatives charged that the Democratic party had moved too far to the left with unrealistic ideas on domestic reforms and a pacifist foreign policy. Neoconservatives reacted against the Great Society programs introduced by Lyndon Johnson in the mid-1960s that aimed to wipe out poverty and discrimination and included food stamps, medical care for the elderly, regional development, urban renewal, prekindergarten education, voting and civil rights for African Americans, and affirmative action to hire minorities. Some liberals said the Great Society was never given a chance because funds for it were siphoned away by the Vietnam war. But disillusioned liberals said it worked badly, that many of the programs achieved nothing. The cities grew worse; educational standards declined; medical aid became extremely costly; and a class of welfare-dependent poor emerged, people who had little incentive to work. Neoconservatives spoke of negative "unforeseen consequences" of well-intentioned liberal programs. One point especially bothered neoconservatives: Affirmative action seemed to give racial minorities preferential treatment in hiring, sometimes ahead of better-qualified whites. This really hit home when affirmative action quotas were applied to academic hiring; liberal, white, male professors sometimes had to taste their own medicine in getting turned down for teaching jobs that went to blacks, Hispanics, and women.

Many neoconservatives were horrified at the extreme relativism that had grown in the 1960s. The popular ideas—such as "It's all right if it feels good" and "It just depends on your point of view" and "multiculturalism"—drove many liberals to neoconservatism. Ironically, some neoconservatives were college professors who had earlier tried to broaden their students' views by stressing the relativity of all viewpoints and cultures. Instead, students became vacuous rather than enlightened.

Libertarianism

Slowly growing since the 1960s is an ideology that's so liberal it's conservative—or vice versa. **Libertarians** would return to the original Adam Smith, with essentially no government interference in anything. They would deliver what Ronald Reagan only talked about. They note that modern liberals want a controlled economy but personal freedom while modern conservatives want a free economy but constraints on personal freedom. Why not have freedom in both areas? Libertarians oppose subsidies, bureaucracies, taxes, intervention overseas, and big government itself. As such, they have plugged into a very old American tradition and gained respectability. Although no Libertarian candidates have won elections, their Cato Institute in Washington has become a lively thinktank whose ideas can not be ignored.

> ### KEY TERMS
>
> **libertarianism** U.S. ideology of the late twentieth century in favor of shrinking all government power in favor of individual freedom.
>
> **feminism** Ideology of psychological, political, and economic equality for women.

Feminism

Springing to new life in the 1960s with a handful of female writers, by the 1970s the women's movement had become a political force in the United States and Western Europe. **Feminist** writers pointed out that women were paid less than men for the same work, were passed over for promotion to leading positions, were subjected to psychological and physical abuse from men, were denied bank loans and insurance unless their husbands would cosign, and were in general second-class citizens.

The problem was psychological, argued feminists. Women and men were forced into "gender roles" that had little to do with biology. Boys were conditioned to be tough, domineering, competitive, and "macho," but girls were taught to be meek, submissive, unsure of themselves, and "feminine." Gender differences are almost entirely learned behavior, taught by parents and schools of a "patriarchal" society, but this could be changed. With proper child rearing and education, males could become gentler and females more assertive and self-confident.

Feminists started "consciousness-raising" groups and railed against "male chauvinist pigs." Feminism started having an impact. Many employers gave women a fairer chance, sometimes hiring them over men. Women moved up to higher management positions (although seldom to the corporate top). Working wives became the norm. Husbands shared in homemaking and child rearing. Politically, however, feminists did not achieve all they wished. The Equal Rights Amendment (ERA) to the Constitution failed to win ratification in a sufficient number of state legislatures. It would have guaranteed equality of treatment regardless of gender. Antifeminists, some of them conservative women, argued that the ERA would take away women's privileges and protections under the law, would make women eligible for the draft, and would even lead to unisex lavatories. Despite this setback, women learned that there was one way they could count for a lot politically—by voting. In the 1980 election a significant "gender gap" appeared, and now women generally vote more Democratic than do men. The women's vote helped Bill Clinton win twice.

Environmentalism

> **KEY TERM**
>
> **environmentalism** Ideology that the environment is endangered and must be preserved through regulation and lifestyle changes.

Also during the 1960s the ecology, or **environmental**, movement began to ripple through the advanced industrialized countries. Economic development paid little heed to the damage it did to the environment. Any growth was good growth: "We'll never run out of nature." Mining, factories, and even farms poisoned streams, industries and automobiles polluted the air, chemical wastes made areas uninhabitable, and nuclear power leaked radioactivity. To the credo of "growth" the ecologists responded with "limits." They seem to say, "We can't go on like this forever without producing an environmental catastrophe." Love Canal, Three Mile Island, and Chernobyl seemed to prove them right. The burning of fossil fuels and rain forests may be creating a "greenhouse effect," trapping heat inside the earth's atmosphere and changing the planet's weather.

The ecologists' demands were only partly satisfied with the founding of the Environmental Protection Agency (EPA) in 1970. Industrial groups, however, found that EPA regulations restricted growth and ate into profits; under President Reagan, the EPA was rendered ineffective and became a scandal. Regulation was only part of the environmental credo. Many argued that consumption patterns and lifestyles in the advanced countries should change to conserve the earth's resources, natural beauty, and clean air and water. Americans, only about 6 percent of the world's population, consume close to half the world's manufactured goods and a third of its energy. In addition to being out of balance with the poor nations of the world, this profligate lifestyle is unnecessary and unhealthy, they argued. Ecologists urged public transportation and bicycles instead of cars, whole-grain foods and vegetables instead of meat, and decentralized, renewable energy sources, such as wind and solar energy, instead of fossil- or nuclear-fueled power plants.

Some environmentalists formed a political party, the Citizens party, but their main impact was within the two big parties, both of which could not ignore the environmental vote. In the 1980s new parties, the Greens (as environmentalists like to call themselves), sprang into life across Western Europe. In Germany and Sweden, bearded and blue-jeaned Greens were elected to parliament, determined to end nuclear power, toxic waste, and the arms race. Many young Europeans found the Greens an attractive alternative to the old and stodgy conventional parties.

Is Ideology Finished?

In 1960, Harvard sociologist Daniel Bell argued that the century-long ideological debates were coming to a close. The failure of tyrannical communism and the rise of the welfare state were producing what Bell called the "end of ideology": There simply was not much to debate about. Henceforth political debate would focus on almost technical questions of how to run the welfare state, said Bell, such as what to include under national health insurance. In 1989, political scientist Francis Fukuyama went even farther: Not only had the great ideological debate ended with the victory of capitalist democracy but history itself could be ending. Widely misunderstood, Fukuyama did not mean that time would stand still but rather that the human endpoint propounded by Hegel— free people living in free societies—was now coming into view. Not only had we beaten communism, suggested Fukuyama, there would not likely be any other ideologies to challenge ours. With the end of ideology would come the end of history in the sense of the struggle of great ideas. (Life could get boring, sighed the puckish Fukuyama.)

Is either the Bell or Fukuyama thesis accurate? There are grounds for doubt. First, the collapse of communism in Europe by itself does not disprove Marx's original ideas, although those now propounding them must carefully distance themselves from the Soviet type of socialism. (We use *socialism* here to mean state control of industry, not *welfarism*, which is but a variation on capitalist democracy.) Socialist thought is still alive on some U.S. college campuses. Some still debate the possibility of a benign socialism. And there are other ideologies besides socialism, some mentioned here, and new and dangerous ideological challenges emerged just as communism collapsed: neofascism, breakaway nationalism, and Islamic fundamentalism. And within free democracy itself there are numerous ideological viewpoints: free market or government intervention, more welfare or less, a secular or religious state, and spreading democracy abroad or avoiding overseas involvement. Fukuyama need not worry about boredom.

Key Terms

communism (p. 100)

conservatism (p. 95)

environmentalism (p. 108)

fascism (p. 103)

feminism (p. 107)

ideology (p. 91)

imperialism (p. 100)

liberalism (p. 94)

libertarianism (p. 107)

maoism (p. 102)

modern liberalism (p. 96)

neoconservatism (p. 106)

pragmatic (p. 93)

revisionist (p. 99)

social democracy (p. 99)

titoism (p. 102)

Key Websites

If you want to find sites that cover everything from anarchism to socialism, start here.
http://dir.yahoo.com/Social_Science/Political_Science/Political_Theory/

This site has links to all types of socialist ideologies, including anarchism, social democracy, and maoism, among many others.
http://www.dsausa.org/rl/Docs/Lingo.html

The Heritage Foundation is a conservative think-tank whose mission is to formulate and promote conservative public policies based on principles such as free enterprise, limited government, and a strong national defense.
http://www.heritage.org/

This site discusses the philosophy of civil disobedience; it also has detailed biographies of Dr. Martin Luther King, Mahatma Gandhi, and Henry David Thoreau.
http://www.kids-right.org/philosop.htm

Further Reference

Boaz, David. *Libertarianism: A Primer*. New York: Free Press, 1997.

Coleman, Daniel A. *Ecopolitics: Building a Green Society*. New Brunswick, NJ: Rutgers University Press, 1994.

Gellner, Ernest. *Nationalism*. New York: New York University Press, 1998.

Harding, Neil. *Leninism*. Durham, NC: Duke University Press, 1996.

Huberman, Leo, and Paul M. Sweezy. *Introduction to Socialism*. New York: Monthly Review Press, 1968.

Kohn, Hans. *Political Ideologies in the Twentieth Century*, 3rd ed., rev. New York: Harper & Row, 1966.

Kramnick, Isaac, and Frederick M. Watkins. *The Age of Ideology: Political Thought, 1750 to the Present*, 2nd ed. Englewood Cliffs, NJ: Prentice Hall, 1979.

Kristol, Irving. *Neoconservatism: The Autobiography of an Idea*. New York: Free Press, 1995.

Laqueur, Walter. *Fascism: Past, Present, Future*. New York: Oxford University Press, 1997.

Sassoon, Donald. *One Hundred Years of Socialism: The West European Left in the Twentieth Century*. New York: New Press, 1996.

Walicki, Andrzej. *Marxism and the Leap to the Kingdom of Freedom: The Rise and Fall of the Communist Utopia*. Stanford, CA: Stanford University Press, 1995.

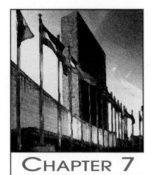

CHAPTER 7

Political Culture

Americans and Canadians appear so similar in tastes and lifestyles some people think they are essentially the same. They are not, especially in politics. Americans are more insistent about their individual rights and limits on government authority than Canadians. Canadians are more law-abiding and willing to let government assume a paternalistic role in guiding the economy and society. Americans sometimes find Canadians a little too obedient; Canadians think Americans are too wild and lawless. Canada has a distinct **political culture**.

The Environment of Government: Political Culture

Each society imparts its set of norms and values to its people, and the people in turn have distinct ideals about how the political system is supposed to work, about what the government may do to them and for them, and about their claims and obligations. These beliefs, symbols, and values about the political system is the political culture of a nation—and it varies considerably from one nation to another.

The political culture of a nation is determined by its history, economy, religion, and folkways. Basic values, laid down early, may endure for centuries. America was founded on the basis of "competitive individualism," a spirit of hustle and looking out for yourself, which is still very much alive. The millennia-old Hindu emphasis on caste persists in present-day India despite government efforts to abolish it. The French, after centuries of *étatisme*, still expect a big

> ### QUESTIONS TO CONSIDER
>
> 1. What is political culture?
> 2. How is political culture different from public opinion?
> 3. Why does democracy need trusting citizens?
> 4. Explain the three types of political culture found by Almond and Verba.
> 5. If Americans are participatory, why do they vote so little?
> 6. What happened to U.S. attitudes starting in the 1960s?
> 7. How do elite and mass political cultures differ?
> 8. How can you tell if a group forms a distinct subculture?
> 9. What are the most potent agents of political socialization?

> ### KEY TERM
>
> **political culture**   The psychology of a nation in regard to politics.

state to supervise the economy. Russians, after centuries of autocracy, have trouble understanding democracy. Political culture is a sort of collective political memory.

As defined by political scientist Sidney Verba, political culture is "the system of empirical beliefs, expressive symbols, and values, which defines the situation in which political action takes place." What are these beliefs, symbols, and values that determine how a people interprets the proper role of government and how that government operates? Much of this goes a long way back. Americans always liked minimal government. In Japan, where the vestiges of a traditional feudal class system still exist, those who bow lower indicate they are of inferior status. The Japanese still tend to submit to the authority of those in office, even when they dislike their corruption and incompetence. Americans, who traditionally do not defer to anyone, consider it their democratic birthright to have a say in the way the country is governed, even if they know little about the issues. In political culture, Japan and the United States are vastly different.

Political Culture and Public Opinion

What is the difference between political culture and public opinion? Obviously, the two overlap, for both look at attitudes toward politics. Political culture aims to tap basic, general values on politics and government. Public opinion, on the other hand, focuses on views about specific leaders and policies. Political culture looks for the underpinnings of legitimacy, the gut attitudes that sustain a political system, whereas public opinion seeks responses to current questions.

The methodologies of political culture and public opinion also overlap: Random samples of the population are asked questions, and the responses are correlated with subgroups in the population. The questions, however, will be different. A political culture survey might ask how much you trust government; a public opinion survey might ask how much you like the current administration. The political culture study is more likely to ask the same questions in several countries in order to gain a comparative perspective. Both may want to keep track of responses over time to see, in the case of political culture, if legitimacy is gaining or declining or, in the case of public opinion, how a president's popularity compares with that of predecessors.

Political culture studies often go beyond surveys, however. Some use the methods of anthropology and psychology in the close observation of daily life and in the deep questioning of individuals about their feelings. Public opinion studies rarely go beyond the clipboard with quantified data, whereas political culture studies can use history and literature to gain insights into a particular country. For instance, the observations of nineteenth-century European visitors provide evidence of continuity in American political and social attitudes. Indeed, the brilliant comments of the Frenchman Alexis de Tocqueville, who traveled through the United States in the 1830s, still generally apply a century and a half later. Tocqueville was one of the founders of the political culture approach in political science.

It used to be widely assumed that political culture was nearly permanent or changed only slowly, whereas public opinion was fickle and changed quickly. Recent studies, however, have shown that political culture is rather changeable, too. Periods of stable, efficient government and economic growth solidify feelings of legitimacy; periods of indecisive, chaotic government and economic downturn are reflected in weakening legitimacy. Public opinion, if held long enough, eventually turns into political culture. In the 1960s, public opinion on Vietnam showed declining support for the war. Over precisely this same time period, confidence in the U.S. government also declined. Public opinion on a given question was infecting the general political culture, making it more **cynical** about the political system.

> **KEY TERM**
>
> **cynical** Untrusting and suspicious, especially of government.

To be sure, a country's political culture changes more slowly than its public opinions, and certain underlying elements of political culture tend to persist for generations, perhaps for centuries. One can easily recognize the America of Tocqueville in the America of today; basic values haven't changed that much. The French still take to the streets of Paris to protest perceived injustice, just as their ancestors did. Italians continue their centuries-old cynicism toward anything governmental. Russians, who have never experienced free democracy, still tend to favor strong leaders and to ignore minority rights. Although not as firm as bedrock, political culture is an underlying layer of attitudes that can support—or fail to support—the rest of the political system. This is one reason why Russian democracy is having difficulty getting established.

Participation in America

Even in America, relatively few actively participate in politics. How, then, can Almond and Verba offer the United States as their model of a "civic culture"? (See box on pp. 114–115.) One of their key findings was that for democracy to work, participation need only be "intermittent and potential." In effect, they offer a "sleeping dogs" theory of democratic political culture. Leaders in a democracy know that most of the time most people are not paying close attention to politics. But they also know that if aroused—because of scandal, high unemployment, inflation, or unpopular war—the public can vote them out of office at the next election. Accordingly, leaders usually work to keep the unaroused public quiet. Following the **rule of anticipated reactions**, leaders in democracies constantly ask themselves how the public will likely react to any of their decisions. They are quite happy to have the public *not* react at all; they wish to let sleeping dogs lie.

> **KEY TERMS**
>
> **rule of anticipated reactions** Politicians forming policies based on how they think the public will react.
>
> **turnout** Percent of eligible voters who vote in a given election.

This theory helps explain an embarrassing fact about U.S. political life, namely, its low voter **turnout**, the lowest of all the industrialized democracies. Only about half of U.S. voters bother to cast a ballot in presidential elections, even fewer in state and

Classic Works   THE CIVIC CULTURE

The pioneering study of cross-national differences in political beliefs, symbols, and values was made by Gabriel Almond and Sidney Verba. Interviewing some 5,000 people in five different nations in 1959 and 1960, the authors sought to measure national political attitudes by testing three important variables: what impact the people felt government had on their lives, what obligation they felt they had toward government, and what they expected from government. Almond and Verba discerned three general political cultures: participant, subject, and parochial.

Participant   In a **participant** political culture, people understand that they are citizens and pay attention to politics. They are proud of their country's political system and are generally willing to discuss it. They believe they can influence politics to some degree and claim they would organize a group to protest something unfair. Accordingly, they show a high degree of **political competence** and **political efficacy**. They say they take pride in voting and believe people should participate in politics. They are active in their communities and often belong to one or more voluntary organizations. They are more likely to trust other people and to recall participating in family discussions as children. A participant political culture is clearly the ideal soil in which to sustain a democracy.

Subject   A notch lower than the participant political culture is the **subject** political culture, in which people still understand that they are citizens and pay attention to politics, but more passively. They follow political news but are not proud of their country's political system and feel little emotional commitment toward it. They feel uncomfortable speaking about politics. They feel they can influence politics only to the extent of speaking with a local official. It does not ordinarily occur to them to organize a group. Their sense of political competence and efficacy are lower; some feel powerless. They say they vote, but many vote without enthusiasm. They are less likely to trust other people and to recall voicing their views as children. Democracy has more difficulty sinking roots in a culture where people are used to thinking of themselves as obedient subjects rather than as active participants.

Parochial   At yet another notch lower is the parochial political culture, in which people may not even feel that they are citizens of a nation. They identify with the immediate locality, hence the term **parochial** (of a parish). They take no pride in their country's political system and expect little of it. They pay no attention to politics, have little knowledge of politics, and seldom speak about political matters. They have neither the desire nor the ability to participate in politics. They have no sense of political competence or efficacy and feel powerless in the face of existing institutions. Attempting to grow a democracy in a parochial political culture is very difficult, requiring not only new institutions but also a new sense of citizenship.

THE CIVIC CULTURE (CONTINUED)

Now, as Almond and Verba warn, there is no country that has a purely participant, subject, or parochial political culture. All nations are mixtures in varying degrees of the three types. The United States, they found, was heavily participant with some subject and even parochial attitudes. One of the problems with U.S. political culture, they suggest, is the relatively weak subject component, causing Americans to be not particularly law-abiding. Britain was closer to a happy balance between participatory and subject political cultures: sufficiently participant to be a democracy and sufficiently subject to obey authority. In Germany, the subject culture dominated; people obeyed authority but didn't want to get involved in politics. The same applied to Italy, with a bigger dose of parochial attitudes. Both Germany and Italy, at the time of Almond and Verba's studies only a decade and a half after World War II, illustrated the difficulty of starting a democracy in a relatively weak participant culture. Mexico was a strange mixture in which people made statements that sounded participatory but in practice behaved in a subject and parochial manner. Almond and Verba called Mexico an "aspirational" political culture—where hopes exceed reality.

All countries are mixtures of political cultures. If a country were purely parochial—with no one interested in anything political—it would either fall apart or succumb to foreign conquest. Without some participation you haven't got a country. The masses of people in the countryside can be parochial with only a few loyal subjects and political participants to guide them. That is the picture of traditional China: Eighty percent of the population toiled as peasants, then a layer of gentry and merchants to run things, and a tiny layer of mandarins and court officials to supervise the empire. Even traditional political systems were not completely parochial.

Today, it is hard to find purely parochial political cultures. All corners of the globe have been penetrated by communications, and even poor and uneducated people are often aware of current events. The white regime of South Africa wrongly supposed that the country's black majority was still tribal and parochial, with little interest (apart from a few troublemakers) in politics. On the contrary, they had long been demanding to participate in their nation's politics, and when not allowed to do so, turned to violence. Industry, education, transportation, and communication have awakened previously parochial people to the possibilities of politics. Modern times have phased out parochial political cultures.

On the other hand, would a purely participant political culture be possible or even desirable? Probably not. What would happen if everyone were eager to participate in politics? There would be the danger of political turmoil as too many citizens passionately pursue political causes. When that occurs, as during revolutions, the intense participation burns itself out after a period of tumult. The sudden growth of feelings of participation accompanies and contributes to the revolutionary upheavals of newly free countries. It is perhaps just as well that few people are truly political animals; most concern themselves with politics only intermittently and devote their chief attention to personal concerns. It is in the mixture of all three attitudes that democracy finds stability: Parochial concerns for family, church, and job give individuals meaning and perspective; subject attitudes give the political system obedience and support; and participant attitudes keep leaders attentive and responsive to the attitudes of the people.

KEY TERMS

participatory   Willing or interested in taking part in politics. (See p. 114.)

political competence Knowing how to accomplish something politically. (See p. 114.)

political efficacy   The feeling that one has at least a little political input (opposite: feeling powerless). (See p. 114.)

subject   The feeling among citizens that they should simply obey authority but not participate much in politics. (See p. 114.)

parochial   Narrow; having little or no interest in politics. (See p. 114.)

local contests. In Western Europe, voter turnout is usually about three-quarters of the electorate and sometimes tops 90 percent. How, then, can the United States boast of its democracy? Theorists reply that a democratic culture does not necessarily require heavy voter turnout. Rather, it requires an attitude that, if aroused, the people will participate—vote, contribute time and money, organize groups, and circulate petitions—and that elected officials know this. Democracy in this view is a psychological connection between leaders and led that restrains officials from foolishness. It is the attitudes of the people, and not their actual participation, that makes a democratic culture.

Another of Almond and Verba's key findings was the response to the question of what citizens of five countries would do to influence local government over an unjust ordinance. Far more Americans said they would "try to enlist the aid of others." Americans seem to be natural "group formers" when faced with a political problem, and this trait could be an important foundation of U.S. democracy. In more "subject" countries, this group-forming attitude was weaker.

Other studies show Americans are prouder of their system and more satisfied with the way democracy works in their country compared to the citizens of other lands. A 1995 Gallup survey found that 64 percent of the Americans polled expressed some degree of satisfaction. Sixty-two percent of Canadians responded likewise, as did 55 percent of Germans, 43 percent of French, 40 percent of Britons, 35 percent of Japanese, and only 17 percent of Mexicans and Hungarians. Americans may complain a lot about government, but their faith in democracy is still the strongest in the world.

The Decay of Political Culture

American political culture has shown great staying power. For centuries, Americans have valued freedom, religion, and personal responsibility far more than other countries. But at the close of the twentieth century observers were expressing concern over what they saw as the decay and decline of U.S. political culture, something that had been underway since the 1960s. Surveys showed a sharp decline in trust in government (Figure 7.1). These were the years of the Vietnam war, Watergate, and inflation—all of which made people distrust Washington. In the 1980s, under the "feel-good" presidency of Ronald Reagan, the trusting responses went up but never recovered the levels of the 1960s. The growth in cynicism made America harder to govern and is reflected in an electorate that seems to be permanently unhappy with Washington. American political culture is not as legitimate as it used to be.

One of the key factors, some claimed, was the decline of the American ten-

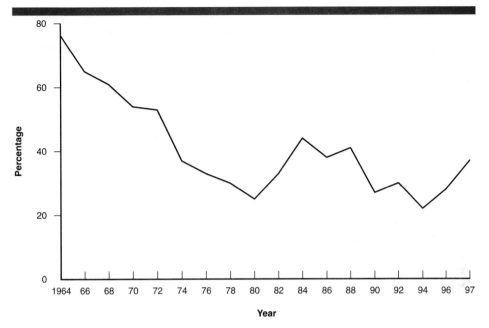

Figure 7.1 Americans' Trust in Government, 1964–1997
Sources: 1964–1996, American National Election Studies of the University of Michigan; 1997, Pew Research Center for People and the Press.

dency to form associations, anything from volunteer fire departments to labor unions. In the 1830s, Tocqueville noted: "Americans of all ages, all conditions, and all dispositions constantly form associations." He was quite amazed at this tendency, for it was (and still is) largely absent in France, and he held it was one of the bases of democracy, a point confirmed much later by the *Civic Culture* study. But several observers claim that these grassroots associations are fading. Harvard political scientist Robert Putnam noted, for example, that the number of people bowling has increased, but league bowling has declined. His eye-catching article, "Bowling Alone," became required reading in the Clinton White House. Putnam had more substantial examples of the decline of associations: union membership, parent-teacher associations, volunteers for the Boy Scouts and Red Cross, and membership in fraternal orders.

Those who see the decline of voluntary associations fear political and economic repercussions. With individuals stridently demanding their "rights" without a corresponding sense of having to contribute something, the demands on government become impossible; there is simply not enough money. Democracy becomes less a matter of concerned citizens meeting face-to-face to discuss a community problem than disgruntled citizens demanding "Gimme!" Furthermore, argued Francis Fukuyama (who earlier brought us the "end of history" theory), trust or "spontaneous sociability" underpins economic growth and stability. If you can trust others, you can do more and better business with them. Hence "high trust" societies lead to prosperous countries.

Political culture changes. True, it does not change as rapidly as public opinion, but political culture at any given moment is a combination of long-remembered and deeply held attitudes plus reactions to current situations. Since the original Almond and Verba *Civic Culture* study, British political culture has turned untrusting and cynical, West (but not East) German political culture became more trusting and participatory, and American political culture went through a decline in the 1960s and 1970s and a partial recovery in the 1980s. All these changes are responses to government performance. Political cultures do not fall from heaven; they are created by government actions and inactions.

Elite and Mass Cultures

The political culture of a country is not uniform and monolithic. One can usually find within it differences between the mainstream culture and subcultures (discussed following) and differences between elite and mass attitudes. Elites, used here more broadly than the "governing elites" discussed in Chapter 5 (a tiny fraction of 1 percent), in political-culture studies means those with better education, higher income, and more influence (several percent). Elites are much more interested in politics and more participatory. They are more inclined to vote, to protest injustice, to form groups, and to run for office. One consistent finding of the *Civic Culture* study has been confirmed over and over again: The more education a person has, the more likely he or she is to participate in politics.

Delegates to a typical Democratic convention—who are clearly very interested in politics—illustrate the differences between elite and mass culture. Usually half the delegates have some postgraduate education (often law school). Nationwide, only 4 percent of self-identified Democrats have gone to graduate school. Of the convention delegates, typically over half come from households with annual incomes of $80,000 or more. Nationwide, only 5 percent of Democrats are so favored. In other words, the people representing the Democratic party at the convention are not closely representative of the party rank and file. The Democrats pride themselves on being the party of the common people, but Democrats with more education and money still take the leading roles. There is nothing necessarily wrong with this: Better-educated and better-off people are simply more interested in political participation. The same is true of the Republican party or probably any party you care to name.

Why should this be so? Here we return to the words mentioned earlier: *political competence* and *political efficacy*. Better-educated people know how to participate in political activity. They have a greater sense of self-confidence in writing letters, speaking at meetings, and organizing groups. They feel that what they do has at least some political impact. The uneducated and the poor lack the knowledge and confidence to do these kinds of things. Many of them feel powerless. "What I do doesn't matter, so why bother?" they think. Those at the bottom of the social ladder thus become apathetic.

The differences in participation in politics between elites and masses are one of the great ironies of democracy. In theory and in law, politics is open to all in a democracy. In practice, some participate much more than others. Because the better-educated and better-off people (more education usually leads to higher income) participate in politics to a greater degree, they are in a much stronger position to look out for their interests. It is not surprising that in the 1990s Congress cut welfare spending, because recipients, who generally lack political skills, have trouble making their voices heard. There is no quick fix for this. The right to vote is a mere starting point for political participation; it does not guarantee equal access to decision making. A mass political culture of apathy and indifference toward politics effectively negates the potential of a mass vote. An elite political culture of competence and efficacy amplifies their influence.

Political Subcultures

Just as there are differences between elites and masses, so also are there differences among ethnic, religious, and regional groups in a country. When the differentiating qualities are strong enough in a particular group, we say that the group forms a **subculture**. Defining subculture is a bit tricky, as not every group in society is a subculture. The Norwegian-Americans of "Lake Wobegon," Minnesota, do not form a subculture because their political reactions and orientations are **mainstream**. But African Americans are on average poorer and less educated than white Americans, and the black vote is solidly Democratic. In attitudes toward the criminal justice system, blacks sharply diverge from whites, as the 1995 murder trial of O. J. Simpson dramatically illustrated. Most blacks, convinced the police and courts are racist and rig evidence, were glad to see Simpson acquitted. Most whites, convinced the police and courts are just and fair, thought the jury (with its black majority) had ignored the evidence. Many whites had naively believed that U.S. society had made great strides since the 1950s in **integrating** African Americans; the Simpson trial and the reactions to it showed how great a gap remained. Accordingly, African Americans form a political subculture.

> ### KEY TERMS
>
> **subculture** A minority culture within the mainstream culture.
>
> **mainstream** Sharing the average or standard political culture.
>
> **integration** Merging subcultures into the mainstream culture.

Groups with a different language who dislike being ruled by the dominant culture constitute subcultures. Many of the French-speakers of Quebec would like to withdraw from Canada and become a separate country. The Bengalis of East Pakistan, ethnically and linguistically distinct from the peoples of West Pakistan, did secede in 1971. The Basques of northern Spain and the Roman Catholics of Northern Ireland are sufficiently different to constitute political subcultures. The Scots and Welsh of Britain harbor the resentments of the "Celtic fringe" against the dominant English: They vote heavily Labour, whereas the English vote heavily Conservative. They, too, constitute subcultures.

Where subcultures are very distinct, the political system itself may be threatened. The Soviet Union and Yugoslavia ceased to exist because citizens were more loyal to their ethnic groups than to the nation. In India, some Sikhs seek

Case Studies   QUEBEC: "MAÎTRES CHEZ NOUS"

The French arrived in North America about the same time the English did, but France was more interested in the lucrative fur trade than in colonization and sent few French settlers; as a result the population of New France stayed tiny compared to that of the English colonies to the south. The two empires collided in the French and Indian War, which essentially ended when the British conquered Quebec City in 1759. After the historic battle on the Plains of Abraham—which was actually quite small, with only a handful killed, including both commanders—the English let the French Canadians keep their language and Roman Catholic religion. It was a magnanimous gesture, but it meant that more than two centuries later Canada faced an angry and defiant Quebec separatist movement.

Culturally and politically, Quebec province fell asleep for two centuries, an island of tradition in an otherwise dynamic North America. Quebec missed the French Revolution and thus stayed far more conservative than France. Quebec has been called "France without the Revolution." Economic leadership moved into the hands of English-speakers, and Montreal became a mostly English-speaking city. Many **francophones** became **marginalized**, living as poor and isolated farmers with little education. An unstated deal was struck: **Anglophones** would run the economy while francophones, a majority of the population, would obey local politicians and the Catholic Church.

In the 1960s, Quebec woke up with its "Quiet Revolution." Francophone attitudes shifted dramatically, away from traditional politicians and the priests. It was almost as if a new generation of Québécois said, "You have held us down and backward long enough. We want to be modern, rich, and *maîtres chez nous* (masters in our own house)." Out of this shift in attitudes emerged the Parti Québécois (PQ) of René Levesque (pronounced Leveck) with its demand to separate Quebec from Canada. The PQ argues that Quebec really is a different culture and is tired of being under the thumb of English-speaking Canada.

The PQ and related Bloc Québécois became the province's largest parties. A 1980 **referendum** on separation failed 60–40 percent, but the 1995 referendum failed only by a whisker. A third referendum, which is promised, could pass. For some Americans, Quebec served as an example of what goes wrong with bilingualism and multiculturalism: They can lead to national fragmentation.

independence for the Punjab, their home province, and resort to arms. Prime Minister Indira Gandhi's Sikh bodyguards assassinated her in 1985. Recalling a term we used earlier, such countries as Lebanon and India are still undergoing a crisis of identification. Should a nation attempt to integrate its subcultures into the mainstream? Such efforts are bound to be difficult, but if left undone the subculture in later years may decide it really doesn't belong in that country. The Spaniards in Peru who conquered the Incas let them retain their language and culture. But now the Spanish-speaking Peruvians of the cities know little of the Quechua-speaking Peruvians of the mountains. Thirty percent of Peruvians speak no Spanish. Any nonintegrated subculture poses at least a problem and at worst a threat to the national political system.

Starting in the 1870s, France deliberately pursued national integration through its centralized school system. Many regions were backwaters and spoke strange dialects. The French education ministry sent schoolteachers into the villages almost like missionaries. The teachers followed an absolutely standard curriculum—the education ministry could tell what was being taught across France at any given minute—that was heavy on rote learning and on the glory and unity of France. Gradually, in the phrase of Eugen Weber, they turned "peasants into Frenchmen." After some decades, a much more unified and integrated France emerged, an example of *overt political socialization* (see discussion following).

> ## KEY TERMS
>
> **francophone**   A French speaker. (See p. 120.)
> **marginalized**   Pushed to the edge of society and the economy; often said of the poor and subcultures. (See p. 120.)
> **anglophone**   An English speaker. (See p. 120.)
> **referendum**   Mass vote on an issue rather than on candidates. (See p. 120.)

The United States has relied largely on voluntary integration to create a mainstream culture in which most Americans feel at home. Immigrants found they had to learn English to get ahead in the New World. The achievement-oriented consumer society tends to standardized tastes and career patterns. The melting pot worked, but not perfectly. Many Americans retain small subculture distinctions—often in the areas of religion and cuisine—but these may not be politically important. Italian Americans did not rally behind Geraldine Ferraro, the first Italian American to run for national office as the vice-presidential candidate on the Democratic ticket in 1984. Their failure to do so pointed out how well Italian Americans had become integrated into the mainstream: They really didn't care that one of their own was at last on the ballot. Asian Americans integrated rapidly into the U.S. mainstream. Now some 4 percent of the total U.S. population, they hold several of the 535 elected seats on Capitol Hill.

Not all American groups have been so fortunate. Blacks and Hispanics are not yet fully integrated into the American mainstream. Should they be better integrated into American society? This has been one of the great questions of post-World War II U.S. politics. With the 1954 *Brown v. Board of Education of Topeka* decision, the Supreme Court began a major federal government effort to integrate U.S. schools. It encountered massive resistance. In some instances federal judges had to take control of local school systems to enforce integration by busing. The pro-integrationist Kennedy and Johnson administrations argued that America, in its struggle against communism, could not field a good army and offer an example of freedom and justice to the rest of the world if some Americans were oppressed and poor. Integration was portrayed as a matter of national security.

Should integration be forced in the area of language? Should African Americans be forced to abandon their black dialect in favor of standard English, and should Hispanics be forced to learn English? If they don't, they will be severely handicapped their whole lives, especially in employment prospects. But some blacks, Hispanics, and Native Americans cling to their language as a statement of

Integration came hard to Little Rock, Arkansas, in 1957. Black students needed a National Guard escort to get past jeering white students at Central High School. The problem was not confined to the South or to the 1950s, however. (AP/Wide World Photos)

ethnic identity and pride. The U.S. Constitution does not specify any national language, nor does it outlaw languages other than English. In some areas of the United States, signs and official documents are in both English and Spanish. In 1986, California voters approved a measure making English the state's official language by a wide margin. People could, of course, continue to speak what they wished, but official documents and ballots would be in English only. In 1998, California voted to end bilingual education in order to speed the assimilation of subcultures. California is often an indicator of nationwide trends, and other states passed similar laws.

Political Socialization

In the **socializing** process, children acquire manners, rules, and slang that often last lifelong. Although some is formally taught, it is mostly absorbed by imitating others. In the same way, political socialization teaches political values and specific usages. Learning to pledge allegiance to the flag, to stand up to sing the national anthem, and to acknowledge the authority of political figures, from presidents to police officers, are imparted by families, friends, schoolteachers, and television. Children raised in cultural ghettoes, such as minorities in America's inner cities, pick up their subcultures, which are sometimes at odds with mainstream culture. Political socialization is thus crucial to stable government.

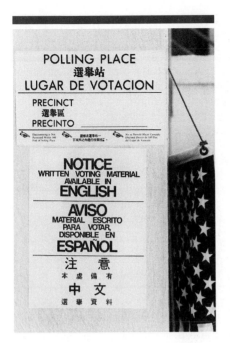

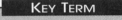

A trilingual sign in California emphasizes the multi-cultural character of the population of that state. In an effort to promote cultural unity, Californians voted in 1986 to make English the state's only official language. (Michael Roskin)

The Agents of Socialization

The Family   Everything the child encounters is a potential agent of political socialization, but what he or she encounters earliest—the family—usually out-weighs all others. Attempts at **overt socialization** by government and schools generally fail if their values are at odds with family orientations. Many Communist countries had this problem: The regime tried to inculcate socialist values in a child, but the family conditioned the child to ignore these messages. Where family and government values are generally congruent, as in the United States, the two modes of socialization reinforce one another.

> **KEY TERM**
>
> **overt socialization**
> Deliberate government policy to teach culture.

Psychologists tell us that long after we've left home, our parents continue to exert a profound influence on us, including our political behavior. Most people vote as their parents did. More basically, the family forms the psychological makeup of the individual, which in turn determines many of his or her political attitudes. It imparts a set of norms and values, including political aspects, and it transmits beliefs and attitudes, such as party loyalty and trust or cynicism about government.

Conditioning and training in the early years have the strongest effect. A study of the shaping of political attitudes found that the most decisive of these attitudes are shaped in the years from ages three to thirteen. Parents are figures of great power and authority in the child's world, and from them the child accepts many norms, values, and attitudes unconsciously and uncritically. The psychological set children acquire as a result of family relationships affects their political behavior

Classic Works | THE AUTHORITARIAN PERSONALITY

One of the boldest attempts to link individual character traits with political attitudes was a 1950 book, *The Authoritarian Personality* by Theodore Adorno and others, mostly refugees from Nazi Germany. Based heavily on the Freudian theory that personality is laid down in early childhood, Adorno and his colleagues devised a twenty-nine-item questionnaire that allegedly showed pre-fascist political views; hence its name, the F-Scale. Persons who scored high on it were conventional in lifestyle to the point of rigidity; were intolerant, prejudiced, and aggressive toward outsiders and minorities; submitted to and liked power; and were superstitious and mystical. The Adorno study attracted great interest but was soon criticized over its methodology and its too-facile connection of personality and politics. Many people have all or some of the F-Scale's characteristics but are good democrats. Although it has faded from view, some still find the study accurate and insightful.

in adult life in many different ways. In general, people give back to the world as adults what they got from it as children. One extensive study found that American college students with authoritarian personalities had almost invariably been treated roughly as children. But parental overprotection may be just as harmful, causing children to fear leaving the shelter of the family. This fear may later be expressed politically as distrust and dislike of public figures. Almond and Verba found that those who remembered having had a voice in family decisions when they were children had a greater adult sense of "political efficacy." Those who took part in family decisions were, on the average, more inclined to feel that expression of their political beliefs could influence the government.

Most of the political socialization that takes place in the family is informal, as when the father "lays down the law" and refuses to hear any argument, or when the mother thinks aloud that there's no use complaining about the unfair amount of housework she has to do without any help from her husband. And parental attitudes and actions about political matters—for instance, their level of interest in election campaigns or their readiness to seek special favors (getting a traffic ticket "fixed")—probably are more important in shaping the child's future political behavior than any of the specific ideas about government and politics that the parents consciously try to impart.

The School A more deliberate type of socialization occurs in school. Most governments use schools to teach its citizens that they are a national community. Many African nations try to unify their tribes, usually with different languages and histories, by teaching in French or English about a mythical past when they were a great and united nation. It often does not work, as seen recently in the Congo (formerly Zaire). The Communist nations also relied heavily on the schools for systematic inculcation of new political loyalties and concepts. As we saw in 1989, though, this effort was unsuccessful; family and church overrode the attempts of schools to make East Europeans into believing Communists. U.S. schools did a brilliant job of turning immigrants from many lands into one nation, something critics of bilingual education say must be restored.

The amount of schooling a person receives also affects political attitudes. Uniformly, people with many years of education show a stronger sense of responsibility to their community and feel more able to influence public policy than do less-educated citizens. As Table 7.1 shows, even though there may be differences among the political cultures of separate nations, there is a striking correlation between a person's formal education and his or her attitudes toward politics and society. Persons with more schooling are more participatory. College graduates are more tolerant and open-minded, especially on questions of race, than high-school dropouts, who are often parochial in outlook. This is both because education imparts more open-minded attitudes and because educated people generally enjoy higher incomes and status, which by themselves encourage interest and participation.

Peer Groups   School is a powerful socializing force but may not have lasting effects unless other influences push the individual in the same direction. For example, working-class children in Jamaica who went to school with children of higher social classes tended to take on the political attitudes of those classes, but when they attended school with only working-class peers, their attitudes did not change. The relative strength of peer-group influence appears to be growing. With both parents working, children may be getting less socialization from families and more from their peers. Upholders of "family values" see this as the underlying cause of youthful drug-taking and violence.

The Mass Media   The mass media, especially television, are a fourth important socializing force, possibly gaining in influence. Many fear the influence is negative. Harvard political scientist Robert Putnam argues that heavy TV watching makes people passive and uninterested in community or group activities. As American children watch thousands of hours of television a year—the "plug-in babysitter"—they witness myriad crimes and murders. Some critics charge this tends to make them heartless and violent. TV reaches kids early; even three-year-olds can recognize the president on television and understand that he is a sort of

Table 7.1   Percentage Who Say People Should Be Active in Their Local Community, by Nation and Education

Nation	Overall	Primary Schooling	Some Secondary	Some University
United States	51	35	56	66
United Kingdom	3	37	42	42
West Germany	22	21	32	38
Italy	10	7	17	22
Mexico	26	24	37	38

Source: Gabriel A. Almond and Sidney Verba, *The Civic Culture* (Princeton, NJ: Princeton University Press, 1963), p. 176. Reprinted by permission of Princeton University Press.

"boss" of the nation. Senators and members of Congress, who receive much less coverage, are treated with relative indifference, a view the children may hold the rest of their lives.

As with schools, the mass media may be unsuccessful if the messages they beam are at odds with what family and religion teach. Even Soviet researchers found that families were much bigger influences on individuals' political views than the all-pervasive Soviet mass media. Iran's mass media, all firmly controlled by the shah, tried to inculcate loyalty to him, but believing Muslims took the word of their local *mullahs* in the mosques and hated the shah. Mass media can't do everything.

The Government   Government itself is an agent of socialization. Virtually everything it does takes into account its citizens' reactions, and many government activities are intended explicitly to explain or display the government to the public, always designed to build public support and loyalty. Great spectacles of state, such as the crowning of a British king or queen, have a strengthening effect, as do parades with flags flying, impressive displays of military power, and proclamations of kings, presidents, prime ministers, and other dignitaries. The power of government to control political attitudes is limited, however, because messages and experiences reach individuals through conversations with primary groups of kin or peers, who put their own spin on messages. Alienated groups may socialize their children to dislike the government, in spite of the government's efforts to the contrary.

Key Terms

anglophone (p. 121)	political competence (p. 116)
cynical (p. 113)	political culture (p. 111)
francophone (p. 121)	political efficacy (p. 116)
integration (p. 119)	referendum (p. 121)
mainstream (p. 119)	rule of anticipated reactions (p. 113)
marginalized (p. 121)	socialization (p. 122)
overt socialization (p. 123)	subculture (p. 119)
parochial (p. 116)	subject (p. 116)
participatory (p. 116)	turnout (p. 113)

Key Websites

The Pew Research Center is an independent opinion research group that studies attitudes toward the press, politics, and public policy issues. They are best known for regular national surveys that measure public attentiveness to major news stories, and for polling that charts trends in values and fundamental political and social attitudes.
http://www.people-press.org/

This site examines the nature of civil society and culture. It addresses the contemporary crisis of liberal democratic culture in the postmodern period.
http://www.civsoc.com/index.htm

The National Civic League (NCL) hopes to transform democratic institutions by citizen democracy. It attempts to accomplish its mission through technical assistance, publishing, research, and an awards program. This website hosts information about NCL's current programs, publications, and membership.
http://www.ncl.org/

The Center for Voting Democracy advocates proportional voting as a fairer way to conduct U.S. elections.
http://www.wideopen.igc.org/cvd/

The WebActive site is a guide to almost every known activist group with a presence on the WWW, regardless of their philosophy or agenda.
http://www.webactive.com/

Further Reference

Almond, Gabriel A., and Sidney Verba. *The Civic Culture: Political Attitudes and Democracy in Five Nations*. Boston, MA: Little, Brown, 1965.

Carter, Stephen L. *Civility: Manners, Morals, and the Etiquette of Democracy*. New York: Basic Books, 1998.

Codevilla, Angelo M. *The Character of Nations: How Politics Makes and Breaks Prosperity, Family, and Civility*. New York: Basic Books, 1997.

Diamond, Larry, ed. *Political Culture and Democracy in Developing Countries*. Boulder, CO: Lynne Rienner, 1994.

Fukuyama, Francis. *Trust: The Social Virtues and the Creation of Prosperity*. New York: Free Press, 1995.

Inglehart, Ronald. *Modernization and Postmodernization: Cultural, Economic, and Political Change in 43 Societies*. Princeton, NJ: Princeton University Press, 1997.

Langton, Kenneth E. *Political Socialization*. New York: Oxford University Press, 1969.

Lipset, Seymour Martin. *American Exceptionalism: A Double-Edged Sword*. New York: Norton, 1996.

Nye, Joseph S., Philip D. Zelikow, and David C. King, eds. *Why People Don't Trust Government*. Cambridge, MA: Harvard University Press, 1997.

Putnam, Robert D. *Making Democracy Work: Civic Traditions in Modern Italy*. Princeton, NJ: Princeton University Press, 1993.

Tocqueville, Alexis de. *Democracy in America*. New York: Washington Square Press, 1964.

Verba, Sidney, Kay Lehman Schlozman, and Henry E. Brady. *Voice and Equality: Civic Voluntarism in American Politics*. Cambridge, MA: Harvard University Press, 1995.

CHAPTER 8

Public Opinion

Widely reported, eagerly watched by the politically attuned, and a multibillion dollar industry, **public opinion** clearly plays a major role in modern democracy. But can or should it play a leading role? Few political scientists would wish it to, and for good reasons.

Public opinion does play an important role. In a democracy, elections provide a formal means of popular control of government but only a very crude expression of the public's will. An election can register only the verdict of the voters on an official's overall performance; rarely is one issue so important that it determines an election. Public-opinion surveys fill in the details so elected officials know that people worry about specific problems, such as Social Security or violence in schools. Public opinion can thus be seen as a backup and detail device for inputting the mass will into politics.

In many cases, public opinion is created, not followed, by the executive. Why else

QUESTIONS TO CONSIDER

1. Does government follow or create public opinion?
2. Which is more important in forming U.S. opinion now, social class or religion?
3. What is the theory of political generations?
4. Explain the three classic opinion curves.
5. Why did the *Literary Digest* miscall the 1936 election?
6. Why did the polls miscall the 1948 election?
7. What is a random sample?
8. What does presidential "popularity" really measure?
9. What are intensity and volatility?

would some of our government leaders spend as much time as they do addressing the nation in front of TV cameras? When Richard Nixon announced in late 1971 that he would be the first American president to visit the People's Republic of China, he revolutionized public opinion about China (it quickly grew more favorable). Spanish Prime Minister Felipe González, head of a party that opposed Spain joining NATO, changed his mind and supported Spain's affiliation, although public-opinion polls showed that most Spaniards didn't want Spain in NATO. González urged support for NATO in a 1986 referendum, and Spaniards swung around to support him. U.S. opinion split evenly on the eve of the 1991 Persian Gulf war, but once the war started, Americans massively supported President Bush's policies. Governments can create public opinion.

KEY TERM

public opinion Citizens' reactions to current, specific issues and events.

Key Concepts   WHAT PUBLIC OPINION IS AND ISN'T

Political culture and public opinion are closely linked but are not the same thing. Political culture focuses on longstanding values, attitudes, and ideas that people learn deeply. Most Americans firmly believe that government power is dangerous and must be controlled and that democracy is the only just form of government. Public opinion concerns people's reactions to specific policies and problems rather than long-term values, such as sending troops overseas, voting intentions, or crime and drugs.

Public opinion is also not the same as individual opinion. A woman's opinion of her neighbor's religion would not be part of public opinion, but her feeling that adolescents should pray in public schools would. Public opinion refers to political and social issues, not private matters of taste.

Public opinion also does not necessarily imply strong, clear, united convictions of most citizens, which is rare. So-called public opinion often involves several small, conflicting groups, plus many who are undecided, plus an even larger number with no interest or opinion on the matter. On most subjects, public opinion is an array of diverse attitudes that can change quickly.

Public opinion may not demonstrate awareness or knowledge. Many respondents are ignorant of basic facts. A 1996 poll found that many Americans believed unemployment was more than 20 percent—a fantastically high figure, something from the Depression—when it was actually a very low 5 percent. Some respondents manufacture answers in order to sound well-informed. In 1948 a poll asked respondents what they thought of the "Metallic Metals Act." Fifty-nine percent supported the act, provided that discretion be left to individual states. Sixteen percent thought the act should not be imposed on the American people, and only 30 percent admitted they had no opinion on the matter. It was a fake question; people answered because they did not wish to appear ignorant.

With these considerations in mind, do numbers make right? Most Americans are opposed to raising taxes on gasoline. Does that mean that government should never do it? Should elected leaders always bow to public opinion? President Truman often shrugged off public opinion and was vilified for it. Decades later, many celebrated him as a leader who did the right thing without fear of public disapproval. Some say current politicians pay too much attention to public opinion. If you are always following, how can you lead?

Public opinion is often led or manipulated by interest groups. Bringing grievances to public attention, especially when the media watches, can generate widespread sympathy. The televised brutality of sheriffs' deputies in Selma, Alabama, toward blacks demanding the right to vote turned public opinion in favor the Voting Rights Act of 1965.

Any government is vulnerable to public opinion. Mahatma Gandhi, by a simple drama of nonviolent protest, used public opinion to win independence for India. A gaunt, bespectacled old man in a loincloth, he led protests, wove his own cloth, and threatened to starve himself to death if the British did not pull out of

The role of public opinion: This sign (reading "We won't give up Havel!") and a petition drive at Prague's Wenceslaus Square aimed to keep Czech President Vaclav Havel in power in 1992. He resigned later that year rather than preside over the dissolution of his country, but returned to office after the split. (Michael Roskin)

India. So powerful was the support he generated that the British realized they could no longer effectively govern India.

Government by sheer violence and coercion cannot last for any length of time. Even Nazi Germany, with all its brutal apparatus for suppressing dissent, depended on the dream of Germany's world supremacy—not night raids by the Gestapo—to rouse patriotic fervor. The Hitler regime kept careful tabs on how the German public felt about its policies and their morale, but the officials in charge were afraid to send in negative reports, so the regime received rose-colored accounts.

The Shape of Public Opinion

Within broad limits, social scientists have been able to discover roughly who thinks what about politics. It is important to bear in mind, however, that no social category is ever 100 percent for or against something. Indeed, 60 or 70 percent is often considered quite high. What we look for are *differences* among social categories, the significance of which can be tested by the rules of statistics. We look for different shades of gray, not for black and white. Once we have found significant differences, we may be able to say something about **salience**, the degree to which categories and issues affect the public opinion of a country. In Scandinavia, for example, social class is salient in structuring party preferences: The working class tends to vote Social Democratic, and the middle class votes for the more conservative parties. In Latin Europe, social class is weakly salient, with the working class scattering its vote among parties of the left, right, and center. In Latin Europe, religion and region are typically most salient.

Social Class

Karl Marx saw **social class** as massively salient. Workers, once they were aware of their situation, would become socialists. More recently, and with qualifications, social scientists have found that social class still matters, even in the relatively classless United States. Over the decades, the American manual worker has tended to vote Democratic; the better-

KEY TERM
social class   A broad division of society, usually based on income and often labeled lower, middle, and upper.

off or professional person has tended to vote Republican. But these are only tendencies, and they are often muddied by other factors. Poor people are often very conservative on religious and social issues, and affluent people can be liberal or even radical. During hard times, when bread-and-butter issues, such as jobs, become salient, the American working class tends to rediscover the Democratic party, as it did in 1992. When these issues lose their salience, however, the working class often finds that noneconomic issues gain in importance. Then questions of morality (abortion, prayer in schools) and foreign policy (relations with China, defense spending) may siphon off part of the working class to the Republicans.

Social class can be hard to measure. There are two general ways, the objective and subjective. An objective determination of social class involves asking a person his or her approximate annual income or judging the quality of the neighborhood. The subjective determination of class involves simply asking the respondent what his or her social class is. Often this diverges from objective social class. A majority of Americans are used to thinking of themselves as middle class even if they aren't. Sometimes even wealthy people, thinking of their modest origins, call themselves middle class. The way a person earns a living may matter more than the amount he or she makes. Typically, American farmers are conservative about politics, and miners and steelworkers are not. Different political attitudes grow up around different jobs.

Sometimes social class works in precisely the opposite way envisioned by Marx. The liberalism of some affluent U.S. suburbs stands Marx on his head. Spanish researchers found an *inverse* relationship between social class and preferring the left; that is, better-off persons were more leftist than poorer Spaniards. In the Spanish study, it was education that was most salient: A university education tended to radicalize Spaniards.

Class matters, especially in combination with other factors, such as region or religion. In Britain, class plus region structures much of the vote; in France, it is class plus region plus religiosity (practicing Catholic vs. nonpracticing); in Germany, it is class plus region plus denomination (Catholic or Protestant). As Yale's Joseph LaPalombara put it, the question is "Class plus what?"

Education

Educational level is related to social class; that is, children of better-off families usually get more education, and education in turn leads to better-paying jobs. Unlike the Spanish case, where university study tended to radicalize, education in the United States seems to have a split impact: It makes people more liberal on **noneconomic issues** but often more conservative on **economic issues**. Abundant survey data show that college-educated people are more tolerant, more supportive of civil rights, and more likely to understand different viewpoints. But when it comes to economic issues, many of these same people are skeptical of efforts to redistribute income in the form of higher taxes on the upper brackets—which happen to be them—and welfare measures for the nonworking. There are, to be sure, some educated people who are consistently liberal on both economic and noneconomic questions, but in the United States the categories sometimes diverge. The same is often true of the American working class: Its members want a bigger share of the national income but are intolerant in the areas of race, lifestyle, and patriotism. When college youths, mostly from middle-class families, protested the Vietnam war, they sometimes ran into the snarls and fists of unionized construction workers, a graphic illustration of the split between economic and noneconomic liberalism.

Region

Every country has a south, goes an old saw, and this is certainly true in politics. What is uncertain, however, is whether a country's south is more conservative or more leftist than its north. France south of the Loire River and Spain south of the Tagus have for generations gone left. The south of Italy, though, is a bastion of conservatism, as is Bavaria in Germany's south. In Great Britain, England is heavily conservative, whereas Scotland and Wales go for Labour. And of course the U.S. South was famous for decades as the "solid South," which went automatically for the Democrats—no longer the case.

A country's outlying **regions** usually harbor resentment against the capital, creating what are called **center-periphery tensions**. Often an outlying region was conquered or forcibly assimilated into the nation and has never been completely happy about it. Regional memories can last for centuries. This is true of the south of France; the U.S. South; the south of Italy, Quebec, and Scotland. Often the region feels economically disadvantaged by the central area. The region may have a different ethnic makeup, as in Catalonia and the Basque country in Spain, Wallonia in Belgium, Quebec in Canada, Slovenia in Yugoslavia, and several parts of India.

Once a region gets set in its politics, it stays that way for a long time. Region plays a big role in the politics of Britain, France, Germany, and the United States. The "sunbelt" of southern and western states is generally conservative on both economic and noneconomic issues and jealous of states' rights. The "frostbelt" of northern and eastern states, where industry has declined, tends to be more liberal, especially on questions of government spending programs. In the early 1980s, when President Reagan cut both taxes and welfare expenditures, conservative, southern Democrats, dubbed "boll weevils," supported him, and some liberal, northern Republicans, nicknamed "gypsy moths," opposed him, providing a vivid illustration of the effects of region on U.S. politics.

Religion

Religion is often the most explosive issue in politics and contributes a great deal to the structuring of opinion. Religion can mean either denomination or religiosity. In Germany, Catholics tend to go to the Christian Democratic Union, whereas Protestants tend to go to the Social Democrats or Free Democrats, although the question of social class is also bound up with this choice. In Germany, it's a question of denomination. In France, where most citizens are at least nominal Catholics, it's a question of religiosity, as many French are indifferent to religion. The more often a French person goes to Mass, the more likely he or she is to vote for a conservative party. Few Communist voters are practicing Catholics. In Poland, the Roman Catholic church encouraged Poles to oust the Communist regime and support pro-Church parties. One of the biggest divisions in Catholic countries is between clericalists and anticlericalists; the former are for a church role in politics, the latter against. France, Italy, and Spain have long been split over this issue, with the conservative parties more favorable to the Catholic church and the parties of the left hostile to church influence.

Religion plays a considerable role in the United States, too, although here it overlaps with ethnicity. Catholics, especially Polish Catholics, have been among the most loyal Democrats of all. In the great immigrations of previous decades, big-city Democratic machines stood ready to welcome and help immigrants from Catholic countries, and in turn these people and their descendants stayed heavily Democratic. For a long time it was believed that no Catholic could be elected president of the United States; John F. Kennedy in 1960 put that view to rest, and now being Catholic probably does no harm to a candidate. Many Catholics and fundamentalist Protestants now have a common cause in fighting abortion.

Of major importance to U.S. politics was the rise of the "religious right" during the 1980s. A 1996 survey estimated that 14 percent of Americans were in the religious right. Many mainstream denominations became more conservative, and rapidly growing fundamentalist groups became highly political. Ministers such as Jerry Falwell mobilized their television flocks against pornography, abortion, and gay rights and for the Republican party. The powerful Christian Coalition is considered the single most conservative force inside the Republican party.

American candidates, especially for the presidency, like to be known as churchgoers, but since the rise of fundamentalism, many also wish to be known as "born-again" Christians. In 1980, both Ronald Reagan and Jimmy Carter claimed to have been born again in Christ. Former Senator Eugene McCarthy, who tried for the Democratic nomination in 1968, reflected that he was the last presidential contender who had been born only once. Bill and Hillary Clinton attended church most Sundays with the President clutching a family bible. Americans like their leaders to at least appear religious.

Age

There are two ways of measuring age in terms of political opinions: strictly chronologically and generationally. Conventional wisdom sees young people as radical, ready to change the system, with older people more moderate or even conservative. With few responsibilities in youth, young people can be idealistic and rebellious, but with the burdens of home, job, and children of their own, people become more conservative.

This "life cycle" theory doesn't always work because sometimes whole generations are marked for life by the great events of their young adulthood. Survivors of wars and depressions carry nervous remembrances of these upheavals for decades, coloring their views on war, economics, and politics. Sociologist Karl Mannheim called this phenomenon **political generations**. Many who lived through the Vietnam war still worry about the use of U.S. troops overseas. Likewise, older people who had personally experienced the Depression of the 1930s were more supportive of federal welfare measures than younger people who had been raised in postwar prosperity. In one 1992 survey, younger Americans voiced more conservative and pro-Republican views than did older Americans.

KEY TERMS
political generations Theory that great events of young adulthood permanently color a generation's political views.
gender gap Tendency of American women to vote more Democratic than do men.

Gender

Even before the women's movement, gender made a difference in politics. Traditionally, and especially in Catholic areas, women were more conservative, more concerned with home, family, and morality. This still applies in Catholic Spain and Portugal. But as a society modernizes, men's and women's views change. Women leave home to work, become more aware of social and economic problems, and do not necessarily adopt their husbands' political views. In the United States, an interesting **gender gap** appeared in the 1980s as women became several percentage points more liberal and Democratic than men. And this was precisely because women had found the federal government necessary to support home and family. Further, many women disliked the Republican administrations' emphasis on war preparation. In 1996, women were 11 percentage points more likely to vote for Clinton than were men. It may be that in the modern political world, women will be the natural liberals.

Ethnic Group

Ethnicity is related to region and religion but sometimes plays a distinct role of its own, especially in the multiethnic United States, where some ethnic groups form political subcultures (see Chapter 7). America was long touted as a "melting pot" of immigrant groups, but research has revealed the staying power and lively consciousness of ethnic groups for many generations. American politics is often described in ethnic terms, with WASPs (white Anglo-Saxon Protestants) and other northern Europeans generally conservative and Republican, and people of southern and Eastern European origin, blacks, Hispanics, and Asian Americans generally more liberal and Democratic. This simplification does not take into account the complexity of individuals and of politics, but some working politicians still find it a valuable guide.

Ethnic politics changes over the decades. After the Civil War, most African Americans were Republican, the party of Lincoln. Then, with Franklin D. Roosevelt and the New Deal, most African Americans became Democrats and stayed that way. In the nineteenth century, American Jews were mostly Republican, for the Republicans sharply criticized the anti-Semitic repression of tsarist Russia. But the Jewish immigrants of the turn of the century, introduced to U.S. politics by Democratic machines such as New York's Tammany Hall, went Democratic. More recently, many Jews, influenced by neoconservatism (see Chapter 6), swung back to the Republicans. Ethnic politics is not set in stone.

Public-Opinion Patterns

What do the people as a whole think about a particular issue? In general, they can be for, against, or undecided. But the factors of uncertainty and changeability are so prominent in many areas that we can't always be confident that the "patterns" tell us a dependable story.

A wishing wall was put up in Washington for President Clinton's inauguration. Citizens pinned up notes urging legislation on everything from hunger and child abuse to global warming and nuclear weapons. (Michael Roskin)

Key Concepts   CLASSIC OPINION CURVES

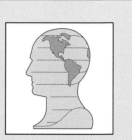

The way people feel about an issue is often summarized statistically in a curve that shows the distribution of different opinions sampled along a range from one extreme position to the opposite extreme. A noncontroversial issue—a matter on which there are only a few doubters and dissenters—will show opinions **skewed** to one side, a much smaller number with qualified opinions in the middle, and few or none at the opposite extreme. For example, if a cross-section of America is asked whether measures should be developed to prevent environmental pollution, the answers could be mapped out along a very stable, one-sided curve, sometimes called a "J-curve" for its lopsidedness.

Stable Curve

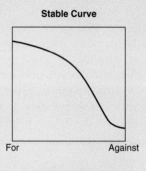

For   Against

"Should we develop more
effective defenses against
environmental pollution?"

On many issues, however, there is less consensus and little certainty. Here, public opinion may take the form of a bell-shaped curve, or **unimodal** distribution, which shows relatively few people totally committed to a position at one extreme or the other, with the majority in the moderate area in between. Asked whether the size of the armed forces is too small, too large, or about right, it is unlikely that the majority will answer with either of the extremes. Conflicting factors, such as the wish to keep taxes low, fear of a chaotic world, and personal attitudes toward military service in general, will cause the "too smalls" to be about equal to the "too larges"; most people will reply with "about right."

Bell-Shaped Curve

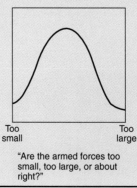

Too   Too
small   large

"Are the armed forces too
small, too large, or about
right?"

CLASSIC OPINION CURVES (CONTINUED)

A third characteristic pattern views can take is that of extreme division, or **bimodal** distribution, sometimes called a "U-curve." If issues are profound, this kind of opinion distribution can lead to extremist takeovers, as it did in Germany and Spain in the 1930s. Protestant and Catholic opinion in Northern Ireland generally forms a U-curve, leading to violent civil conflict that was terribly difficult to end.

Extreme Division

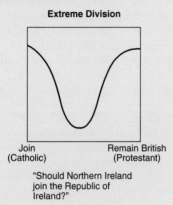

Join   Remain British
(Catholic)   (Protestant)

"Should Northern Ireland
join the Republic of
Ireland?"

Some thinkers argue that bell-shaped opinion curves are a basic ingredient of democracy. If many citizens take extreme positions, the center disappears, and major conflict looms. In the 1930s, German and Spanish political views turned bimodal, and democracy collapsed in both lands. Most democratic countries have unimodal distributions of opinion on basic issues; that is, people cluster in the center. Democracy is a centrist thing.

Often opinion distribution does not fall into well-defined patterns, mainly because most people, most of the time, pay little attention to political and government issues. They have little sustained interest in issues that do not directly touch their lives, and therefore they acquire little information about these issues. Most public surveys, for example, will find that nearly half of those questioned don't know who their representative in Congress is.

Thus, in the case of most issues, only a small portion of the total public is attentive enough to news reports and editorials to form a decisive opinion. And in many situations, a general public opinion curve will be a rather dim reflection of the opinion pattern within this "attentive public." With all of the uncertainties, personality quirks, and just plain ignorance involved in public opinion, how are surveys able to reflect an accurate picture of what the people are thinking?

KEY TERMS

skewed A distribution with its peak well to one side.

unimodal A single, center-peaked distribution; a bell-shaped curve.

bimodal A distribution with two large clusters at the extremes and a small center.

Key Concepts   A SHORT HISTORY OF POLLING

In 1824, the *Harrisburg Pennsylvanian* asked passersby whether they would vote for John Quincy Adams or Andrew Jackson. The tally was printed on the theory that these "straws in the wind" foresaw the election results. Many other newspapers, using a variety of both careful and haphazard methods, conducted "straw polls" in various elections thereafter. But the popular magazine *Literary Digest* was the first to develop a survey of great prestige that accurately predicted the 1916, 1920, 1924, 1928, and 1932 presidential elections. The *Literary Digest* used a huge sample on the theory that the more people questioned the more dependable the result. It conducted its survey by mail, drawing close to 10 million addresses from lists of subscribers, car owners, and phone books. All went well until 1936, when 2.4 million people replied that they wanted Franklin D. Roosevelt out of office. The *Literary Digest* predicted the Republican candidate, Alfred M. Landon, as victor with 59.1 percent of the vote. Roosevelt's landslide victory—with over 60 percent of the vote—signaled the demise of both the straw-poll method of sampling and of *Literary Digest* itself.

As it happened, 1936 was also the first year that practitioners of the newly developed techniques of "scientific polling" were on the political scene, branching out from the field of market research. George H. Gallup's **survey** results, syndicated in several newspapers, forecast Roosevelt's victory. Gallup publicly predicted that the *Digest* poll was riding for a fall and identified the reason: Its sample was drawn heavily from higher-income people, many of whom were angered by Roosevelt's social and economic policies. The new technique used by Gallup was to select a **sample** as *representative*, rather than as large, as possible.

This scientific sampling method has dominated the field since then, with a very successful record. But even it failed in the 1948 election, when almost every poll predicted that Thomas E. Dewey would defeat Harry S Truman by a landslide. (It looked so certain to one leading pollster that he stopped taking samples in mid-September.) Truman won with 49 percent in a four-way contest. The Social Science Research Council found the error in assuming that respondents who said they were undecided would wind up voting in the same ratio as those who had made up their minds. In fact, these voters decided much more heavily in favor of Truman—close to 75 percent. The major polls have further refined their methods since that time and today make special efforts to detect late swings to one candidate or the other. It should be noted, however, that they do not even claim to be able to predict divisions within closer than two to three percentage points. The margin of victory in several presidential elections has been less than 1 percent, so it is clear that even the most accurate polls cannot confidently predict the winner in close elections. Such elections are called "too close to call."

Public-Opinion Polls

Any effort to gauge the attitude of the public by means of a representative sample is called a survey or poll. Published polls, particularly in election years, are carefully watched. Almost daily we see statistics and percentages on what

America thinks of crime, of unemployment, of abortion, and of one candidate as opposed to another. This is useful stuff for policymakers and candidates. But debate has developed over some of their political side effects. For example, do the polls give undue attention and influence to uncertain opinions? Do journalists create self-fulfilling prophecies by treating the polls as authoritative verdicts, which people read about, then follow? And should public-opinion surveys be treated, as some propose, as a truly democratic method of deciding public policies? Are polls reliable enough to determine policy? Who uses polls, what purpose do they serve, and can we trust them?

KEY TERMS
survey   A public-opinion poll.
sample   Those persons to be interviewed in a survey, usually a small fraction of a population.
quota   Drawing a sample to match categories of the population.
randomization   Drawing a sample at random, with everyone having an equal chance of being included.

Polling Techniques

How can a sample of as few as 1,000 people be used to predict the actions of a hundred million? The answer is complex, but it revolves around a technique that can be summarized as follows.

Selecting the Sample   In deciding whom to sample, the pollster must choose between two major approaches. One, the stratified-**quota** sampling, tries to include a proportionally representative cross-section of the society. This is very difficult to carry out because interviewers must question precisely x number of blue-collar workers, y number of older women, and z number of Republicans. If they query too many or too few of various groups, they lose proportionality.

The second major approach is to do a truly random sample with no picking and choosing among dozens of categories. In a random sample, the number of blue-collar workers (or any other category) contacted will be very close to their percentage of the population. **Randomization**, aided by the advent of the computer, produces more dependable results than the quota system.

The method most often used, "area sampling," has one hundred to two hundred regular interviewers in different areas around the country each interview fifteen to twenty persons in a designated locality. The sample, which is both random and highly representative, involves an initial decision of which geographic districts should be sample areas, the classification of these districts into groups according to population characteristics, and random selection of which categories to use and which people to question from each category. The resulting sample is quite close to that which a completely random selection would obtain and is considerably less expensive.

Reaching the Sample   Polling costs can be high, and most pollsters want to hold them down. Unfortunately, the least expensive methods tend to be the least accurate. The cheapest method is to mail out ballots to a sample and tally the replies, but people who are involved enough to make the effort to reply will not be representative, the *Literary Digest* error. Telephone polling can avoid this problem, but it rarely establishes sufficient rapport to obtain really candid replies. For telephone surveys, a computer actually dials the numbers nationwide at random, even unlisted ones. One problem with this method: Not everyone is reachable by phone. The most dependable method is still the costly face-to-face interview, which requires interviewers to be carefully selected and trained. Because face-to-face is costly, political questions are often appended to commercial or product questions—"Do you eat Krunchy Flakes?"—for that is what pays the bill.

Asking the Questions   The unbiased wording of questions to avoid slanting responses is also important. In 1974, for example, Gallup found that more Americans thought President Nixon should be brought "to trial before the Senate" than be "impeached" for alleged Watergate wrongdoings. The two expressions mean exactly the same, but "impeached" in the public mind connotes convicted and ousted from office. In 1992, answers to a badly worded question (it had a double negative) suggested that one in five Americans doubted the Nazi Holocaust had really happened. When the question was worded clearly in 1994, only 2 percent denied the Holocaust had happened. The pollster must also avoid tones of voice or sympathetic looks that might encourage one response over another and skew the results.

How Reliable Are the Polls?

Public-opinion surveys have achieved great reliability. Overall, the opinion-research business takes in over $1 billion a year in the United States alone, and the number of private polls commissioned by candidates in primary and general elections each year is now in the thousands.

A major limitation of polls, however, especially for election forecasting, is the unpredictability of voter turnout. Many respondents who say they intend to vote actually don't. These voters and the undecideds are likely not to divide the same way as those who do vote and have already decided. This underlay the mistaken predictions of Truman's defeat in 1948. Election results may be different if there is a heavy turnout. Pollsters must adjust raw findings for this factor, but there is no way to be certain how big the turnout will be and what, if any, will be the effect of last-minute events such as rain storms and foreign-policy announcements.

Public opinion is **volatile**, able to change quickly under the impact of events. In 1965, as Lyndon Johnson escalated the war in Vietnam, an aide told him that "we have overwhelming public opinion on our side." Johnson, a crafty political pro who had long read the polls, replied, "Yes, but for a very underwhelming period of time." He was right; majority support for the war in 1965 turned into majority opposition in 1968. Nothing is permanent in public opinion; volatility must be taken into account.

Finally, a survey that is accurate in its overall results can-

---

KEY TERM

volatility Tendency of public opinion to change quickly.

not assure reliability when broken down into finer categories. A sample adequate for a national finding will probably not involve a big enough sample from any one category, such as region, income, or religion, to provide the same degree of reliability. Nationwide polls may include only ten Japanese Americans, not enough for a good sample of their views. For that, pollsters need special surveys concentrating on areas where many Japanese Americans live.

American Opinion

Presidential Popularity

One of the oldest and most important items in U.S. public opinion polls asks how the president is handling his job, not how much the respondent likes the president. In practice, however, the respondent who likes the president will approve of the president's job performance, so the term *popularity* is generally used for this poll.

Typically, presidents start with high popularity and then decline. During their first year they enjoy a **honeymoon** with the press and the public. The high point of their popularity often comes early in their term of office. After some years, however, problems accumulate: The economy turns sour or foreign policies don't work. This brings a popularity low point. Presidents seldom leave office as popular as they were during their first year.

> ### KEY TERMS
>
> **honeymoon**   High popularity of presidents early in their terms.
>
> **rally event**   Occurrence that temporarily boosts a president's popularity.

When a president comes under intense pressure or takes a major action, his popularity enjoys a temporary upturn. Americans rally to a president who faces a difficult decision, and they like decisive responses. Political scientist John Mueller called these **rally events**. Subsequent research found that these events on average occur every fourteen months and boost a president's popularity 8 percentage points for ten weeks. President Carter initially gained 19 percentage points over the seizure of American hostages in Iran, and the sympathy lasted thirty weeks. Unfortunately for Carter, by the time he was up for reelection the next year, the rally in opinion had turned negative, because he was unable to resolve the crisis. Similarly, President Bush enjoyed a 14-point boost when Iraq invaded Kuwait and another 18-point gain when he began the Persian Gulf war. But by 1992, Bush's approval rating was below 50 percent, owing to a lingering recession.

Some suspect that presidents, especially later in their terms of office, may deliberately try to appear decisive in a dramatic way to boost their sagging popularity. Foreign policy provides the natural arena for such dramatic moves and (as we will consider in the next chapter) the best television coverage. A meeting with foreign leaders, a bold strike against terrorists, or the rescue of American hostages provides a welcome lift in popularity for a president. Notice in Table 8.1

how the highest popularity ratings of Presidents Truman, Kennedy, Nixon, Carter, Reagan, and Bush came with a dramatic foreign-policy event. Even a failure, the 1961 attempted Bay of Pigs invasion to overthrow Castro, caused Americans to rally around President Kennedy. When a humiliating situation lasts a long time, however, presidential popularity sinks, as Carter and Reagan both found in dealing with Iran. Similarly, a war that drags on a long time destroys popularity; Truman experienced this in Korea and Johnson in Vietnam. Economic recession is also bad for popularity; four Republican presidents (Eisenhower, Ford, Reagan, and Bush) were rated low during economic downturns. A good economy is great for presidents; Clinton's approval stayed high during the prosperous late 1990s even though many suspected him of immoral or unethical behavior.

Presidential popularity based on one situation tends to spill over into other areas of presidential activity. As might be expected, President Reagan's popularity jumped several points in the wake of the successful U.S. takeover of Communist Grenada and the rescue of American students there in the fall of 1983. At that same time, approval of Reagan's economic policies also climbed, although little in the economy had actually changed.

Table 8.1 Highs and Lows of Presidential Popularity

	High	Low	After 5 Years
Truman	87%	23%	37%
event	end of World War II	Korean War	
Eisenhower	79%	49%	60%
event	reelection	recession	
Kennedy	83%	56%	—
event	Bay of Pigs invasion	—	
Johnson	80%	35%	43%
event	election	Vietnam War	
Nixon	68%	24%	27%
event	Vietnam peace	Watergate scandal	
Ford	71%	37%	—
event	takes oath	recession	
Carter	64%	26%	—
event	human rights	Iranian hostage crises	
Reagan	68%	35%	65%
event	Geneva summit	recession	
Bush	86%	33%	—
event	Gulf War	recession	
Clinton	73%	37%	59%
event	prosperity	gays in military	

Source: *New York Times*, February 2, 1986; March 5, 1991; November 20, 1992; February 3, 1998. Copyright by The New York Times Company. Reprinted by permission. And Pew Research Center, news release of February 6, 1998.

Liberals and Conservatives

The long stretch of Republican presidents did not necessarily reorient Americans to a conservative ideology. Americans, politically, continued to distribute themselves as the familiar bell-shaped curve, with most people at the center (Table 8.2). Such a distribution, social scientists find, is virtually the norm for all industrialized democracies, a fact that probably makes democracy possible. During the Reagan years, the percentage of Americans identifying themselves as conservatives did not increase, and more Americans expressed support for environmental and welfare legislation, typically liberal causes. The percentage who thought the poverty programs of the 1960s—one of Reagan's favorite targets—generally made things better actually increased during the Reagan years. Americans had not repudiated the moderate welfare state. The American people liked Reagan, but they did not become Reaganites.

To explain this seeming inconsistency we return to the difference between economic and noneconomic liberalism discussed earlier in this chapter. Americans are not very clear about what they mean by "liberal" or "conservative." Retired people, for example, support Social Security and Medicare—attitudes that might make them economic liberals—but many retired people call themselves conservatives because they oppose the erosion of traditional values. They use "conservative" in the noneconomic sense. College-age people, on the other hand, may disdain the welfare state and celebrate market economics—making them economic conservatives—but they may call themselves liberal in reference to their open-mindedness on social, racial, and lifestyle questions. Reagan was able to hold together these two strands for several years. There had been little overall growth in "conservatism"; rather, Reagan had appealed to the economic conservatism of some and to the noneconomic conservatism of others. Under Bush, this coalition fell apart.

Who Pays Attention?

Public opinion is fragmented; groups are interested in different questions. Farmers are concerned about produce prices, steel and auto workers about imports, women about wage equality, and minorities about job opportunities. In 1998, for example,

Table 8.2   Americans' Description of Self

Very Liberal	5%
Somewhat Liberal	12
Moderate	48
Somewhat Conservative	24
Very Conservative	8
Don't Know	3

Source: *New York Times,* February 28, 1984. Copyright © 1984 by The New York Times Company. Reprinted by permission.

Classic Works   ALMOND'S THREE PUBLICS

In his 1950 *The American People and Foreign Policy*, political scientist Gabriel Almond proposed that there were three American public opinions, not just one:

1. A *general public* of a majority who don't know or care about much beyond their immediate concerns. For example, they show little interest in foreign policy unless the country is in a war or international crisis.
2. An *attentive public* of a minority who are among the better-educated and who follow more abstract political concerns, such as foreign policy. They are the audience the elite plays to; and, in turn, this attentive public passes on views that mobilize the general public.
3. A *policy and opinion elite* of a few highly influential people who are involved in politics, often professionally. These members of Congress, appointed officials, and top journalists devise foreign and domestic policies and articulate them to the attentive and general publics.

Especially regarding foreign affairs, Almond makes a strong case. The number of Americans who follow the news is decreasing. Survey after survey finds ignorance of world affairs. Attentive and elite opinion—such as business, media, and religious leaders and academics—favor NAFTA, NATO expansion, and the U.S. mission in Bosnia far more than the general public.

---

amid news of a federal budget surplus, younger people said spend it on education and other social problems, and older people said spend it to fix Social Security, but few wanted a tax cut. A time when some groups are satisfied may be a time when others are dissatisfied. Blacks and poor people didn't much notice the good economic times of the late 1990s; better-off Americans praised the economy.

KEY TERM

attentive public Those citizens who follow politics, especially national and international affairs.

The **attentive public** (see box above), although fewer in number, may have more importance politically because they have ideas that they articulate, demonstrating political competence. Sometimes they can rouse the general public. Opposition to the Vietnam war and to South Africa's apartheid started with a few critics who wrote and spoke in churches, newspapers, and classrooms. In the early 1990s, while few people were paying attention, some of the attentive public were raising questions about atrocities in Bosnia and starvation in Somalia. The attentive public can act as "spark plugs" among the apathetic and slow-reacting general public. This is why all regimes treat intellectuals with caution and sometimes with suspicion. For this reason, Communist regimes expended great effort to ferret out a handful of dissident intellectuals. In Washington, administration officials devote much time and energy in trying to win over the attentive public to minimize criticism that might influence the general public and the next election. As we will consider in

Chapter 9, relations between the White House and the news media often resemble a cat-and-mouse game. All over the country, the attentive public can offer the general public new ways of looking at issues. And the regime may not like attention drawn to certain issues.

Political elites, aware of the ignorance and low interest of the general public, may convince themselves to not pay much attention to public opinion. A 1998 Pew study found that members of Congress, presidential appointees, and senior civil servants believed most Americans do not know enough to form sound opinions on vital issues of the day. Elites, in other words, believe elites have to decide many questions because they are the only ones following them. Unfortunately for democracy, they may be right.

The general public's indifference and fragmentation mean that their views are often hard to discern and may have little impact on decision making. Elected leaders are apt pay attention to the group with the most intensely held views. Polls show that most Americans would permit abortion, but few are strong-

> ### KEY TERM
> **intensity**   The firmness and enthusiasm with which an opinion is held.

ly supportive of abortion. The "pro-life" foes of abortion, although a minority nationwide, have such great **intensity** about the subject that they can often drown out the greater numbers who are not passionately concerned. Jews make up less than 3 percent of the U.S. population, but among them are such intense supporters of Israel that most elected officials take a pro-Israel stance. Most Americans favor some form of gun control, but they are mostly lukewarm about the issue. The opponents to gun control are red hot and thus quite influential. Intensely held views of a few often override large numbers of indifferent people.

The disproportionate influence of the attentive public and passionate opinion holders underscores one of the problems of public opinion. Often there is little "public" opinion, just the opinion of scattered and small groups who pay attention to issues and care intensely about them. Should their views be excluded as nonrepresentative of the public, or should they take on added weight as the views of the only people who really care about the issues? Which is the more democratic approach? Most people would be inclined to say democracy means going with the greatest numbers, even if their views are lukewarm. When it comes to a question that deeply concerns them, however, many people do not wish to have a simple head count, arguing that the majority view is ignorant or mistaken and should not be heeded. We will consider some of these questions when we discuss interest groups in Chapter 10.

Is Polling Fair?

Polls do not merely monitor public opinion; they also help make it. Critics charge that published or broadcast poll results can distort an election. For example, the news media may give considerable attention to polls that indicate one candidate is leading another by a wide margin. Such publicity, underdog candidates claim, can be devastating to their campaigns. Would-be supporters of the underdog candidate may lose interest. They may even jump on the leader's bandwagon. Even more important, campaign funds may dry up because the candidate behind in the polls looks like a loser. Few political scientists think average voters are likely to change their votes because a poll shows their candidate is losing. But it does seem probable that poor poll showings, especially early in the campaign, can act as a self-fulfilling prophecy of defeat for some candidates. Those who lead in the early polls get more donations, more news coverage, and thus more supporters. Those behind in the early polls are sunk at the start. We will consider the problem of media coverage in the next chapter.

One current controversy is the effect of "exit polls," which question voters just as they leave the balloting area. With the three-hour time difference between the East and West Coasts, exit polls enable television to predict winners in the East while westerners still have hours in which to cast a ballot. Does the early prediction in the East affect the vote in the West? Democrats charged that during the two Reagan landslides many West Coast people were persuaded not to bother to vote because the early East Coast exit polls had already given the contest to Reagan. This development robbed state and local Democratic candidates in the West of votes that might have been theirs if more people had voted. Some urged a delay in broadcasting the results of exit polls, and in 1992 broadcasters voluntarily delayed reporting exit polls. No evidence was found that exit polls influenced the presidential vote, but they might have influenced other contests for the House, the Senate, or the state legislature. Polls, especially when their results are broadcast so quickly, are not neutral in their impact, but no constitutionally legal way has been found to control them.

Should America Be Governed by Polls?

Considering the preceding discussion, it would seem in most cases that America should not be governed by polls. First, public attention varies widely. On many issues, the general public has no knowledge or opinion. In such a situation, the intense concern of a minority might dominate the poll results. Leaders, especially with modern means of communication, can influence public opinion in their direction. This encourages government leaders to try to create the kind of feedback they want to hear. Typically, public opinion follows executive decisions. Public opinion does not usually lead executive decisions.

The wording of the questions and selection of the sample (the people to be polled) can seriously skew results. We must be sure that the survey was done by reliable professionals with standardized questions and a random sample. Polls conducted by partisans of a cause or candidate can seriously mislead and should be ignored. Equally serious is the problem of volatility: the changeable nature of poll results. What the public likes one month, it may dislike the next. Decisions made on the basis of a given survey may meet with public displeasure when the consequences of the decision sink in. Accordingly, public officials who are tempted to "go with the polls," who think, "All those voters can't be wrong," may be stepping into a trap that hurts both themselves and their country. The polls, if

Political Communication and the Media

The **mass media** have always loomed large in American politics. In the 1780s, the *Federalist Papers* were published in daily newspapers throughout the colonies to win support for the new constitution. Andrew Jackson's victory in 1828 over John Quincy Adams marked the end of one of the most bitter "media campaigns" in America's history. In it, mudslinging reached its high point (or low point) when Jackson and his wife were accused of moral irregularities, and the press played a key role in the exchange of propaganda. In the early twentieth century, we had a media candidate in Teddy Roosevelt: He tailored his rough-and-ready image to fire the imagination of the people, with great success. And Franklin D. Roosevelt used his famous "fireside chats" on radio, along with hundreds of press conferences, to win support for his policies. Today, the mass media are a recognized component of American politics, and modern campaigns depend on television so much that many critics complain that candidates no longer run for office on issues; instead, professional marketing consultants package them and sell them like any product.

QUESTIONS TO CONSIDER

1. How do the mass media and face-to-face communication differ?
2. What journals constitute the elite media?
3. Where does most newspaper and radio news come from?
4. What are the weaknesses of television news coverage?
5. Can money buy television time and hence buy elections?
6. Has television created political apathy?
7. Which country has the freest mass media?
8. What can you do to stay well-informed?
9. Is it generally a good thing that the media and government are adversaries?

Communication in Politics

Political scientists have long recognized the dependence of politics on communications. Karl W. Deutsch, for example, claims the rate of modernization of developing nations and the rise and decline of

---

KEY TERM

mass media   Modern means of communication that reach very wide audiences.

metropolitan areas around the globe can be measured from patterns and flow of mail, telephone calls, and migration paths of the labor force. The political system and the communication system precisely parallel one another, and it is doubtful that one could exist without the other.

Levels of Communication

All political action is a reaction to communication of one kind or another. There are, however, different levels and types of communication. **Face-to-face** communication is the most basic and most effective for altering or reinforcing political opinions because it allows for dialogue where mass media cannot. Until the early 1930s, face-to-face communication was the main method of political campaigning. Candidates **stumped** (in the old days, many spoke from tree stumps) their districts and addressed small groups of voters, appealing for their support with the help of ward bosses, precinct captains, and political organizers. However, the rise of television and the complexity of modern society have today largely bypassed grassroots stumping, except as a means of getting free media coverage.

The Mass Media The mass media reach an infinitely larger audience, and therefore yield a greater voter or public opinion return, than face-to-face communication. A speech that gets on television can reach millions of people at once, but a speech given at even the largest rally may be heard by only a few thousand people. If even a small percentage of television viewers respond positively to what the speaker says, that response can become tens of thousands of votes, perhaps enough to swing an election.

But the mass media are essentially a one-way avenue of communication. If a viewer dislikes the current president, he or she can turn the channel; if the viewer disagrees with his message, the president can't counter those objections with a custom-made response. Studies of the impact of the mass media on individual thinking and behavior show that mass media can effectively reinforce existing political opinions but can't really convert anyone. Radio and television do have stronger persuasive power than the printed word because they are closer to face-to-face communication, but their impact still depends partly on the influence of chats with friends after the program is over.

Television may have somewhat eroded the role of opinion leaders as television newscasters have become opinion leaders on a grand scale. Television not only serves by transmitting direct political messages but also serves indirectly as an instrument of social change by bringing news events into the homes of the people. Most observers agree that the civil rights movement of the 1960s would not have achieved the success it did without television. Racial discrimination in the South was largely unnoticed—perhaps deliberately unnoticed—in the print media and radio. But television news showing fire hoses and police dogs used to attack

Classic Works

THE TWO-STEP FLOW OF MASS COMMUNICATIONS

How do the mass media penetrate an audience? Paul Lazarsfeld and Elihu Katz were among the first to perceive a two-step pattern in this process. They found that every community has respected **opinion leaders**—teachers, ministers, community and civic leaders, outstanding businesspersons, and professional leaders—what Almond called the attentive public (see Chapter 8). These people take political cues from the mass media and pass them on to their less attentive friends in normal daily contact. In this way, political messages filter down to most. The effectiveness of mass media appeals depends on these opinion leaders, and it is they whom successful politicians must reach, influence, and convince.

peaceful marchers turned most Americans in favor of equal black rights. Likewise, the graphic television coverage of the Vietnam war—the world's first television war—turned many people against the war and against President Johnson.

Who Uses the Media? Fewer Americans are interested in news coverage than they were a generation ago. Fewer watch television news (down from 60 percent in 1990 to 42 percent in 1996) or read a newspaper. And within the media, news is shifting away from politics and world affairs and toward human interest and "news you can use" about health, business, and lifestyles. This decline precisely parallels the decline in Americans' interest in politics in general, confirming the close connection between communications and politics. The causes of this decline are debated. Some see a shift in values, especially among a new and **introspective** generation. Others think it is just the temporary effect of relatively good times in which there is neither war nor economic anxiety to focus peoples' attention on the news.

KEY TERMS
opinion leaders   Locally respected people who influence the views of others.
introspective   Looking within oneself.

The various modern media appeal to different audiences who can be distinguished by education, income, and age. The better educated individuals are, the more they will use the mass media. College graduates and better-off people tend to read newspapers, magazines, and books as well as listen to the radio and watch television and motion pictures. But grammar and high-school graduates, who use the mass media more for entertainment, generally favor television, radio, and motion pictures more than the print media. Ninety percent of the people in high-income brackets are regular magazine and book readers, but only half of the people in low-income groups are.

Age or maturity also affects the use of the mass media. In general, people between the ages of thirty and fifty pay more attention to the editorial and news content of newspapers and magazines than do teenagers and young adults, who tend to use newspapers for entertainment. Young readers follow sports, rock stars, and feature articles rather than hard news. The college student who keeps up on the news and editorial opinion is rare.

Modern Mass Media

Newspapers   In 1910, the United States had more than 2,600 daily newspapers, and 57 percent of all American cities had two or more competing papers. Today, only 1,550 newspapers remain, and only thirty-three U.S. cities have two or more separately owned papers. Does this decline in competition mean that the people are being denied access to a healthy variety of political and editorial opinion? The charge that the fabled "free press" is really just a business is backed up by certain facts. Some 75 percent of U.S. newspapers are owned by centrally controlled syndicates or chains, and corporation ownership of most large newspapers gives them a **status-quo** orientation.

> ### KEY TERMS
>
> **status quo**   The present situation.
> **elite press**   Highly influential newspapers and magazines read by elites and the attentive public.

THE ELITE MEDIA

The *New York Times*, the *Washington Post*, and the *Wall Street Journal* are read by a small fraction of the U.S. population, but they carry by far the most clout. Decision makers in Washington and indeed across the country read them and take both their news stories and their editorials seriously. Leading thinkers fight battles on their "op-ed" pages (opposite the editorial page) or in their letters to the editor. That is why these papers have influence out of all proportion to their circulation. They are what is known as the **elite press**. The people who read them are generally wealthier and better educated and have more influence than the reader of a hometown paper. The elite press pursues "investigative reporting," looking for government and partisan wrongdoing, something the average paper usually shuns. The *New York Times* jolted the nation when it published the Pentagon Papers on the Vietnam war in 1971. The dogged pursuit of the 1972 Watergate burglary by the *Washington Post* brought down the Nixon administration in 1974. The editorials of the *Wall Street Journal* influence economic decisions in Washington.

The small-circulation magazines of opinion are also among the elite press. The conservative *National Review*, the liberal *New Republic*, the leftist *Nation*, and the neoconservative *Commentary* have considerable impact on opinion leaders, the sorts of people who influence others. President Reagan named Jeane Kirkpatrick ambassador to the UN on the strength of an article of hers he had read in Commentary. Students are often ignorant of the elite press, but those who themselves aspire to leadership status would be well advised to follow one or more of these journals.

The News Services

Most hard news in newspapers and on radio, and even a good deal of television's news, is not produced in-house but comes from a printer hooked up to the New York offices of the Associated Press (AP), hence the old-fashioned name **wire service**. The elite newspapers disdain wire-service copy, as it's matter of pride for them to have their own reporters covering the story. But most papers in America are little more than local outlets for the Associated Press, which provides them with photos, sports coverage, even recipes, as well as news. Often, editors on small-town papers read just the first two paragraphs, so that they can write a headline, and slap the stories into their papers nearly at random.

The AP is a cooperative, with members paying assessments based on their circulation. They also contribute copies of local stories to the AP, which may rewrite them for nationwide transmission. The AP is one of the few news services not owned, subsidized, controlled, or supervised by a government. It is free of government influence and proud of it. Britain's Reuters gets discreet government subsidies; France's AFP has government supervision, as does Germany's DPA; and China's Xin Hua is wholly a creature of Beijing.

The AP is free, but it has other problems that limit its quality and influence. First, it moves fast; every minute is a deadline. This means it can give little time to digging. Second, the wire services' definition of news is something from an official **source**. All wire-service stories are carefully attributed to police, the White House, the State Department or Pentagon, and so on. If it's not official, it's not news. This causes the wire services to miss many explosive situations in the world because they do not like their reporters to talk to opposition people, the average citizen in the street, or the merchants in the bazaar, who might have a completely different—and sometimes more accurate—perspective than official spokespersons. The American news media failed to notice the coming of the Iranian revolution for this reason. Often, the best news stories are not about a key event or statement but about what people are saying and thinking, which the wires don't cover.

But most newspapers do not present the news in an obviously partisan manner. The reasons are both practical and idealistic. Sixty-five to 90 percent of newspaper revenue comes from advertising, and fees from advertisers depend on the newspapers' circulation. Thus, keeping circulation high is the main concern, and the result is usually a middle-of-the-road news policy calculated to not antagonize most people. This often makes newspapers bland.

Journalism itself has a long tradition of objectivity in news reporting (although the editorial page may be another story). The profession's own idealism no doubt influences newspaper people to present the news fairly and honestly. Further, most news printed in U.S. newspapers is from a wire service, and wire services take special pains to be objective and to refrain from editorializing.

How much political impact, then, do U.S. newspapers have? Not as much as they used to. Fewer households take newspapers now than half a century

Key Terms

wire service News agency that sells its product to many media.

source Who or where a news reporter gets information from.

ago, and only about half of adult Americans read a daily paper. The content of newspapers is mostly advertisements (one important reason people read them) and wire-service copy. The editorials of most newspapers carry little weight. The exceptions are the "elite" media.

Radio   Like newspapers, radio is not what it used to be. Between the two world wars it zoomed in popularity, and radio news, comments, and political addresses—such as Franklin D. Roosevelt's famous "fireside chats," which served as models for both Jimmy Carter and Ronald Reagan—were quite influential. But with the rise of television in the 1950s, radio became a medium of background music. Radio news dwindled into brief hourly spots, much of it "rip and read" from the wire-service printer. Radio now has little political impact, although it too has an elite exception: the radio magazine "All Things Considered" on National Public Radio, full of in-depth explorations of world events, economics, politics, and reasoned opinion. This daily broadcast brought back to radio some better-educated people of all political persuasions.

The Giant: Television

When most Americans say "the media," they mean television, for television towers over everything else in terms of impact. Most Americans get their political information from television, and most say they believe information obtained from television more than that in newspapers. Television has touched almost everything in American politics and has changed almost everything it has touched. Election campaigns now revolve heavily around the acquisition of television time; winners are usually those who can raise the most money to hire the best media consultants. Television has become a suspect in the decline of both U.S. election turnout and political parties. Some observers see television as contributing to the more complete trivialization of U.S. politics, which now focus on "sound bites" of a few seconds length. Calm analysis is out; the catchy phrase is in.

Television News

Television, by very definition, favors the visual. "Talking heads" provide no more news than does radio. (Talking heads do provide something very important, though—a sense of personality and hence credibility, a sort of imitation face-to-face communication.) News producers therefore devote more attention to a news story with "good visuals" than without. As with the wire services, abstract, deeper topics tend to go by with little coverage, but dramatic action—if there was a camera crew on hand to catch it—gets played up. Television, like most of the rest of the U.S. news media, ignored the deep hatred that was brewing against the shah of Iran for years but caught the dramatic return of the Ayatollah Khomeini. Television never did explain what the Vietnam war was about, but a brief film clip of a Saigon general shooting a Vietcong assassin in 1968 helped sicken Americans

Media execution: AP photographer Eddie Adams snapped the summary execution of a captured Vietcong assassin in 1968. Adams later said he was sorry he took the history-making photo, which tended to make the Vietcong look heroic. In truth, the Vietcong assassin had just murdered the family of one of the assistants to South Vietnam's police chief, who took speedy revenge. Images can mislead. (Eddie Adams, AP/Wide World Photos)

against the war. Just as the wire services are hooked on official sources, television news is hooked on the eye-catching. This makes television inherently a more emotional medium than the others. Television coverage can go straight to the heart, bypassing the brain altogether; that is its great power.

Unfortunately, television camera crews are expensive to maintain in the field, especially overseas, so they usually arrive where the action is only *after* having been notified by the wire services. Television prefers to know in advance what's going to happen; then it can schedule a camera crew. This makes television news lopsided with press conferences, speeches, committee hearings, and official statements. Some critics characterize these happenings as **media events**, things that would not have occurred without television coverage. A media event is not fake, but it is planned in advance with an eye to catching the attention of television crews. Not only is this understood by officials, but protest groups, too, stage marches, sit-ins, and mass arrests to get television exposure for their cause. Chanted protesters at the 1968 Democratic convention in Chicago: "The whole world is watching!" The next time you watch television, count the number of film clips of events that were obviously scheduled in advance as opposed to those that weren't; the former will probably outnumber the latter by a big margin.

> **KEY TERM**
>
> **media event** News happening planned in advance to insure media coverage.

Deep analysis is also not television's strong point. An average news story runs one minute; a two- or three-minute story is considered an in-depth report. Walter Cronkite, long dean of television newspeople, emphasized that television news was just a "headline service," meaning that if viewers wanted detail and depth they would have to go elsewhere. Many Americans, of course, don't look deeper and are left with the tardy, the eye-catching, and the media event as their daily diet of information. Thus, it is not surprising when polls repeatedly discover that Americans are poorly informed about the great issues of the day.

Television and Politics

All agree that television has changed politics, and in several ways. Incumbency, especially in the White House, has always brought recognition. Television has enhanced this recognition, but not always to the incumbent's satisfaction. Television news is heavily focused on the president and, to a lesser extent, on the rest of the executive branch. Congress gets much less coverage, the courts even less. This deepens a long-term American tendency to president-worship. The president—especially with the way television socializes small children—is seen as an omnipotent parental figure, a person who can fix all problems. That in itself should make a current president very happy. But then things go wrong; the president doesn't fix the problems; an ultracritical press implies that presidential policies may be making them worse. The flip side of being treated as all-powerful is catching all the blame. The media (especially television) whip up president-worship and then whip up mass dissatisfaction with the president's performance. Expectations, heightened by the media, are very high, and disappointments are correspondingly bitter. Some critics charge that the media are wrecking the U.S. political system with that kind of coverage, making the country unstable and ungovernable.

Nomination by Television   Television also contributes importantly to the presidential selection process. With all eyes focused on the early presidential primaries—especially New Hampshire—commentators grandly proclaim who is the "real winner" and who is picking up "momentum." The lucky candidate thus designated as front-runner goes into the remaining primaries and the national convention with a **bandwagon** effect, enhanced recognition, and lots of television coverage. In the nominating process, television has become a kind of kingmaker. It is no wonder that candidates arrange their schedules and strategies to capture as much television exposure as possible.

KEY TERM
bandwagon   The tendency of front-runners to gain additional supporters.

The television coverage of candidates focuses on their personalities, not on issues. Television, with its sharp closeups and seeming spontaneity, gives viewers what they think is a true glimpse of the candidate's character. Actually, this may not be so; some candidates play the medium like professionals (Ronald Reagan), and others tense up and hide their normal personalities. How a candidate performs on television is a poor indicator of how he or she will perform in office, but it is the one most American voters use.

First presidential debates: In the 1960 election campaign, Richard Nixon debated John Kennedy live and nationwide, a television first. Kennedy's more relaxed performance helped him win. (UPI/Corbis)

While television is playing this major role in nominating and electing candidates, the political party is bypassed. Party organizations and bosses are not very important, as candidates on television go right over their heads to the voters. Since the leading contender or two have already picked up their "momentum" going into the convention, they don't need party professionals to broker a nominating deal. Politics has come out of the proverbial smoke-filled back rooms and into the glare of television lights, not always for the better. The party and its chiefs used to know a thing or two about politics and were often capable of putting forward tried and tested candidates. With television, a candidate can come from out of nearly nowhere and win the top national office with little political experience. We must be careful, though, in blaming television for the weakening of the parties. American parties, with the exception of a few urban machines, were never as strongly organized as most European parties. Moreover, American parties began declining a long time ago, not just with the advent of television. Other factors, such as special-interest groups, political action committees, and direct-mail solicitation, have also undermined party strength. Television is not the sole culprit.

Television and Apathy Observers long suspected that television induces passivity and apathy. Harvard political scientist Robert D. Putnam (see his discussion of "bowling alone" on p. 117) believes he's proved "the culprit is television." Systematically reviewing the possible causes of the decline of "civic engagement" in the United States, Putnam finds older people, those born before World War II, are more trusting and more inclined to join groups and participate in politics. The reason: They were raised before the television age. Younger people, raised on television, lack these qualities. Says Putnam: "Each hour spent viewing television is associated with less social trust and less group membership, while each hour reading a newspaper is associated with more."

A related charge is that television has lowered election-day turnouts. There is a close coincidence in time; turnout dropped 13 percentage points from 1960, when television first established itself as the top means of campaigning, until 1988. Television saturates viewers so far in advance that they lose interest. Perhaps this loss of interest has occurred because the top two candidates usually sound so similar that many voters see little difference. Negative campaigning also disgusts many voters. Charges and countercharges in political spots come so thick and fast that the voter is **cross-pressured** into indecision and apathy. In Western Europe, where paid-for political television spots are generally prohibited and campaigns are much shorter—usually about a month instead of the year and more in the United States—voter turnout is much higher, sometimes topping 90 percent. Only America does not regulate television political ads.

> ### KEY TERM
>
> **cross-pressured** To be subjected to two or more opposing political forces; said to incline one to apathy.

One thing U.S. television does for sure: It costs candidates a bundle. (Total spending on the 1992 U.S. elections: over $3 billion, a figure that has grown since then.) Depending on the time of day and locale, a one-minute spot can go for $100,000. The cost factor in itself has transformed American politics. Members of Congress can sometimes get by with little television advertising, but virtually all senatorial and presidential candidates need it. About half of presidential campaign chests are estimated now to go for television. Political consulting—the right kind of themes, slogans, and speeches presented in the right kind of television spots—has become a big business. In most contests, the winner is the one who spent the most money, most of it on television spots. This heightens the importance of special-interest groups and political action committees, which in turn has weakened the role of the parties and perhaps deepened feelings of powerlessness among average voters.

Many Americans are ignoring party labels, either calling themselves "independents," splitting tickets, or voting against their party registration. The trend, alarming to some political scientists, is called voter "dealignment," citizens *not* lining up with a party. Lacking party identification, these voters are increasingly open to persuasion via the media, especially television. This development, some suggest, produces great volatility as voters, massaged by media professionals, shift this way and that in response to candidates' televised images.

Television: Ownership and Control

The U.S. government exercises the *least* control of communications of any industrialized country. Since the invention of the telegraph, the American government has stood back and let private industry operate communications for profit. In

Europe, in contrast, telegraphy was soon taken over by the postal service, as were telephones. The U.S. government—partly because of First Amendment guarantees of free speech and partly because of the U.S. ethos of free enterprise—simply does not like to butt in. For European nations, with traditions of centralized power and government paternalism, national control of electronic communications is as normal as state ownership of the railroads.

The U.S. attitude of **nonpaternalism** has led to the freest airwaves in the world, but it has also brought some problems. With the rapid growth of radio in the 1920s, the **electromagnetic spectrum** was soon jammed with stations trying to drown each other out. To bring some order out of the chaos, the Radio Act of 1927 set up a five-member Federal Radio Commission (FRC) appointed by the president to assign frequencies, call letters, and maximum power. Stations had to get licenses and could lose them. Most important, the 1927 act put the government on record

KEY TERMS

nonpaternalism Not taking a supervisory or guiding role.

electromagnetic spectrum The airwaves over which signals are broadcast.

IS TELEVISION A "VAST WASTELAND"?

Decades ago FCC Commissioner Newton Minow despaired that television was culturally a "vast wasteland," and the phrase stuck. In theory, the FCC licenses radio and television stations to serve "the public interest," but in practice no station has its license revoked for broadcasting junk. The FCC lays down no rules about program content except for obscenity on the air. Programs can be as trashy or as lofty as the owners want. Most owners, in their appraisals of the viewing audience, emphasize the former. The FCC claims it can do nothing to make programs more cultural, educational, or morally uplifting.

Most broadcasting in America is private and profit-oriented. Profits derive from advertising, which depends on audience size. Station owners argue that they automatically serve the public interest in offering the programs most people want. They are also, of course, serving their own interests. If most people want twenty-four hours of rock and roll, that must be the public interest for that area. If most people like violent and sexy detective shows, television must provide them. Thus do self-interest and altruism happily merge.

Critics bemoan this kind of reasoning, pointing out that broadcasters are not merely *following* public tastes but *setting* them by offering only competing junk. About the only outlet for the critics' frustration, though, is public broadcasting. During the 1950s, noncommercial FM and television stations, financed by universities and community donations, began to offer programming at higher cultural and educational levels. The Ford Foundation and Congress came in with more support. In 1967, Congress set up the Corporation for Public Broadcasting (CPB), with National Public Radio (NPR) and the Public Broadcasting Service (PBS) under it. This is as close as the United States has come to establishing a link between government and broadcasting, and it's not very close. Government funding, especially with the budget cuts of recent administrations, accounts for only a minority of NPR's and PBS's finances. Public broadcasting presents all political viewpoints. NPR and PBS are the only exceptions to private ownership and profit orientation in American broadcasting.

Case Studies   THE EUROPEAN MEDIA

The American airwaves are lightly regulated. Could it—or should it—be otherwise? The European experience offers a range of possibilities, all involving greater government control or supervision than the United States has. Television in the Soviet Union was strictly government controlled and was carefully aimed. It was patriotic, upbeat, and positive, calculated to inculcate feelings of loyalty and hard work and to uplift culturally. Instead of the "hands-off" American attitude, the Soviet approach was to use television as an instrument of education and guidance. Soviet programming accordingly stressed the glorious but trying events of World War II, factories and workers happily producing more and more goods, and opera and ballet that would be seen only on PBS in the United States. Soviets familiar with American television regarded it as debauchery, an example of capitalism run amok. The concept of giving viewers what they want was alien to them, and Soviet programming had little pop music and light entertainment. Political pronouncements were generally reserved for the party newspaper, *Pravda* (Truth), and its government counterpart, *Izvestia* (News). The Soviets regarded newspapers as more authoritative than television. When, in 1988, Soviet television showed spontaneous coverage of a major party congress that included criticism and accusations of wrongdoing, Soviet viewers were wide-eyed with interest and amazement. This policy of *glasnost* (openness) contributed a lot to the collapse of the Soviet system. Once truth started coming out, the system could not stand.

French television is also government controlled, although not as heavy-handed as in the ex-Soviet Union. Before he returned to power in 1958, General Charles de Gaulle watched a great deal of television and concluded that it was the perfect way to control a country. As the powerful president of the Fifth Republic, which he created, from 1958 to 1969, de Gaulle did indeed use television as a tool of governance and guidance. In military uniform and with his sonorous voice and superb command of the language, de Gaulle put down two rebellions and won four referendums with his televised calls for loyalty. The government office de Gaulle established, the ORTF, is still at work today, although many French viewers and journalists are aware that it slants the news. The French left protested this rigging of information, but when the Socialists swept to power in 1981 they did not free the ORTF, rather they proceeded to slant things *their* way. The trouble with government-controlled broadcasting, though, is that listeners and viewers will try to go elsewhere. In France, they tune in to radio and television from Luxembourg and Monaco, which are more objective than the French programs. To a certain extent, government control of radio and television is self-defeating, for these media lose credibility. In 1986, a conservative French government "privatized" some of the airwaves by selling the largest of France's three state-owned television networks, TF1.

The northern European systems are better at putting some distance between the government and broadcasting. The British Broadcasting Corporation (BBC), created in 1927, is run by a board of governors who are nonpartisan but are nonetheless named by the government. The BBC is supported by annual licenses that listeners and viewers must buy; it carries no commercial advertising. During Britain's brief (three-week) campaigns, air time is allocated to the three main parties—Conservative, Labour, and Liberal Democrat—in proportion to their strength in Parliament. Whereas the nonpaternalistic U.S. system lets programming

---

THE EUROPEAN MEDIA (CONTINUED)

sink to a low level, the BBC system, supervised by cultivated and educated governors, rises high, often too high for the British public; many find it staid and boring. Since 1954, Britain has permitted private, commercial television in the form of the Independent Television Authority, which offers programs more at the mass level. Swedish and German broadcasting are mainly financed by user license fees. They are governed by nonpartisan boards of media people, cultural leaders, and civil servants. The German system has both nationwide and state networks, diffusing control and introducing a certain amount of competition. Advertising is permitted but grouped into several-minute spots throughout the day. Advertisers do not sponsor programs and have nothing to say about content. Paid political advertising is not permitted, but time is allocated to parties during election campaigns for political messages.

The U.S. broadcast media are, paradoxically, free but expensive. They are under virtually no government control, but listeners and viewers pay a price in having programming skewed to earn broadcasters the maximum amount of money. The price is junk programming that does indeed leave America culturally, educationally, and informationally underdeveloped.

---

for the first time as recognizing that the airwaves were public property and should serve "the public interest, convenience and necessity." The Communications Act of 1934 superseded the FRC and created the Federal Communications Commission (FCC), which monitors broadcasting to this day. The 1934 act recognizes the danger of partisanship and now provides for five FCC commissioners appointed by the president and approved by the Senate. The commissioners serve staggered seven-year terms, and no more than three can be members of the same party.

The FCC doesn't supervise the content of programs, but it does have a political impact. Section 315 of the 1934 act, known as the "equal-time provision," tells broadcasters that if they give or sell air time to one candidate, they must do the same for others. Station owners, of course, don't like to give away air time. They also fear that public interest programs featuring the candidates of the two big parties will lead to a demand for equal time by minor or frivolous candidates. News broadcasts are exempt from the equal-time rule, so debates between the two leading presidential contenders are conducted by a panel of newspeople to get around the equal-time provision. Broadcasters may also not be too happy about selling air time, for it must go at the lowest rate, which in turn must be offered to the opponents. Broadcasters long sought modifications of the equal-time provision.

Another FCC power, more vague than "equal time," is the "fairness doctrine" first published in 1949 by the commission. Recognizing that broadcast editorials are part of the public interest, the fairness doctrine requires broadcasters to offer air time for those with opposing views to respond. Enforcement, though, is left to the broadcasters, and many public-spirited interest groups feel that broadcasters simply try to avoid all controversy so that they won't have to make air time available to anyone. The Reagan-appointed members of the FCC abolished both the equal-time and fairness provisions, arguing that they tended to limit political debate on the airwaves.

Are We Poorly Served?

As may be judged from some of our earlier discussions, the U.S. mass media do not serve Americans very well. First, news coverage is highly selective, over-concentrating on some areas while ignoring others. This is called "structural bias." The president and staff occupy over half the news time given to the federal government. Why is this? The president is inherently more dramatic and eye-catching than the other branches of government. Reporters, editors, and producers are afraid that if they devote more than a little time to Congress and the courts, readers and viewers will become bored. Another reason is that what the president does is visually more exciting than what Congress or the courts do. The president gets in and out of helicopters, greets foreign leaders, travels overseas, or gets involved in scandals; all provide good television footage. Congress may get some attention when one of its committees faces a tense, controversial, or hostile witness. Then the committee members hurl accusatory questions, the witness stammers back denials, and sometimes shouting erupts. That's good drama; the rest of Congress is pretty dull. And the courts face the biggest obstacle of all: No cameras are allowed in most courtrooms. Accordingly, Americans grow up with the notion that the White House does most of the work and has most of the power, whereas Congress and the courts hardly matter.

One part of the U.S. government is especially undercovered: the civil service, in its myriad departments, agencies, and bureaus. Here is where much of the governance of America takes place. But "faceless bureaucrats" make boring interviewees—some are not allowed to be interviewed—and federal regulations are unintelligible. Still, many of next year's news stories are buried in the federal bureaucracy. What agency using what criteria allowed a nuclear power plant to operate? The media don't pay any attention until a Three Mile Island occurs. What department shoveled out millions in contracts to presidential-campaign contributors? The wrongdoings of federally insured savings and loan associations went on for several years, little noticed by the media. What federal agency decides whether commercial airlines are observing adequate safety standards? The news media don't even try to cover such things; they wait until something goes wrong and then evince shocked surprise. The very stuff of politics is there in the federal agencies, but few pay attention. Drastically undercovered—almost as if they are under a news blackout—are state governments, and they are increasingly important, but editors figure that few citizens care.

On the world scene, too, the news media wait for something to blow up before they cover it. Except for the elite media previously mentioned, there is little background coverage of likely trouble spots. Thus, when war engulfs a disintegrating

Yugoslavia or an economy collapses in East Asia, most Americans are surprised. They shouldn't be; even moderate news coverage of these places over the years would have kept Americans informed about the increasing problems. But the U.S. media often do not keep reporters in these countries and rarely even send them on quick visits. Troubled Mexico, with all its implications for the United States, is still largely uncovered. We live in a revolutionary world, but the U.S. media pay little attention until the shooting starts. Providers of "good visuals" rather than analysis and early warning is the way they define their role, and this sets up Americans to become startled and confused.

The biggest problem with the U.S. media is that they do not try to give a coherent, comprehensive picture of what is happening. Operating under tight deadlines, flashing the best action footage, and basing reports heavily on official sources, the media bombard us with many little stories but seldom weave them together into a big story. They give us only pieces of a jigsaw puzzle. Part of this problem is due to the nature of any news medium that comes out daily: Newspapers and television take events one day at a time. Such news is usually incomplete and often misleading. We see people shooting, but we don't know why. The media world is, in Shakespeare's phrase, "full of sound and fury, signifying nothing."

What Can Be Done?

The mass media—except for the elite media—do not provide *meaning*. Some, such as the wire services, deliberately shun analysis and interpretation in their stories; that would be unobjective or editorializing. Reporters are typically unequipped to explain the historical background or long-term consequences of the stories they cover. Reporters are expected to be generalists, to be able to cover everything and anything. All you have to do is write down what the official source says. It is for this reason that editorials and columns of opinion often contain more "news" than the straight news stories, for the former set the news into a meaningful context, but the latter just leaves the bits and pieces scattered about. Unfortunately, most Americans make do with the bits and pieces as they make decisions on candidates, economic matters, and sending troops abroad.

Can anything be done? Professional newspeople generally agree that the public is ill informed, and some will even admit that their coverage could be wider and deeper. But the limiting factor, they emphasize, is the public itself. Most people don't want to be well informed, especially about things distant or complicated. Audience surveys find that people care least about foreign news and most about local news. Newspapers can go broke pushing too much world news; many, in fact, are going the way of the checkout-counter weeklies with the splashy and the trashy. Most people aren't intellectuals and don't like complicated, in-depth analyses. The shooting they care about; the reasons behind it they don't. Do the media have any responsibility, though, in educating the mass public so that citizens can better comprehend our complicated world? Some idealists in the media do feel a responsibility, but they are usually offset by the hardheaded business types, who have the last word. After a while, the idealists become cynical. We cannot expect any major improvements soon. For you, however, the student of political science who is already among the more attentive, the answer is the elite media. Use the mass media for sports coverage.

The Adversaries: Media and Government

The role of the press as critic in the healthy functioning of U.S. democracy has long been recognized. Thomas Jefferson wrote in 1787, "Were it left to me to decide [between government without] newspapers and newspapers without government, I should not hesitate a moment to prefer the latter."

KEY TERM
adversarial Inclined to criticize and oppose, to treat other persons or institutions with enmity.

Over the centuries, the press has criticized government. In the late 1960s and early 1970s, however, a new **adversarial** relationship between media and government emerged that is with us today. To be sure, not all the media entered into the fray; most newspapers with their wire-service stories continued to quote official sources. But the elite media and television often adopted hostile stances toward the executive branch.

The causes are not hard to see: Vietnam and Watergate. In both episodes the executive branch engaged in considerable lying to the media in order to soothe public opinion. Many media people resented being used in this way and struck back by means of sharp questioning in press conferences and investigative reporting. The presidency of Richard Nixon didn't help matters; he had long feared and hated the press. On losing the governor's race in California in 1962, he slouched off, muttering that the press "won't have Nixon to kick around any more." Before presidential press conferences, Nixon used to calm his nerves by relaxing in a darkened room. He liked to operate in secrecy and then spring his decisions on the public in direct telecasts without any newspeople getting in the way. In turn, the press resented him all the more.

In Saigon, the U.S. military held afternoon press briefings, dubbed the "five o'clock follies," in which upbeat spokesmen tried to show progress in the war. Journalists soon tired of the repetitive, misleading, and irrelevant briefings and took to snooping around themselves. What they found wasn't pretty: a corrupt, inept Saigon regime that was not winning the hearts and minds of its people; a Vietcong able to roam and strike at will; and tactics and morale inadequate to stop them. One young *New York Times* reporter was so critical of the Diem regime that his stories undermined American confidence in Diem and paved the way for Diem's 1963 ouster and murder by his own generals. Such is the influence of the elite media.

Television, too, showed a picture different from what U.S. officials wanted: the bodies of young GIs covered with mud and blood in full color. Because television inherently favors the visual, it beamed gory film clips into America's living rooms. Television also developed, perhaps unwittingly, a devastating style of coverage in which scenes of horror were juxtaposed with calm reassurances of top officials. The contrast silently indicated that the officials were either fools

Case Studies · THE MEDIA AND WATERGATE

In 1972 a news story began that brought the fall of the Nixon administration and, for at least portions of the media, a new self-image as guardians of public morality. Persons connected to the White House were caught burglarizing and planting telephone "bugs" in the Democratic campaign headquarters in the Watergate office and apartment complex. Dogged investigation by two young *Washington Post* reporters, who later wrote the book *All the President's Men*, revealed a massive cover-up led by the Oval Office. The more Nixon promised to come clean, the guiltier he looked. Nixon was never impeached. A House special committee voted to recommend impeachment; then Nixon resigned. The House certainly would have voted impeachment, and the Senate probably would have convicted.

Would the same have happened without media coverage? Ultimately, the legal moves came through the courts and Congress, but the media made sure these branches of government would not ignore or delay their duties. Did the media bring Nixon down? The Nixon people thought so, but then they always loathed the press. Others have argued that the same would have happened without the investigative reporting, but more slowly and with less drama. The point is that media and government are so intertwined that they are part of the same process and hard to separate.

Since Watergate, some branches of the media, namely the elite press and the national television networks, have adopted generally adversarial stances toward the executive branch. Criticism of the occasional changes of course under later presidencies was immoderate and sometimes unreasonable. Typically, presidents now claim the press is out to get them. Presidential policies are almost automatically doubted and criticized. The media see scandal everywhere in Washington and then descend in a "feeding frenzy" that leaves no reputation untarnished.

or liars. In 1971, CBS News accused the Defense Department, in a documentary, of spending millions of tax dollars to win public and congressional support. "The Selling of the Pentagon" raised a storm of controversy, with administration accusations of tricky editing that made interviewees look as if they were saying things they weren't. By this time, media and government were in a snarling match.

That same year, another bombshell burst: *The Pentagon Papers* appeared, first in the *New York Times*, then in the *Washington Post*. (See the box on p. 68.) The papers were a multivolume, top-secret study commissioned by former Secretary of Defense Robert McNamara to document decision making on the Vietnam war. Daniel Ellsberg, a former Pentagon official who had turned against the war, made photocopies and delivered them to the newspapers. In the Xerox age, there are no more total secrets. The Nixon administration was outraged—although the Papers made the Johnson officials the chief culprits—and ordered their publication halted, the first time the U.S. government ever censored newspapers. The

Supreme Court immediately threw out the government's case, and the presses ran again. By this time, there was open warfare between government and the media.

   Has the press gone too far? Some people are fed up at the high-handedness with which the media impugn all authority. The media seem to think they are always right, the government always wrong. One favorite target of media criticism was the former U.S. commander in Vietnam, retired General William Westmoreland. CBS News produced a documentary that said Westmoreland and his staff deliberately lied about Communist troop strength. Westmoreland sued, and even though he lost, the media world trembled. The threat of libel suits has a **chilling effect** on the news media's efforts to uncover wrongdoing in public life.

> **KEY TERM**
>
> **chilling effect**   Media losing interest in a subject for fear of lawsuits.

   In the late 1990s, evidence of exaggerated or fabricated news stories soiled the reputation of several news organizations and increased public distrust of the media in general. CNN and *Time* magazine in 1998 admitted they had no solid support for a lurid story of U.S. armed forces using nerve gas in a secret 1970 raid to kill American defectors in Laos. They simply failed to quote those interviewed who said that no such thing ever happened. Some newspapers and magazines admitted their writers had made up quotes and sources. Many people felt it was about time to take the media down a peg.

   What is the proper role of the media in a democracy? That they can and should criticize is clear: This keeps government on its toes. But how much should they criticize? Should they presume wrongdoing and cover-up everywhere? Should many reporters model themselves after Woodward and Bernstein of Watergate fame and try to ferret out scandals at every level of government? The press is largely protected from charges of libel, for "public" persons are presumed to be open to scrutiny. This has left some public figures feeling helpless and bitter at the hands of an all-powerful press and has increased cynical attitudes about politics in general. Public opinion has grown critical of the too critical media. Perhaps the United States can find some happy middle ground.

Key Terms

adversarial (p. 164)

bandwagon (p. 156)

chilling effect (p. 166)

cross-pressured (p. 158)

electromagnetic spectrum (p. 159)

elite press (p. 152)

face-to-face (p. 150)

introspective (p. 151)

mass media (p. 149)

media event (p. 155)

nonpaternalism (p. 159)

opinion leaders (p. 151)

source (p. 153)

status quo (p. 152)

stump (p. 150)

wire service (p. 153)

Key Websites

Associated Press.
   http://www.ap.org/
The Atlantic Monthly.
   http://www.theatlantic.com/atlantic/
National Public Radio.
   http://www.npr.org/
National Review.
   http://www.nationalreview.com/
The New York Times.
   http://www.nytimes.com/
Public Broadcasting System.
   http://www.pbs.org/
USA Today.
   http://www.usatoday.com/
The Wall Street Journal.
   http://www.wsj.com/
The Washington Post.
   http://www.washingtonpost.com/
This site helps you keep up with day-to-day U.S. political news, polls, and issues.
   http://www.cnn.com/ALLPOLITICS/

Further Reference

Cappella, Joseph N., and Kathleen Hall Jamieson. *Spiral of Cynicism: The Press and the Public Good*. New York: Oxford University Press, 1997.

Diamond, Edwin, and Robert A. Silverman. *White House to Your House: Media and Politics in Virtual America*. Cambridge, MA: MIT Press, 1995.

Entman, Robert M. *Democracy Without Citizens: Media and the Decay of American Politics*. New York: Oxford University Press, 1989.

Gans, Herbert J. *Deciding What's News*. New York: Vintage Books, 1980.

Graber, Doris A., Denis McQuail, and Pippa Norris, eds. *The Politics of News: The News of Politics*. Washington, D.C.: CQ Press, 1998.

Hess, Stephen. *News and Newsmaking*. Washington, D.C.: Brookings Institution, 1996.

Iyengar, Shanto, and Richard Reeves, eds. *Do the Media Govern? Politicians, Voters, and Reporters in America*. Thousand Oaks, CA: Sage, 1997.

Page, Benjamin I. *Who Deliberates? Mass Media in Modern Society*. Chicago, IL: University of Chicago Press, 1996.

Sanford, Bruce W. *Shooting the Messenger: America's Hatred of the Media*. New York: Free Press, 1997.

Schudson, Michael. *The Power of News*. Cambridge, MA: Harvard University Press, 1995.

Seib, Philip. *Headline Diplomacy: How News Coverage Affects Foreign Policy*. Westport, CT: Praeger, 1996.

West, Darrell M. *Air Wars: Television Advertising in Election Campaigns, 1952–1996*, 2nd ed. Washington, D.C.: CQ Press, 1997.

CHAPTER 10

Interest Groups

Interest groups are especially numerous, vocal, and visible in the United States, but we have no monopoly on them. They are an element in the political life of every highly organized modern society. Even in countries where social, economic, and political life is dominated by central planning, interest groups exist, though in muted form. Observers detected interest groups even in the Soviet Union under the conservative Brezhnev, quarreling, for example, over whether heavy or light industry will be emphasized in economic plans. And opposing the regime, groups of dissidents sprang up despite the Kremlin's efforts to promote uniformity.

QUESTIONS TO CONSIDER
1. Can democracy exist without interest groups?
2. Are all citizens equally capable of organizing effective interest groups?
3. Does government sometimes create interest groups?
4. Are interest groups and their money too powerful?
5. What are PACs and "soft money"?
6. What was new and different about Roger Tamraz?
7. Which is more effective, lobbying Congress or the administration?
8. Can interest groups bypass democracy?

What Is an Interest Group?

The term **interest group** covers a wide spectrum of people and issues. In his landmark work *The Governmental Process*, David B. Truman defines an interest group as "a shared-attitude group that makes certain claims upon other groups in society" by acting through the institutions of government. Some interest groups are transient, but others are permanently organized. Many are solely interested in influencing the government's public policy, but others are only sporadically concerned with political decisions. Some work directly through the executive or administrative agencies, but others work through the judicial or legislative sectors or even through public opinion. But one crucial factor is common to all interest groups: They are all non-publicly accountable organizations that attempt to promote shared private interests by influencing public-policy outcomes that affect them.

KEY TERM
interest group   An association that tries to influence policy.

HOW INTEREST GROUPS DIFFER FROM POLITICAL PARTIES

It may seem that interest groups resemble political parties. But interest-group leaders are not elected by the general public, nor are they answerable to the people for their decisions. Both try to influence public policy. But unlike political parties, interest groups lie outside the electoral process and are thus not responsible to the public. The survival of the party depends on the people's support. Private interest groups may try to influence the nomination of candidates who are sympathetic to their cause, but the candidates run under the party banner—not the interest group banner.

Goals   The goal of the political party is to acquire power though elections. The interest group, however, is concerned with specific programs and issues and is rarely represented in the formal structure of government. The interest group tries to steer political parties and their elected officials toward certain policies rather than enacting those policies itself. Interest groups often try to win the favor of all political parties. Environmentalists want the support of both the Republicans and the Democrats in their fight to minimize ecological damage. But at times they may take a stand in favor of one party if they are convinced that that party will further their objectives with greater vigor. In most elections, environmentalists support the Democrats, but they are not wedded to them.

Nature of Memberships   Most political parties want broad enough support to win an election, drawing into their ranks different interests. Their membership is much more varied than that of the interest group. Even the conservative Republican party includes people in all income brackets and occupations, and some of its members are more liberal than many Democrats. The Democratic party, on the other hand, seen as the more progressive party of the working class, also counts all walks of life among its supporters, including wealthy people.

Interest groups generally have a more selective membership. Members of a labor union are likely to share similar living and working conditions and to have comparable educational and cultural backgrounds. Interest groups for a specific problem or issue, such as ecology or the banning of nuclear weapons, may draw their members from a wider spectrum, but even they tend to have more similarities than members of parties.

Almost Unlimited Number   For several reasons, including the length of a ballot, the number of political parties must be limited; even in multiparty political systems, all the parties can usually be counted on the fingers of both hands. But there is no functional limit on the numbers of interest groups, and some countries, such as the United States, offer a particularly fertile environment for their development. As Tocqueville observed in the 1830s, "In no country of the world has the principle of association been more successfully used or applied to a greater multitude of objects than in America." Tocqueville is still accurate. Just open a Washington, D.C., phone book to "National ..." and behold the hundreds of national associations, institutes, leagues, and committees. Much of Washington's prosperity is based on its obvious attraction as a headquarters for interest groups.

Who Belongs to Interest Groups?

In every highly organized technological society, life is maintained by a multitude of industries. There are also differences in the cultural, economic, educational, ethnic, and religious backgrounds of people. These varied categories of people and enterprises represent the raw material of interest groups.

David Truman argued that wherever there are divergent interests, there exists the potential for an interest group. Interest groups play a central role in a democratic government, and we pay considerable attention to the pressure system of organized special interest groups attempting to influence government policies. Because of our highly developed pressure system, the United States is often defined by theorists of Truman's school as a "pluralist democracy," in which a multiplicity of interest groups, all pushing their own claims and viewpoints, creates a balance of opposing interests that prevents any one group from dominating the political system. In this optimistic view, government policy is the outcome of competition among many groups, which represent the varied interests of the people. This is the classic pluralist picture discussed in Chapter 5.

The U.S. system does indeed include many rival pressure groups. But in contrast to David Truman's theory, many observers have noted that the members of these groups tend to be drawn overwhelmingly from the middle and upper classes, and that group activities are dominated by individuals with business-related interests. The mere fact of competition among rival interest groups does not guarantee a democratic system. As E. E. Schattschneider noted, "The flaw in the pluralist heaven is that the heavenly chorus sings with a strong upper-class accent." Many critics of our interest group system would agree that middle- and upper-class interests are disproportionately represented in comparison to the lower classes, which have relatively little voice.

Elite theorists argue that if David Truman's group theory really operated, the poor would organize in groups as soon as they became aware that they were poor and didn't want to be. Yet, with only sporadic exceptions, the poor, who seem to have so much to gain from collective action, have been slow in joining together to promote their common interests. When organizations or aid programs have been developed to tackle the problems of poverty, the ideas, money, and leadership often have come from outside the community. Better-off and better-educated people are much more likely to participate in politics, and this includes organizing and running interest groups. In this area, too, the poor get shortchanged.

Left on their own, the lower classes are more likely to act explosively rather than as organized groups with reasonable approaches. They have a strong sense of grievance, which has been demonstrated time after time through history. The storming of the Bastille at the start of the French Revolution is one example of how poverty-nurtured resentments boiled over into violence. In recent U.S. history, the riots in large-city ghettos reflected the anger that race-related poverty produced in many African Americans. The ghetto riots, while serving to publicize the grievances and anger that exist in certain poor communities, resulted in great destruction that hurt the people living in those communities more than anyone else. They cost their perpetrators a great deal without offering any real challenge to the power and influence of business and industry, labor unions, or other groups that the poor regard as blocking their progress. Not all sectors of society can effectively form and use interest groups.

Interest Groups and Government

Interest groups try to influence government. But what if there is no government? To take an extreme example, consider Somalia, where in the early 1990s there was no government. There were, to be sure, plenty of groups: dozens of clans and mafias, each with its own militia engaging in nearly constant fighting. Would we call these "interest groups"? Probably not. Although some interest groups engage in occasional violence, they do so in a context of trying to influence government. In Somalia, there was no government to influence; the groups fought to guard their respective "turfs." Not all clashes of groups automatically qualify as "interest-group activity."

Interest groups presuppose an existing government that is worth trying to influence. Government, in fact, virtually calls many interest groups into life, for they are intimately associated with government programs. There are farm lobbies because there are farm programs, education lobbies because there are education programs, and veterans' lobbies because in years past the government chose to go to war.

Once government is funding something, the groups that benefit develop constituencies with a strong pecuniary interest in continuing the programs. As government has become bigger and sponsored more programs, the number of interest groups has proliferated. By now, virtually every branch and subdivision of the

---

Case Studies	NDEA: HOW GOVERNMENT CREATED AN INTEREST GROUP

In 1957, the launch of the Soviets' *Sputnik*, the first earth-orbiting satellite, jolted Americans and their Congress, because it seemed to prove the Soviets were ahead of us (actually, they weren't). Congress acted. The 1958 National Defense Education Act (NDEA) put millions of dollars into university science, engineering, and foreign-area and language programs. A decade later, as enthusiasm for the last two subject areas waned (partly because of the Vietnam war), a vigorous lobby dedicated to "world education" and funded by universities that received NDEA grants tried to persuade Congress to continue the program. Congress had created a program, the program created an interest group, and then the interest group worked on Congress. This is one reason that programs, once set up, are hard to terminate.

U.S. government has one or more interest groups watching over its shoulder, demanding more grants, a change in regulations, or their own agency. The Departments of Education and Energy were created under these circumstances, and Ronald Reagan vowed to abolish them. He couldn't: The interests associated with them—in part created by them—were too powerful.

Sometimes interest groups participate in government legislation and implementation. In Britain, "interested members" of Parliament are those who openly acknowledge that they represent industries or labor unions. This is not frowned on and is considered quite normal. (Quietly selling government influence to British interest groups, however, is considered "sleaze," and has become a source of scandal.) In Sweden, interest groups are especially large and powerful. Swedish "royal commissions," which initiate most new legislation, are composed of legislators, government officials, and interest-group representatives. After a proposal has been drafted, it is circulated for comments to all relevant interest groups. Some Swedish benefits for farmers and workers are administered by their respective farm organizations and labor unions. Some call this **corporatistic**, meaning that interest groups are taking on government functions. Top representatives of business, labor, and the cabinet meet regularly in Sweden to decide a great deal of public policy. Critics charge that this too-cozy relationship bypasses parliamentary democracy altogether.

> **KEY TERM**
>
> **corporatism** The direct participation of interest groups in government.

Bureaucrats as an Interest Group

Government and interest groups are related in another very important but sometimes overlooked way: The bureaucracy has become one of the biggest and most powerful interest groups of all. Civil servants are not merely the passive implementers of laws; they also have a great deal to say in the making and application of those laws. Much legislation originates in the specialized agencies. Many of the data and witnesses before legislative committees are from the executive departments and agencies.

Needless to say, these bureaucracies develop interests of their own. They see their tasks as terribly important and so naturally think they need a bigger budget and more employees every year. When was the last time a professional civil servant—as opposed to a political appointee—recommended abolishing his or her agency or bureau? Bureaucrats have a lot of knowledge at their fingertips, and knowledge is power. When the Reagan administration came in, it said it would abolish the Department of Energy (DOE). One of the authors of this book asked a friend, an official of the department, why he wasn't worried. "They won't abolish us," he asserted knowingly. "They can't. DOE manufactures nuclear bombs, and the administration needs the DOE budget to disguise how big the nuclear-bomb budget is." He was right; Reagan did not abolish the Department of Energy.

It was earlier proposed that interest groups are offshoots of society and the economy. That is only partly true, for they are also offshoots of government.

Government and interest groups, to paraphrase Thomas Hobbes, were born twins. The more government, the more interest groups.

To say that every political system has interest groups doesn't say very much, for interest groups in different systems operate quite differently. One key determinant in the way interest groups operate is the government. Here we can refine our definition of pluralism discussed in Chapter 5. Pluralism is determined not by the mere existence of groups, each trying to influence government, but by the degree to which government permits or encourages the open interplay of groups. Pluralism has a normative component, an "ought" or a "should."

Antipluralism in Europe   The United States and Britain, for example, are considered highly pluralistic, for interest-group activity is acceptable and desirable. Many observers consider lobbying the normal functioning of a healthy democracy, with nothing **furtive** about it. In France, on the other hand, interest-group activity, although it does exist, is frowned on and considered a bit dirty. France is heir to centuries of centralized and paternalistic government. The French are used to Paris ministries setting national goals and supervising much of the nation's economic activity. Further, the philosopher Jean-Jacques Rousseau still has a powerful hold on the French mind. Rousseau argued, among other points, that there must be no "partial wills" to muddy and distort the "general will," that which the whole community wants. Rousseau presumed there was such a thing as a general will, something pluralists deny. Accordingly, interest groups are seen as trying to pervert the good of the whole community. The French bureaucratic elites pay little attention to interest groups, considering them "unobjective." French interest groups operate in a more constrained atmosphere than their American or British counterparts.

KEY TERM

furtive   Secretive; concealing one's activities.

Communist China took this a step farther. Until recently, open interest-group activity has been taboo. Chinese interests still make their case quietly, within the confines of party discussions, and do not lay claim to more than their area of professional interest. Few spontaneous, nongovernment interest groups appear openly to propose major or systemic change. The way groups function is structured by government, which can permit a lot or very little open activity.

Effective Interest Groups

Political Culture

Interest groups are most likely to flourish in democratic societies in which occupational and other contacts put individuals in touch with a wide range of people and where political participation is emphasized. The percentage of people who join organized groups differs greatly from one country to another.

In their study of political cultures, Almond and Verba noted that people in the United States, Great Britain, and Germany were more likely to participate in voluntary associations than were citizens of Italy and Mexico. Civic participation in every country increased with educational level, and in all except the United States, more men than women were participants. Not all of the groups were political, but even nonpolitical groups, by discussion among members, have some political influence. Members of a bicycle club become involved in politics when they discuss the need for more bicycle paths. One of the significant findings of the study was that in societies where many join groups, people have a greater sense of political competence and efficacy. It is with concern that political scientists have noted a decline in the U.S. tendency to form groups (see Chapter 7 on political culture).

The Rise of Big Money

Money is probably the single most important factor in interest-group success. Indeed, with enough money, interests hardly need a group. Money is especially important for elections, and groups try to secure the victory of candidates known to favor their cause. Most democracies have recognized the danger in too close a connection between interests and candidates, the danger that we will have the "best Congress money can buy." Some, such as Germany and Sweden, provide for almost complete **public financing** of the major parties in national elections. Spain, which rejoined the democracies only in 1977, subsidizes parties after the election according to how many votes they received and parliamentary seats they won.

The United States has been reluctant to go to public financing of campaigns for several reasons. First, there is the strong emphasis on freedom. The U.S. Supreme Court generally interprets the First Amendment to include dollars as a form of free speech. If a person wants to give money to a candidate, that is a political statement. Second, U.S. campaigns are much longer and more expensive than in other democracies, the result of our weak, decentralized parties and nominating system. In Western Europe, elections can be short and cheap because the parties are already in place with their candidates and platforms. And third, given these two previous conditions, American legislators have not been able to find a formula for public financing that really works in the manner intended. Some efforts turn out to have negative **unforeseen consequences**.

Some individuals and political action committees (see box on p. 176) contribute to parties and interest groups not directly working for a candidate's election campaign. This **soft money**, uncontrolled and unlimited, enables parties and groups to produce "issue ads" aimed *against* the other side without mentioning their own candidate's name, a big loophole in federal campaign laws. Soft money thus contributes to the trend toward negative advertising in political campaigns. Congress said it wanted to reform soft-money

KEY TERMS
public financing   Using tax dollars to fund something, such as election-campaign expenses.
unforeseen consequence   A negative or counterproductive result when laws or policies do not work as expected.
soft money   Campaign contributions to parties and issue groups as a way to skirt federal limits on contributions to individual candidates.

political action committee
A U.S. interest group set up
specifically to contribute money
to election campaigns.

contributions but failed to do so when legislation came up in 1998, and for an obvious reason: Congressional incumbents and their parties benefit enormously from soft money.

Some critics say this is money politics out of control; defenders say it is just pluralist democracy and the amounts are peanuts compared to the overall U.S. economy. Can or should anything be done about interest groups and money? Some suggest we go to a European-type system in which the parties are well-organized and campaigns are short and relatively cheap. But that is simply not the U.S. nominating and electoral system, which is complex and long. And Europe's interest groups still give plenty (sometimes under the table) to their favored candidates. Another solution might be to limit the amount that any company could give to a PAC and that any PAC could give. The Supreme Court rejected such limits in 1985. Public financing of all candidates—presidential nominees who gain at least 5 percent of the national vote are already entitled to federal financing—would be terribly expensive. Many U.S. taxpayers do not check off the option on their tax returns to contribute a few dollars to presidential campaigns, even though it costs them nothing. For the foreseeable future, it will not be possible to break the tie between interest groups and candidates in the United States.

Case Studies   THE RISE OF POLITICAL ACTION COMMITTEES

In 1971 and 1974 (following Watergate) Congress, thinking it was instituting important reforms, sharply limited the amount of money that individuals and corporations could contribute directly to candidates in an effort to curb the influence of "big money" in politics. (Currently, individuals may give up to $1,000 directly to a campaign.) But there was no prohibition on individuals and businesses organizing committees and donating money to them that in turn would go to desirable candidates. **Political action committees** (PACs) grew like mushrooms, from 600 in 1974 to over 5,000 now. During presidential elections, they now give in total a billion or so dollars to candidates and parties (less when only Congress is up for election). Incumbent U.S. representatives receive on average some quarter of a million dollars from PACs, perhaps half their total campaign expenses. Challengers get perhaps a tenth of that. Incumbent senators get from PACs on average some $2 million, again about half their total campaign expenses. (The rest comes from individuals, corporations, and foundations.)

Although PACs were originally an idea of labor unions, business PACs now greatly outspend labor PACs. Large corporations, many with defense contracts, are heavy PAC contributors. The bulk of contributions go to incumbents, which enables members of Congress to lock themselves into power nearly permanently. Especially favored by PACs are incumbents on committees relevant to the PACs interests (for example, farm PACs give to members of the House Agricultural Committee). The rise of PACs illustrate how interests "work around" whatever reforms are put into place.

The Rise of Single-Issue Groups

Perhaps the second greatest factor in the influence of interest groups (after money) is the intensity of the issue involved. The right issue can mobilize millions, give the group cohesion and commitment, and boost donations. There have always been American interest groups pursuing one or another idealistic objective,

KEY TERM

single-issue interest group   Interest association devoted to one cause only.

but during the 1970s the rise of **single-issue interest groups** changed U.S. politics. Typically, interest groups have several things to say about issues, for their interests encompass several programs and departments. Organized labor in the form of the AFL-CIO tries to persuade government on questions of Social Security, medical insurance, education, imports and tariffs, and the way unemployment statistics are calculated. The AFL-CIO has a long-term, across-the-board interest in Washington. The same can be said for many business groups.

But to the single-issue groups only one issue matters, and it matters intensely. Typically, their issues are moral—and therefore hard to compromise—rather than material. The most prominent single-issue group is the right to life, or antiabortion, movement. In 1973 the Supreme Court ruled that states could not arbitrarily restrict a woman's right to an abortion. Many Roman Catholics and Protestant fundamentalists were shocked, for they believe that human life begins at the moment of conception and that aborting a fetus is therefore murder. "Pro-life" people oppose, for a start, allowing any state or federal medical funds to be used for abortion, and they would like to amend the Constitution to outlaw abortion. They are opposed by the "pro-choice" forces. Abortion rights are linked to the women's movement, and feminists argue that whether or not to have an abortion is a matter for the individual woman to decide and no one else; the right

The abortion battle is being fought on the streets of this nation as well as in the courts. Abortion is a highly emotional issue that activates strongly committed interest groups on both sides. (U.S. Department of Health and Human Services)

to choose returns to women an element of control over their lives and hence is part of their liberation from second-class status.

The antiabortionists make life miserable for many senators and representatives. They care about nothing else in a representative's record—where he or she stands on taxes, jobs, defense, and so on. They want to know where he or she stands on abortion, and a compromise middle ground—the refuge of many politicians faced with controversial issues—is not good enough. How can you be a "moderate" on abortion? Some elections turn on the abortion issue. Meanwhile, the pro-choice forces organize and grow militant enough to offset the pro-life forces.

Other single-issue causes have appeared, such as prayer in public school and homosexual rights. Taken together, these two and the abortion question are sometimes referred to as the "morality issue." Gun control grew into a major issue, fanned by the assassinations of John and Robert Kennedy and Martin Luther King, Jr. The powerful National Rifle Association (NRA) opposes such groups as Handgun Control. None of these issues makes elected representatives any happier. They like to be judged on a wide range of positions they have taken, not on one narrow issue on which it is hard to compromise.

Size and Membership

Their size and the degree of commitment of their members obviously give groups clout. The biggest and fastest growing U.S. interest group is the American Association of Retired Persons, claiming over 30 million members, many of them educated, forceful, and strongly committed to their cause of preserving and

---

Case Studies   HOW POWERFUL ARE U.S. UNIONS?

Unions in the United States are not very powerful, at least in comparative perspective. Since the 1950s, the percent of American workers in labor unions has dropped by half. Approximate percentages of the workforce that is unionized:

Sweden	80%
Germany	30
Britain	25
Japan	20
United States	15
France	10

U.S. unions seem powerful because they attract much attention whey they strike at key firms, such as UPS and General Motors. Actually, their biggest numbers are among government employees at all levels, including schoolteachers, who are often prohibited from striking. Business in the United States has far more clout than unions. U.S. unions are now striving for new members to get back some of their former strength.

enhancing Social Security and Medicare. When AARP speaks, Congress trembles. Their opposition to cuts in Medicare encouraged President Clinton to veto the Republican measure in 1995.

Size alone, however, is not necessarily the most important element in interest-group strength. Money and intensity are often able to offset sheer size. Groups that claim to speak for large numbers are not appreciated if it is known that only a small fraction of the group are committed members. The National Association for the Advancement of Colored People (NAACP) claims to speak for millions of African Americans, but its actual membership is much smaller. All things being equal, a large group has more clout than a small one—but things are never equal.

The **socioeconomic status** of members gives groups clout. Better-off, well-educated people with influence in their professions and communities can form groups that get more respect. The socioeconomic status of American Jews boosted the impact of the American-Israel Public Affairs Committee (AIPAC) and other Jewish groups. As Japanese Americans climbed educationally and professionally, their Japanese American Citizens' League (JACL) started having more of an impact and won apologies for the highly unconstitutional internment of West Coast Japanese in World War II; JACL then worked on getting compensation. Respect leads to clout. This means, paradoxically and unfairly, that disadvantaged groups with the biggest grievances are among the least likely to be listened to.

> ### KEY TERMS
>
> **socioeconomic status** Combination of income and prestige criteria in the ranking of groups.
>
> **access** Ability of an interest group to get listened to.

Access

Money, issue, and size may not count for much unless people in government are willing to listen. To be sure, these ingredients help, but it is often the careful cultivation of relationships with members of Congress and civil servants over the years that makes sure that doors are open. When a group has established a stable and receptive relationship with a branch of government, it is said to enjoy, in the words of Joseph LaPalombara, structured **access**. Greek-American members of Congress are, quite naturally, receptive to Greek arguments on questions concerning Turkey, Macedonia, and Cyprus. Michigan legislators are likewise disposed to discuss the problems of the automobile industry. Arab Americans complained bitterly that Jews enjoyed too much access on Capitol Hill and organized their own groups to try to gain such access. There is nothing wrong with access as such; it is part and parcel of a working democracy.

But what happens when groups are shut out, have no access? The pluralists tend to think this can't happen in a democracy, but apparently it does. Black and Indian militants argued that no one was listening to them or taking their demands seriously. Only when violence began in urban ghettos and on Indian reservations did Washington begin to listen. When the wealthy and powerful have a great deal of access, the poor and unorganized may have none. The consequences sometimes lead to violence.

Briefly jolting Congress was the 1997 testimony of a Arab-American multimillionaire, Roger Tamraz. With a grin, Tamraz detailed to a Senate panel how he contributed $300,000 to the Democrats in 1996 in soft money to get around restrictions. (He also gives to Republicans.) Why did he do that, asked the panel. "To get access," happily admitted Tamraz, namely to the White House, which he hoped would help him with a huge pipeline deal in Central Asia. Tamraz denied any wrongdoing and told the panel: "You set the rules and we're following the rules. This is politics as usual." He was right and added with a smile, "I think next time I'll give $600,000." The only thing unusual about Tamraz is the way he spoke the truth; most lobbyists deny they seek access.

Strategies of Interest Groups

Approaching the Lawmakers

Although lobbying is not the only strategy of interest groups, it is the one that receives the most attention. The campaign contributions and favors to legislators given by some rich corporations convey the impression that lobbyists are buying Congress. Indeed, any major interest threatened by new laws spares no expense to make sure they are not passed, and they are usually successful. Big tobacco, which is especially generous to incumbent Republican candidates, routinely blocks or dilutes anti-smoking legislation. One favor big companies provide cooperative congresspersons: trips in the corporate jet. The average lobbying group, however, simply doesn't have large sums of money to toss around, so most see themselves as providers of information.

Lobbying Techniques   The approaches and techniques commonly used by lobbyists vary widely according to the types of interest the lobbyists represent and the way in which they conceive of their jobs. Political scientist Samuel C. Patterson identified three types of lobbyists: the "contact man," the "informant," and the "watchdog." The contact man promotes the interests of his group by establishing friendships with legislators to whom he can present his group's case on a person-to-person basis. The informant lobbies in public rather than in private meetings, offering testimony supporting her group's case at legislative hearings and disseminating published materials on the group's behalf. The watchdog keeps close track of what is happening in the legislature so he can alert his group to take action when the time is appropriate.

Criteria for Successful Lobbying   The success of a lobbyist's approach depends on several factors, one of which is the receptivity of legislators. Surveying lobbyists' evaluations of their various techniques, Lester Milbrath

Union made: The sign in a union hall reminds a Democratic candidate for the Senate where his support comes from. Many interest groups support candidates in the expectation of future consideration. (Michael Roskin)

found that those rated most effective by the lobbyists themselves involved direct communication between the lobbyist and the legislature. The highest-rated strategies included not only the personal presentations of viewpoints and "research results" made by the contact-man type of lobbyist to individual legislators but also the lobbyist's testimony at legislative hearings. Rated less effective were the techniques—such as contacts by constituents and close friends, letter and telegram campaigns, public relations campaigns, and publicizing voting records—that involved no personal communication between legislators and lobbyists. The lowest-rated strategies were those of "keeping channels open" between interest groups and legislators. Under this category would fall campaign work, social get-togethers, and financial contributions.

Approaching the Administration

Depending on the issue, the executive branch of government may be a better target for interest group pressure and persuasion. The interest group may not need or want a new law, merely favorable interpretation of existing rules and regulations. For this, they turn to administrators. Antipollution groups, for instance, seek tighter definitions of clean air; industry groups seek looser definitions of clean air. Interest groups concentrate their attention on the department that specializes in their own area of interest. Farm groups deal with the Department of Agriculture, public service companies deal with the Federal Power Commission, and so forth. As a rule, each department pays careful heed to the demands and arguments of groups in its area. In fact, at one time or another, many government bureaucracies have been "captured" or "colonized" by powerful pressure groups within their respective spheres of authority.

In dealing with the bureaucracy, interest groups employ about the same tactics they use with legislators, including personal contacts with officials, supplying research and factual materials, public relations and publicity campaigns, and entertaining. Some provide money; in most of the world corruption of public officials is the norm. The U.S. federal bureaucracy, it must be said, is one of the least corrupt in the world; officials caught on the take are usually political appointees and not career civil servants. One special occasion for interest groups to make their influence felt in the bureaucracy is when candidates are up for appointment to top-level government posts, including positions in the president's cabinet. At such times, interest groups may influence the choice of a nominee who is to serve in areas they regard as sensitive to their own interests.

Approaching the Judiciary

Interest groups may also seek to realize their goals through the judicial process. This is stronger in the United States than in most other countries, as the U.S. judicial system has far more power than most judiciaries, which are considered merely part of the executive branch. In countries where rule of law is strong, the courts become an arena of interest-group contention, as in Germany, where groups have made cases on abortion and worker rights before the Federal Constitutional Court.

Every year in the United States the state and federal courts hear numerous cases filed or supported by such interest groups as the American Civil Liberties Union, Sierra Club, and NAACP. In recent years the U.S. Supreme Court has dealt with several delicate and important social issues brought to it by interest groups, including women's rights, the death penalty, abortion, and school prayer. Interest

---

Case Studies	How the NAACP Used the Courts

Aware of the importance of the U.S. judicial system, especially of the Supreme Court, the National Association for the Advancement of Colored People (NAACP) focused much of its fight against racial segregation on the courts. It paid off. The legal staff of the NAACP, whose chief attorney was Thurgood Marshall (later an associate justice of the U.S. Supreme Court), successfully challenged the constitutionality of all state laws requiring racial segregation in public schools in the famous *Brown* decision of 1954. Then it went on to challenge the legality of state laws on segregation in public transportation, restaurants, lodging, and other areas. The vast changes in U.S. civil rights happened more through the courts than through legislation.

groups have generally used two methods to pursue their goals through the judicial process. The first is to initiate suits directly on behalf of a group or class of people whose interests they represent (such suits are commonly referred to as **class actions**). The second method is for the interest group to file a brief as a "friend of the court" (**amicus curiae**) in support of a person whose suit seeks to achieve goals that the interest group is also seeking.

> ### KEY TERMS
>
> **class action**   A lawsuit on behalf of a group.
>
> **amicus curiae**   A statement to a court by persons not party to a case.

Other Tactics

Government is not the only target of interest-group action. Organized interests may often choose to take their case to the public with peaceful—or not so peaceful—appeals.

Appeals to the Public   Even powerful interest groups realize the importance of their public image. For this reason, many interest groups invest considerable sums in public-relations programs and publicity campaigns to explain how they contribute to the general welfare and why their programs and policies are good for the country. For example, railroads used television to explain their case for "fair" government policies so they could stay alive and compete with trucking. The "right-to-work" lobby placed many magazine ads attacking unions for preventing nonunion people from getting or keeping jobs.

Even while investing large sums in publicity, some interest groups maintain what is popularly referred to as a "low profile," preferring to promote their objectives without advertising themselves. In such cases, groups may rely on planted news stories that promote their objectives indirectly and behind-the-scenes pressure to prevent the publication of material that they judge to be detrimental to them. The Tobacco Institute, for example, discreetly funds research that casts doubt on findings that smoking is bad for your health. The American Petroleum Institute seeks no news coverage but lets its officers be quoted as unbiased experts in the field, supposedly above the political fray.

Demonstrations   Certain special-interest organizations, such as the American Cancer Society and the Heart Fund, may have access to free advertising space and time, but most interest groups do not, and many lack the funds to purchase such publicity. Under these circumstances, a disadvantaged group may try nonviolent demonstrations as a way of publicizing and promoting their cause. The precedent for such demonstrations in modern times was provided by Mahatma Gandhi, who used this tactic against the British Raj before India gained its independence in 1947. Gandhi, who derived his inspiration for nonviolent protest from an essay on "civil disobedience" by Henry David Thoreau, written in protest against the United States-Mexican War of 1846–1848, also provided a model for the African-American leader Martin Luther King, Jr., who headed the nonviolent civil rights movement during the 1950s and 1960s.

Citizens protest plans for a toxic-waste incinerator, claiming it would bring poisonous fumes to nearby towns. In this case, well-organized local citizens beat a well-heeled corporation, which was forced to drop its plans. (Michael Roskin)

Protesters against nuclear power plants, facing the financial and political resources of power companies, felt that marching, picketing, and sometimes blocking plant entrances through sit-ins was their only option. With news media coverage of their protests, they were able to gain adherents, contributors, and sometimes access in Washington. Their powerful opponents, of course, often prevailed, leading some protesters to become frustrated and bitter.

Violent Protest   A group that loses faith in the efficacy of conventional political channels and modes of action often sees violent protest as its only alternative. Although violent protest occurs more than we would like in this country, it is not a mode of action that interest groups normally use. Rather, it is a reaction that requires a psychological buildup, nurtured by poverty, discrimination, frustration, and a sense of personal or social injustice. An outbreak of violence usually begins spontaneously as a result of an incident that sparks the pent-up anger of a frustrated group, and the momentum of mob behavior escalates the violence. The riots in minority ghettos in large cities typify such violence, which has occurred in Britain, France and other countries, as well as in the United States. The more articulate rioters claim they are simply *opposing* the violence they suffered daily at the hands of police, all levels of government, and an economy that keeps them underpaid or unemployed. Does violent protest work? Perhaps it was no coincidence that the social legislation of the Great Society was passed during a period of U.S. urban riots. The British got out of India and Palestine when outbursts of violence made the areas difficult to govern. The white government of South Africa started offering reforms only when blacks turned to violence. In certain circumstances, violence works. Americans are certainly no strangers to violence. As black radical H. "Rap" Brown put it, "Violence is as American as cherry pie."

Interest Groups: An Evaluation

Interest groups are an intrinsic part of every modern democracy. Yet how well do they serve the needs of the average citizen? Interest groups help represent a wider range of interests in the legislative process, and that's good. Many smaller organizations, however, have neither the members nor the money to make an input. Unless they are able to form coalitions, they cannot defend their interests from larger, more powerful groups. The mere fact that interest groups can articulate demands does not mean that the demands will be heeded. Resources are highly unequal among interest groups. Some are rich and powerful and have a lot of influence. Others are ignored.

There is a further problem in a system in which interest groups are accorded a prominent place: What about those individuals who are not organized into groups? Who speaks for them? Many citizens are not members or beneficiaries of interest groups. They vote for elected leaders, but the leaders usually pay more attention to group demands than to the unorganized multitude who elected them. If legislators and executives are attuned to interest groups, who is considering the interests of the whole country? At times, it seems as if no one is. Then we may begin to appreciate Rousseau's emphasis on the "general will" over and above the "particular wills" that make up society.

To try to remedy such defects, the "citizens' lobby," Common Cause, was formed in 1970. Claiming to represent the will of all in promoting good government, Common Cause, funded by voluntary subscriptions, successfully fought for public funding of presidential campaigns, an end to the congressional seniority system, and disclosure of lobbying activities. In a similar vein, Ralph Nader set up several public-interest lobbies related to law, nuclear energy, tax reform, and medical care. Although groups such as these have done much good work, they raise an interesting question: Can a society as big and complex as America's possibly be represented as a whole, or is it inherently a mosaic of groups with no common voice?

Another problem is whether interest groups really speak for all their members or represent the views of a small but vocal minority within the group? Interest-group leaders, like leaders of political parties, often have stronger ideas on issues than their followers in order to retain a favorable bargaining position. Strikes called by union leaders do not always have the full sympathy of the workers, many of whom are more interested in collecting their weekly paychecks than in bargaining for a new contract. And many women who are in favor of equal pay for equal work find the concept of abortion, as presented by many women's leaders, to be an anathema.

Stalemating Political Power

Interest groups compete with one another, and in the process they may help to limit the power and influence that any group can exercise within Congress or a government agency. However, by dispersing political power, interest groups can also stalemate government action. Certain issues have been aptly characterized as "hot potatoes" because government action in either direction will arouse a loud outcry from one group or another. Typically, such issues are ardently supported and vehemently opposed by competing groups with enough voting power and influence to drive politicians to equivocation. Government may in effect get stuck, trapped between powerful interests and unable to move on important national problems. Italy has been called a "stalemate society" for this reason.

In two-party systems especially, issues tend to be muted by political candidates who try to appeal to as broad a segment of the voting public as possible. The result is a gap between the narrow interest of the individual voter and the general promises of an electoral campaign—a gap that interest groups attempt to fill by pressing for firm political actions on certain issues. But how well do interest groups serve the needs of the average citizen? The small businessperson, the uninformed laborer, and minority groups with limited financial resources tend to get lost in the push and pull of larger interests and government. The successful interest groups, too, tend to be dominated by a vocal minority of well-educated,

---

Case Studies   BRITAIN: TOO-STRONG INTEREST GROUPS

Harvard political scientist Samuel Beer argued that British interest groups became too strong and too closely connected to government programs. Elections became little more than attempts by the two main parties to promise more and more to all manner of interest groups. Because the groups' demands were inherently in conflict, this led to what Beer called "the paralysis of public choice." Parties were no longer able to articulate overarching policies for the good of the entire nation; they were too intent on winning over this or that group.

Beer's analysis explains why many Britons elected and reelected Margaret Thatcher, for she pointedly ignored the demands of both business and labor groups to do what she believed best for the country. Many Britons thought it was high time somebody said no to the interest groups. Labor Prime Minister Tony Blair won election only because he made it clear that his party was no longer dominated by labor unions; he called his party "New Labor" and said it looked after the interests of all. Britain is a case in which interest groups became too powerful. Is this also true in the United States?

middle- and upper-class political activists. In some cases interest groups have become so effective that they overshadow parties and paralyze policymaking with their conflicting demands. The precise balance between the good of all and the good of particular groups has not yet been found.

Key Terms

access (p. 179)   political action committee (p. 176)
amicus curiae (p. 183)   public financing (p. 175)
class action (p. 183)   single-issue interest group (p. 177)
corporatism (p. 173)   socioeconomic status (p. 179)
furtive (p. 174)   soft money (p. 175)
interest group (p. 169)   unforeseen consequence (p. 175)

Key Websites

American Associated of Retired Persons.
   http://www.aarp.org/
American Civil Liberties Union.
   http://www.aclu.org/
Common Cause.
   http://www.commoncause.org/
The Feminist Majority Foundation.
   http://www.feminist.org/
Mothers Against Drunk Driving.
   http://www.madd.org/
The National Rifle Association.
   http://www.nra.org/
Examples of how organizations put pressure on sovereign governments without the use of force are Amnesty International and Human Rights Watch. These organizations advocate the basic human rights of people around the world by enlisting public and international community support in challenging governments that engage in abusive practices.
   http://www.hrw.org/hrw/ and **http://www.amnesty.org/**

Further Reference

Berry, Jeffrey M. *The Interest Group Society*, 3rd ed. New York: Longman, 1997.
Browne, William P. *Groups, Interests, and U.S. Public Policy*. Washington, D.C.: Georgetown University Press, 1998.

Cigler, Allan J., and Burdett A. Loomis, eds. *Interest Group Politics*, 4th ed. Washington, D.C.: CQ Press, 1994.

Hrebenar, Ronald J. *Interest Group Politics in America*, 3rd ed. Armonk, NY: M.E. Sharpe, 1997.

Johnson, Haynes, and David S. Broder. *The System: The American Way of Politics at the Breaking Point*. Boston, MA: Little, Brown, 1996.

Key, V. O., Jr. *Politics, Parties, and Pressure Groups*. New York: Crowell, 1958.

Olson, Mancur, Jr. *The Logic of Collective Action: Public Goods and the Theory of Groups*. New York: Schocken Books, 1968.

Rauch, Jonathan. *Demosclerosis: The Silent Killer of American Government*. New York: Random House, 1994.

Sabato, Larry J., and Glenn R. Simpson. *Dirty Little Secrets: The Persistence of Corruption in American Politics*. New York: Times Books/Random House, 1996.

Wald, Kenneth. *Religion and Politics in the United States*, 3rd ed. Washington, D.C.: 1996.

Wright, John R. *Interest Groups and Congress: Lobbying, Contributions, and Influence*. Needham Heights, MA: Allyn & Bacon, 1996.

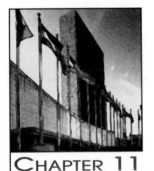

Political Parties and Party Systems

To many Americans, a **political party** doesn't mean a great deal. The two major U.S. parties often seem to be alike. Both parties share much in the way of basic values, ideologies, and proposals. Elections usually turn on the personality of the candidates rather than party affiliation. Many American political scientists worry that the parties are becoming so weak that they may fail to perform necessary political functions to keep the system running correctly.

This weakness of American parties is curious, for the United States was the first country to develop mass political parties, which appeared with the presidential election of 1800, decades before parties developed in Europe. Europeans, however, may have developed political parties more fully. Americans have tended to forget that parties are the great tools of democracy. As E. E. Schattschneider put it, "The rise of political parties is indubitably one of the principal distinguishing marks of modern government. Political parties created democracy; modern democracy is unthinkable save in terms of parties." If American parties are weakening, it may bode ill for the long-term future of American democracy. For what will take their place? Political action committees? Television campaigns? Neither prospect is appealing.

Almost all present-day societies, democratic or not, have parties that link citizens to government. Occasionally, military dictators—such as Franco in Spain, Pinochet in Chile, or generals in Brazil—try to dispense with parties, blaming them for the country's political ills. But even these dictators set up tame parties to bolster their rule, and after the dictators

> ### QUESTIONS TO CONSIDER
>
> 1. Can you have a democracy without competing parties?
> 2. What is "interest aggregation" and how do parties do it?
> 3. What good is party centralization, as in Britain?
> 4. How can a party seemingly commit electoral suicide?
> 5. How did Communist parties differ from democratic parties?
> 6. How may parties be classified on an ideological spectrum?
> 7. What is a "catchall" party?
> 8. Outline the several types of party systems.
> 9. How do competitive party systems handle corruption?

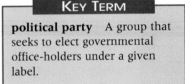

> ### KEY TERM
>
> **political party** A group that seeks to elect governmental office-holders under a given label.

189

departed free parties came out into the open almost immediately. Love them or hate them, countries seem unable to do without political parties.

Functions of Parties

In democratic systems, parties perform several important functions that help hold the political system together and keep it working.

A Bridge between People and Government

To use a systems phrase, political parties are a major "inputting" device, allowing citizens to get their needs and wishes heard by government. Without parties, individuals would stand alone and be ignored by government. By working in or voting for a party, citizens can make some impact on political decisions. At a minimum, parties give people the feeling that they are not utterly powerless, and this belief helps maintain government legitimacy, one reason even dictatorships have a party.

Aggregation of Interests

If interest groups were the highest form of political organization, government would be chaotic and unstable. One interest group would slug it out with another, trying to sway government officials this way and that. There would be few overarching values, goals, or ideologies that could command nationwide support. (Some worry that the United States already resembles this situation.) Parties help tame and calm interest group conflicts by **aggregating** their separate interests into a larger organization. The interest groups then find that they must moderate their demands, cooperate, and work for the good of the party. In return, they achieve some of their goals. Parties—especially large parties—are thus, in part, coalitions of interest groups.

> **KEY TERM**
>
> **interest aggregation** The melding of separate interests into the general demands put forward by a political party.

Integration into the Political System

As the aggregation of interest groups goes on, parties pull into the political system groups that had previously been left out. Parties usually welcome new groups into their ranks, giving them a say or input into the formation of party platforms. This gives the groups both a pragmatic and a psychological stake in supporting the overall political system. Members of the group feel represented and develop a sense of efficacy in the system and loyalty to the system. The British Labour party and the U.S. Democratic party, for example, enrolled workers with platforms stressing union rights, fair labor practices, welfare benefits, and educational opportunities. Gradually, a potentially radical labor movement learned to play by the democratic rules and support the system. Now, ironically,

Case Studies — FDR's Coalition Party

A classic example of party as coalition was the Democratic party that Franklin D. Roosevelt built in the 1930s, which helped get him elected four times. It consisted of unionized workers, farmers, Catholics, Jews, and blacks. Labor unions, for example, working with the Democrats, got labor legislation they could never have obtained on their own. As long as this coalition held together, the Democrats were unbeatable; since then the coalition has badly decayed. In the 1980s, Ronald Reagan aggregated economic and noneconomic conservative groups into the Republican party, but it too did not last.

British and American workers are so successfully integrated into the political systems that many vote Conservative or Republican. In countries where parties were unable to integrate workers into the political system, labor movements turned radical and sometimes revolutionary. In the United States, parties have also integrated successive waves of immigrants and minorities into American political life.

Political Socialization

As parties are integrating groups into society, they are also teaching their members how to play the political game. Parties introduce citizens to candidates or elected officials and teach people to speak in public, to conduct meetings, and to compromise, thus deepening their political competence and building among them a sense of legitimacy for the system as a whole. Parties are also the training grounds for leaders. Historically, some European parties attempted to set up distinct political subcultures—complete with party youth groups, soccer leagues, newspapers, women's sections, and so on. The effort was self-defeating, however, for as these parties socialized their members to participate in politics, the more they came out of the subcultures. The fading remnants of this effort can still be found in Italy in both the renamed Christian Democrats, now the Popular party, and the renamed Communists, now the Democratic Party of the Left. Some American parties even provided social services. New York's Tammany Hall served as a welcome wagon for European immigrants, helping them find jobs and housing, while enrolling them as Democrats.

Mobilization of Voters

The most obvious function of parties is getting people to vote. In campaigning for their candidates, parties are **mobilizing** voters—whipping up voter interest

KEY TERM

mobilization Getting people ready and willing to participate in something, as in rousing people to vote.

and boosting turnout. Without party advertising, many citizens would ignore elections. Most political scientists believe there is a causal connection between weak U.S. political parties and low voter turnout. In Sweden, strong and well-organized parties often produce voter turnouts of 90 percent or higher. Some critics object that party electoral propaganda trivializes politics, but even this propaganda has a function. By simplifying and clarifying issues, parties enable voters to choose among complex alternatives.

Organization of Government

The winning party gets government jobs and power and tries to shift policy to its way of thinking. The party with the most seats in the U.S. House of Representatives or Senate appoints the chamber's leaders and committee chairpersons. A new president can appoint some 3,000 people to high-level jobs in the executive departments. This allows the victorious party to put its stamp on the direction policy will take for at least four years. Party control of government in the parliamentary systems of Western Europe is tighter than in the United States because parliamentary systems give simultaneous control of both the legislative and executive branches to the winning party. What a prime minister wants, he or she usually gets, and with minimal delay, because party discipline is much stronger. In no system, however, is party control of government complete, for the already established bureaucracies of government have considerable power of their own (see Chapter 16). Parties *attempt* to control government; they don't always succeed.

Parties in Democracies

In evaluating party functions, two major factors must be considered: the degree of **centralization** in the party's organization and the extent to which a party actively participates in government policy.

Centralization

The control party leadership can exert on its elected members varies widely among democratic systems. At one extreme is Israel, whose highly centralized system of candidate selection calls for each party to draw up a national list of nominees to the parliament, or Knesset. Since Israel's system of elections uses proportional representation, 120 candidates are nominated, but only the names listed at the top of the ballot can be expected to win seats. Party chiefs can place tried and trusted people higher on the list; newcomers, lower. This helps ensure party discipline. Germany also uses party lists, but the country is divided into sixteen states in which state parties have the dominant say. Such a system decentralizes party control. In Britain, the parties select their candidates by a process of bargaining between each party's national headquarters and its local constituency organizations. The national headquarters may suggest a candidate who is not from that district—often

KEY TERM
centralization Degree of control exercised from one place, usually the nation's capital.

the case in Britain—and the local party will look the
person over to approve or disapprove the candidate.
The local party may also run its own candidate after
clearing the nomination with national headquarters.
The varying degrees of centralization of these systems

gives their parties **coherence**, discipline, and ideological consistency. When you
vote for a party in Israel, Germany, or Britain, you know what it stands for and
what it will implement if elected. Once elected, members of these parliaments do
not go their separate ways but vote according to party decisions.

Voters have less assurance of party discipline in the United States, where
parties have historically been decentralized and weak. In most cases, candidates
rely on themselves to raise funds and campaign. Candidates for the House and
the Senate, in effect, create a new local party organization every time they run.
Between elections, U.S. parties lie dormant. The Republican National
Committee and Democratic National Committee may not have many resources
to distribute to candidates. Candidates appeal directly to voters through television and other media. Increasingly, television advertisements fail even to mention the candidate's party affiliation. Candidates are thus in a position to tell
their national parties, "I owe you very little. I didn't get much party help to win,
and I won't necessarily obey you now that I'm in office." This makes U.S. parties radically decentralized and often incoherent. Elected officials answer to
their conscience, to their constituents, and to their PACs, and not to their political parties. Starting with President Reagan and continuing with the Republican
Congress elected in 1994, the Republican party became more coherent and
cohesive, but within a few years it too quarreled internally.

Setting Government Policy

One key to responsible party government is the extent to which the majority party
can enact its legislative program. Here, the American party system is exposed to its
severest criticism from advocates of strong parties. In parliamentary systems, the
majority party must resign when it can no longer muster the votes to carry on its
legislative program. In contrast, the problem in the United States is often one of
identifying exactly where the majority lies. The platform of the presidential campaign is not binding on the members of the president's party in Congress. Often
the party of the president is not the majority party in one or both houses.
Furthermore, just what is and who determines an American party's legislative program? The president? The Speaker of the House? The Senate majority leader?

In the United States, the legislative program is usually initiated centrally, with
the president. But it must be acted on by the 535 individual senators and members of Congress, all of whom are ultimately responsible for their own vote, as
they are for their own reelection. Is the president, then, to be blamed for failing
to fulfill campaign promises, or does the fault lie rather with a party discipline
that is too loose? Schattschneider argued that because U.S. national parties are so
decentralized, not one of them can agree on a strong national platform, and the

result is that the American government is "a punching bag for every special and local interest in the nation." Most Americans, however, would prefer our senators and representatives to vote according to their consciences rather than the dictates of a more distant party leadership, as is the style in Europe.

Case Studies — PARTIES THAT IGNORE VOTERS

Can a political party in a democracy ignore voters? According to democratic theory, no, for they will soon be punished and forced to change their tune. But according to "neo-institutional" theory, they can be so self-absorbed that they rumble on with little regard to what voters want. An old, established party with strong traditions and leadership patterns may be so focused on what's happening *inside* the party that they neglect public opinion *outside* the party. The party as institution can take on a life of its own apart from trying to win elections. The Communist parties of Eastern Europe and the ex-Soviet Union didn't "get it," that they were unpopular and ripe for ouster.

Two recent examples: The Canadian Progressive Conservatives (PC) and Japanese Liberal Democrats (LDP). In 1983, the PC under Brian Mulroney won elections with a majority of the House of Commons's 295 seats. Mulroney and the PC adopted Thatcherite free-market policies and stayed with them even though unemployment climbed and their popularity declined. The PC and Mulroney campaigned on the new free trade agreement (NAFTA) and won again in 1988, but with a reduced majority. A worsening economy, the Quebec problem, and alleged favoritism to certain firms brought the PC into public disrepute. Why didn't the PC change? Why didn't Mulroney resign? Eventually he did, but late in his second five-year term; he passed power to Kim Campbell, Canada's first woman prime minister, a short-lived sacrificial lamb. In the 1993 elections, the PC almost disappeared, winning only two (2!) seats out of 295. The Liberals took over Ottawa, and a new Reform party displaced the PC in Canada's west.

In Japan, the LDP under Ryutaro Hashimoto also ignored what voters were thinking. They talked about financial reforms to get Japan out of its worst slump in decades, but delivered little. Factions inside the LDP blocked and vetoed one another. Going into the 1998 elections to the (less-important) upper house of Japan's parliament, the LDP was confident of victory. Japanese voters dislike change, they thought, and would always return the LDP, which governed Japan with only one break since the war. But Japanese voters were fed up with the LDP and brought it down to minority status in the upper chamber. Hashimoto resigned in shame and was replaced by Keizo Obuchi, a colorless figure but one who lined up key factions in the LDP.

How could ruling parties seemingly shoot themselves in the foot? Don't they read the polls? They do, but dominating their parties matter more to them than the electorate. Too busy playing games inside the party, they don't notice that the party is crumbling. They institutionalized the internal patterns of their parties so strongly that they forgot their original purpose, to win elections. Actually, every time a major party loses big, it is a sign that they are too self-absorbed: the U.S. Republicans under Goldwater in 1964, the British Conservatives under Major in 1997, and the German Christian Democrats under Kohl in 1998.

Party Participation in Government

It is true that a parliamentary system of government is more conducive to what Schattschneider regards as responsible party government than the American system. Our system, with its rigid set of checks and balances, can make it difficult for parties to bridge the separation of powers in order to enact platforms. But this is not entirely the fault of the American party system. It is inherent in the constitutional separation of powers between the executive and legislative branches. Occasionally, when a powerful president controls both the White House and Congress, party platforms may turn into law, as when Lyndon Johnson got his **Great Society** program through the Democratic Congress of 1965–1966. No European parliamentary system had ever passed so many sweeping reforms so quickly.

> **KEY TERMS**
>
> **Great Society** Ambitious program of social reforms initiated by President Johnson.
>
> **political appointee** One who gets a government job by virtue of support for winning party or candidate.

Still, party participation in government is stronger in Western Europe because in parliamentary systems the winning party is the government, or more precisely, the leadership team of the winning party becomes the cabinet. This parliamentary system allows for more clear-cut accountability and voter choice than does the decentralized American party system. In both systems, parties participate in government by providing jobs for party activists in departments and agencies. In Britain, about 100 members of the winning party's parliamentary faction take on cabinet and subcabinet positions, compared to the 3,000 Americans who can receive **political appointments** when a new president takes office.

The Party in Communist States

Communist systems—that is, countries ruled by Communist parties—have become rare. In Eastern Europe and the Soviet Union, most Communist parties were voted out of power. China, Vietnam, North Korea, and Cuba tried to preserve the classic Communist system of a party-controlled state, but they too appeared ripe for change.

The "classic" Communist system founded by Lenin and developed by Stalin in the Soviet Union featured the interlocking of a single party with government and the economy. The Communist party did not rule directly; instead it supervised, monitored, and controlled the personnel of the state and economic structures. Members were hand-picked from among the most intelligent, energetic, and enthusiastic. Most Soviet officials wore two hats, one as government functionary and another as Communist party member. Every level of government, from local to national, had a corresponding party body that nominated its candidates and set its general lines of policy. At the top of the state structure, for example, was the legislature—the Supreme Soviet. Corresponding to it in the

Politburo   Russian for "political bureau"; the top group ruling a Communist party.

opportunist   A person who is out for himself or herself.

apparatchik   Russian for "person of the apparatus"; full-time Communist party functionary.

mass party   A party that attempts to gain as many adherents as possible.

cadre party   A party run by a few political professionals.

devotee party   A party based on a single personality.

party system, the Central Committee oversaw the nomination of candidates to the Supreme Soviet, set its agenda, and guided its legislative outcomes. Supervising the Central Committee, the **Politburo** of a dozen or so top party leaders was the real heart of Soviet governance. Guiding the Politburo was the party's general secretary, who could appoint loyal followers to high positions and thus amass great power.

Why did Soviet President Mikhail Gorbachev deliberately undermine this structure? A single party that attempts to control everything important in society develops severe problems over the years. Because it gives members the best jobs, housing, and consumer goods, the party fills up with **opportunists**, many of them corrupt. The party **apparatchiks** also become highly conservative. The system favors them, and they have no desire to reform it. With such people supervising it, the Soviet economy ran down and fell farther behind the American, West European, and Japanese economies. A Communist party that was to lead the Soviet Union into a radiant future came to be seen as leading the country backwards. Gorbachev came to the conclusion that to save his country he had to break the Communist party's monopoly on power. Gorbachev failed to understand (as did many Western political scientists) how brittle the system was. Unable to reform, it collapsed.

The Soviet experience suggests that single parties that monopolize power are not workable long-term solutions. Without the invigorating elements of debate, competition, and accountability, Communist-type parties become corrupt,

Classic Works   DUVERGER'S THREE TYPES OF PARTIES

One of the first scholars to formulate a scheme for classifying political parties was French political scientist Maurice Duverger, who developed three descriptive categories: mass, cadre, or devotee. The **mass parties** include Western democratic parties, which vie for members by attempting to cut across class lines and which seek the largest membership possible. In contrast, **cadre parties**, such as the Chinese or Vietnamese Communist parties, draw their support from a politically active elite and have strongly centralized organizations. Duverger uses the term **devotee** for parties such as the Nazis under Hitler, where the party's formal structure is built around one person. Such parties, now rare, are now found in Yugoslavia under Milošević's Socialist party and Iraq under Saddam Hussein's Ba'ath (Arab Renaissance) party.

inflexible, and unable to handle the new challenges and complex tasks of a modern world. Study Communist systems while you can, for soon there may be none left.

Classifying Political Parties

One important way to classify parties is on a left-to-right spectrum, according to party ideology (see Chapter 6). Left-wing parties, such as Communists, propose leveling of class differences by nationalizing major industries (that is, putting them under government control and ownership). Center-left parties, such as the socialist parties of Western Europe, favor welfare states but not nationalizing industry. Centrist parties, such as the German and Italian Liberals, are generally liberal on social questions but conservative (that is, free market) on economics. Center-right parties, such as the German Christian Democrats, want to rein in (but not dismantle) the welfare state in favor of free enterprise. Right-wing parties, such as the British Conservatives under Thatcher, want to dismantle the welfare state, break the power of the unions, and promote vigorous capitalist growth. Sweden has a rather complete political spectrum (see Figure 11.1).

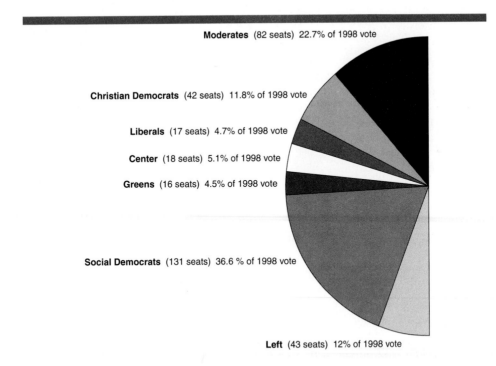

Moderates (82 seats) 22.7% of 1998 vote

Christian Democrats (42 seats) 11.8% of 1998 vote

Liberals (17 seats) 4.7% of 1998 vote

Center (18 seats) 5.1% of 1998 vote

Greens (16 seats) 4.5% of 1998 vote

Social Democrats (131 seats) 36.6 % of 1998 vote

Left (43 seats) 12% of 1998 vote

Figure 11.1 *An ideological spectrum: Swedish parties, their number of seats (out of 349), and their percent of the national vote in the 1998–2002 Riksdag (parliament).*

Classic Works | Kirchheimer's "Catchall" Party

Accompanying the general drift of most democracies to two-plus party systems has been the growth of big, sprawling parties that attempt to appeal to all manner of voters. Before World War II, many European parties were ideologically narrow and tried to win over only certain sectors of the population. Socialist parties were still at least partly Marxist and aimed their messages largely at the working class. Centrist and conservative parties aimed at the middle and upper classes, agrarian parties at farmers, Catholic parties at Catholics, and so on. These were called **Weltanschauung** parties because they tried not merely to win votes but also to promote their view of the world.

After World War II, Europe changed a lot. As prosperity increased, people began to think that the old ideological narrowness was silly. In most of Western Europe big, ideologically loose parties that welcomed all voters either absorbed or drove out the *Weltanschauung* parties. The late German political scientist Otto Kirchheimer coined the term **catchall** to describe this new type of party. His model was the German Christian Democratic party, a party that sought to speak for all Germans: businesspersons, workers, farmers, Catholics, Protestants, women, you name it. The term now describes virtually all ruling parties in democratic lands; almost axiomatically, they've got to be catchall parties to win. The British Conservatives, Spanish and French Socialists, and Japanese Liberal Democrats are all catchall parties. And, of course, the biggest and oldest catchall parties of all are the U.S. Republicans and Democrats.

Most political scientists welcome this move away from narrowness and rigidity, but with it comes another problem. Because catchall parties are big and contain many viewpoints, they are plagued by factional quarrels. Struggles between parties have in many cases given way to struggles within parties. Virtually every catchall party has several factions. Scholars counted many factions in the Italian Christian Democrats and Japanese Liberal Democrats, parties that resembled each other in their near-feudal division of power among the parties' leading personalities. A good deal of American politics also takes place within rather than between the major parties.

Financing Political Parties

Every party must finance its activities, and these are increasingly expensive. In 1976, an estimated $540 million was spent on all U.S. political campaigns—presidential, congressional, state, and local. Just four years later, in 1980, an estimated $1 *billion* was spent for all political campaigns. Sixteen years later, in 1996, it was $2.2 billion. And it keeps growing. (In contrast, total spending in the 1997 British general elections was only $82 million, but it too is growing rapidly.) In every democratic country, parties have become desperate to raise money. Some do it crookedly. Almost every democratic country has recently suffered scandals related to party fund-raising. The problem may be incurable, related to the political competition that is the crux of democracy. Said California political boss Jesse

Unruh, "Money is the mother's milk of politics," something that British, French, German, Russian, Japanese, and many other politicians would in candor agree with.

Most democracies have laws that restrict or sharply regulate political contributions from external sources, such as corporations and unions. Germany, Spain, Sweden, and Finland use government funds to subsidize political parties in proportion to each party's electoral strength. This obviously discriminates against new parties. The U.S. Congress in 1974 passed a similar plan (the Presidential Campaign Fund), which allowed taxpayers to authorize the Internal Revenue Service to donate $3 of their income tax payment to the fund; this fund subsidized presidential nominees in proportion to the votes they received, provided they got a minimum of 5 percent of the nationwide vote. But only one taxpayer in four authorizes the checkoff, far too little to cover campaign expenses. The Fund was ended by the Republican Congress in 1995. Political action committees (PACs; discussed in Chapter 10) have filled the vacuum with a vengeance. Now U.S. parties rely more and more on PACs, deepening the influence of interest groups.

> ### KEY TERMS
>
> **Weltanschauung** German for "worldview"; a party that attempts to sell a particular ideology. (See p. 198.)
>
> **catchall** A large, ideologically loose party that welcomes all. (See p. 198.)
>
> **party system** How parties interact with each other.
>
> **electoral system** How each country conducts its elections; two general types: single-member district and proportional.

Party Systems

There is a logical distinction between "parties" and "party systems." *Parties*, as discussed, are organizations aimed at influencing government, usually by winning elections. **Party systems** are the interactions of parties with each other and with the overall political system. Much of the health of a political system depends on the party system, whether it is stable or unstable, whether it has too many parties, and whether they compete in a "center-seeking" or "center-fleeing" manner. An unstable party system can wreck an otherwise good constitution. Stable, moderate party systems made democracy possible in West Germany after Hitler and in Spain after Franco. In turn, much of the country's party system depends on its **electoral system**—whether it is based on single-member districts or on proportional representation.

Classifying Party Systems

The One-Party System The one-party system, generally associated with totalitarian regimes of the left or right, is a twentieth-century phenomenon. The Soviet Union, China, and many of the emerging nations of Africa and Asia are or were one-party states. These are characterized by a single party that controls every level of government and is the only party legally allowed in the country.

Key Concepts | WHAT IS A "RELEVANT" PARTY?

Columbia University political scientist Giovanni Sartori asks pointedly just what counts as a party? Every group that calls itself a party? Every group that wins a certain percentage of votes or at least one seat in parliament? We should count as "relevant parties," Sartori argues, those which the main parties have to take into account either in campaigning for votes or in forming coalitions. If a party is so small and weak that no major party needs to worry about trying to win over its adherents, it is irrelevant. Likewise, if it is unnecessary in forming a governing coalition, it is irrelevant. Thus, British Trotskyists and Irish Communists are ignored by all and don't count as parties, but Sweden's Liberals and Israel's small religious parties, each with only a few percentages of the vote, may be nec-essary coalition partners and thus count as relevant parties.

Using Sartori's definition of "relevant" parties, would we include various American third-party efforts? Although the Democrats in 1948 denied the importance of the States' Rights party (Dixiecrats) and in 1968 the importance of Wallace's forces, in both elections they took them into account. In 1968, Democratic nominee Hubert Humphrey visited the South and emphasized that the Democratic party was a "very big house" that could accommodate many view-points, a lame attempt to make southern voters forget the strong civil rights reforms of the Johnson administration. In 1980, the independent candidacy of John Anderson probably forced President Carter to emphasize foreign and ecological policies he might otherwise have minimized. In 1992, Ross Perot forced Bush and Clinton to pay more attention to the feder-al budget deficit. In these cases, we could say the United States had relevant third parties. The tiny Communist, Socialist Worker, and Socialist Labor parties no one has to take into account, so under Sartori's definition we should not consider them relevant. The jury is still out on the Libertarian party, an extreme freemarket party that pledges the near dismantling of the federal government.

The leaders of such parties rationalize that they are still democratic because they represent what the people really want and need. No fair election or honest public-opinion poll can substantiate this claim. When allowed, as in East European countries, citizens repudiate the one-party system. Some developing lands, especially in Africa, argue that having several parties spells chaos and vio-lence, for they would form along tribal lines.

The Dominant-Party System   In contrast to one-party systems, opposition parties in dominant-party systems are free to contest elections, but they rarely win. Some democratic nations have dominant-party systems. Since winning independence in 1947, India has been governed mostly by the Congress party. Although it has occasionally been voted out, the opposition parties are often too fragmented to win or govern effectively. Similarly, the Liberal Democratic party of Japan so consistently won that Japan was called a "one-and-a-half party system," with the much smaller Socialists being the half party. Many Japanese now hope that a two-party system will emerge. In Mexico, the Party of Revolutionary Institutions (PRI) has also dominated at the national level since 1929, but not completely democratically. The more conservative National Action party (PAN) and more radical Democratic Revolutionary party threatened civil disobedience if PRI's voting fraud did not cease. Mexico, a dominant-party system with a touch of single-party dictatorship, seems to be giving way to true multiparty competition.

The Two-Party System   Most familiar to us is the two-party system, found in the United States and Britain. Here, two major parties have a fairly equal chance of winning. Although third parties, such as that of Ross Perot's presidential attempts and Britain's Liberal Democrats, seldom win, they serve to remind the two big parties of voter discontent. Often one or both of the two main parties will then offer policies calculated to win over the discontented. In this way, even small third parties can have an impact. Some observers argue that new political ideas come mostly from third parties, as the big parties are too stuck in their ways.

The Multiparty System   On the other end of the continuum from one-party nations are those with several competing parties. The Swedish party system (as we saw in Figure 11.1) shows how its parties, arrayed on a left-to-right spectrum, receive seats in parliament in proportion to their share of the vote. This system is often criticized as being unstable. Israel and Italy are examples of the shortcomings of having many parties, as each has been unable to keep any

---

MULTIPARTY SYSTEMS ARE MORE FUN

In a multiparty system, you get to choose from a bigger menu. With several relevant parties to choose from, as in Sweden (see Figure 11.1 on p. 197), you can find a party that matches your preferences much better than just the two big U.S. parties, which give you a choice between Coca Cola and Pepsi Cola. In most of Europe, people concerned about the environment can vote for a Green party. Serious Christians can vote for a Christian Democratic party. People with a leftist slant can vote for a Socialist party, conservatives for a Conservative party.

True, U.S. ballots (depending on the state) may list more than a dozen parties, ranging from Green to Libertarian to Socialist Workers, but if you vote for them you know you are throwing your vote away. Such is the impact of our winner-take-all electoral system (see following), so a vote for a third-party in the United States is simply a protest vote. Voters in much of Europe and in Israel know they are not throwing their votes away; if their party gets some minimum threshold (5 percent in Germany, 1.5 percent in Israel), the party wins some seats in parliament. The interesting choices on European ballots helps explain Europe's higher voter turnout.

KEY TERMS

cabinet instability Frequent
changes of cabinet.

immobilism Getting stuck
over a major political issue.

two-plus party system
Country having two big and
one or more small parties.

government in power for a long time. It is usually true that
the existence of many political parties makes it harder for any
one party to win a governing majority, but this is not always
the case. The Netherlands, Sweden, and Norway generally
manage to construct stable multiparty coalitions that govern
effectively. The number of parties is not the only reason for
cabinet instability. Much depends on the political culture,
the degree of agreement on basic issues, and the rules for
forming and dissolving a cabinet. Scholars have spent considerable effort debating which is better, two-party or multiparty systems. It's hard to say, for both have fallen prey to indecision and
immobilism. In the meantime, there has been a drift in both systems toward
a middle ground, "two-plus" party systems.

The Two-Plus Party System   Many democratic countries now have two large
parties with one or more relevant smaller parties. Germany has large Christian
Democratic and Social Democratic parties, but the Free Democratic and Green
parties win enough votes to make them politically important. Austria was long
dominated by two big parties, but recently a third party, the highly nationalistic
and anti-immigrant Freedom party, made major gains. Britain is often referred to
as a two-party system, but it has long had third parties of some importance: the
Liberal Democrats, the Scottish Nationalists, and Plaid Cymru (the Welsh nationalists). Even Spain, which has a history of multiparty fragmentation, now has a
two-plus party system: a large Socialist party, a large center-right Popular
party, and a scattering of smaller parties.

To be honest, we should also call the U.S. system two-plus, for it too has long
had third parties, some of which were mentioned earlier. In 1912 Teddy
Roosevelt stalked out of the Grand Old Party (GOP) with his "Bull Moose
Republicans," splitting his party and giving the election to Wilson and the
Democrats. In 1948, some southern Democrats ran as "Dixiecrats." In 1968,
Governor George Wallace of Alabama won nearly 10 million votes for his implic-
itly racist American Independent party. The label "two-party" doesn't do justice
to the complexity of U.S. politics.

As long as there are at least two parties, we call the system a "competitive
party system." Even if there are only two parties, and they are not far apart ideologically (as in the United States), the essence of a competitive party system
continues—which is to impede corruption. A single party that locks itself in
power, whatever its ideological rationale, inevitably becomes corrupt. Corruption
can be kept in check only by the "out" party or parties hammering away at
alleged corruption in the administration of the "in" party. The utility of a competitive party system was underscored in 1989 in East Germany, where
Communist leaders were revealed to have skimmed millions from foreign-trade
deals and stashed them in Swiss banks for personal use. Such antics are generally short-lived in competitive party systems, for the "ins" are soon out.

Classic Works | SARTORI'S TYPES OF PARTY COMPETITION

Giovanni Sartori (see box on p. 200), among others, is not satisfied with simply counting the number of parties to classify party systems. Also important is the degree and manner in which the parties *compete*. The term *multiparty system* does not differentiate between those systems that are stable and those that are unstable. Sartori's scheme does; it delineates party systems of "moderate pluralism" from those of "polarized pluralism."

In the former, there are usually five parties or fewer, and they compete in a "center-seeking" or centripetal manner; that is, their platforms and promises appeal to middle-of-the-road voters. Left-wing parties curb their radicalism and right-wing parties dampen their conservatism, for both know that the bulk of the voting public is somewhere nearer the center. Thus, political life in moderate pluralism tends to be calm and stable, with ideological considerations toned down.

When the number of parties is greater than five or six, Sartori believes, there is the danger of polarized pluralism. Here, the parties may compete in a "center-fleeing" or centrifugal manner. Instead of moderating their positions, parties become ideologically extreme and engage in a "politics of outbidding" with their rivals. Many of the parties offer more and more radical solutions, either radical left or radical right. Some of the parties are "antisystem" or revolutionary. Parties that try to stick to the center find themselves attacked from both sides. Such a situation causes political instability, sometimes leading to civil war, as in Spain in the 1930s, or to military takeover, as in Chile in 1973.

The Party System and the Electoral System

How a given nation gets its party system is often difficult to determine. Much is rooted in its unique historical developments. Some very different countries have similar party systems: Culturally segmented India produced a dominant party system (under the Congress party), as did culturally homogeneous Japan (under the Liberal Democrats). Single-factor explanations will not suffice, but political scientists generally agree on the importance of the electoral system, which we shall review in greater detail in Chapter 13.

Single-member election districts, such as U.S. congressional districts, where a simple plurality wins, tend to produce two-party or two-plus systems. The reason is not hard to understand: Small third parties are grossly underrepresented in such systems and often give up trying. Such is the case in the United States and Britain, based on the original English model. The British call this the "first past the post" (FPTP) system, as it resembles a horse race; even a nose better wins. There is a big premium in single-member districts on combining political forces to form the party with a majority or at least a plurality. If one party splits, it often throws the election to the party that hangs together. The factions within a party may not love each other, but they know they've got to stay together to have any political future. This factor goes a long way toward explaining why the two big American parties stay together despite considerable internal differences.

Proportional representation allows and perhaps even encourages parties to split. Proportional systems use multimember districts and assign parliamentary seats in proportion to the percentage of votes in that district. In the Anglo-American single-member districts, the winner takes all. In multimember districts, winners take just their percentage. Accordingly, not such a big premium is placed on holding parties together; a splinter group may decide that it can get one or two people elected without having to compromise with other viewpoints. Israel's proportional representation system helps in this way to produce its many small parties. As we will discuss in Chapter 13, modification of electoral laws can change a country's party system, pushing a country from a multiparty to a two-plus system, as in Germany, from a multiparty system to a "two-bloc" system, as in France, or from an exceedingly fragmented multiparty system to a moderate one, as in Poland.

The U.S. Party System: Could It Be Different?

There's a great deal of valid criticism of American political parties. Because they are so dependent on affluent donors and PACs, they are open to immoderate special-interest influence. Because they are so weakly organized and so highly decentralized—in effect, every congressional district and state has its own parties, little related to each other—the parties do not cohere well at the national level and are rarely able to articulate clear-cut platforms and policy goals. Because there are only two main parties, each usually aiming for the political center, they are not able to offer voters an extensive menu to choose from. Most political scientists agree that U.S. parties, especially in contrast to their West European counterparts, are weak.

Can anything be done about this? Parties and party systems are rooted in their countries' history, society, and institutions. The U.S. Constitution never recognized parties, and the Founding Fathers warned against them. American society is not terribly fragmented; it may not need more than two parties to express the general divisions within the population. And, of course, the single-member district with a simple plurality win favors a two-party system. Realistically, we can expect no major change in America's two-party system.

But could there be changes in the way the two parties function? Already there may be some move toward party centralization. President Reagan made the Republicans a more thoroughly conservative party with a reasonably clear program. This continued when disciplined House Republicans passed their "Contract With America" in 1995. These policy initiatives have forced the Democrats to get their often incoherent act together. Some of the "reforms" the Democrats had carried out in the 1970s proved to have weakened and divided the party; the reforms themselves had to be reformed. Technology is helping to centralize the parties. Computerized mailing lists are a powerful inducement for state and local party organizations to cooperate with national headquarters. The national party committees can also channel PAC money to loyal candidates. In the long run, this may make the two parties more cohesive and ideologically consistent.

There may be a certain advantage in *not* having strong parties. Strong parties may fall into the hands of oligarchic leaders who control too much and stay on too long, getting the party stuck in rigid and outmoded viewpoints. The U.S. system, by virtue of its very fluidity, may be better able to process demands from a wider range of citizens. The lack of programmatic coherence confers the benefit of flexibility.

Key Terms

apparatchik (p. 196)

cabinet instability (p. 202)

cadre party (p. 196)

catchall (p. 199)

centralization (p. 192)

coherence (p. 193)

devotee party (p. 196)

electoral system (p. 199)

Great Society (p. 195)

immobilism (p. 202)

interest aggregation (p. 190)

mass party (p. 196)

mobilization (p. 191)

opportunist (p. 196)

party system (p. 199)

Politburo (p. 196)

political appointee (p. 195)

political party (p. 189)

two-plus party system (p. 202)

Weltanschauung (p. 199)

Key Websites

The ANC is the majority party in South Africa's Government of National Unity.
   http://www.anc.org.za/
The Communist Party U.S.A.
   http://www.hartford-hwp.com/cp-usa/
Democratic National Committee.
   http://www.democrats.org/index.html
Green Parties of North America.
   http://www.greens.org/
This site details the events in the development of Green party politics. It also provides links and sources to various Green political parties, gathering information and opinions throughout the world.
   http://utopia.knoware.nl/users/oterhaar/greens/intlhome.htm
Libertarian Party.
   http://www.lp.org/lp.html

The Party of European Socialists (PES) brings together the Socialist, Social
Democratic, and Labour parties of the European Union, Cyprus, Norway,
and the countries of Central and Eastern Europe.
http://www.pes.org/

Republican National Committee.
http://www.rnc.org/

Ross Perot's Reform Party. (Jesse Ventura became the first Reform Party candidate to win statewide office as Governor of Minnesota.)
http://www.reformparty.org/

Further Reference

Aldrich, John H. *Why Parties? The Origin and Transformation of Political Parties in
America*. Chicago, IL: University of Chicago Press, 1995.

Alexander, Herbert E. *Financing Politics: Money, Elections, and Political Reform*, 4th
ed. Washington, D.C.: CQ Press, 1992.

Beck, Paul Allen. *Party Politics in America*, 8th ed. New York: Longman, 1997.

Duverger, Maurice. *Political Parties: Their Organization and Activities in the Modern
State*, 3rd ed. London: Methuen, 1964.

Epstein, Leon D. *Political Parties in Western Democracies*. New York: Praeger, 1967.

Keefe, William J. *Parties, Politics, and Public Policy in America*, 8th ed. Washington,
D.C.: CQ Press, 1998.

Mair, Peter. *Party System Change: Approaches and Interpretations*. New York: Oxford
University Press, 1997.

Rosenstone, Steven J., Roy L. Behr, and Edward H. Lazarus. *Third Parties in
America: Citizen Response to Major Party Failure*, 2nd ed. Princeton, NJ:
Princeton University Press, 1996.

Sartori, Giovanni. *Parties and Party Systems: A Framework for Analysis*. New York:
Cambridge University Press, 1976.

Schattschneider, E. E. *Party Government*. New York: Holt, Rinehart & Winston,
1942.

Ware, Alan. *Political Parties and Party Systems*. New York: Oxford University Press,
1996.

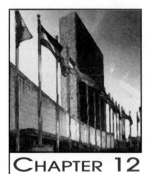

CHAPTER 12

Voting

In this chapter we ask three general questions about voting behavior, each followed by a more specific question about voting in the United States. First, we ask why people vote. This leads us to the puzzle of why voting turnout in the United States is so low. Second, we ask how people vote. This brings us to the question of whether party loyalties in the United States are declining or merely shifting. Finally, we ask what wins elections. This takes us to some of the strategies used in U.S. elections.

Why Do People Vote?

Although they are committed to democracy and participation, Americans vote considerably less than citizens of other democracies. In the 1996 election, only 49 percent of those eligible to vote in the United States bothered to cast a ballot. And historically, voter **turnout** in the United States was never very high; its peak in 1960 was still only 63 percent. Election turnout in Sweden, Germany, and Italy sometimes tops 90 percent. Black South Africans in 1994 had not been allowed to vote, yet turnout was 86 percent, perhaps a measure of how much they appreciated the right to cast a democratic ballot.

In nonpresidential elections, U.S. turnout is even worse, perhaps a quarter to a third. Why do Americans have such a poor voting record? Typically, more than half of U.S. nonvoters say they aren't interested in or are dissatisfied with the candidates. Many feel their vote won't make a difference; even more feel that none of the candidates is

> **QUESTIONS TO CONSIDER**
>
> 1. Should we view U.S. non-voting with alarm?
> 2. If educated people participate more, why has U.S. voting declined precisely as education has increased?
> 3. What age group votes the least? Why?
> 4. How does party identification help decide elections?
> 5. Why is there a "gender gap" in U.S. voting?
> 6. How well does income predict how a person votes?
> 7. Are we seeing electoral realignment, dealignment, or neither?
> 8. Has much of the world gone to U.S.-style elections, where the candidates' personalities matter most?
> 9. How does the economy influence elections?

> **KEY TERM**
>
> **turnout** Percent of those eligible who vote.

really good. Another reason is the U.S. party system, in which the two large parties may not offer an interesting or clear-cut choice; both tend to stick to centrist positions. In addition, television saturates voters so long in advance—often with primitive, dirty political spots—that many voters are disgusted with both parties by election day. Fewer than one adult American in twenty is involved enough in politics to attend a political meeting, contribute money, or canvass a neighborhood.

U.S. nonvoting has inspired a major debate among political scientists. One school views the decline with alarm, arguing that low electoral participation means that many Americans are turning away from the political system, which in turn is losing its legitimacy and authority. If this keeps up, democracy itself could be threatened. Another school is more sanguine, arguing that the decline may mean that Americans are basically satisfied with the system, or at any rate not sufficiently dissatisfied to go to the effort of registering and voting. Indeed, countries with very high voter turnouts may be suffering from a sort of political fever in which partisan politics has become dangerously intense.

Why the difference between European and American turnout? One obvious reason is that in Europe registration is automatic; upon reaching eighteen local authorities register you. In contrast, America's residency laws and registration procedures can present an obstacle to the would-be voter. The citizen, not the government, has to make sure that any change of name or residency is officially recorded. This may require a visit to city hall or county courthouse months before the election. By the time that campaign excitement mounts, the deadline for registration is often past. Further, elections are held on working days (in much of Europe, voting takes place on Sundays), and the lineup of local, state, and national candidates is often enough to baffle all but those who have the choices in advance. European ballots are simple, usually just a choice of party, and all European countries strictly control and limit television political advertising; some allow none. America might take a hint.

Who Votes?

The typical voters in almost every democracy tend to be middle-aged, better educated, and have white-collar jobs. They are more likely to live in a city than in the country. And they are more likely to identify strongly with a political party. Nonvoters tend to show the reverse of these characteristics: young, lacking education, and have blue-collar or no jobs. Income and education, race, age, gender, and area of residence are key factors in who votes.

Income and Education   People with high incomes vote more than the less affluent, just as people who are well educated vote more compared to high-school dropouts. Are they in fact the same individuals? Not quite, for a wealthy person who did not finish high school is almost as likely to vote as a wealthy college graduate. These two characteristics often come together (good education makes it easier to earn a good salary) and reinforce each other. High income gives

Classic Works   DOWN'S THEORY OF VOTING

In a landmark 1957 work, *An Economic Theory of Democracy*, Anthony Downs theorized that people will vote if the returns outweigh the costs. That is, if the stakes seem important enough, the citizen will go to the trouble of voting. Thus, the person whose property taxes stand to be raised if a new school bond is passed is much more likely to vote on the issue than his or her neighbor who rents an apartment and will not be hurt by the tax. The cost of political information, both financial and personal, is also influential in determining whether a person will vote. The price of a newspaper, the sacrifice of switching from a favorite television show to watch the news, and the time involved in attending a political meeting all tend to prevent political information from being distributed equally to everyone because each person places a different value on personal time and political awareness. The result is that the poor and the uneducated in every society are the least likely to vote.

people a stake in election outcomes, and education raises levels of interest and sophistication.

Assembly-line workers living in small towns may see little difference between candidates. They are accustomed to paying taxes, following rules, and making a living. They see little or no difference in the way they fare under a Democratic administration as opposed to a Republican one and have little stake in the election's outcome. In contrast, corporation presidents feel involved in the election. They see a direct relationship between who wins and their personal fortune, which will be affected by changes in international monetary policy, personal and corporate tax rates, interest rates, and a score of other policies. Blue-collar workers may also be affected by a change in administration, but they are less likely to know it.

The difference between voters and nonvoters is a feeling of *efficacy*, the feeling that one has at least a little power. It tends to be low for workers and high for executives. Better-off and better-educated people have seen interest groups succeed in changing government policy, if only by successfully influencing the local school board. Blue-collar workers are likely to see political life from inside a "silent majority" subculture. Friends, neighbors, and family rarely had much wealth and have never organized to pressure the government successfully.

Well-educated people have broader interests in elections beyond personal economic stakes. The college-educated person—whether wealthy or not—tends to be more interested, better informed, and more likely to participate in elections. As our discussion in Chapter 7 indicates, schooling provides a sense of the importance of political participation and a more abstract intellectual curiosity, which makes people more likely to follow political news and feel involved in events. Much research shows that education is the strongest determinant of who votes.

Race   Despite federal laws and black organizations, black voting rates are lower than white. The gap may eventually close as black income and education levels rise. The 1965 Voting Rights Act overcame some of the barriers placed in the way of black registration, chiefly in the South. Many blacks have gone through political consciousness-raising and learned the value of participation and voting. Some previously racist white politicians got the message and became respectful toward their black constituents. Latinos faced similar problems and also showed low turnouts. Race, accordingly, is still a factor in U.S. election turnout.

Age   Young people—those under twenty-five—typically feel less politically involved than those who are older; accordingly, they vote less. About half of U.S. citizens eighteen to twenty-five are currently not registered to vote. (This is probably not the case in your political science class, first because you are college students and second because you're at least a little interested in politics.) Nonvoting among the young parallels our discussion of income and voting. Young people, with lower incomes and little property, don't feel economically involved with election outcomes. When they start paying substantial taxes, they become much more interested. Focused on the concerns of youth, many have no time or interest in political questions, which seem abstract and distant. When jobs become a major issue, however, younger people quickly take an interest.

In 1971 the Twenty-sixth Amendment lowered the U.S. voting age from twenty-one to eighteen at almost the same time that most other democracies did. The results were similar: The newly **enfranchised** young people didn't vote as much as their elders, and when they did vote, their preferences weren't much different. Middle-aged and older people are more likely to vote than the young, probably because the middle-aged person is at a peak in earning power and the old

KEY TERM

franchise   Right to vote.

Black voter registration in recent decades has enfranchised a group of citizens who previously had little political clout but who now are courted by candidates of both parties. (Laima E. Druskis)

THE PUZZLE OF EDUCATION
AND VOTING IN THE UNITED STATES

All studies agree that education makes people more participatory. But the declining U.S. turnout is happening precisely as U.S. educational levels are *growing*. America has the highest percentage of both young people in college and college-educated citizens. That should make us very participatory and with rising voter turnouts.

No one has really cracked this seeming puzzle. Education may not mean what it used to. The sheer numbers of U.S. college graduates have diluted its former elite status. A college degree, in terms of getting a job nowadays, is more like a high-school diploma before World War II. Many majors are vocational or career-related and do not awaken intellectual curiosity or knowledge of the nation and world.

And perhaps voting does not mean what it used to. Even well-educated citizens may not see a great choice during elections and feel indifferent to parties and candidates. Potential voters may be turned off by negative campaigning and conclude that all politicians are dirty. As we considered in Chapter 9, some blame television for a decline in political participation.

"Postmaterialism" offers another explanation. According to this cultural theory, in all the industrialized nations the economy has moved away from manufacturing and into knowledge and information industries. With this has come a profound shift of values, away from society and toward self. Only personal things matter in the New Age: relationships, correct diet, outdoor activities, and music. Social problems and political questions no longer interest many. If the postmaterialism theory is accurate, we will be seeing even less political involvement, and education will increasingly incline people to avoid politics. This explanation, if it's true, does not bode well for democracy.

person is concerned about Social Security and Medicare. In recent U.S. elections, those over 70 usually have the highest turnout.

Gender   Traditionally, men were more likely to vote than women in almost every society. Women had only comparatively recently won the right to vote. (Switzerland's female population was enfranchised only in 1971.) Since 1920, when female **suffrage** was granted in the United States, the gap between men's and women's voter turnout narrowed and then even reversed; in the 1996 U.S. elections women constituted 52 percent of those voting.

KEY TERM

suffrage   Right to vote.

Area of Residence   City dwellers are more likely to vote than rural residents. This fact probably reflects the easier accessibility of polling stations in the cities, where a few blocks can make up a voting district with the same population as a rural district of many square miles. Turnout in rural France has traditionally been high, as small-town French politics are more intimate than the depersonalized politics of the big city. People who have lived in the same place for a long time are more likely to vote than are transients or newcomers, for longtime residents feel more involved in local affairs and more likely to participate in groups and activities in the community.

Voter turnout in the United States is somewhat lighter in the South than in the North and West, a reflection of lower living standards and a lack of party competition. But the South and its politics have changed, and now turnout in the South is approaching that of other areas. Other nations are also characterized by regional differences in voter participation. In France, the areas south of the Loire River have a lower voter turnout than the northern areas of the country.

How Do People Vote?

The reasons that people vote as they do are many and complex. Loyalty to a party, fitting into a group, liking one candidate and distrusting another, and feelings about issues can effect voters' election decisions. Factors can be divided into *long-term* and *short-term* **variables**. Loyalty to a political party is a long-term influence and can affect a person's votes for his or her lifetime. Short-term variables may cause a person to vote one way for one election year but not three or four years later. Margaret Thatcher shrewdly called British elections in 1983 to catch the glow of military victory in the Falklands and again in 1987 during an economic upswing and disarray in Labour's ranks. Her Conservatives won both times. Similarly, in 1976 in the United States, Jimmy Carter benefited from a "morality factor" awakened by the Watergate scandal. As we shall see, economic conditions may push a voter to one candidate. The economic downturn of 1992 hurt incumbent President Bush. Such short-term variables rarely mean a permanent shift in party loyalty.

KEY TERMS

variables Factors that explain differences (for example, age explains why some people vote more than others).

party identification Long-term voter attachment to a given party.

Party Identification

Party identification—party ID, for short—is the tendency many people have to associate themselves mentally with one party over many years. Strong party identifiers habitually vote for that party without question. Weak identifiers can be swayed sometimes to vote for another party. People with no party ID are up for grabs and may shift their votes with every election. Remember, party ID is something that people carry around in their heads; it is not something that parties carry around.

Party ID is heavily influenced by one's parents and is instilled early in life. Some schoolchildren confidently state that they are Democrats or Republicans and may never change the affiliation they inherited from their parents. Like the early learning of a religion, preference for one party is difficult to shake. Another reason is that it is easier to vote along party lines, especially important with complicated U.S. ballots. It provides a shortcut for election decision-making—a "standing decision." Persons who call themselves Democrats are predisposed toward Democratic candidates, whether they know them or not. When asked how they feel about Republican candidates, they will often express suspicion of them and their views.

Party ID is an important element in electoral stability. People who stick pretty much to one party are like a foundation, allowing politicians to anticipate what people want and to try to deliver it. Weak party ID produces great "volatility" in voting, as citizens, like ships without keels, blow this way and that in the political winds. It is with some concern, then, that political scientists notice a decline in the number of party identifiers in the United States.

Party Identification in Europe   American political parties have some effect on the way most people vote, but most European parties are more influential in determining an individual's election choice. Since World War II, Britain has largely been characterized by a consistent split between Labour and Conservative supporters. The "swing" from one major party to another during national elections ranges from only about 1 percent to 5 percent. In voting for members of Parliament, some two-thirds of British voters can be counted on to stick with the same party. Norwegian party identifiers are more likely to vote along party lines than American Democrats or Republicans. The smaller political parties of Norway permit voters to express a personal ideology, unlike U.S. parties. French voters, on the other hand, are less likely than Americans to have a party ID, partly the result of the splitting, merging, and renaming that French parties engage in. Such changes do not give party IDs time to take root. Result: French voting is volatile.

Who Votes How?

No one can totally predict the voting in a free and fair election, but using the same social categories discussed in Chapter 8 (on public opinion) and earlier in this chapter (on voting turnout), political scientists can generally describe what kinds of people tend to identify with the various parties. Bear in mind that no social category votes 100 percent for a given party; people are highly individualistic and often go their own way, disregarding group norms. This fact accounts for some poor Republicans and some rich Democrats. If more than half of a given social category votes for one party, there is probably a significant relationship between the social category and the party. If three-quarters votes for a party, there is a strong relationship. We are making statements here that indicate a tendency, not an absolute relationship. Political scientists learn to say things like "Catholics *tend* to vote Democrat," and not "All Catholics are Democrats." Notice in Table 12.1 (on p. 214) that 53 percent of Catholics in 1996 voted for Clinton, but 37 percent voted for Dole. Beware of absolute statements.

Once practicing politicians (and sometimes political scientists) detect a tendency in a group to identify with a certain party, they call it a **voting bloc**. The candidates' strategy is then to secure enough blocs to

KEY TERM
voting bloc Group with a marked voting tendency.

Table 12.1   Who Voted How in 1996

	Clinton	Dole	Perot
Overall	49%	41%	8%
Men	43	44	10
Women	54	38	7
Whites	43	46	9
Blacks	84	12	4
College graduate	44	46	8
High school graduate	51	35	13
Less than high school	59	28	11
18–29 years old	53	34	10
30–44 years old	48	41	9
45–59 years old	48	41	9
60 and older	48	44	7
White Protestant	36	53	10
Catholic	53	37	9
Jewish	78	16	3
Union household	59	30	9
Family income			
under $15,000	59	28	11
$15–$30,000	53	36	9
$30–$50,000	48	40	10
over $50,000	44	48	7
over $75,000	41	51	7
over $100,000	38	54	6
East	55	34	9
Midwest	48	41	9
South	46	46	7
West	48	40	8

Source: Copyright © 1996 by The New York Times Company. Reprinted by permission.

deliver a majority of the electorate, and they tailor their campaign to win over the blocs most likely to vote for them. The concept of voting blocs is an oversimplification; there is no such thing as a solid bloc.

Class Voting   As discussed in Chapter 8, social class is one determinant of party identification and voting behavior. Even in the United States, where class distinctions are blurred, blue-collar workers tend to register and vote Democratic, especially in families in which the breadwinners are union members. Notice in Table 12.1 how "union households" was one of the few categories that went over 55 percent for Clinton in the 1996 election. In most European countries, this tendency is stronger, for unions are often connected to social-democratic or labor parties. The gigantic Swedish and German unions, respectively the LO and DGB, can reliably deliver the labor vote to the Social Democrats.

The middle and upper classes tend to have more conservative political leanings. In 1996, notice that the higher the family income, the greater the tendency to vote for Dole. Better-off Britons, French, German, and Swedes are also more likely to support their respective conservative parties. Two things muddy class voting. Some working-class people—because they consider themselves middle class, have a family tradition, or have individual convictions—vote for conservative parties. A majority of the U.S. and British working class voted, respectively, Republican in 1988 and Conservative in 1987. Conversely, some middle- and even upper-class people—because they are of working-class origins, have a family tradition, or have individual convictions—vote for parties on the left. Such people are especially important in providing working-class parties with educated leadership. This two-way crossover—working class identifying with conservatives and middle class identifying with the left—dilutes class voting. All over the world, class voting has receded; it just happened first in the United States.

Regional Voting   Some regions identify strongly with certain parties. Often these are areas that were conquered and subjugated centuries ago, and the inhabitants still harbor resentments. South of the Loire River, the French tend to vote Socialist. Scotland and Wales vote heavily Labour. The Southern United States used to be solidly Democratic, but by the 1980s, regional loyalties had so shifted that the South is now the strongest area for the Republicans, and the East—which following the Civil War had been a Republican bastion—is now weakest for them.

Religious Blocs   Religion can have an even deeper impact than region. In France, for example, devout Catholics vote mostly conservative; nonreligious people vote mostly left. The same applies to Italy, where the Popular party was founded by and is still linked to the Roman Catholic church. The Catholic areas of Germany are more likely to vote Christian Democrat than are the Protestant areas. In the United States, Catholics and Jews tend to vote Democrat, whereas white Protestants tend to vote Republican, tendencies that were borne out in 1996.

Age Groups   It's not necessarily true that younger people are more radical than their elders. Rather, they tend to catch the tide that is flowing in their youth and stay with it. Young people socialized to politics during the Depression tended to identify with the Democratic party all their lives. By the same token, Republicans hope that the enthusiasm for Reagan among young voters in the 1980s will give them a permanent sense of identification with the Republican party. Age groups react in part to the economic situation. Many young voters felt that Republican policies of growth would lead to jobs, but many retired voters feared Republican cuts in Social Security and Medicare. This leads to retired voters being more liberal than young ones. One study found that age predicts how a person will vote better than race, income, or gender.

Gender Gap   It also used to be assumed that women were more traditional and conservative than men, but that tendency has been reversed in the United States. Women now vote Democrat by several percentage points more than men. Women tend to like the Democrats' support for welfare measures and for abortion rights and to dislike the Republicans' opposition to such views.

Racial Minorities   Blacks are the most loyal Democrats by far; over 80 percent of those who vote generally vote for Democrats. A majority of Hispanic voters also identify with the Democrats, but Asian Americans in 1996 went slightly for Dole. The affinity of racial minorities for the Democrats, however, may cost the party white votes. Republicans are delighted to portray the Democrats as the party of minorities, feminists, and labor unions—and to portray themselves as the party of everyone else.

Urban Voting   Big cities strongly tend to vote liberal or left wing. This is explained, partly, by the concentration of the working-class vote in cities—for big cities have big factories. In addition, cities are also centers of education and sophistication, places where intellectuals are often drawn to liberal and leftist causes. Country and suburban dwellers tend to embrace conservative values and vote for conservative parties. England votes overwhelmingly Tory, but the city of London does not. Germany's Bavaria is a conservative stronghold, but not Munich. Italy was long dominated by the Christian Democrats, but not Italy's cities, most of which had leftist mayors. In 1996, voters in cities of half a million or more went massively for Clinton.

Electoral Realignment

For some decades political scientists have debated a theory of **critical** or **realigning elections**. Typically people retain their party identification for a long time, sometimes all their lives. But, according to this theory, in several watershed presidential elections, the party loyalties of many voters dissolve, and they establish new, durable party identities. These "critical elections" do not determine how every election will go, but they set the terms of debate and the main topics to be debated. They give one party dominance, although not absolute control. The critical or realigning elections in U.S. history are usually seen as the following:

> **KEY TERMS**
>
> **critical election**   An election showing a realignment.
> **realignment**   Major, long-term shift in party ID.

1800—the emergence of Jefferson's Democratic Republicans
1828—the emergence of Jacksonian populist Democrats
1860—the emergence of Lincoln's Republicans
1896—the emergence of business Republicanism
1932—the emergence of Roosevelt's New Deal Democrats

Between these critical elections, party identifications are stable and most people vote according to them. This is called the "normal vote" or "maintaining elections." Occasionally, enough voters will disregard their party identification to elect the weaker party: Democrat Grover Cleveland in 1884 and 1892, Democrat Woodrow Wilson in 1912 and 1916, and Republican Dwight Eisenhower in 1952 and 1956. These have been called "deviating elections" because the party shift was only temporary; afterward voters went back to their long-term party ID.

A Reagan Realignment?

Republicans anticipated that the Reagan sweeps of 1980 and 1984 marked a realignment in party identification in their favor. Party registration rose for Republicans and declined for Democrats until the parties were about equal in size. Young people, in particular, who are the future of any party, registered and voted Republican. Even more important, Reagan and his intellectual supporters restructured the ideological debate in a conservative direction (see Chapter 6). It was no longer fashionable, as it had been from FDR to Carter, to talk about using the powers of government to fix social ills and provide welfare programs. Instead, the political debates concerned how to lower taxes, cut government spending, limit government regulation, reduce the federal deficit, and restore growth through free enterprise. Before Reagan, even Republicans went along with the welfare state, and some of the biggest expansions of welfare programs occurred under Nixon. After Reagan, even the Democrats demanded fiscal responsibility.

But realignments don't come with name tags. It might not be possible to tell if there has been a realignment until some decades later. Furthermore, it may be difficult to spot the precise election in which realignment occurred. Looking at the results of the 1968 election, which brought Nixon to the White House, and carefully dissecting regional trends, Kevin Phillips concluded in 1969 that a Republican majority was emerging. Which, then, was the critical election, 1968 or 1980? If it was 1968, it would mark Carter's election in 1976 as a "deviating election," and, indeed, Carter's victory was largely the result of the Watergate scandal. What was missing from the Nixon years, however, was the ideological conservatism that came with Reagan. We might say that the ingredients for a realignment in favor of the Republicans came with the 1968 election but did not fully coalesce until 1980. What we have then is not a single "critical" election but a time period in which realignment occurred.

If there was a Republican realignment it took some time to reach congressional races. Even during the Reagan landslides, the House of Representatives stayed in Democrat hands, and in 1986 the Senate moved back under Democratic control. In 1994, both houses came under Republican control, but in 1996 the White House stayed in Democratic hands. How, then, can we tell if there has been a realignment? If the Republicans regain the presidency, and if they perpetuate their power in Congress, there will be a strong case for realignment. The Clinton victories in 1992 and 1996, both based heavily on the economy, suggest that the theory of electoral

KEY TERM

dealignment   Major, long-term decline in party ID.

realignment will have to be reexamined. If voters react mostly to current situations and candidates' personalities, the basic supposition of party identification will have to be reconsidered. Perhaps party ID is not as important as it once was. Instead of realignment, we may be seeing **dealignment**.

Key Concepts   ELECTORAL DEALIGNMENT

Since the mid-1960s, the number of voters committed to neither major U.S. party has increased sharply. In 1948, under 20 percent of U.S. voters called themselves independents. Some polls show more people calling themselves independent than Democrat or Republican. What happened to produce this major change, and what does it mean for American politics?

Studies in the 1950s showed "independents" tended to be least involved in and least informed about politics. This is no longer the case, as many independents are now well informed and politically concerned. Independents tend to be young and college-educated. They also came of age during extraordinary times. In 1964 they heard the Democratic candidate for president promise not to send Americans to fight in Vietnam. In 1974 they saw a Republican president resign in shame. Their faith in conventional party politics was shaken; both major parties appeared to be dishonest. Subsequent scandals did not improve their image.

Some political scientists noted that this process—which proceed during both bad and good economic times—coincided with three trends: (1) declining voter turnout, (2) declining party loyalty, and (3) declining trust in the government in Washington. Do the three items hang together? Which causes which? Declining political trust is probably the underlying cause, giving rise to the other two.

If things keep on like this, is there a danger for U.S. democracy? There well could be. Presidents are not voted in by a majority of those eligible, only by a majority of those actually voting. With only about half of those eligible voting, presidents often win with only one-quarter or less (if there is a third-party candidate) of the total electorate behind them, hardly a claim for a "mandate." Further, the high numbers of independents, when they decide to vote, easily shift their loyalties more on the basis of mood and the candidate's personality than on issues. This voter volatility makes the country hard to govern, for it deprives elected officials of stability and predictability. Voters become too fickle for any president to please them. Interest groups and media replace parties.

Some researchers doubt there is any significant trend toward electoral dealignment and independent voting. Many voters who call themselves "independent" actually lean to one party or the other, and they vote for that party rather reliably. Instead of the third of the electorate that says they're independent, claim these researchers, only 15 percent are genuine neutrals, and this amounts to only 11 percent who actually cast ballots (because genuine independents tend to vote less). The size of the independent vote is exaggerated and nothing to worry about, they charge. By the time you count the weak identifiers, party ID in the United States is largely unchanged.

Bill Clinton and running mate Al Gore took their show on the road in the 1992 election campaign, crossing parts of the country by bus and stopping for speeches every day, a technique reminiscent of the old "whistle stop" campaigns conducted by rail in earlier decades. (Wilfredo Lee, AP/Wide World Photos)

What Wins Elections?

In theory, elections are when citizens get to choose and guide their government. In modern elections, however, the element of rational choice is heavily manipulated by the twin factors of personality and the mass media. People vote without clearly realizing what they are voting for or why, and this could become a threat to democracy.

Modern parties showcase their leaders' personalities. Especially in the advanced industrialized world, ideology is seldom emphasized. Ads and television spots feature the leaders' images, sometimes without even mentioning their parties. The leader is presented

KEY TERM
charismatic   Having strong personal drawing power.

as **charismatic** and decisive but calm and caring. Ronald Reagan was an excellent example of a winning political personality, and leaders in other countries have adopted similar approaches. British Prime Minister Tony Blair won in part by copying the style of Bill Clinton. French presidential candidates project an image of a caring, almost fatherlike intellectual who is above the political fray, almost nonpartisan. German candidates for chancellor project a tried-and-true, reliable and upbeat image but also say little about what policies they will pursue. The pattern worldwide: Keep it general, keep it happy, don't mention parties, and smile a lot.

A good part of a candidate's personality is the degree of optimism he or she exudes. Victory in U.S. elections almost always goes to the candidate who presents the most upbeat image of America. Pessimistic candidates, who worry about things going wrong, tend to lose. The two University of Pennsylvania psychologists who conducted this study, Harold Zullow and Martin Seligman, in May 1988, gave Bush an optimism rating of 4.6 and Dukakis only 2.1, thus accurately predicting the November results.

The leaders' personalities are sold through the mass media, especially through television, where the candidate's image can be carefully controlled; even physical appearance can be altered. "Photo opportunities" instead of traditional question-and-answer sessions avoid embarrassing probes by journalists. The "photo op" shows seemingly spontaneous candidate activity; words explaining the activity can be added later. The "photo op" itself is largely wordless. The candidates' professional "handlers" worry that their candidates will slip their leashes and start acting like themselves. This can ruin a carefully built-up image. Journalists must be kept distant. And this is happening worldwide. One British observer argued, "The general election of 1987 proved that television very largely *is* the campaign." In France, journalists complain about the *hypermédiatisation* of French politics. The dominance of television is clearly not just an American problem.

The really big medium of modern campaigning is the televised political spot commercial. Here, everything is professionally controlled: set, lighting, music, makeup, narration—a mini-drama more perfect (and often more expensive) than many regular programs. The television spot, highly developed in America, now occurs in Europe. Labour's Neil Kinnock set new European standards for the rich images of his 1987 television spots, which were adjudged much better than Prime Minister Margaret Thatcher's (who nonetheless won). The following year, French presidential elections also featured what the French call *le clip politique*. French political scientist Jean-Paul Gourevitch discerns three types: (1) the "jingle clip," a simple attention-getting device; (2) the "ideological clip," which sets an idea in images; and (3) the "allegorical clip," which portrays the hero-candidate in an epic. The same could be said of U.S. television spots.

If things keep going like this, what will happen to democratic elections? Increasingly, they will be won by the candidate with the sunniest personality and best media ads. This generally means the candidate with the most money, for the mass media, especially television, are terribly expensive. Candidates, desperate for money, sell themselves to private interests. Parties become little more than fund-raising organizations. And notice that this is not just an American problem; it started in the United States but has since spread to Europe.

Retrospective Voting

Most people do not carefully evaluate issues in a presidential election, but they do accumulate an overall evaluation of the performance of an incumbent president. That is, they feel the president has done a good job or a poor one. Especially important are their perceptions concerning the health of the economy and government steps to boost economic growth. Morris P. Fiorina called the accumulated or package views of voters toward incumbent presidents **retrospective voting** because it views in retrospect a whole four

---

KEY TERM

retrospective voting Voters making decisions based on overall incumbent performance.

Key Concepts · ELECTIONS AND THE ECONOMY

Political scientists have long suspected that modern elections are in large degree referendums on the economy. "Consumer confidence" in the economy, a survey of expected prosperity tracked by the Conference Board, accurately predicted the last seven elections. When the consumer confidence index was 99 or above, the incumbent party's candidate won; when 87 or below, the incumbent party's candidate lost. Since World War II, U.S. economic growth of (a rather robust) 4 percent or higher during the year preceding the presidential election guarantees that the incumbent or his party's candidate will be elected. Less than 4 percent and they're in trouble. The recessions of 1980 and 1991 doomed, respectively, Carter and Bush. Presidents will do almost anything to avoid a recession during an election year.

Some thinkers worry that a too-direct relationship between the economy and elections increases voter volatility and prevents presidents from doing what needs to be done for long-term economic growth. It is as if voters angrily warn presidents: "Give me prosperity, or else!" That kind of voter input, warn some, is a perversion of democracy.

	Consumer Confidence Index	Vote for Incumbent Party's Candidate	
1972	112	62%	(Nixon wins)
1976	87	49	(Ford loses)
1980	84	42	(Carter loses)
1984	99	59	(Reagan wins)
1988	117	54	(Bush wins)
1992	53	38	(Bush loses)
1996	106	49	(Clinton wins)

years of performance in office. When voters think the government in general is doing a good job they reward the incumbent's party: Johnson in 1964, Nixon in 1972, Reagan in 1984, Bush in 1988, and Clinton in 1996. When they think the government in general is doing a poor job they punish the incumbent's party: Humphrey in 1968, Ford in 1976, Carter in 1980, and Bush in 1992.

Retrospective voting is colored, naturally, by party identification, issues, and the candidate's personality. For weak party identifiers plus the many independents, the feeling of overall performance is apt to be the most powerful determinant of voting. Further, if an administration scores well in the minds of such people in retrospect, they may start identifying with that party. Voting behavior is complex. When people say they "like" candidates, what does it mean? Do they like the candidates' party affiliation, their stand on issues, their personal images,

or the performance of the economy? Unraveling such puzzles is the crux of campaign strategy.

Candidate Strategies and Voter Groups

Campaign strategies are geared toward two goals: keeping "one foot on home
base" by not alienating the normal party supporters and, at the same time, trying to win over votes from the undecided and from as many of the opposition as
possible.

How does the candidate plan campaign strategy? In most cases, the campaign
is designed to fit the opinions and needs of the **constituency**. For this, constituency public-opinion polls are indispensable. Candidates must be aware of
pockets of party strength and resistance, what various groups are thinking about,
what districts have the lowest turnouts (and therefore merit
less of the candidates' time), and which issues could inflame
constituents. Only when the candidate has some awareness of
the direction and intensity of voter opinion will he or she be
able to plan an effective campaign. Important in this is a
knowledge of "voting blocs."

KEY TERM
constituency The people or district that elects an official.

Voting blocs fall into roughly the same categories as the public-opinion blocs
discussed in Chapter 8. Class, religion, and geographic characteristics are the most
important influences in opinion formation, and these provide general guidelines
for predicting voting behavior. Urban and rural voters will oppose each other on
a mass-transit bond; blacks and whites may vote differently on a school-busing
issue. Election victories are often the result of a major coalition formed by several smaller blocs of voters. On a national scale, the Democrats used to represent a
coalition of labor, blacks, Catholics, Jews, and urban voters; the Republicans
received their support from a coalition of rural and farm voters, the remaining
Protestants, and nonunion workers. By the 1960s, though, these traditional blocs
had begun to break up, and neither party has managed to reconstruct them. The
breakup of the blocs, it should be noted, coincides with the declining voter
turnout and party loyalty discussed earlier.

Increasingly, candidates recognize that "blocs" are not what they used to be,
that many Americans do not fit demographic, ethnic, or religious pigeonholes.
Instead, attitudes on free enterprise, welfare, patriotism, civil rights, and other
issues cut across the old voting blocs. Trying to make this approach more systematic, an innovative approach for the 1988 and 1996 elections broke the U.S. electorate into several "voter groups" based on their attitudes. The Pew Research
Center study held that traditional classifications such as "liberal" or "conservative"
don't count for much because people are often liberal on some things and conservative on others. Neither does party ID matter much in an era of dealignment and
rapid shifts between parties. In contrast to the traditional type of voter survey,
exemplified in Table 12.1, the Pew studies hold that clusters of *values* count for
more than income, religion, education, region, and so on. "White" or "professional" may not explain much about how a person votes, but a pro-business

"Enterpriser" cluster of values (in Table 12.2) strongly predicts a Republican voter, as do the "Moralists." "Seculars" and "New Democrats" tend strongly to the Democrats.

The Pew Research approach offers certain practical advantages to candidates. By knowing what issues appeal to which voter groups, they can target their campaign messages to them. Republicans can put out themes of enterprise to secure the large Enterpriser portion of the electorate. On the other hand, they know that the "Partisan Poor," strongly concerned with social welfare, will be hard to budge from the Democratic column, so Republicans can concentrate their efforts elsewhere. And both parties know that the two center groups, "New Economy Independents" and "Embittered," are up for grabs, and they can be enough to turn an election.

Table 12.2   Voter Groups in 1996

	Clinton	Dole	Perot
The Dividend Right/% Likely Voters			
Enterprisers/19% Pro-business, antigovernment, worry about economic issues	6%	88%	3%
Moralists/18% Pro-school prayer, antiabortion, worry about social issues	20	66	7
Libertarians/7% Pro-business and antigovernment, but highly tolerant, open to a third party	39	34	12
The Detached Center/% Likely Voters			
New Economy Independents/10% Don't like either major party or government but support environment and some welfare	53	14	16
Embittered/5% Poor and poorly informed; mistrust government, the main parties, and corporations	45	37	11
The "Not So" Left/% Likely Voters			
Seculars/9% Liberal, nonreligious, tolerant, well-educated, heavily Democratic	90	2	2
New Democrats/12% Religious but tolerant, both pro-business and pro-government, lean to the Democrats	86	5	4
New Dealers/10% Older, pro-government, pro-union socially conservative, worry about foreign competition	74	10	12
Partisan Poor/10% Militantly Democratic, pro-social spending, worry about drug abuse, unemployment, social justice	92	4	3
Total Sample	**50**	**38**	**6**

Note: ("Don't Knows," non-voting, and "voted for others" omitted.)
Source: Pew Research Center.

Key Terms

charismatic (p. 219)

constituency (p. 222)

critical election (p. 216)

dealignment (p. 218)

franchise (p. 210)

party identification (p. 212)

realignment (p. 216)

retrospective voting (p. 220)

suffrage (p. 211)

turnout (p. 207)

variables (p. 212)

voting bloc (p. 213)

Key Websites

The Administration and Cost of Elections Project explores alternatives in election administration, functions, processes, and costs throughout the world.
http://www.aceproject.org/

The Daily Worldwide Elections News website provides exhaustive daily coverage of elections held around the world. It includes links to detailed election returns, many daily newspapers, and analysis.
http://www.klipsan.com/elecnews.htm

The Vote Smart website tracks all sorts of information, including biographies of candidates, the performance of elected officials, issues, voting records, campaign finances, and evaluations by special interests.
http://www.vote-smart.org/

This site has the most recent election results from almost every country in an easy-to-use clickable map.
http://www.agora.stm.it/elections/election.htm

Congress created an independent regulatory agency—the FEC—to disclose campaign finance information, to administer the public funding of presidential elections, and to enforce the limits, prohibitions, and other provisions of the election law. This is the Federal Election Commission's official site.
http://www.fec.gov/

Further Reference

Flanigan, William H., and Nancy H. Zingale. *Political Behavior of the American Electorate*, 8th ed. Washington, D.C.: CQ Press, 1994.

Jamieson, Kathleen Hall. *Dirty Politics: Deception, Distraction, and Democracy*. New York: Oxford University Press, 1992.

Lawrence, David G. *The Collapse of the Democratic Presidential Majority: Realignment, Dealignment, and Electoral Change from Franklin Roosevelt to Bill Clinton*. Boulder, CO: Westview, 1996.

Leduc, Lawrence, Richard G. Niemi, and Pippa Norris, eds. *Comparing Democracies: Elections and Voting in Global Perspective*. Thousand Oaks, CA: Sage, 1996.

Miller, Warren E., and J. Merrill Shanks. *The New American Voter*. Cambridge, MA: Harvard University Press, 1996.

Nelson, Michael, ed. *The Elections of 1996*. Washington, D.C.: CQ Press, 1997.

Newman, Jody, and Richard A. Seltzer. *Sex as a Political Variable: Women as Candidates and Voters in U.S. Elections*. Boulder, CO: Lynne Rienner, 1996.

Page, Benjamin I., and Robert Y. Shapiro. *The Rational Public: Fifty Years of Trends in Americans' Policy Preferences*. Chicago, IL: University of Chicago Press, 1992.

Simpson, Dick. *Winning Elections: A Handbook in Modern Participatory Politics*. New York: Longman, 1996.

Tullock, Gordon. *On Voting: A Public Choice Approach*. Williston, VT: Edward Elgar, 1998.

CHAPTER 13

The Basic Structures of Government

Political institutions are the working structures of government, such as legislatures and executive departments. Many political scientists also count parties as institutions, if they are important and stable. Institutions may or may not be housed in impressive buildings, which helps bolster their authority. The U.S. Supreme Court, even if it met in a tent, would be an important institution as long as its decisions were obeyed. As we will consider later, it was not clear what the powers of the Supreme Court were to be when it began, but forceful personalities and important cases slowly gave it power. Like most institutions, the Supreme Court **evolved** into importance.

As we considered in Chapter 1, authority is a fluid thing, which requires continual maintenance. A political institution is congealed or partly solidified authority. Over time, people have become used to looking to political institutions to solve problems, decide controversies, and set directions. Institutions, because they are composed of many persons and (if they're effective) last many generations, take on lives of their own apart from the people temporarily associated with them. This gives the political system stability; citizens know where they stand.

Institutions are bigger than individual leaders. When President Nixon resigned under a cloud of scandal in 1974, the institution of the presidency was scarcely touched. If there had been a series of such presidents, and if they had refused to resign, the institution itself would have been severely damaged. Sometimes dictators have tried to make themselves into "institutions," but it hasn't worked; no matter how powerful dictators are during their lifetimes, the

---

QUESTIONS TO CONSIDER

1. How can a party be a political institution?
2. How does "Who's got the power?" help locate institutions?
3. Why are Europe's monarchies among the most democratic countries?
4. What are the problems of territorially unitary systems?
5. Why do some federal systems fall apart?
6. In what ways is U.S. government extremely complex?
7. How do electoral systems contribute to party systems?
8. How does the German electoral system combine the best of two distinct types?

KEY TERMS

political institution
Established and durable relationships of power and authority.
evolve To slowly develop.

institutions they have tried to build unravel upon their deaths. Josip Tito ruled Yugoslavia—sometimes with an iron hand—for thirty-five years. He attempted to ensure that the system he had set up would survive after him, but it was too much based on himself. Eleven years after his death, Yugoslavia split

apart in bloody fighting. Dictators seldom build lastingly; they are rarely able to **institutionalize** their personal power.

Powerful inhabitants of an office, however, can sometimes put their personal stamp on the institution. George Washington retired after two terms, and until FDR no president tried to serve longer. Washington institutionalized term limits into the presidency that were not codified into law until the Twenty-second Amendment in 1951. In another example, the first chancellor of the Federal Republic of Germany, Konrad Adenauer, offered such decisive leadership that the institution of chancellor has been powerful ever since.

One way to study institutions is to locate the most powerful offices of a political system: Who's got the power? Constitutions may help locate power but do not tell the whole story. The U.S. Constitution indicates the executive and the legislative powers are in equal balance. This is what the Founding Fathers intended, but over the past two centuries power has gravitated into the hands of the president.

The French constitution, set up by Charles de Gaulle in 1958, seems to give the presidency near-dictatorial powers. But French legislative elections have produced parliaments of one party facing a president of another. Before this first occurred in 1986, it was hard to predict how French institutions would handle the "deadlock" problem, a common feature of the U.S. system. The French constitution was unclear on this point, but Socialist President Mitterrand solved it by trimming his role and letting Gaullist Prime Minister Chirac take a bigger role. When the same situation, called "cohabitation," occurred again, French institutions took it in stride; they had evolved to accommodate a different power relationship. Ironically, later President Chirac had to cohabit with Socialist Prime Minister Jospin. Constitutions are themselves institutions, gradually evolving in practice if not in wording.

Monarchy or Republic

An example of such evolution is the modern constitutional **monarchy**. Calling a country a monarchy or a republic is to describe its "form of state." A **republic** is simply a form of state that does not have a monarch. The word republic does not imply "good" or "democratic." All but a few countries in the world are republics. Most of the remaining monarchies are figurehead constitutional monarchies such as those of northwestern Europe—Britain, Norway, Sweden, Denmark, Holland, and Belgium. The traditional,

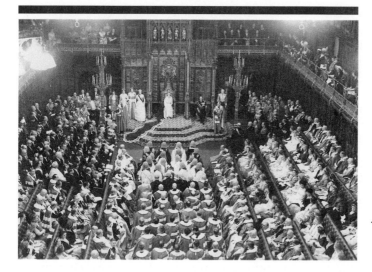

The constitutional monarchy of Great Britain, with its colorful ceremonies and pageantry, gives the appearance of a traditional monarchy, but the monarch is a figurehead and the real power is in the hands of the Parliament and the prime minister. (British Information Service)

working monarchies still found in the Arab world—Morocco, Saudi Arabia, Jordan, Kuwait—are probably doomed unless they can accomplish the extremely difficult task of turning themselves into limited constitutional monarchies. Failure to do so has in recent decades led to the overthrow of traditional monarchies and their replacement by revolutionary regimes in Egypt, Iraq, Libya, Ethiopia, and Iran.

New republics, such as those of the Third World, have to face the multiple crises of nation building (discussed in Chapter 2) without a dominant institution that can confer legitimacy. If their fragile new institutions can survive the first decades, they gradually gain legitimacy. In time, respect for republican institutions may succeed in uniting most elements of the society, as has happened in the United States. As Edmund Burke pointed out two centuries ago, in the world of institutions, old is good, for an institution that has survived and adapted over a long time has also implanted itself into citizens' hearts and minds.

Unitary or Federal Systems

Another basic institutional choice concerns the territorial structuring of the nation. There are really only two choices: unitary or federal. A unitary system accords its component areas little or no autonomy; most governance radiates from the capital city. The subdivisions—departments in France, provinces in Italy, counties in Sweden, prefectures in Japan—are largely administered by national authorities with only small local inputs. Federal systems are composed of units—U.S. and Brazilian states, German *Länder*, and Swiss cantons—that have considerable political lives of their own and cannot be legally erased or easily altered by the central power.

How is it that the limited constitutional monarchies of northwestern Europe can combine an old form of state with modern democracy? Indeed, these countries are some of the freest and most democratic in the world. The answer seems to be that monarchies perform an integrative function, holding together divergent social groups during the delicate modernization phase. The traditional sectors of society—the clergy, army officers, and great landowners—usually oppose democracy and may be tempted to carry out coups to stop democratization. But these sectors are also monarchist, and if the king or queen goes along with democratization, the traditional sectors will probably support it also. The monarch thus serves as a bridge between the traditional political system of the Middle Ages and the modern participatory system, easing the way from one to the other.

Consider the histories of countries that retained their kings and queens but gradually limited their powers until they were figureheads. Then consider those countries that deposed their monarchs. Britain temporarily deposed its monarchy in the seventeenth century, but it was soon reestablished. Since then Britain's political evolution has been mostly peaceful and gradual. The French Revolution repudiated monarchy and alienated French conservatives. Since then French politics has been a nasty tug of war between conservative and radical forces with rare periods of stability. Sweden retained its monarchy and evolved into a modern social-welfare state. Germany lost its monarchy after World War I, when the kaiser abdicated and fled to Holland; after the shaky fourteen years of the Weimar Republic, Hitler took over with his Nazis. Monarchs can confer legitimacy on new democratic institutions. When King Juan Carlos of Spain blocked a military coup in 1981, the head of the Spanish Communist party announced his support for monarchy. The king had thus bridged most sectors of Spanish society, even those that had previously been antimonarchist.

Unitary Systems

Unitary governments generally control local authorities and touch people's daily lives in more ways than a federal government would. For example, in France, elementary school curricula are drawn up by the central ministry in Paris in order to reduce regional differences. Unitary states have a national police force and one court system, whose judicial officers are appointed by the national government. In Britain, counties and cities elect councils that control policing, education, and health and welfare matters. Curiously, Conservative Prime Minister Thatcher opposed their autonomy, as they were often bastions of the welfare state she tried to dismantle.

Local nationalism grew in several unitary systems during the 1970s, and for several reasons. Economics was one. Local nationalists usually claim that their region is shortchanged by the central government. The region may have a distinct language or culture that its people want to preserve. Many feel that important political decisions are not under local control, that they are made by distant bureaucrats. Often regions harbor historical resentments at having long ago been conquered and forcibly merged with the larger nation. Several unitary systems grope for solutions to the regional problem.

Devolution in Britain   The Celtic Scots and Welsh, pushed to the peripheries of Britain centuries ago by the invading Angles and Saxons, retain a lively sense of their differences from England. Many Scots and Welsh resent being ruled by London. The Scots wanted to retain a bigger share of the North Sea oil revenues—"It's Scotland's oil!" was their cry—and the Welsh wanted to make their Cymric language equal to English in schools and on television. During the 1970s, the Scottish and Welsh nationalist parties grew until they won several seats in Parliament. In 1997 the new Labour government of Tony Blair passed **devolution** bills that gave home-rule powers to Scotland and Wales. The Scottish parliament, first elected in 1999, has the power to raise taxes and run Scotland's education, medical services, judicial system, and local government, much like a U.S. state.

> **KEY TERM**
>
> **devolution**   The shifting of some powers from the central government to component units.

Decentralization in France   France was historically a much more unitary system than Britain. Everything is—or, until recently, was—run from Paris. Both monarchs and republicans pursued centralization with single-minded determination. Most of France's ninety-six *départements* were named after rivers to try to erase the historical memories of the old provinces. It didn't completely work, for France, like Britain, has distinctive regional subcultures: the Celtic Bretons (who fled from Britain centuries ago to escape the Saxons); the southerners of the Midi, whose speech is still flavored with the ancient *langue d'oc*; and the Corsicans, who still speak an Italian dialect. Breton and Corsican separatists sometimes promote their cause with violence.

Case Studies   THE SHAKY LIVES OF CONFEDERATIONS

There is, theoretically, a third alternative to unitary and federal systems: the confederation, a nation so loosely formed that the component parts can override the center. Confederations tend to have short lives; they either fall apart or become federations. This was the fate of the United States under the Articles of Confederation. Similarly, in the Confederate States of America each state had such independence that they could not effectively wage the Civil War. Switzerland still calls itself a confederation (Confederatio Helvetia), but it is actually a federal system. The European Union (EU) started as a confederation but with the growth of the powers of Brussels (its headquarters), especially with economic and monetary union (the new *euro* currency), is rapidly becoming a federation.

In 1960, better to coordinate economic development, President de Gaulle decreed twenty-two regions
consisting of two to eight *départements* each. These were
mere administrative conveniences, however. Starting
in 1981, Socialist President François Mitterrand instituted genuine **decentralization**. Certain economic-
planning powers were transferred from Paris to the
regions. The Paris-appointed prefects lost some of their

> **KEY TERM**
>
> **decentralization** The
> shifting of some administrative
> functions from the central
> government to lower levels; not
> as strong as devolution.

powers, especially on economic matters. The hitherto powerless departmental legislatures picked up these powers. Elected regional assemblies took over much economic planning. France thus reversed five centuries of centralization.

Autonomy in Spain   Spain, too, decentralized its highly centralized system.
Here the problem was more urgent, for regional resentments, long buried under
the dictatorial rule of Francisco Franco (1939–1975), came out in anger. Spain's
regional problems were among the most difficult in Europe, second only to
Yugoslavia (see following). Basques and Catalans, in the north of Spain, speak
non-Castilian languages and are intensely proud of their distinctive cultures. In
addition, many areas of Spain were granted *fueros* (local rights) in medieval times,
which they treasured for centuries. On top of great regional diversity, Spanish
centralizers attempted to plant a unitary system on the French model. The result
was great resentment that appeared whenever Spain experimented with democracy. Breakaway movements appeared in 1874 and in the 1930s, only to be
crushed by the Spanish army, which regards the unity of the country as sacred.

With this background, Spain held its breath in the late 1970s and 1980s as the
post-Franco Spanish democracy instituted seventeen regional governments called
autonomías. The big problem was in the Basque country, where a terrorist movement, Euzkadi ta Azkatasuna (ETA), demanded complete Basque independence.
To appease regionalist feeling, which also appeared in more moderate forms in
Catalonia, Galicia, Andalusia, and other areas, the Madrid government allowed
regions to become autonomous, with regional parliaments, taxation power, language rights, and control over local matters. Most Spaniards approved of the
autonomías, which go much further than French decentralization.

Pros and Cons of Unitary Systems   Authority in unitary states may be
absurdly overconcentrated. Local government may not be able to install a traffic
light or bus stop without permission from the capital. This, in turn, may cause citizens to feel it is pointless to become active in local affairs and lead to political
alienation in general. On the other hand, centralization of power can be a significant advantage in facing the problems of modern society. Clear lines of authority without excess bickering among units of government can be useful. In unitary
systems, the central government can marshal economic resources and coordinate
planning and development. Taxation is the same throughout the country, so firms
and individuals cannot flee to low-tax states, as in the United States. Education
standards can be high and uniform, as in Japan.

Federal Systems

Federalism preserves a considerable degree of local authority while simultaneously allowing the central government enough power to run the country. This combination varies among federal nations. Some, such as the ex-Soviet Union and Mexico, became so centralized that some wondered if they were still federal. The crux of a federal system is that the component states have some powers that cannot be easily overridden by the central government. The states are typically represented in an upper house such as the U.S. Senate or German Bundesrat. (Unitary systems do not really need upper houses, but most have them.) In federal systems, the central government has exclusive control over foreign, defense, and monetary policy. The states typically control education, police, and highways. Because the division of these powers is seldom clear or permanent, a federal government rests on a delicate balance between centralized power and local autonomy.

There are several reasons for starting a federal union. The first is national security; small and weak states cannot defend themselves against powerful aggressors. (This was one of the main arguments of the Federalist writers.) The pooling of diplomatic and military resources of the states made Bismarck's Germany a major power. Federal unions serve economic purposes. The United States created a continentwide market without tariff barriers, a feat the EU is now copying. Federalism is often the only way to protect national unity. As Britain freed India in 1947, New Delhi set up a federal system that allowed such states as Bengal, Punjab, Marathastan, and Rajastan to maintain their own cultures while joining in the Indian nation. These states were jealous of their identities and would not have entered the federal union without a guarantee of local autonomy.

Pros and Cons of Federal Systems   Citizens are closest to their local government; they may influence officials and see how decisions are made and what their effects are. Subnational governments can experiment with new programs. If they work they can be copied nationwide; if they fail not much harm is done. It is for this reason that the U.S. states have been called "laboratories of democracy." On the other hand, local governments may lack the money to finance programs, and their officials are sometimes incompetent and corrupt. Local decision making can lead to duplication of services and poor coordination.

The relationship of the states or provinces to other levels of government varies among federal systems. In Germany, each of the sixteen *Länder* (states) has its own constitution and government for Land affairs. The Landtag (state legislature) can even affect the national policy, because it elects members of the Bundesrat (the upper house of the national legislature). States in the Indian federation likewise have control over such items as education, agriculture, and public health, but share authority with New Delhi in judicial matters. India is unique among federal states because its national government can proclaim a state of emergency, suspend the constitution, and take over the government of any state. "President's rule" is sometimes declared after riots and disorders in India's states.

Each of America's fifty states can legislate in any area not delegated to the federal government or to the people. Usually, education, welfare, civil law, property taxes, and licensing of professions are all state functions. However, in the twentieth century, the federal government expanded in the areas of civil law, welfare, and economic regulation. Dependent on federal grants and revenue sharing, the states find themselves having to meet federal standards in many areas. Washington, for example, threatened to withhold federal highway funds if states did not make twenty-one the legal drinking age. They did.

From the beginning, the United States has debated the proper role of the federal government and worried that "sectionalism" could pull the Union apart, which it did. Southern insistence on "states' rights" led to a clash with President Lincoln over slavery and then to civil war. In the 1960s, controversial U.S. Supreme Court decisions prompted a campaign to curb the power of the federal courts. Some insist that the concentration of power in Washington perverts American federalism and encroaches on individual freedoms. At the same time, local governments and citizens continue to rely on a strong federal government for help in solving complex—and expensive—problems. Federalism is not an easy system to maintain and does not necessarily solve the problems of large and diverse countries. Consider the following.

Ex-Soviet Federalism On paper, the Soviet Union was a highly decentralized federation: Its fifteen "republics" were supposed to have the right to secede. In practice, under the tight control of the Communist party—although usually staffed by local talent (Georgians ran Georgia, Uzbeks ran Uzbekistan, and so on)—they followed Moscow's orders. Few understood that beneath a centralized veneer lurked disunion. Gorbachev totally underestimated the strength of local nationalism, and when he allowed *glasnost* (media openness) in the late 1980s, many Soviet republics began to clamor for independence, especially the Baltic states of Lithuania, Latvia, and Estonia, which had been brutally annexed by Stalin in 1940. With the collapse of the Soviet Union at the end of 1991, all fifteen republics proclaimed themselves sovereign and independent, and many countries, including the United States, granted each of them diplomatic recognition.

Twelve of the old Soviet republics—all but the three Baltic states—enrolled in the "Commonwealth of Independent States" (CIS), a weak and uncertain entity with headquarters in Minsk, capital of Belarus. The CIS was supposed to promote trade among members. With the ruble rendered worthless, however, this trade shrank. Fighting between two CIS members, Armenia and Azerbaijan, over disputed territory, took thousands of lives, and the CIS was unable to settle their quarrel. Some observers suspect the CIS is merely a cover for the eventual takeback of the old Soviet territory by Russia, which is openly advocated by Russian nationalists.

The bulk of the old Soviet Union continued as the Russian Federation, which is composed of eighty-nine autonomous republics, districts, regions, and even cities, most of which have signed a federation treaty with Moscow. Several areas,

Key Concepts   NATIONALITY AND CITIZENSHIP

Communist countries split nationality and citizenship. You could have Uzbek nationality but Soviet citizenship, Macedonian nationality but Yugoslav citizenship, or Slovak nationality but Czechoslovak citizenship, and this was marked in your internal passport, which everyone had to have. This system—devised by Stalin as "national in form, socialist in content"—was supposed to satisfy the "national question." Instead, it asked for trouble by locking people into a nationality and reminding them of it. Actually, the old tsarist system was better; it listed everybody as Russian. Legally, we have only one nationality, American, a point that helps cement us together.

home to some of the more than one hundred ethnic groups within Russia, refused to sign and billed themselves as independent. In the Caucasus, Chechnya fought a long and bloody war with the Russian army and persuaded Moscow to leave it alone.

Could the three Communist federations—the Soviet Union, Yugoslavia, and Czechoslovakia—have devised a more genuine federalism that would not have fallen apart? Or were these federations of unlike components doomed from the start? The Communists, by pretending to have solved the "national question," merely suppressed it until it came out later.

Ex-Yugoslav Federalism   Yugoslavia, founded only in 1918, was a new and somewhat artificial country whose components were rarely content. It fell apart once before, in World War II. The Communist Partisans who fought the Nazis thought federalism was the answer. Under the maverick Communist Tito, Yugoslav federalism went farther than the Soviet variety. Each of Yugoslavia's six republics really did run local affairs and sent equal numbers of representatives to both houses of parliament. Yugoslavia's collective presidency had one member from each republic. This ultrafederal setup, however, did not calm local nationalism; it inflamed it. Each republic wanted its own railroads, steel mills, and control of its economy. Under Tito, the Communist party and security police could hold Yugoslavia together, but after he died in 1980 the republics started going their separate ways. The most advanced republics, Slovenia and Croatia, resented being governed and taxed by a regime they didn't like in Belgrade, which is also the capital of Serbia. They declared their independence in 1991, and fighting broke out as ethnic Serbs set up a mini-republic inside Croatia. The bloodshed was much worse after Bosnia, with a Muslim plurality (but not a majority), declared its independence in 1992. Serbian forces brutally practiced "ethnic cleansing" and murdered thousands. The problem was that 3 million ethnic Serbs lived outside of Serbia in areas where Serbs were massacred in World War II.

Feeling endangered, Serbs felt entitled to take whatever lands they were living on for an eventual Greater Serbia. Serbia and Montenegro continue as a rump federation calling itself Yugoslavia. The situation calmed after a U.S.-brokered and NATO-enforced peace was agreed to in 1995, but then trouble flared up in Kosovo, a part of Serbia whose inhabitants are 90 percent ethnic Albanians.

Canadian Federalism Canada is another federation with centrifugal tendencies. Quebec is not alone in seeking independence; so do some of the western provinces. As we considered in Chapter 7, the British allowed the French-speaking Québécois to keep their language, and francophones became second-class citizens, poorer than other Canadians and discriminated against because almost all private and government business was conducted in English.

In the 1960s the Parti Québécois (PQ) sprang up, dedicated to Quebec's independence from Canada. To appease them, the federal government in Ottawa in 1969 made Canada bilingual, with French and English having equal rights. This wasn't enough for the PQ which made French the only official language of Quebec, turning the English-speaking minority into second-class citizens. Trying to hold the federation—which came to look a bit like a confederation as the provinces overruled the center—together, Ottawa and the provincial governments laboriously developed two new federal accords (Meech Lake in 1987 and Charlottetown in 1992), which were then rejected. The stumbling block was a separate status for Quebec as a "distinct society." Quebeckers said it didn't go far enough; other Canadians said it went too far. Quebec separatists, still in control

Linguistic nationalism shows in Quebec, where now all shop signs must be in French. Here a Montreal greengrocer had to paint over his fruit market sign with "marché de fruits," but was allowed to keep "Simcha's" in English, as it is an established business name. (Michael Roskin)

of the province's government, plan on another referendum on separation. A "yes" vote could have disastrous consequences for all of Canada.

Federalism is difficult. These three cases remind us that federalism cannot cure everything. If the components are too different from one another culturally, economically, linguistically, or historically, a federal system may not hold together. A shared political culture, as in the United States, Australia, and Germany, is a big help. With that as a foundation, the right balance must be found between central and state governments. The United States is still searching for its correct balance.

The United States: Balkanization of Government

There are approximately 80,000 local governments in the United States, plus fifty state governments and the national government. These governments often get in each other's way, a situation called, half in jest, "balkanization," after the many little countries that emerged in the Balkans when the Turks were pushed out in the past century. Balkanization in the United States has led to immoderate jurisdictional conflicts over whose rules apply in which situation.

One difficulty is the size of American cities and counties. Since World War II, much of the middle class has moved from cities to suburbs, leaving the cities with a shrinking tax base, precisely when poorer people—who cannot pay much in taxes but need many social services—are moving in. If the entire metropolitan area had a single government, the affluent suburbs (many of whose residents earn their livings in the city) could be taxed to share the burden. But suburbs, with their own representatives in state and federal legislatures, block such moves, and the cities become poorer, more blighted, and more desperate. Instead of solving their own problems on a metropolitan basis, the cities go hat in hand to Washington to ask for financial help.

The Growth of Federal Power   The Founding Fathers would have difficulty recognizing the balance of powers between state and federal governments today. They expected, first, that the amount of actual governing would be small, and second that most of it would be done by the states under their "reserved" powers. For most of the nation's history this was so. States and localities raised their own revenues and spent them on modest programs; federal help was minor. As late as 1932, federal grants were less than 3 percent of state and local revenue.

But things were changing. The passage of the Sixteenth Amendment in 1913 allowed the federal government to tax income. Although little used at first, it meant that Washington gained an extractive power much stronger than the states'. Soon small federally funded programs for highways, education, and public health appeared. With FDR's New Deal in the 1930s, federal programs increased in number and funding. With Lyndon Johnson's Great Society in the 1960s (Johnson was a great admirer of Roosevelt), federal programs expanded, and Richard Nixon greatly increased the funding for them. Now, many billions of dollars flow from Washington to state and local governments. States and localities came to depend on federal grants for a portion of their revenues.

State and local governments often don't like being dependent on Washington, but they need the money. It's easier for the federal government to collect taxes through its progressive income tax (the richer you are, the bigger percentage you pay) than it is for states and cities through their income, sales, and property taxes. The public demand for services has outstripped the financial ability of most states and localities. Theoretically, states and cities could decline federal grants, but no one likes to turn down offers of money, even if there is some red tape involved.

The net impact was a growth of federal power. Because it provided money, it could set standards. The content of school lunches; design and construction of hospitals, highways, and airports; and women's collegiate athletics come under federal supervision. Some have suggested that this development makes the United States less federal than it used to be. Perhaps so, but reversing the process is difficult. Should toxic and nuclear waste disposal be left to state discretion? Is education a purely local concern? Standards and dollar support vary wildly across the fifty states, leaving the U.S. population inadequately educated.

The New Federalism   The federal grants process is terribly complex, consisting of some five hundred different programs. Firms offer computerized grant-finding services, and states, cities, hospitals, and universities hire people for their "grantsmanship"—their ability to locate and win grants. Most of these grants are **categorical**, aimed at a specific problem, which takes control and discretion away from state and local authorities. Funds for flood control cannot be used for sewage processing; funds for schoolbooks cannot be used for athletic equipment. State and local officials have complained of being locked into federal programs that don't take local needs into consideration.

KEY TERMS
categorical grant   Federal aid narrowly aimed at a specific need.
block grant   A general category of federal aid to states.
revenue sharing   The division of federal taxes with the states.
New Federalism   Nixon's and Reagan's program of returning powers to the states.

Presidents Nixon and Reagan thought they had the answer: Move away from the categorical grants to broader **block grants** and **revenue sharing**. Both presidents called their programs the **New Federalism**, connoting a return of some power and control to the states. The federal government had become too powerful, they argued, so power should be given back to the states. It didn't quite work that way.

Congress, under President Nixon's leadership, designated $6.9 billion a year to go directly from the federal treasury to the states as revenue sharing, which states could spend as they needed without federal guidelines or supervision. The trouble was that this made states and cities *more* dependent on Washington, not less. Further, because revenue sharing is distributed by formula, it goes to rich cities and poor cities alike. One city may desperately need revenue to keep up police and fire services, whereas another may use it just to improve its parks.

Because revenue sharing gives money with virtually no strings attached, it erodes federal control. Revenue sharing isn't "aimed" at problems; it leaves that up to state and local officials, who mostly use the money for general budget (police and fire departments, streets, and schools). Germany has gone the furthest with revenue sharing; a set percentage of federal income taxes every year are sent to the Land governments.

An intermediate ground between categorical grants (too narrow) and revenue sharing (too wide) appeared in 1974 with block grants. These take several related categorical grants, roll them into one, and let state and local officials use them within the general category. President Reagan, for example, reduced dozens of categorical grants into a few block grants and called this the New Federalism. Congressional Republicans in the mid-1990s sought increased block grants as a way to shrink Washington's powers. There is a catch. Whereas the block grants are simpler and have fewer federal strings attached, they also provide less money. In 1978, some 25 percent of state and local government outlays were federal aid. By the turn of the century, federal funding of state and local outlays was down to about half that. This decline left many states and municipalities, which had taken on new tasks, so desperate for funds they had to raise taxes. The question of how much federal money to give and how to give it is a permanent problem of U.S. federalism, for it is one facet of the problem we discussed earlier, that of the proper balance between central and state governments in federal systems.

The Unitary-Federal Mixture

No country is perfectly unitary, nor is any perfectly federated. Even strongly unitary systems have certain elements of local input and control, and federal systems keep considerable power for the center. The interesting trend of our time is the tugging of unitary systems in a federal direction. Britain, France, and Spain are two examples of highly centralized governments moving to quasifederalism. It would be premature to say that eventually unitary systems will resemble federal systems, for both systems carry with them centuries of institutional and cultural baggage. Our task is not simply to classify countries as "unitary" or "federal," but to see how they actually operate in practice. Then we will find all manner of interesting deviations from the model, borrowings, and attempts to modify systems.

Electoral Systems

As considered briefly in Chapter 11, electoral systems go a long way to determining the party system. In choosing their electoral system, countries are partly determining the number of parties, the ease of forming a stable government, and the degree of citizen interest in politics. There are two general types of electoral systems with many variations.

Single-Member Districts

The simplest electoral system is the Anglo-American **single-member district**, wherein one member of Parliament or of Congress is chosen to represent the entire district by winning a plurality (not necessarily a majority) of the votes. The system is sometimes called

"single-member districts with plurality win" or "first past the post" (FPTP). This system puts pressure on interest groups and political factions to coalesce into two big parties. If there were, say, four parties who received 25, 25, 24, and 26 percent of the vote respectively, the last party would win the election. Losing parties that aren't too far apart ideologically quickly recognize their advantage is to combine forces for the next election. Then this new party wins, forcing other small parties to combine. The message: merge or lose. In South Korea in 1987, for example, two liberal candidates split the opposition vote and handed the election to the conservative incumbent. Woodrow Wilson won in 1912 only because Theodore Roosevelt split the Republican party. Countries with single-member districts and elections decided by a plurality of the vote tend to have two-party systems, such as the United States and Britain.

Third parties can and do exist in such systems, but without much hope of winning. They may have an impact as protest groups or as pressure groups on the big parties. The British Liberal Democrats win nearly one vote in five, but because they are dispersed rather evenly throughout the country, they win few seats. Single-member systems are unkind to third parties.

Advantages of Single-Member Districts   Single-member district systems tend to the center of the political spectrum, for this is where the votes are. This tendency inhibits the growth of extremism. If, for one election, leaders out of touch with mainstream views should capture control of the party, the party will likely lose. After the election, the party will probably soon dump the extremists. This is what happened with the Republicans under the conservative Goldwater in 1964, the Democrats under the liberal McGovern in 1972, and the British Labourites under left-wing Michael Foot in 1983. As was mentioned in Chapter 8, public opinion in most democracies arrays itself as a bell-shaped curve. Parties that depart too far from the center penalize themselves.

FPTP systems also generally give a clear parliamentary majority to one party, and therefore coalitions are rarely necessary. Victories are magnified in single-member systems. A relatively small "swing" of votes from one party to another can translate into many parliamentary seats, perhaps enough to form a parliamentary majority and a new government. In 1997, for example, Labour won 43 percent of the vote but 63 percent of the seats in Parliament. (Remember, FPTP systems are not supposed to be proportional to votes.) The United States, with its constitutionally mandated separation of powers, muddies the advantage of this system by frequently giving the White House to one party and the Congress to another.

Disadvantages of Single-Member Districts   The single-member districts create a somewhat artificial majority in parliament, which makes governing easier but does not fairly or accurately reflect public opinion or voting strength. In each district the winner takes all. The losing party, even if it received 49 percent of the vote, gets no representation. This is particularly unfair to third parties, especially if their supporters are not sufficiently concentrated to form a plurality in a few districts, the fate of the British Liberal Democrats.

Single-member districts teach parties to stick to the political center. This makes politics safe but dull. The two big parties, in trying to win over the many votes in the middle, often end up sounding rather alike. The resulting voter boredom helps explain the low voter turnout in U.S. elections, discussed in the last chapter. The European multiparty systems have much higher voter turnouts, partly because voters can choose from a more interesting menu of parties.

Case Studies   THE FRENCH VARIATION

France also uses single-member districts, but with two rounds of voting. Any candidate in parliamentary elections, held every five years, can enter the first round; in most districts half a dozen do. If they get an outright **majority** (over 50 percent, not the same as the simple plurality in the Anglo-American system), they are elected on the first round, not usually the case. In most districts they have to go to a second round a week later. This time only candidates with at least 12.5 percent can run, and simple **plurality** suffices to win. By previous agreement between parties, however, some candidates withdraw and urge their supporters to vote for the candidate closest to them ideologically. On the right side of the French political spectrum, the center-right Republicans will have agreed with the conservative Gaullists that the weaker candidate will drop out on the second round. To run both on the second round would split the conservative vote and give the election to the Socialists. On the left side, Socialists make the same deal with Communists: The weaker vote-getter (in most districts, the Communist) drops out and throws his or her support to the Socialist candidate. For presidential elections, held every seven years, the runoff comes two weeks later, with only the top two candidates running; they make the same sort of deal with the parties who have dropped out.

The French system—"single-member districts with runoffs"—permits many parties to exist and to run in the first round. Then the system narrows the choice in the second round and forces politicians to make the same choices as in the Anglo-American system; that is, it forces parties to combine. The first round of the French system is the functional equivalent of American primary elections. If the French were to drop the first round and go straight to the second round, they would encourage the formation of just two big parties, as in the United States and Britain. Some French thinkers argue, however, that French history, society, and ideologies are more complex and thus need more than two parties to represent them. Some East European countries adopted the French-style single-member districts with runoff.

Proportional Representation

Proportional representation (PR) systems overcome the disadvantages of single-member systems but bring in problems of their own. These systems are based on multimember districts; that is, each district sends several representatives to parliament, not just one, as in single-member systems. In the small countries of the Netherlands and Israel, the entire country is one big district. In Sweden the district is a county, in Spain a province. If the district is entitled to ten seats, each party offers voters a *party list* of ten candidates. Each voter picks one list, and the party gets seats in proportion to the votes it receives. If the party won 30 percent of the votes in a ten-member district, it would send the first three names on its party list to parliament. A party with 20 percent would send its first two names.

Mathematical problems immediately appear. Rarely does the vote divide itself neatly. More typically, one party might win 42 percent of eleven seats. Would the party get 4.62 seats? How do you send a fraction of a person to parliament? There are a couple of ways to handle this. The most common is the d'Hondt system, which uses a mathematical formula to divide the seats; it overrepresents the larger parties at the expense of smaller ones. Sweden also uses a mathematical formula plus an interesting provision for nationwide seats. Its twenty-eight districts elect only 310 of the Riksdag's 349 seats. Naturally, mathematical discrepancies appear, so the remaining thirty-nine seats are parceled out to rectify any variances from the parties' national percentages.

To minimize the problem of splinter, nuisance, or extremist parties, most PR systems require parties to win a certain percentage of the vote in order to obtain any seats at all. These are called "threshold clauses." Germany and Poland require a party to get at least 5 percent of the vote nationwide; Sweden and Italy require 4 percent.

Advantages of Proportional Representation The chief advantage of PR is that the country's legislature accurately reflects the main currents of public opinion and party strength. Parties are not driven by the need to capture the middle of the electoral spectrum as in Anglo-American systems. Parties can thus articulate their ideologies and principles more clearly because they aren't trying to please everybody. If a small part of the population—as low as 1.5 percent in Israel—really believes in something, they can run as a party and win a seat or two. They are not forced to amalgamate into bigger parties and dilute their views, as happens in "first past the post" systems.

Disadvantages of Proportional Representation PR systems encourage party splintering, or more accurately, where political views are splintered it permits small groups to organize as parties and win seats in parliament. This tendency, however, is waning, and two-plus party systems have emerged even in PR systems. Sweden and Spain have one or two large parties plus a few smaller ones.

Case Studies   THE GERMAN HYBRID

The German system combines the best of both worlds. The Bundestag is elected on the basis of both single-member districts and proportional representation. On a split ballot, Germans vote for both an individual to represent their district and a party to represent their *Land* (state) in proportion to the votes received. Overall strength in the Bundestag is set by the second vote, the one for parties, so seats are always proportional to votes. Half of the seats, though, are reserved for the 328 winners of the district contests. The net effect of Germany's split representation system has been to produce a two-plus party system (discussed in Chapter 11) and great governing stability. The German system is a modification of the PR system and was designed after World War II to prevent a repetition of the weak and unstable Weimar system, which had proportional representation that treated the country as one big district. In the 1990s, Russia, Italy, New Zealand, and Japan adopted German-style **hybrid** systems that combine single-member districts with PR for their parliamentary elections.

KEY TERM

hybrid   A combination of two or more systems.

Their political systems are not terribly splintered. Israel, on the other hand, is plagued by splinter parties; as many as fifteen parties are elected to the Knesset. If the chief party falls short of half the seats in PR systems it must form a coalition with other parties. These coalitions are often unstable and unable to decide important issues. Some Israelis protest their country's PR system and urge reforms that would reduce the number of parties. It's not true that multiparty systems are always unstable. Where one party is big enough to govern alone, the system is quite stable. Nonetheless, the Anglo-American systems confer an almost automatic majority and thus stability.

Choosing Institutions

Political institutions are, in large measure, artificial creations. Most of them, of course, have evolved over time, but at key points in a nation's history, people have had the opportunity to choose their institutions. This brings an element of creativity into politics. Institutions neither fall from heaven nor rise from earth. They are crafted by a handful of people who can do a good job or a poor one. They are guided both by past experience and by reason. Often they are taking a leap in the dark. The Founding Fathers had little in the way of precedent when they constructed a presidential federal republic. Modified by time, usage, amendments, statutes, and court decisions, their handiwork has endured. The drafters of Germany's Weimar constitution in 1919 were less fortunate. On paper, the Weimar constitution looked like a perfect democracy, but some of the institutional choices were poor: no monarch, a weak president, a PR electoral system that encouraged splinter parties and cabinet instability, and a provision for emergency powers that could be misused. One wishes we could have warned them of their fateful choices.

When political science was young, it focused heavily on constitutions, as if selecting the right institutions could confer moderation and stability on a political system. Well, often the right choices can help. We may wonder if political science, in trying to imitate the natural sciences, has strayed too far from its origins. There was something noble and challenging about trying to devise workable, durable constitutions. In a tumultuous world, there can be few higher tasks than the development of effective political institutions.

Key Terms

block grant (p. 237)

categorical grant (p. 237)

decentralization (p. 231)

devolution (p. 230)

evolve (p. 226)

hybrid (p. 242)

institutionalize (p. 227)

majority (p. 240)

monarchy (p. 227)

New Federalism (p. 237)

plurality (p. 240)

political institution (p. 226)

proportional representation (p. 241)

republic (p. 227)

revenue sharing (p. 237)

single-member district (p. 239)

Key Websites

This comprehensive site links to many local government and party web pages around the world.
http://world.localgov.org/

NGA is the only bipartisan national organization of the nation's governors. Its members are the governors of the fifty states, the commonwealths of the Northern Mariana Islands and Puerto Rico, and the territories of American Samoa, Guam, and the Virgin Islands. Through NGA, the governors identify priority issues and deal collectively with issues of public policy and governance at both the national and state levels.
http://www.nga.org/

The National Association of State Budget Officers (NASBO) has served as the professional membership organization for state finance officers for over fifty years. NASBO is the instrument through which the states collectively are advancing state budget practices. As the chief financial advisors to our nation's governors, NASBO members are active participants in the public policy discussions at the state level.
http://www.nasbo.org/

The Brookings Institution functions as an independent analyst and critic, committed to publishing its findings for the public. In its conferences and activities, it serves as a bridge between scholarship and public policy, bringing new knowledge to the attention of decisionmakers and giving scholars insight into public policy issues.
http://www.brook.edu/

Rand is a nonprofit organization that hopes to improve policy and decision-making through research and analysis. It does this by analyzing choices and developments in many areas, including national defense, education and training, health care, criminal and civil justice, labor and population, science and technology, community development, international relations, and regional studies.
http://www.rand.org/

Further Reference

Donahue, John D. *Disunited States*. New York: Basic Books, 1997.

Duchacek, Ivo D. *Comparative Federalism: The Territorial Dimension of Politics*, rev. ed. Lanham, MD: University Press of America, 1987.

Lijphart, Arend. *Electoral Systems and Party Systems: A Study of Twenty-Seven Democracies, 1945–1990*. New York: Oxford University Press, 1994.

Rae, Douglas. *The Political Consequences of Electoral Laws*, rev. ed. New Haven, CT: Yale University Press, 1971.

Redish, Martin H. *The Constitution as Political Structure*. New York: Oxford, 1995.

Reeve, Andrew, and Alan Ware. *Electoral Systems: A Comparative and Theoretical Introduction*. New York: Routledge, 1991.

Riker, William H. *Federalism: Origin, Operation, Significance*. Boston, MA: Little, Brown, 1964.

Rivlin, Alice M. *Reviving the American Dream: The Economy, the States and the Federal Government*. Washington, D.C.: Brookings Institution, 1992.

Sartori, Giovanni. *Comparative Constitutional Engineering: An Inquiry into Structures, Incentives and Outcomes*. New York: New York University Press, 1994.

Shapiro, David. *Federalism: A Dialogue*. Evanston, IL: Northwestern University Press, 1995.

Siegan, Bernard H. *Drafting a Constitution for a Nation or Republic Emerging into Freedom*, 2nd ed. Fairfax, VA: George Mason University Press, 1994.

Walker, David B. *The Rebirth of Federalism: Slouching toward Washington*. Chatham, NJ: Chatham House, 1995.

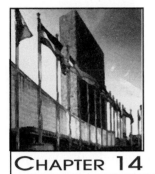

CHAPTER 14

Legislatures

Political institutions, it is theorized, become more specialized, complex, and differentiated as they become more modern. Primitive hunting bands may have nothing more than a single leader who decides everything. Tribes may add councils of elders to debate major problems and adjudicate disputes. City-states such as Athens have assemblies that combine legislative, executive, and judicial functions. The Romans developed a senate, but it, too, combined several roles, and its powers declined as Rome went from republic to empire. In the Middle Ages, the prevailing feudal system was a balance among a monarch, nobles, and leading churchmen, and it is in feudalism that we first get a glimpse of the "balance of power."

Countries with limits on government have usually had **feudal** pasts, which teach that dispersion of power is good and concentration of power is bad. Countries with mostly **absolutist** traditions have trouble founding democracies. An example of this balancing of power is the oath the nobles of medieval Aragon (in northeast Spain) pledged to a new king, "We, who are as good as you, swear to you, who are no better than we, to accept you as our king and sovereign lord provided you observe all our statutes and laws; and if not, no."

Ambitious monarchs, who were often at war, desperately needed revenues. Some of them started calling assemblies of notables to levy taxes. In return for their "power of the purse," these assemblies were allowed a modest input into royal policies. Such were the beginnings of the British **Parliament**, which is divided into two houses (Lords for peers and church leaders and Commons for knights and burghers), and

QUESTIONS TO CONSIDER

1. How did parliaments first come to be?
2. What is the difference between presidential and parliamentary systems?
3. Is it too hard to oust a U.S. president?
4. What is executive-legislative "deadlock"?
5. What good is a bicameral legislature in a unitary system?
6. Do legislatures originate the laws they pass?
7. Is the U.S. "pork barrel" necessary to make the system work?
8. Have legislatures declined in importance? Why?

KEY TERMS

feudalism System of political power dispersed among layers.

absolutism Post-feudal concentration of power in a monarch.

parliament A national legislature; when capitalized, the British Parliament, specifically the House of Commons.

the Swedish **Riksdag**, which originally had four chambers (for nobles, clerics, burghers, and farmers). The French **Estates General**, with three houses (for nobles, clerics, and commoners), got off to a weak start and was soon forgotten as French monarchs gathered more and more personal power in what became known as absolutism.

In Britain, Sweden, and some other European countries, though, legislatures slowly grew in power and were able to resist the absolutist demands of monarchs. In Britain in the sixteenth century, Henry VIII, who broke with Rome because he wanted a divorce, developed a partnership with Parliament because he needed its support in passing laws to get England out of the Catholic church and the church out of England. By the seventeenth century, Parliament considered itself coequal with the monarch and even supreme in the area of taxes. The English Civil War was a quarrel between royalists and parliamentarians over who had top power. In 1649, Parliament decided the issue by executing Charles I.

John Locke, the English philosopher who lived through this momentous period, extolled the power of the "legislative" as the most basic and important. During the Age of Enlightenment in the eighteenth century, political theorists such as Montesquieu and Jefferson declared that liberty could be secured only if government were divided into two distinct branches, the legislative and the executive, with the ability to check and balance the other. Modern governments are

Mother of Parliaments: Westminster, on the banks of the Thames River in London, represents the slow, gradual march to democracy over many centuries. (British Department of the Environment)

Key Concepts	HEAD OF STATE VERSUS HEAD OF GOVERNMENT

Two terms that sound almost alike often confuse students, especially Americans. A *head of state* is the theoretically top leader, but one with often only symbolic duties, such as the queen of England or king of Sweden. These monarchs symbolically represent their nations by receiving foreign ambassadors and giving restrained speeches on patriotic occasions. In republics, their analogues are presidents, some of whom are also little more than figureheads. The republics of Germany, Italy, and Israel, for example, have presidents as heads of state, but they don't do much in the way of practical politics. (They are also not well known. Can you name them?)

The *head (or chief) of government* is the real working executive, called prime minister, premier, or chancellor. They typically also head their parties, run election campaigns, and supervise the running of government. In Britain, this is Prime Minister Tony Blair, in Germany Chancellor Gerhard Schröder. The United States combines the two offices, for our president is both head of state and head of government.

generally still divided into these two branches, but only in the United States do they check and balance each other. Theoretically, at least, the legislature enacts laws that allocate values for society and the executive branch enforces the statutes passed by the legislature. (A coequal judicial branch is rare; it is a U.S. invention and found in few other systems.) But these responsibilities often overlap, and the separation of powers is rarely clear-cut.

Presidential and Parliamentary Systems

Presidential democracies most clearly show the separation of power between the executive and legislative branches. These systems, a minority of the world's governments, have a **president** who combines the offices of head of state with chief of government. He or she is elected more or less directly by the people (in the United States the quaint electoral college mediates between the people and the actual election), is invested with considerable powers, and cannot be easily ousted by the legislative body. In **parliamentary systems**, the head of state (figurehead monarch or weak president) is an office distinct from the chief of government (**prime minister**, premier, or chancellor). In this system, the prime minister is the important figure.

Notice that in parliamentary systems voters elect only a legislature; they cannot split their tickets between the legislature and executive (see Figure 14.1). The legislature then elects an executive from its own ranks. If the electoral system is based on proportional representation (see Chapter 13), chances are there will be several parties in parliament. If no one party has a majority of the seats, two or more parties will have to form a coalition. Whether one party or several, a majority of parliament must support the cabinet. Usually a monarch (as in Britain and Spain) or weak president (as in Germany or Israel) "asks"—there's no real choice in the matter—the head of the largest party to become prime minister and "form a government." **Cabinet** and **government**, used interchangeably, are what Americans call an **administration** (the Blair government but the Clinton administration). The prime minister, after consulting with the parties likely to support him or her, names a team of ministers for the cabinet who are themselves members of the

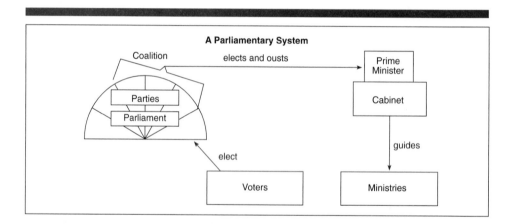

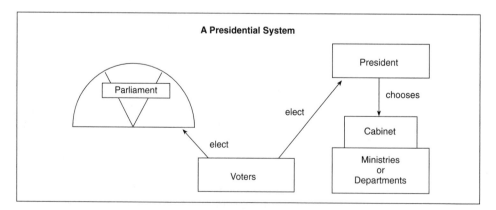

Figure 14.1 Parliamentary versus Presidential Systems

parliament. These ministers then guide the various ministries or departments of government that form the executive branch. The prime minister and cabinet are "responsible" (in the original sense of the word, "answerable") to the parliament. (Prior to democratization in the nineteenth century, ministers were responsible only to the monarch.)

Presidents in presidential systems are not responsible to legislatures. The close connection between the legislative and executive is broken. Presidents are elected on their own and choose cabinet ministers or department secretaries from *outside* the ranks of the legislative body. In the United States, of course, top executive and judicial officers must be approved by the Senate. The two branches of government cannot control, dissolve, or oust the other, as can happen in parliamentary systems. This gives presidential systems great stability. The president may be unpopular and face a hostile Congress, but he or she can still govern with existing constitutional and statutory powers already in hand.

Pros and Cons of Each System

The United States takes great pride in its **separation of powers**, the famous "checks and balances" that the Founding Fathers insisted on. Having just won independence from George III and his executive dictatorship, they set one branch of government as a check against the power of another. It was an extremely clever arrangement and has admirably preserved America from tyranny. But it is terribly slow and cumbersome, what political scientist Edward S. Corwin called an "invitation to struggle"

KEY TERM

separation of powers
Legislative and executive branches checking and balancing each other.

between the executive and legislative branches. The two branches can effectively stymie each other. Congress can fail to pass something the president wants, and the president can veto something Congress wants. Some scholars think such an executive-legislative *deadlock* is virtually the norm for the U.S. presidential system.

Important questions, such as campaign-funding reform, can get stuck for years between the two branches of government. The president cannot dissolve Congress and hold new elections, which are set by the calendar. Congress cannot oust a president except by the impeachment procedure. Only two presidents, Andrew Johnson and Bill Clinton, have ever been impeached, and they were not convicted by the Senate. Richard Nixon resigned before the House of Representatives could vote to impeach him. The repeated showdowns of the sort between the Clinton administration and the Republican-dominated Congress are standard in U.S. history.

West Europeans consider the American system inefficient and unintelligible, and they are actually equipped with more modern systems that evolved after the U.S. Constitution was devised. Their parliamentary systems have a **fusion of power** that does not set the branches against each other. In fact, it's sometimes hard to distinguish between legislative and executive branches, for the top executives are themselves usually members of parliament. In the British, German, Japanese, and Dutch systems, the prime ministers must be elected to parliament, just like an ordinary legislator, before he or she can become chief of government. As leaders of the biggest parties, they are formally called on (by the monarch or figurehead president) to form a government. The individuals forming this government or cabinet have both their seats in parliament and offices in the executive departments. They report back often to parliament. At any time, about a hundred British **MPs** (members of Parliament) also serve at various levels in the executive ministries and departments. Thus legislators are also executives. The cabinet, in effect, is a committee of parliament sent over to supervise the administration of the executive branches of government.

> ### KEY TERMS
>
> **fusion of power** The executive as a leading offshoot of the legislature.
>
> **MP** British term for member of Parliament, namely, the House of Commons.
>
> **opposition** Those parties in parliament not supporting the government.
>
> **backbencher** An ordinary member of parliament with no leadership or executive responsibilities.

When Britain's parliament is in session, the cabinet members show up to answer questions from their fellow MPs. Britain's House of Commons holds a Question Hour most afternoons at the beginning of the session. The members of the two main parties sit facing each other across an aisle on, respectively, the "government benches" and "**opposition** benches." The front bench of the former is reserved for cabinet ministers, the front bench of the latter for the opposition's "shadow cabinet," who are the MPs who would become ministers if their party should win the next election. MPs without any executive responsibilities sit behind the cabinets and are called **backbenchers**. Most questions to the prime minister and his or her cabinet come from the opposition benches—first written questions and then oral follow-ups. The answers are criticized, and the opposition tries to embarrass the government with an eye to winning the next election. Most parliamentary systems operate in a similar fashion.

In the U.S. system, with its separation of powers, committees of the Senate or House can summon cabinet members and other officials of the executive branch to committee hearings. But appearing before a committee is not the same as a grilling before the entire legislative body. The president, of course, as equal to and separate from Congress, cannot be called to testify.

There are several advantages to a parliamentary system. The executive-legislative deadlock, which happens frequently in the American system, cannot occur because both the executive and legislative branches are governed by the same party. If the British Conservatives win a majority of the seats in the House of Commons, the leaders of the party are automatically the country's executives. When the Conservative cabinet drafts a new law, it is sent to the House of Commons to be passed. There is rarely difficulty or delay in getting the law passed because the Conservative MPs almost invariably obey the wishes of the party's leaders. If, by some strange circumstance, members of the governing party should disagree with their own leaders in the cabinet, they can withdraw their support and vote "no confidence" in the government. The government then "falls" and must be replaced by a new leadership team that commands the support of a majority of the House of Commons. If a new election gives the opposition party the numerical edge in parliament, the cabinet resigns and is replaced by the leaders of the newly victorious party, formerly known as the "shadow cabinet." Either way, there cannot be a long disagreement between executive and legislative branches; they are fused into one.

The prime minister and cabinet can be speedily ousted in parliamentary systems. Any important vote in parliament can be designated a vote of confidence. If the prime minister loses, he or she takes it as a signal of lack of parliamentary support and resigns. There is no agony of impending impeachment of the sort that paralyzed Washington under Presidents Nixon and Clinton. A new prime minister can be voted in immediately. If the government makes a major policy blunder, parliament can get rid of the cabinet without waiting for its term to expire. When Americans become unhappy with presidents' policies, there is little the system can do to remove them from the White House early. Parliamentary systems don't get stuck with unpopular prime ministers.

Parliamentary systems have other difficulties, however. First, because members of parliament generally obey their party leaders, votes in parliament can be closely predicted. The parties supporting the government will vote for a bill the cabinet has drafted. Parties opposing the government will vote against it. Floor speeches and corridor persuasion have no impact; the legislators vote the way their party instructs. MPs in such systems have lost their independence, and their parliaments have become little more than rubber stamps for the cabinet. The passage of legislation is more rational, speedy, and efficient, to be sure, but the legislature in such systems cannot "talk back" to the executive or make independent inputs. This makes European parliaments rather dull and less important than Capitol Hill in Washington, where legislators often oppose the president, even when of their own party. Many European legislators are jealous of the spunky independence and separate resources that American representatives and senators enjoy.

Second, depending on the party system and electoral system, parliamentary democracies often have many parties, with no single party controlling a majority of seats in parliament. This means the largest party must form a *coalition* with smaller parties in order to command more than half the seats. The head of the largest party becomes prime minister, and the head of the second largest party becomes foreign minister. Other cabinet positions, or portfolios, are assigned by bargaining. Italy and Israel are often examples of coalition governments, and they illustrate what can go wrong: The coalition partners quarrel over policy. One or more parties may withdraw from the coalition, bringing it below the required majority in parliament. The government then "falls" for lack of parliamentary support, with or without a formal vote of no confidence. This leads to instability, frequent cabinet changes, and loss of executive authority. Italy, for example, at last count had fifty-six governments since World War II.

This is not as bad as it sounds—remember, the "government" simply means "cabinet"—and the cabinets are often put back together again after bargaining among the same coalition partners. The trouble is that prime ministers must concentrate on not letting the coalition fall apart, and thus they hesitate to launch new policies that might alienate one of the member parties. The problem here is not one of too much change but of too little: the same parties in the same coalitions getting stuck over the same issues. **Immobilism**, the inability to decide major questions, is the danger of multiparty parliamentary systems. Notice how this parallels the problem of deadlock in presidential systems.

> **KEY TERM**
>
> **immobilism** Inability of coalition governments to solve major questions.

Not all parliamentary systems, to be sure, suffer from immobilism. Britain, Germany, New Zealand, and Spain have cohesive and effective cabinets because they have to share little or no power in coalition governments. The largest parties in these countries are big enough to govern either alone or with only a little help from like-minded parties. The German coalition has fallen only once, in 1982, when the small Free Democratic party abandoned the Social Democrats and went to the Christian Democrats to form a new coalition. The fall of a cabinet because of defection is equally rare in Britain: Since World War II it happened only once, when the small Scottish Nationalist party withdrew its support from the minority Labour government in 1979. In general, the more parties in a coalition, the less stable it is.

What Legislatures Do

Let us take a closer look at the old high-school civics question, how does a bill become law? The first step is to draft and introduce the proposal. In most democratic legislatures, any member may introduce a bill. Without the support of a larger group, however, it may not get very far. In the German Bundestag, as in

much of Europe, individual legislators may not introduce bills on their own; only a *Fraktion* of fifteen
members may propose legislation. Bills often originate
in the executive branch, however, with an agency
drafting a proposal and finding a sympathetic legislator to introduce the bill to the legislative chamber.
When U.S. senators or representatives want to propose a bill of their own, their staffs usually do the

actual writing, with the Office of the Legislative Council checking to ensure proper wording. In parliamentary governments, the executive branch may introduce
legislation directly, since cabinet members hold seats in the legislature.

Key Concepts BICAMERAL OR UNICAMERAL?

Some two-thirds of parliaments in the world have two chambers, an upper house (the U.S.
Senate, the British House of Lords, the German Bundesrat) plus a lower house (the U.S. House
of Representatives, the British House of Commons, or the German Bundestag). These are
called **bicameral** (two chambers) legislatures. Despite its name, the upper house usually has
less and sometimes much less power than the lower house. Typically if the upper house
objects to something passed by the lower house, the lower house can override their objections,
often by a simple majority. Only the two houses of the U.S. Congress are coequal and must
pass identically worded versions of a bill. A smaller number of parliaments are **unicameral**
(one chamber), such as China's National Peoples Congress, Sweden's Riksdag, and Israel's
Knesset. Yugoslavia once experimented with a five-chambered parliament. South Africa had
a curious and short-lived three-chambered parliament with one house each for whites,
mixed-race peoples, and East Indians. The majority black population
was unrepresented in the national parliament of South Africa. (Since
1994, South Africa has had a bicameral parliament with a black
majority.)

The reason for two chambers is clear in federal systems (see
Chapter 13). The upper house represents the component parts, and
the lower house represents districts based on population. This was
the great compromise solution incorporated in the U.S.
Constitution: The Senate represented the states and the House the
people. A federal system requires an upper chamber. Germany's Bundesrat, for example, represents the sixteen *Länder* and is coequal to the lower house on constitutional questions. On
other issues, however, it can be overridden by the Bundestag.

The utility of an upper house in unitary systems is unclear. Britain's House of Lords (its
members or "peers" are chosen by either heredity or by lifetime appointment) is mostly an
elderly debating society that sometimes catches errors in laws passed too quickly and obedi-
ently by Commons. Otherwise, the Commons overrides any objection from the House of
Lords with a simple majority vote. This is also true of the French Senat, an indirectly elected
body that largely expresses farming interests. The New Zealanders, Danes, and Swedes—all
with unitary systems—came to the conclusion that their upper houses served no purpose and
abolished them in recent decades.

The Finnish parliament is unicameral—with no upper chamber—and consists of 200 seats arrayed in a semi-circle, the standard layout for parliaments. Also standard are the buttons on each member's desk to register his or her vote, which is then electronically tabulated and displayed instantly. (Michael Roskin)

The real power of modern legislatures is in their committees, which can make or break a proposal. Democratic parliaments often hold public hearings to get expert testimony and input from interest groups. If the bill is reported favorably out of committee, it goes to "the floor," the full chamber, which must give it a majority vote. In the United States, floor debate may lead to amendments or even to the death of a bill. This cannot happen in parliamentary systems; obedient parties will give some speeches for the media and then pass it. Remember, in these systems parliament passes whatever the government wants. To make the bill law requires the signature of the president (who can veto it) or the prime minister (who rarely vetoes a measure because it is the handiwork of his or her cabinet).

The Committee System

Virtually every legislature has a number of standing or permanent committees and may from time to time create special ad hoc committees to study urgent matters. The British House of Commons has five standing committees plus several specialized committees. These committees are less important than their U.S. counterparts, for the fusion of powers of the British system means that Parliament is not supposed to review carefully, criticize, or reject bills the cabinet has submitted. With separation of powers, the committees of the U.S. Congress are most fully developed. The House of Representatives has twenty-seven standing committees—the Senate, twenty-one—and they often make the news. Assignment to the more prestigious of these committees, such as the House Ways and Means Committee or Judiciary Committee, is a boon to the career of a member of Congress, for they give members more media exposure.

U.S. congressional committees screen the thousands of bills that are introduced at every session and pick out the few that merit serious study and consideration. A government bill in a parliamentary system is automatically important; "private members' bills" may be quickly weeded out in committee. Second, legislatures are so large that bills cannot be drafted by the entire membership; to work out an agreement on the precise wording and scope of legislation, proposals must be referred to relatively small groups of lawmakers. It should not be surprising, therefore, that the bulk of legislative work is not performed on the floor but in committee rooms.

In the United States, each committee has several specialized subcommittees; the two houses have a total of about 250 subcommittees. Changes in the 1970s weakened what were considered to be the tyrannical powers of committee chairpersons by making it easier to establish subcommittees. It worked; committees and their chairpersons are not what they used to be. But now, critics charge, subcommittees and *their* chairpersons have decentralized and fragmented power too much, weakening Congress as an institution. A cure for one problem produced new problems, the story of many political reforms.

These same reforms of the 1970s broke the power of appointment of the senior House and Senate leaders of both parties. Committee chairs and membership were generally assigned on the basis of seniority. Now, when the parties caucus at the beginning of a session in each house, members vote for committee chairpersons by secret ballot, effectively breaking the seniority system. Party committees in each house make committee assignments and usually try to take members' interests and expertise into account. Capitol Hill is now more open and democratic than it used to be, but interestingly, this has not enhanced its power vis-à-vis the executive branch.

In many parliamentary systems, committees are not as specialized and lack the political influence of their American counterparts. The standing committees

A Senate subcommittee hearing chaired by Senator Joseph Biden (D-Delaware) hears testimony from experts and interest groups on the situation of East European minorities. Much legislative work is done in such committees, often with little notice by the press or public. (Michael Roskin)

of the British House of Commons are designed to be flexible and broad and play a less critical role. They work out the details of a bill after a "first reading" on the floor has sent the bill to them. Newer British committees are specialized. Education, overseas aid, race relations, science and technology, and nationalized industries have permanent committees in Commons. The counterpart in the French National Assembly is the commission—again not as compartmentalized as the American committee. In studying a bill, the commission assigns only one member—called the *rapporteur*—to the task, rather than working collectively as in the United States and Britain. In the United States, specialization is the name of the game. The larger committees, such as the Senate Foreign Relations Committee, may have a dozen subcommittees.

Standing committees in the U.S. Congress are balanced so that they will represent both political parties and the states or geographic regions with the greatest interest in the committee's area of specialization. A Nebraskan is often on the Agricultural Committee and a New Yorker on the Education and Labor Committee. Each standing committee is bipartisan, made up of Democrats and Republicans in proportion to each party's seats in that house of Congress.

A Closer Look at Legislatures

The main purpose of legislative bodies, in theory, is to formulate laws. This, however, varies among political systems and is generally in decline. Ideally, legislatures initiate laws, propose constitutional amendments, ratify treaties, control tax revenues, and scrutinize government activities. In authoritarian systems, however, legislatures are usually just rubber stamps for the dictator.

Lawmaking   Although legislatures *pass* laws, few of them *originate* laws—which is why we must take their "rule-initiation function" with a grain of salt. Much legislation actually originates in government departments and agencies, comes to the attention of cabinet officers, and is sent on to the legislature, which may alter it somewhat. In parliamentary systems, especially where one party has a majority of seats, the cabinet gets what it wants. Party discipline makes sure that members of the ruling parties will automatically vote the way party leaders instruct. Votes in such legislatures are highly predictable along party lines; some observers say such parliaments have become rubber stamps for the executive. The U.S. Congress, with its weak and decentralized party system, represents at least a partial rejection of this development. Party discipline is weak, and members sometimes buck their own party. But even in the United States, notice how much of the legislative agenda is determined by items sent over from the White House: economic initiatives, use of troops overseas, expanding or cutting domestic programs, and setting new criteria for pollution or auto safety. Even the budget, the original "power of the purse" that gave legislatures their importance, is now an annual congressional *reaction* to the budget produced by the White House budget office. Accordingly, "lawmaking" is not the only nor perhaps even the most important thing that legislatures do.

Constituency Work   Legislators spend much time helping constituents. Most have staffs to answer letters, make sure people get their government checks, and generally show that the elected representatives really care. Often "lawmakers" are so busy with **constituency casework** that they pay little attention to making laws. In effect, elected representatives have partly transformed themselves into **ombudsmen**, specialists who intervene with government on behalf of people with complaints. Is there anything wrong with this? Is it not a perfectly valid and necessary role for legislators to play? It is, but something gets lost: the wider view that a representative should have in looking out for the common good of the whole country. A legislator immersed in constituency work has no time for or interest in bigger questions, so the initiative goes more and more to the executive branch. What then will become of democracy?

Constituency service is one main way elected representatives keep getting reelected. Incumbents are in a position to do favors. They frequently visit their home districts to listen to local problems and arrange for government help, something an out-of-office challenger cannot do. Thus, legislators in systems as different as the United States and Japan can lock themselves into power.

> ### KEY TERMS
>
> **constituency casework**   The attention legislators pay to the complaints of the people who elect them.
>
> **ombudsman**   Swedish for "agent"; a lawyer employed by parliament to help citizens wronged by government.

Case Studies | THE U.S. PORK BARREL

Legislators everywhere look after the needs of their district. Projects that bring improvements to or spend money in their district are called "pork barrel," after the occasional gifts of plantation owners to their slaves of a barrel of pickled pork parts. Modern pork-barrel projects include highways, bridges, dams, canals, military bases, and parks—anything that makes the folks back home happy.

Is the U.S. pork barrel bigger than in other systems? Likely, although Japanese legislators are also famous for delivering massive public-works projects to their districts. Republicans long denounced Democrat-sponsored pork-barrel legislation but could not resist it when they controlled Congress in the 1990s. And that is the point: Legislators will generally do whatever gets them reelected. Pork is built into our system of democracy. If the United States and Japan wish to reduce the amount of pork, they will have to devise ways to break the close connection between their elected representatives and their home districts. But this close connection is precisely what such systems  prize. Would you want a system in which Congresspersons are distant and uncaring about their districts? Besides, much good and important legislation would not pass if leaders could not use pork as inducements to vote for it. Pork is a little bribe to win legislative compliance. Returning to a theme of Chapter 1, do not get angry at a fact like the pork barrel; instead, analyze it. Why does it exist? What functions does it serve? You may find that it is built into the system.

Supervision and Criticism of Government   The potentially more important role of modern legislatures is keeping a sharp and critical eye on the executive branch. Even if they don't originate much legislation, legislatures can powerfully affect the work of government by monitoring government activity to make sure it is in the nation's interest, uncorrupt, and effective. Virtually every U.S. administration must modify its policies because Congress raises difficult and sometimes embarrassing questions, even though it may have passed little legislation on these matters.

In Britain, the Question Hour allows members of Parliament to grill ministers, sometimes with devastating results. Even if the British cabinet knows that it is almost immune to a vote of no confidence—because it controls the largest party in Commons—its members must be very careful in answering these questions. If they give a bad, unconvincing answer or are caught lying, it can cost the ruling party the next election.

In Israel in 1983, the Begin government had to end its military thrust into Lebanon because of criticism in the Knesset that the campaign was lasting too long, costing too many lives, and not producing a stable solution. In 1998, congressional investigations into overseas Democratic fund-raising embarrassed the Clinton administration. Keeping the government on its toes is one of the best things a legislature can do, even if it doesn't pass any laws.

Education   Legislatures also inform and instruct the citizenry on the affairs of government; they create mass demands by calling public attention to problems. In the mid-1960s, Senator J. William Fulbright (D-Arkansas), chair of the Senate Foreign Relations Committee, educated Americans about the Vietnam war by televising his committee's hearings. All democratic countries carry extensive press reports on parliamentary debate, and many now televise them.

Representation   One of the chief functions of legislatures is to represent people. Although legislators are a far more elite group of people than those they represent, most legislators in democracies consider the interests of all their constituents; it helps get them reelected. Even in the U.S. South, now that African Americans are voting in considerable numbers, members of Congress take care not to offend them. A large part of representation is psychological; people need to *feel* they're represented. When they don't, they become resentful of government power, and the government loses legitimacy. "No taxation without representation," chanted the American colonials. The **apartheid** laws of South Africa, passed by a whites-only legislature, evoked no support and much disobedience from the black majority. Because of this, the apartheid system eventually cracked.

> **KEY TERM**
>
> **apartheid**   System of strict racial segregation formerly practiced in South Africa.

The foregoing are some of the roles performed by legislatures. Note that only one of them is lawmaking, and that is usually just a follow-up on ideas initiated by bureaucrats and executives. Still, if legislatures carry out the other functions mentioned, they're doing a lot.

The Decline of Legislatures

By the late nineteenth century, observers began to notice that parliaments were not working the way they were supposed to. Contrary to Locke's expectations, legislatures seemed to be losing power to the executive. Most political scientists would agree that the trend has continued and grown. Some, however, hold that the original Lockean expectations were too high to begin with and that parliaments provide useful checks on the executive even though they do not originate much legislation. For better or worse, a high-tech age has shifted power away from legislatures.

Structural Disadvantages

In parliamentary systems, party discipline is strong, and legislators obey party whips. Members of the legislative body are unmoved by speeches or debates to vote against their party. If they do, they can lose their party's endorsement and be dropped from the party list at the next election. In effect, they are fired from parliament. Gilbert and Sullivan summed it up in the words of a successful British politician in *Pinafore*: "I always voted at my party's call and never thought of thinking for myself at all." In European parliaments we can usually predict within a vote or two how the issue will be decided: in favor of the government, because the government (or cabinet) commands a majority of seats. In such systems, individual members do little and there is no special excitement in the press and public about parliamentary affairs. Only when coalitions break up or when members of one party defect to another (a rare occurrence) do things get unpredictable and therefore interesting. The European parliaments really are more rational and efficient than the U.S. Congress, but they are also less powerful and less interesting. Efficiency has led to atrophy.

The U.S. **Capitol** Hill has no such problem with efficiency. Its near-feudal dispersion of power with weak party discipline and its tendency to deadlock with the executive have made it most inefficient. Yet it is precisely these impediments that keep Congress lively and important. In few other countries can the national legislature as a whole "talk back" to the executive and even override a presidential veto. In parliamentary systems, the opposition parties criticize the government party, but the government party does not criticize its own cabinet in power. Nevertheless, even in the United States power has drifted to the executive. The president speaks with one voice; Congress speaks with many. Congress is fragmented into committees and subcommittees—with chairpersons vying for media attention—and this fragmentation delays and often prevents agreement. Congress expects and even demands presidential leadership and usually gives presidents most of what they want after some controversy and debate.

One case illustrates Congress's dependency on the president's power.

> **KEY TERM**
>
> **Capitol**   Home of the U.S. Congress (note it is spelled -*ol*, not -*al*).

Despairing of ever being able to cut the huge spending budget, Congress attempted to hand the power to an appointed congressional official in the 1985 Gramm-Rudman Act. The Supreme Court immediately threw out this provision in the law; it was clearly unconstitutional. Congress then attempted to hand the power to cut the budget to the White House with the 1996 "line-item" veto, a major shift in power from the legislative to the executive. The Supreme Court also threw it out; the Constitution does not permit the veto of part of a bill. It was almost as if Congress were saying, "We give up; we're too divided. So here, Mr. President, you take over our constitutional duties." The astonishing thing about the U.S. Congress, the last Mohican of independent parliaments, is that it *wants* to surrender power to the executive.

Lack of Expertise

Few legislators are experts on technical, military, economic, or social problems. Of the 535 senators and representatives in both houses of Congress, typically half are lawyers. European parliaments have fewer lawyers and more schoolteachers, journalists, and full-time party people. But hardly anywhere are technical experts elected to legislatures, and few legislators are professionally equipped to deal with such technical matters as nuclear power, medical care, international currency fluctuations, and environmental pollution. Accordingly, legislators must rely chiefly on experts from the executive departments. Much legislation originates with these specialists, and they are often called as witnesses to committee hearings. The ensuing legislation usually grants these executive specialists considerable discretion in applying the law.

Most parliaments have little or nothing in the way of independent research support; their data come either from the government or from private interest groups. Only the U.S. Congress—again, based on the idea of separation of powers—can generate its own data. The General Accounting Office (GAO), Congressional Research Service (CRS), and Congressional Budget Office (CBO) are all part of the legislative branch. They provide independent evaluations and data to lessen Congress's dependence on the executive. No other legislature in the world has a fraction of this research capability. Still, it remains to be seen if the research agencies of Congress can counterbalance the massive information advantage of the executive branch.

Some hope computers can help legislators overcome this information gap. At first computers were used in legislators' offices simply as advanced typewriters, to speed up the handling of constituent letters. More recently, though, computer networks have been set up to put at the legislators' fingertips all types of government and private data. This could make parliamentarians almost as knowledgeable as bureaucrats, but legislators need the time and interest to review reams of data. In most cases, legislative assistants who specialize in certain areas are the ones who make use of computerized data bases; they then pass on their findings to the elected member.

Psychological Disadvantages

Citizens of any country are more impressed with presidents or prime ministers than with parliaments. There may be a deep human need to respond to a single leading personality. A president can have charisma but not a legislature. American children are socialized to revere the president but to disdain members of Congress. As was mentioned in Chapter 12, even in parliamentary systems voters now respond to the personalities of the candidates for prime minister. Television, by giving a great deal more air time to chief executives than to any other political figure, heightens this tendency. People come to see their president or prime minister as a parental figure, calmly guiding the country toward safety while the silly parliamentarians squabble among themselves. School textbooks in the United States often depict the president as a sort of "daddy." This leads to what some political scientists fear is "president worship."

The Absentee Problem

If you visit a legislature in session you might be disappointed, for usually the chamber is nearly empty. Most of the time, most members don't have to be present, and they aren't. They have a lot of other things to do: helping and visiting constituents, talking with interest groups, and sitting on committees. Why bother listening to speeches in the chamber? They're not going to change anyone's mind, and everyone pretty much knows their content in advance. The speeches are not for other legislators; they're for the mass media.

Absent most of the time, the member is really needed only to vote, and sometimes not even then. British party whips can get a high turnout for an important vote. In Sweden, an electronic system summons members from all over the Riksdag after the speeches are over. They press their *ja* or *nej* button according to their parties' wishes, glance up at the electronic tabulation (which was never in doubt), and then leave. The Riksdag chamber has been full for only five to ten minutes.

Most systems have ways of recording members' votes without their presence. When the French National Assembly votes, a few members of each party move down the rows of absent fellow party members' desks and flick their voting switches to a *pour* or *contre* position, as the party has specified. The press then reports that the measure passed by a vote of around 300 to 200, but that account is deceptive, as typically only three dozen members were present for the vote. Theoretically, the French system could function with just one member present from each party.

The U.S. House and Senate require members to be present to vote, but even if absent they can arrange to have their votes "paired against" that of another absent legislator with the opposite viewpoint. The yes vote cancels out the no vote, so the passage of the measure is unaffected, and the member can still claim to have voted for or against something.

What is the impact of legislative absenteeism? It may indicate that the legislator is busy doing other important things of the sort discussed earlier. It may also indicate just plain laziness. But it surely means that legislators no longer regard legislating as their chief function. By their absence they admit that they are not important, at least not in the way originally seen for legislators. Is there any way to fix the problem? Only by weakening party discipline and party-line voting so that no one could predict how a floor vote would go. If bills were up for grabs, some excitement and tension would return to floor debate, and members would have an interest and incentive to show up and participate. The trade-off would be that the passage of legislation would be more chaotic and unpredictable.

Lack of Turnover

In most democratic parliaments, members tend to become career, lifetime legislators. Once elected, they usually get reelected as long as they wish to serve. This means it's difficult for fresh, young blood with new ideas to enter parliament, and on average parliamentarians are rather old, in their fifties. In the U.S. House, most representatives run for reelection, and almost all win. Incumbency brings terrific advantages: name recognition, favors done for constituents, media coverage, and plentiful campaign funds from PACs and other interest groups. Unless the representative has gotten involved in some scandal, he or she is almost automatically reelected. Challengers are so discouraged that several dozen House incumbents run unopposed. In many other contests opposition is only token. Why waste time and money in a hopeless race?

What happens to democracy when an elected representative is not often ousted until death or retirement? It loses some of its ability to innovate and respond to new currents in public opinion. It gets stodgy. The Founding Fathers made the House term deliberately short, just two years, to let popular views wash freely into the chamber. Alexander Hamilton described the frequent elections to the House in this way: "Here, sir, the people govern. Here they act by their immediate representatives." He might have a hard time believing that usually almost all representatives who wish to run win reelection and that turnover is actually higher in the Senate, a chamber that was designed to be insulated from mass passions. All this raised the question of limits on congressional terms. Elections in the 1990s, however, have brought a major influx of new faces— partly due to the retirements of incumbents—so that now the average representative has served less than twelve years. With turnover like that, mandatory limits seem unnecessary.

The parliamentary systems have similar problems. Few legislators are replaced by elections and most consider their membership in parliament a career. If the system is proportional representation (discussed in Chapter 13), the more senior party people are higher up on the party list, ensuring their election. Young newcomers may be entered at the bottom of their party lists with scant chance of winning. However, PR systems do have the advantage of letting new, small parties into parliament with fresh faces and new ideas. In the 1980s, the Greens (as ecology parties like to be called) entered several West European parliaments, forcing the big, established parties to pay attention to environmental problems.

The Dilemma of Parliaments

The deadlock between Russian President Boris Yeltsin and the Russian legislature, the State Duma, illustrates the dilemma of parliaments. To get things done, power must be concentrated, as in the hands of a powerful executive. To keep things democratic, however, power must be dispersed, that is, divided between an executive and a legislature. Russia urgently needs vast reforms—the economy teetered on the brink of collapse—and Yeltsin claimed to be the leader to carry them out. The Duma, on the other hand, dominated by Communists and nationalists who oppose Yeltsin, disputed and blocked him. Yeltsin, equipped with a constitution he had engineered, practiced one-man rule with dictatorial tendencies. Russia experienced the sort of executive-legislative deadlock well known in the United States.

How this problem is solved will determine much of the future course of democracy in Russia. One man may take over and "get things done," but it may not be democratic. An obstreperous parliament, stacked with special interests, may preserve pluralism and block dictatorship, but at the price of accomplishing little. It is precisely this struggle between the two branches—making sure that neither gains too much power—that builds democracy. We cannot offer the Russians much in the way of specific advice on how to achieve executive-legislative balance. The Russians have no tradition of democracy, parliaments, or limited government, and their problems are far larger and more desperate than ours. We can assure them, however, that executive-legislative problems can be solved and offer ourselves as a modest and ungainly example.

Key Terms

absolutism (p. 245)	immobilism (p. 252)
administration (p. 248)	MP (p. 250)
apartheid (p. 258)	ombudsman (p. 257)
backbencher (p. 250)	opposition (p. 250)
bicameral (p. 253)	parliament (p. 245)
cabinet (p. 248)	parliamentary system (p. 247)
Capitol (p. 259)	president (p. 247)
constituency casework (p. 257)	presidential democracy (p. 247)
Estates General (p. 246)	prime minister (p. 247)
feudalism (p. 245)	Riksdag (p. 246)
fusion of power (p. 250)	separation of powers (p. 249)
government (p. 248)	unicameral (p. 253)

Key Websites

At the House website, you can access individual members' websites, as well as learn about pending bills, the making of laws, the difference between statutes and continuing resolutions, mark-ups, and other minutiae of the legislative process.
http://www.house.gov/

Less robust than the House site, the U.S. Senate site gives you access to all the senators' e-mail and website addresses, and also explains filibusters, unanimous consent agreements, and other parlance of the Senate floor.
http://www.senate.gov/

Thomas: Legislative Information on the Internet. This site concentrates on tracking legislation that is currently going through Congress. It also has schedules for floor activities, roll call of votes, the Congressional record, and historical documents.
http://thomas.loc.gov/home/thomas2.html

This site provides information about the House of Commons and Members of England's Parliament.
http://www.parliament.uk/commons/cminfo.htm

This is the best site to link to any legislative body in the world that has a website.
http://www.agora.stm.it/elections/parlemen.htm

Further Reference

Burns, James MacGregor. *The Deadlock of Democracy: Four-Party Politics in America*, rev. ed. Englewood Cliffs, NJ: Spectrum, 1963.

Copeland, Gary W., and Samuel C. Patterson, eds. *Parliaments in the Modern World: Changing Institutions*. Ann Arbor, MI: University of Michigan Press, 1994.

Deering, Christopher J., and Steven S. Smith. *Committees in Congress*, 3rd ed. Washington, D.C.: CQ Press, 1997.

Dodd, Lawrence C., and Bruce I. Oppenheimer, eds. *Congress Reconsidered*, 6th ed. Washington, D.C.: CQ Press, 1997.

Gregg, Gary L. *The Presidential Republic: Executive Representation and Deliberative Democracy*. Lanham, MD: Rowman & Littlefield, 1997.

King, Anthony. *Running Scared: Why America's Politicians Campaign Too Much and Govern Too Little*. New York: Free Press, 1997.

Laver, Michael, and Norman Schofield. *Multiparty Government: The Politics of Coalition in Europe*. New York: Oxford University Press, 1990.

Lijpart, Arend, ed. *Parliamentary versus Presidential Government*. New York: Oxford University Press, 1992.

Loomis, Burdett A. *The Contemporary Congress.* New York: St. Martin's, 1996.

Suleiman, Ezra N., ed. *Parliaments and Parliamentarians in Democratic Politics.* New York: Holmes & Meier, 1986.

Sundquist, James L. *Constitutional Reform and Effective Government.* Washington, D.C.: Brookings Institution, 1986.

Thurber, James A., ed. *Rivals for Power: Presidential-Congressional Relations.* Washington, D.C.: CQ Press, 1996.

CHAPTER 15

Executives

There have been executives a lot longer than there have been legislatures. Tribal chiefs, kings and queens, and emperors appeared with the dawn of civilization, and most of the time they didn't have legislatures to worry about. Parliaments are relatively new. Even today, powerful executives seem more natural to us than divided and contentious parliaments. Executives have a built-in psychological advantage over legislatures.

Indeed, the word **government** in much of the world means the executive branch. As we considered in the previous chapter, in Europe, *government* basically equals *cabinet*. The "Blair government" is just another way of saying Prime Minister Blair's cabinet plus some additional subcabinet assistants. In the United States (and nowhere else), this is called the *administration*. What Americans call the *government*, meaning all the bureaus and bureaucrats, is known in Europe as the **state**.

QUESTIONS TO CONSIDER

1. Is it too hard to oust a U.S. president?
2. What are the main differences between a president and a prime minister?
3. Have prime ministers tended to become more like presidents?
4. What case can be made for giving a U.S. president a single, six-year term. What case against?
5. Is the U.S. president too powerful?
6. What are the various styles of presidential leadership?
7. Explain Barber's classification of presidential character.
8. Explain Lasswell's psychology of political power.
9. Are cabinets as important as they used to be?

Presidents and Prime Ministers

KEY TERMS

government In the United States, all branches of the federal system; in Europe, a given cabinet.

state In Europe, all branches of the national political system; what Americans call "the government."

As discussed in Chapter 14, there is a considerable difference between parliamentary and presidential systems. A parliament indirectly elects a chief executive from one of its own numbers, a prime (originally meaning "first") minister. The parliament can also oust a prime minister and cabinet by a vote of no confidence, although this is now rare. Still, prime ministers are responsible to parliament. If they represent a party with a majority of seats, they are secure in office and can get legislative programs passed quickly and with little backtalk. Margaret Thatcher of Britain, for example, with a sizable and disciplined majority in the Commons, at times wielded powers that might make an American president jealous.

If no party has a majority, however, a government is formed by a coalition of parties, each of whom gets one or more ministries to run. Sometimes the coalition partners quarrel over policy and threaten to split up. This weakens the hand of the prime minister, as he or she knows that any major policy shift could lead to new quarrels. It's not quite right to say that prime ministers are "weaker" than presidents; it depends on whether prime ministers have a stable majority in parliament.

A presidential system bypasses this problem by having a strong president not dependent on or responsible to a parliament but elected on his or her own for a fixed term. Parliament—for example, the U.S. Congress—may not like the president's policies and may vote down presidential proposals, but parliament may not vote out the president. The president and the parliament stand side by side, sometimes glaring at each other, knowing there is nothing they can do to get rid of one another. It is sometimes said that presidents are "stronger" than prime ministers, and in terms of being able to run the executive branch for a fixed term, they are. But they may not be able to get vital new legislation or budgeting out of their legislatures. This "**deadlock** of democracy," the curse of the U.S. political system, parallels parliamentary immobilism (see p. 252). Neither system can guarantee cooperation between legislative and executive. Any system that could would be a dictatorship.

"Forming a Government" in Britain

Great Britain is the classic of parliamentary systems, one in which we still see its historical roots. The monarch, currently Queen Elizabeth II, initiates a new government (in the European sense) by formally inviting the leader of the largest party in the House of Commons to become prime minister and "form a government." As such, the prime minister appoints two dozen **ministers**, and a greater number of sub-**cabinet** officials. All are MPs and in the prime minister's party, usually chosen to represent significant groups within the party. Theoretically, the prime minister is *primus inter pares* (first among equals) and guides the cabinet to consensus. But the prime minister is really boss and can dismiss ministers. Ministers who oppose government policy are expected to not go public but merely to resign and return to their seats in Commons. Under Tony Blair, the British cabinet merely concurred on decisions he had reached earlier with a small group of close advisors, on the American pattern.

KEY TERMS
deadlock   In presidential systems, executive and legislative blocking of each other.
minister   The head of a ministry; equivalent to a U.S. departmental secretary.
cabinet   All the ministers of a government.
impeachment   An indictment by the House for the Senate to put the president on trial. (See p. 268.)

Case Studies — THE CLINTON IMPEACHMENT

The **impeachment** of President Bill Clinton in late 1998 and his trial before the Senate in early 1999 provided a revealing snapshot of American politics exhibiting the following characteristics:

Moralistic   Many Americans were angered by Clinton's breach of moral standards, both his sexual dalliance and his lying to cover it up. In few other countries are politicians expected to be moral exemplars.

Divided   Approximately two-thirds of Americans approved of how Clinton was handling his job (although not necessarily of his personal conduct) and wanted him to finish his term, while one-third hated him and wanted him out. Few Clinton supporters were passionate, but Clinton detractors felt intensely on the subject.

Partisan   The division was based strongly on political party, with conservative Republicans the most anti-Clinton, liberal Democrats the most pro-Clinton. The votes in both houses of Congress were along party lines. Clinton was acquitted because the Republicans lacked two-thirds of the Senate. In contrast, deliberations on Nixon's impeachment were bipartisan.

Personality-Driven   Americans reacted differentially to Clinton's personality. Most saw him as normal (if immature), but a minority saw him as a lying and immoral "Slick Willy." Clinton's personality served as a litmus test between two U.S. subcultures, which talked to themselves and past each other.

Public   Independent council Kenneth Starr's office made its findings public, and the media eagerly seized upon them, especially the salacious elements. Americans followed the news coverage but were disgusted by it. Many other countries would keep these things out of the mass media.

Legalistic   Everything turned on legal details and definitions that annoyed and bored most Americans. Our system is a paradise for lawyers.

Expensive   Starr's investigation—which started with the Whitewater land deal (found nothing), moved on to campaign fundraising (found nothing that both parties weren't doing), and finally settled on Monica—cost some $40 million. Clinton went millions of dollars into debt defending himself.

Institutionalized   Events unrolled according to the Constitution, with help from the precedent of other (mostly judicial) impeachments. Although there had been no presidential impeachment since Andrew Johnson in 1868, Congress knew the procedures. The strongest institutional demonstration was how difficult it is to remove a U.S. president from office.

Distasteful   Many Americans were turned off by the whole thing. They did not approve of Clinton's antics, but they disliked the immoderate Republican attack on the president even more. It looked like partisan politics run amok and deepened Americans' apathy toward anything political.

"Constructive No Confidence" in Germany

The **chancellor** of Germany is like a British prime minister but even stronger. The chancellor, too, is head of the largest party in the lower house (Bundestag). Once in the office the chancellor can be ousted only if the Bundestag votes in a replacement cabinet. This is called "constructive no confidence," and it has contributed a lot to the stability of Germany's governments. It's much harder to replace a cabinet than just oust it; as a result, constructive no confidence has succeeded only once, in 1982, when the small Free Democratic party defected from the Social Democrat-led coalition to the opposition Christian Democrats. A prime minister supported by constructive no confidence is a more powerful figure than one without it, as one might see in a comparison of the average tenures of Italian and German cabinets (several months as compared to several years).

KEY TERMS
chancellor   Germany's prime minister.
premier   France's and Italy's prime minister.

"Cohabitation" in France

President Charles de Gaulle of France (1958–1969) designed a hybrid system that has both a working president and a prime minister. The president is elected directly by the people for seven years, and a parliament is elected for five years. If both are of the same party, there is no problem. The president names a like-minded **premier**, who then serves as the link between president and parliament. In 1986 and again in 1993, though, a Socialist president, François Mitterrand, with two years left in his term, faced a newly elected parliament dominated by conservatives. The constitution gave no guidance in such a case. Mitterrand solved the problem by naming opposition Gaullists as premiers and letting them dismantle many Socialist measures. Mitterrand reserved for himself the high ground of foreign policy. The French, tongue-in-cheek, called the arrangement "cohabitation," a couple living together without benefit of wedlock. In 1997, the reverse happened: Gaullist President Jacques Chirac called parliamentary elections early, lost them, and had to face a Socialist-dominated National Assembly. The solution was cohabitation again; Chirac named Socialist chief Lionel Jospin as premier. Cohabitation works, and the French don't much mind. France thus handled the problem of deadlock that is almost the norm in the United States. The 1993 Russian constitution incorporated a French-style system with both president and premier, and it quickly led to executive-legislative deadlock.

The "Presidentialization" of Prime Ministers

Observers have noticed a tendency for parliamentary systems to "presidentialize" themselves. Prime ministers with stable majorities supporting them in parliament start acting like presidents, like powerful chiefs only dimly accountable to legisla-tors. They know they won't be ousted in a vote of no confidence, so the only

Case Studies — DIRECTLY ELECTED PRIME MINISTERS?

In 1996 Israelis, under a new law, elected a parliament and a prime minister *separately and directly*, something never before done in the world. Each Israeli voter has two votes, one for a party in the legislature and one for prime minister. By definition, parliamentary systems elect prime ministers indirectly, usually the head of the largest party in parliament. Presidential systems directly elect their chief executives. The new law thus turns Israel's system from purely parliamentary toward presidentialism, but not all the way. The **Knesset** can still vote out the prime minister on a motion of confidence, but if they do the Knesset is automatically **dissolved** and its members must stand for reelection. This makes them reluctant to vote out a prime minister. Israel's government, in the past often dependent on unstable coalitions, enjoys more stability, probably because the prime minister now has the psychological advantage of being the "people's choice." Many Israelis, however, unhappy with the power and policies of Prime Minister Benjamin Netanyahu, wanted to repeal their unique hybrid system.

thing they have to worry about is the next election, just like a president. This is seen strongly in Britain and Germany.

Increasingly, elections in parliamentary systems resemble presidential elections. Technically, there is no "candidate for prime minister" in parliamentary elections. Voters vote for a party or a member of parliament, not for a prime minister. But everybody knows that the next prime minister will be the head of the largest party, so indirectly they are electing a prime minister. For these reasons, virtually all West European elections feature posters and televised spots of the party chiefs as if they were running for president. As in U.S. elections, personality increasingly matters more than policy, party, or ideology.

Executive Terms

Presidents have fixed terms, ranging from four years for U.S. presidents to seven for French presidents. A U.S. president may be reelected once, a French president theoretically without limit. When presidents are in office a long time, even if "elected," they become corrupt and dictatorial, as President Suharto did in thirty-two years at Indonesia's helm. He was forced out only after Indonesia's economy, looted by Suharto's friends and family, collapsed in 1997.

In parliamentary systems, prime ministers have no limits on their tenure in office, providing their party wins elections. As noted, increasingly their winning depends on the personality of their leader, almost as if they were presidential candidates. Britain's Margaret Thatcher, elected for a third time in 1987, said merrily she "might just go on and on, into the next century." By 1990, however, her mounting political problems persuaded her to resign after a total of eleven and a half years in office. Furthermore, most prime ministers can dissolve parliament early. Prime ministers thus can call elections when they believe they'll do best at the polls. A good economy, sunny weather, and high ratings often persuade prime ministers to call elections a year or two early. Powers such as these might make an American president jealous.

On the other hand, prime ministers can get ousted quickly if they lose the support of a majority of parliament. When British Labour Prime Minister James Callaghan lost the support of just eleven Scottish Nationalist MPs in 1979, he slipped below a majority in Commons and was replaced virtually overnight by Tory chief Thatcher. Some Italian premiers have held office only briefly as their coalitions disintegrated. Japanese prime ministers, the playthings of powerful faction chiefs within the ruling Liberal Democratic party, average only two and a half years in office, some just a few months. Theoretically, prime ministers can serve a long time; in practice their tenure depends on political conditions such as elections, coalition breakups, and scandals. Parliamentary systems practice a kind of easy-come, easy-go with their prime ministers, something an American president would definitely not like. Presidents in presidential systems are partially insulated from the ups and downs of politics.

A U.S. president can be impeached, but this is a lengthy and uncertain procedure that has been attempted only three times. Andrew Johnson was

How Long a Presidential Term?

What is the right length for a presidential term? Many U.S. critics, on both sides of the political fence, say four years is too short. Presidents are so worried about getting reelected that much of their first term is wasted in cautious image building. They are afraid to be themselves and to try significantly new policies. Only in his second term can a president "be oneself," according to this view.

Some propose a single six-year term. Once elected, the president would feel free to do what needs to be done, even if it's unpopular, because he or she wouldn't have to worry about reelection. Six years would be long enough to put major policies into place. We should be cautious. Many in France think the seven years of their system is too long. A French president can gain too much power, grow distant, and become ineffectual and scandal-ridden. Chirac, for example, won the presidency in 1995 but quickly became unpopular, and there was nothing to do but wait until 2002.

Another problem: Is it really desirable to let the president "be oneself"? The threat of losing reelection keeps presidents on their toes; they don't want to awaken mass disapproval. This is Friedrich's "rule of anticipated reactions" discussed earlier. Take that constraint away and the president may resort to imprudent and dangerous policies. The president of Mexico is elected (not precisely democratically) for a single six-year term, and some have committed crimes and errors that brought Mexico to the brink of bankruptcy. Maybe they should have been worried about reelection. It is best to err on the side of caution in instituting a major change.

impeached by the House in 1868 but acquitted in the Senate by one vote. Richard Nixon was about to be impeached by the House but resigned just before the vote. Clinton was impeached but not convicted. When faced with a problem character as chief executive, parliamentary systems have a big advantage over the U.S. system. A simple vote of no confidence in parliament and the rascal is out. This helps explain why, even though there are lots of scandals in parliamentary systems, few become as big and paralyzing as Watergate: It's much easier to get rid of the chief.

The Roles of the Executive

Richard E. Neustadt has written that "a President is 'many men' or one man wearing many 'hats,' or playing many roles." Most modern chief executives wear more than one hat, but U.S. presidents are uncommonly strong. Elected independently of the legislature, they are the direct choice of the nation. They are head of state, head of government, party leader, commander in chief of the armed forces, top diplomat, chief executive, and even leading legislator. There is no one to whom presidents can blame for mismanaged affairs. As the sign on Harry Truman's desk put it, "The buck stops here." Since 1789, the powers of the president have grown enormously, as have those of the chief executives of all other nations.

Chief of State

Presidents are the visible symbol of the nation and perform public ceremonies that monarchs and figurehead presidents do in other nations: greet and meet visiting heads of government, receive ambassadors, represent the country at important international conferences, and report to Congress on the state of the nation.

Head of Government

Heads of government—presidents, prime ministers, or chancellors—are responsible for making and carrying out policy decisions. They supervise the bureaucratic machinery at the national level, a staggering job. The U.S. president is responsible for fourteen major departments of government, more than 100 executive bureaus, 500 administrative offices, and 600 divisions employing 2.8 million civil servants. One American worker in fifty is a federal employee (compared to one in 2,000 in Washington's day). The Executive Office of the President, with some 1,700 full-time workers, was formed in 1939 to supervise the bureaucracy on a daily basis.

Party Chief

U.S. presidents are also leaders of their political party, as are the British, French, and German heads of government. They are expected to take the lead in raising campaign funds and in endorsing and campaigning for the party's candidates.

Case Studies — LIMITING THE PRESIDENT'S WAR POWERS

The U.S. Constitution specifies—and the Supreme Court has upheld—the right of presidents to deploy the country's armed forces as they see fit. Congress has long been exasperated with this power and has tried, never successfully, to curb it. Congress fears that the president's power as commander-in-chief infringes on its power to declare war.  In the late 1930s, Congress passed a series of Neutrality Acts designed to keep the country out of the coming war, but FDR circumvented them. In 1973 Congress, which was too timid to move when the Vietnam war was at its height, passed (over President Nixon's veto) the War Powers Act, which is supposed to limit the president's use of troops in overseas combat to ninety days unless Congress approves an extension. This law did not prevent President Reagan from sending U.S. troops into Lebanon, Grenada, and Central America; Bush from sending troops to Panama, the Persian Gulf, and Somalia; or Clinton from sending troops to Haiti and Bosnia. It is likely that no law will seriously check presidential war powers and that the War Powers Act is an unconstitutional legislative veto.

More important, they are expected to lead in formulating the party's legislative program. The president is not as powerful a party leader as the prime minister in a parliamentary government because of the lack of centralization and discipline in the American party system.

Commander in Chief

Virtually all heads of government are commanders in chief of their country's military establishment. In nations new to democracy, this is a problem, as presidents or prime ministers may use the military in extralegal ways, to crush political opponents or lock themselves into power. Most countries have, at least on paper, procedures and command structures to make sure that all orders are constitutional and legal. Presidential systems often make it too easy to go to war. Both U.S. and Russian presidents have used troops in ways their respective parliaments did not approve, and nothing could be done about it. The power of commander-in-chief is one of the most dangerous of any political system.

Chief Diplomat

Likewise, presidents and prime ministers can do almost anything they want in diplomacy without parliamentary approval. They can grant diplomatic recognition to foreign countries, negotiate trade deals, and conclude "executive agreements" that are almost like treaties. Treaties themselves, those most important international contracts, generally must be ratified by the countries' legislatures. In the United States, that means a two-thirds assent from the Senate. The

Case Studies — AN IMPERIAL PRESIDENCY?

"The accumulation of all powers, legislative, executive, and judiciary, in the same hands," James Madison wrote in *The Federalist*, no. 47, "may justly be pronounced the very definition of tyranny." The Founding Fathers held that power must be balanced to prevent one person or group from seizing all control. Checks and balances, John Adams declared, are like "setting a thief to catch a thief." In recent years, however, many political scientists have voiced the fear that the modern presidency has become too powerful. How valid are these fears?

The relationship between Congress and the president has changed profoundly in the last century. Samuel P. Huntington noted that from 1882 to 1909, Congress initiated more than half (55 percent) of significant legislation; between 1910 and 1932, the figure dropped to 46 percent; and from 1933 to 1940, Congress initiated only 8 percent of all major laws. "Since 1933," Huntington wrote, "the initiative in formulating legislation, in assigning legislative priorities, in arousing support for legislation, and in determining the final content of legislation enacted has clearly shifted to the executive branch." Many observers decried the decline of Congress and growth of the presidency.

As the Vietnam war was winding down and Watergate was boiling up, a noted historian produced a book that captured the worried feeling of the time—*The Imperial Presidency*, by Arthur Schlesinger, Jr. Lyndon Johnson had taken the country to war without a declaration of war from Congress. Richard Nixon had expanded that war into Laos and Cambodia, again without a declaration of war. Nixon also "impounded" appropriations made by Congress; he simply refused to spend funds in certain areas, in effect exercising an item veto after bills had been signed into law. Was the president overstepping constitutional bounds? Were we on our way to an imperial presidency, going the way of ancient Rome, from republic to rule by the Caesars? Many thought so.

Congress attempted to reassert some of its authority, passing the War Powers Act in 1973 (see box on p. 273) and moving toward impeachment of Nixon the following year. It looked like the beginning of a new era, with Congress and the president once again in balance. But this didn't really happen, for the U.S. system *needs* a strong president to function properly.

When Jimmy Carter took office in 1977, he attempted to deimperialize the presidency, but this simply led to an ineffective White House. Carter, catching the spirit of the time, ran against Washington in 1976, billing himself as the average American who was not part of the establishment. Symbolically, on his inauguration day he and his family walked down Pennsylvania Avenue instead of riding in the presidential limousine. As an outsider, though, Carter was ignorant of the ways of Washington and quickly alienated a Congress that was dominated by his own party. His important legislation stalled on Capitol Hill and was often diluted by amendments, especially his crucial energy proposals. By the 1980 election, much of the American electorate—and perhaps even some people in Congress—wished for a more forceful and experienced chief executive.

Congress's reassertion of independent authority in the 1970s proved brief, for with the arrival of Ronald Reagan in the White House in 1981, the president once again had a fair

AN IMPERIAL PRESIDENCY? (CONTINUED)

degree of command over Capitol Hill. But this, too, did not work for long. In late 1986 it was revealed that officials of the president's National Security Council totally bypassed Congress in selling arms to Iran and using the money to fund contras attempting to overthrow the Nicaraguan government. Even President Reagan's supporters in Congress turned angry and subjected his appointees to pointed questions in committee hearings. Once again, a Congress disappointed with alleged executive misuse of power was trying to assert a check over an executive branch it had repeatedly invested with enormous powers. The problem is one of structure and not of personality.

Supreme Court has upheld presidential preeminence in foreign relations, and Congress has gone along with it.

Dispenser of Appointments

Since the introduction of the merit system into the U.S. Civil Service at the turn of the century, the power of patronage has been considerably diminished. However, all federal judges and legal officers are appointed by the president, as are top diplomats and upper-echelon management personnel in the federal departments, agencies, offices, bureaus, and divisions. All in all, a new president has some 3,000 jobs to dispense. One of the key ways a president can enforce party discipline in Congress is through patronage appointments. The president says in effect: "I'll appoint your nominee to a federal office if you support my legislative program." Politics is very much a part of appointments.

Chief Legislator

Heads of government are not only responsible for executing the laws but also have great law-making powers. The executive initiates much legislation. In Washington, the State of the Union message and national budget spell out the general direction of policy and suggest programs and laws the president wants. Further, most parliaments draft very general laws and give the chief executive broad discretionary powers in interpreting and implementing them.

Executive Leadership

Back to back, America was treated to two distinctly different leadership styles. President Carter (1977–1981) was a hands-on, detail person; he tried to supervise nearly all parts of his administration. Gifted with great intelligence and energy, he put in long hours and memorized prodigious amounts of material. Critics,

Classic Works | BARBER'S PRESIDENTIAL CHARACTER

Can you tell in advance what a president is going to be like? One political scientist thinks you can, at least in general terms. James David Barber in 1969 virtually predicted how Richard Nixon would handle a major crisis. A political scientist who can predict anything deserves our attention. Barber focuses on something he calls "presidential character" and claims you can get a fair idea of it from a psychological study of individuals' earlier life and how they reacted to problems. For example, virtually all presidents had been in college politics (often student body president), and how they handled their campaigns and student offices then was pretty much how they would handle them as president. Character is laid down early, by college years, and stays consistent, Barber argues.

Barber looks at two key variables: (1) how much presidents like political office and (2) how much energy they put into it. The first variable is divided into two types. A person who really likes the job, relishes the power and perquisites, Barber calls "positive." A person who doesn't especially enjoy the job but is ambitious and driven to achieve it, Barber calls "negative." The second variable is also divided into two types. A person with a lot of energy for the job is called "active"; one with little energy is called "passive." This gives Barber a fourfold table and allows him, based on studies of both their earlier and presidential careers, to place presidents into each square:

	Active	Passive
Positive	Roosevelt	Taft
	Kennedy	Harding
	Bush	Reagan
Negative	Johnson	Coolidge
	Nixon	Eisenhower

Presidents with an active-positive character enjoy being president and put a lot of energy into their tenure. They are flexible, have a sense of humor, and learn and change in office. The passive-positive characters, on the other hand, like being president but do not energetically throw themselves into it. They prefer to delegate matters to subordinates. They are friendly and want to be liked. Passive-negative characters are hard to find in the presidency; they are politicians who have been drafted for the job, don't particularly relish it, and don't have much energy for it. Active-negative characters are the real "meanies" in office. They've got plenty of energy, but they don't really enjoy power in a relaxed, happy way. The office is a heavy burden on them, and they take political opposition personally, as if numerous foes are "out to get them." It was no accident, Barber argues, that America's most troubled postwar presidencies came with—and because of—the active-negative characters of Johnson and Nixon, who got themselves into deeper and deeper trouble.

Many objected that just four classifications is much too simple, that people are a lot more complicated. Moreover, few presidents have not actively sought the position—they have to work very hard to win it. How can a "passive" person advance so high? By the same token, how can a person who does not relish the office want to assume it? Barber

---

argues that people can be driven to achieve the presidency and then discover that they are not especially happy in the office.

Barber, long before the Watergate break-in and investigation, predicted that Nixon would behave in a devious fashion, would dig in his heels and refuse to confess, and would make things worse for himself. This is precisely how Nixon behaved under the pressure of Watergate. He became overtense and ruined his own presidency. Chronically insecure, Nixon felt he had to ensure the election, even though he was certain to win in 1972. Barber urges political scientists and journalists to look into the lifelong character of presidential candidates in order to discern such general patterns. This will give us a much better idea of the person we are electing than following the silly charges candidates hurl at each other during campaigns.

There is a problem with this method, however: How many investigators have the ability and time to do a really exhaustive study of each major candidate? "Character" is a tricky area, open to many interpretations. Suppose half a dozen journalists, political scientists, and psychologists each do a study of candidates and finish with six different analyses? Whom do we believe? We might trust Barber for a good, impartial study, but can we trust others who claim to have insight into a candidate's character? There is a potential for hiding personal likes and dislikes under the heading of "presidential character" studies.

One way to weed out potentially dangerous characters, suggests Barber, is to have each party's leading politicians caucus and select three or four candidates who would then run in nationwide primaries. Practicing politicians—senators, representatives, and governors—know the candidates well enough to screen out problem personalities. In effect, each party would practice "peer review." Legally, however, this would be hard to enforce. Even harder would be getting the problem personalities to go along with the decision. They are usually clever manipulators who would say they were excluded for political reasons. They would raise their own money and campaign for the nomination without their peers' blessings.

---

including management experts, say this is the wrong approach, that chief executives only scatter and exhaust themselves if they try to run everything.

President Reagan (1981–1989) was the opposite; he supervised little, preferring to leave the workings of his administration in the hands of trusted subordinates. He took afternoon naps and frequent vacations. Critics say Reagan paid no attention to crucial matters, letting things slide until they turned into serious problems. The Iran-contra fiasco showed what can happen when subordinates are given only general directions and are allowed to go off on their own. The National Security Council staff thought it was doing what the President wanted when it illegally sold arms to Iran and illegally transferred the profits to the Nicaraguan contras.

President Bush moved into the office so energetically that some feared he would become a Carter-type of detail executive, busy trying to make everything run just the way he wanted it. This impression, however, may have simply resulted from the contrast with Reagan's hands-off approach, which made anyone look energetic. Bush tended to make decisions—especially in foreign policy—with a handful of close, trusted advisers. He would then present the policy to the nation and to Congress as a fait accompli.

Can there be a happy middle ground between hands on and hands off? Some say President Eisenhower (1953–1961) achieved it without letting it show. He superficially appeared to be an early version of Reagan, a hands-off type of president who was too busy golfing to look closely into the affairs of state. The press used to make fun of Eisenhower's relaxed style. Princeton political scientist Fred Greenstein, however, carefully analyzed Eisenhower's schedule and calendar and concluded that he was actually a very active and busy president who made important and complex decisions. He just didn't want to show it, preferring to let others take the credit (and sometimes the blame). Greenstein called Eisenhower's style the "hidden-hand presidency." Greenstein's findings at least partially refute those of Barber (see box on pp. 276–277), who saw Eisenhower as a passive character.

Instead of appearing to be a grandstanding leader, Eisenhower quietly manipulated things to go his way. It fooled most observers at the time, but it was an effective style. In 1954, for example, faced with the question of whether to commit U.S. forces to help the French in the Indochina war, Eisenhower called top senators to the White House. He knew they would be cautious, for we had just ended the unpopular Korean War. The senators did not favor sending U.S. forces, and Eisenhower went along with their view. Actually, he never wanted to send troops, but he made it look as if the senators had decided the issue.

President Franklin D. Roosevelt (1933–1945) used a style that some call deliberate chaos. Setting up numerous agencies and advisers, some of them working at cross-purposes, Roosevelt would let them clash until they either hashed things out or submitted the question to him for a decision. The really important decisions would rise to the top; the others would be settled without him. This, too, was a kind of middle ground between hands on and hands off. The Clinton White House borrowed this spontaneous and creative approach, but Clinton participated personally in many policy deliberations in a more hands-on manner.

Disabled Presidents

Presidential systems have another problem that parliamentary systems do not. If a prime minister becomes disabled or insane in office, he or she can be replaced overnight. Presidential systems don't quite know what to do with a seriously ill chief executive. Ecuador, for example, had difficulty legally replacing a president who had serious mental problems. The U.S. Constitution says that a president unable "to discharge the powers and duties" of office should be replaced by the vice-president, but it doesn't explain how inability can be determined. As a result, several presidents have stayed in office while seriously infirm. In France, President Mitterrand was slowly dying of cancer for most of his two terms (fourteen years) in office, but his physicians went public with it only after his death in 1996.

Woodrow Wilson (1913–1921) had suffered strokes even before he went to the Versailles Peace Conference in 1918. His poor health weakened his diplomatic bargaining power there. He collapsed while touring the United States, trying to drum up support for the Versailles Treaty and the attached League of Nations Covenant. After that, his wife ran things, saying she was just conveying the president's wishes. In 1944, when he was elected for a fourth term, Franklin Roosevelt was suffering from heart failure and hypertension. Near death's door, he went to the historic Yalta Conference in early 1945; perhaps that is why he conceded too much to Stalin. Kennedy had Addison's disease, a failure of the adrenal glands, and had been on steroids for years. Could this have affected his judgment and willingness to take risks?

Why didn't White House physicians speak out? They protected the president, partly because the doctor-patient relationship is privileged and partly because they genuinely liked the president and did not want to see him lose power. Their personal motivation is impeccable, but they may have done their country a real disservice by keeping a sick president in power when he should have stepped aside.

The Twenty-fifth Amendment, ratified in 1967, tried to define presidential inability, but it too has not solved the problem. In 1981 President Reagan was severely wounded in an assassination attempt; he lost half his blood and was in surgery more than two hours. A lung infection and fever kept him bedridden the following week, yet at no time was the Twenty-fifth Amendment invoked to let Vice-President Bush take over. Presidential advisers decided not to alarm the public. Again, the tendency is to close ranks around an ill president, even if that is not what the Constitution specifies or the public interest requires.

President Reagan came close to death in a 1981 assassination attempt. The ability of a young, unbalanced man to purchase a gun, get close to the president, and fire off six shots demonstrated how vulnerable the chief executive is. (Michael Evans, The White House Photo Office)

Even more difficult, what can be done if a president suffers a nervous breakdown or mental disability in office? It may have happened in the 1960s. Richard Goodwin, who worked closely with Lyndon Johnson (1963–1969) as a presidential assistant, argues that Johnson took on the appearance of clinical paranoia under the pressure of Vietnam. In private, Johnson often thundered that "those Kennedy people" were "out to get him." Goodwin suspects that Johnson was always a bit paranoid but hid it and used its energizing effect to climb politically. He always got his way and had a fierce reputation for revenge if he thought someone had crossed him. Once in the Oval Office, Johnson snapped under the strain of Vietnam, a war he didn't want but didn't know how to avoid. Tapes of Nixon's private discussions show a similar paranoia. Nixon reacted to the 1971 leak of the "Pentagon papers" (see pp. 68, 165) by telling his assistant, "We're up against an enemy, a conspiracy. They're using any means. *We are going to use any means.* Is that clear?" The Pentagon papers led to a "Plumbers" unit (to stop leaks), which led to the Watergate break-in, which led to the destruction of the Nixon administration. Paranoids keep making things worse for themselves.

But how can you tell if such behavior is an illness, the temporary effects of difficult decisions, or just the president's normal (if overbearing) personality? Who should be in a position to declare the president psychologically disabled? There was then and is now nothing to be done about a president who gets a "little funny" in office; you just have to wait until the term is up.

Classic Works | LASSWELL'S PSYCHOLOGY OF POWER

The mental problems of presidents lead us back to a classic work by Harold Lasswell of Yale, who introduced concepts from Freudian psychology into political science. In his 1936 *Politics: Who Gets What* and other works, Lasswell held that politicians start out mentally unbalanced, that they have unusual needs for power and dominance, which is why they go into politics. Normal people find politics uninteresting. If Lasswell is even approximately right, many executives should be removed from office, and only people who don't want the job should be elected. This is the kind of analysis that cannot be applied in practice; it is fascinating but useless.

It was Plato who first wrote that even sane people who become too powerful in high office go crazy. They've got to, for they can trust no one. They imagine, probably accurately, that they have many enemies, and they amass more and more power to crush these real and imaginary foes. It's an insightful description of Hitler and Stalin. According to Plato, tyrants must go insane in office;  there's no such thing as a sane tyrant. The problem is not personal psychology but the nature of a political office that has grown too powerful. The solution, if Plato is right (and we think he is), is to limit power and have mechanisms to remove officeholders who abuse it. In the U.S. system, the threats of electoral defeat and impeachment tend to keep the presidency and its occupants healthy.

Cabinets

Chief executives are assisted by cabinets. A cabinet member heads one of the major executive divisions of government called a *department* in the United States and a **ministry** in most of the rest of the world. The former is headed by a *secretary* and the latter by a *minister*. Cabinets range in size from a compact fourteen in the United States to twenty or more in Europe.

The United States enlarges its cabinet only slowly and with much discussion, for it takes an act of Congress, and the provision for its own budget, to do so. For most of its history, the United States had fewer than ten departments. Health and Human Services, Housing and Urban Development, Transportation, Energy, Education, and Veterans Affairs were added only since the 1960s. In Western Europe, chief executives can add, delete, combine, and rename ministries at will; their parliaments routinely regard this as an executive right. In the 1980s, for example, most West European governments added environmental ministries. The U.S. Environmental Protection Agency stayed at the sub-cabinet level, and environmental responsibilities were divided between it and several departments.

What's the right size for a cabinet? It depends on how the system is set up and on what citizens expect of it. The United States has been dedicated to keeping government small and letting the marketplace make decisions. When this led to imbalances—for example, bankrupt farmers, unemployed workers, and business collapses—the U.S. system added the Departments of Agriculture, Labor, and Commerce. The Department of Energy was added after the "energy shocks" of the 1970s. Slowly, U.S. cabinets have been creeping up to West European size.

Who Serves in a Cabinet?

There is another difference between parliamentary and presidential systems. In parliamentary systems like Britain and Germany, ministers are drawn from parliament and keep their parliamentary seats. They are both legislators and executives. Usually they have had years of political experience in winning elections and serving on parliamentary committees. The chair of Germany's Bundestag defense committee, for example, could be a good choice to become defense minister. In a presidential system like that of the United States or Brazil, secretaries or ministers are generally not working politicians but businesspersons, lawyers, and academics. They may have some background in their department's subject area, but few have won elective office. President Bush named four members of Congress to his cabinet, Clinton named three. This made U.S. cabinets look a bit European, but the secretaries had to first resign their seats in Congress.

Which is better, a cabinet member who's a working politician or one from outside government? The elected members of West European parliaments who becomes ministers may have a great deal of both political and subject-area knowledge. They know the relevant members of parliament personally and have worked closely with them. Ministers and parliament do not view each other with suspicion, as enemies. The ministers are criticized in parliament, but from the opposition benches; their own party generally supports them.

Outsiders appointed to the cabinet, the traditional U.S. style, may bring with them fresh perspectives, but they may also be politically naive, given to brash statements and unrealistic programs that get them in trouble with Congress, where members of their own party do not necessarily support them. Their lack of political experience in the nation's capital leads to another problem.

The Rise of Noncabinet Advisers

In the United States especially, the cabinet counts for less and less. A cabinet meeting has little utility and takes place rarely. Few Americans can name three or more cabinet members. What has happened? Why has the cabinet fallen into neglect? Part of the problem is that few cabinet secretaries are well-connected political figures. And their jobs are rather routine: Get more money from Congress to spend on their department's programs. Cabinet secretaries are in charge of administering established programs with established budgets, "vice-presidents in charge of spending," as Coolidge's vice-president Charles G. Dawes called them. As such, they are not apt to be consulted on much. They are largely administrators, not generators of ideas.

A more basic problem is what has happened to government in modern times: It moves fast and combines several subject areas. The president typically wants people who can produce new ideas and a quick estimate of what's happening close at hand. Thus Washington, and to a growing extent other capitals, have seen the rise of noncabinet advisers who are often more important than cabinet secretaries. These people make up the Executive Office of the President (EOP), and most of them do not have to be confirmed by Congress or answer to Congress, unlike secretaries. Most answer only to the president and are located either in the White House; the adjacent, ornate Executive Office Building; or the New Executive Office Building across Pennsylvania Avenue from the White House. The EOP keeps getting bigger.

In recent years, for example, great attention has focused on the "White House chief of staff," an office mentioned nowhere in the Constitution or in statutes. The chief of staff, however, is the president's gatekeeper, possibly the president's brains. No one, not even a cabinet secretary, gets in to see the president without approval by the chief of staff, and most of the president's activities and agenda are determined by this person. Information flows to the president as the chief of staff deems necessary. Invariably, the White House chief of staff is a long-term and close associate of the president who knows—or thinks he knows—exactly what the president wishes.

In foreign affairs, a "national security adviser" holds sway. In 1947 Congress provided for a National Security Council (NSC), consisting of the president, the secretaries of state and defense, and a few others. They were to meet to coordinate foreign policies. There was no mention of a staff for the NSC, but over the years a large and powerful staff grew, supervised by a national security adviser. The NSC staff gets all the relevant State, Defense, and CIA cables and reports and structures them into policy alternatives for the president. In some cases, the national security adviser, who is close at hand and can preserve secrecy better, has become more important than the secretary of state or defense. This was the case with the most famous national security adviser, Henry Kissinger, in the Nixon administration.

There are other White House offices that wield more power than departments. The Office of Management and Budget (OMB) commands compliance from all departments because it decides whose budgets will be cut the most. This office often knows as much about specific programs as the departments who run them and is better able to initiate new policies because it can see the whole picture of government activity. Those who control the budget control policy. (This is also the case with the British Treasury Ministry, but it is a full-fledged ministry.) The chair of President Clinton's new National Economic Council is the architect of economic policy, more so than the secretaries of treasury, commerce, or labor.

There is no plot here. There is a gradual drift of power away from official departments and into the hands of the chief executive's personal staff. It is a tendency in many governments. British Prime Minister Blair was criticized for ignoring his cabinet. The culprit is the complexity of modern government and the speed with which decisions have to be made. Chief executives must have advisors and assistants close at hand, and they become powerful, secretive, and unaccountable to parliaments.

The Danger of Expecting Too Much

In both presidential and parliamentary systems, attention focuses on the chief executive. Presidents or prime ministers are expected to deliver economic growth with low unemployment and low inflation. They are expected to keep taxes low but government benefits high. They are held responsible for anything that goes wrong but told to adopt a hands-off management approach and delegate matters to subordinates. The more problems and pressure, the more they have to delegate.

How can they do it all? How can they run a government, economy, subordinates, and policies? They can't, and increasingly they don't. Instead, the clever ones project a mood of calm, progress, and good feeling, and this makes most citizens happy. President Reagan was a master of this tactic. The precise details of governance matter little; they are in the hands of appointed advisers and career civil servants, and few citizens care about them. What matters is getting reelected, and for this personality counts for more than policy, symbols more than performance.

Worldwide, power has been flowing to the executive, and legislatures have been in decline. The U.S. Congress has put up some good rear-guard actions, but it, too, has been generally in a slow retreat. Some observers have argued that this can't be helped, that a number of factors make this shift of power inevitable. If this is true, what can we do to safeguard democracy? Democracies still have a trump card, and some say it is enough: electoral punishment. As long as the chief executive, whether president or prime minister, has to face the electorate at periodic intervals, democracy will be preserved. The "rule of anticipated reactions," of which we spoke in Chapter 5, will keep them on their toes. Perhaps the concept of checks and balances was a great idea of the eighteenth century that doesn't fit the twentieth. Maybe we will just have to learn to live with executive dominance.

Key Terms

cabinet (p. 267)	government (p. 266)	minister (p. 267)
chancellor (p. 269)	immobilism (p. 267)	ministry (p. 281)
deadlock (p. 267)	impeachment (p. 267)	premier (p. 269)
dissolve (p. 270)	Knesset (p. 270)	state (p. 266)

Key Websites

The CIA site provides the chronological history of leaders around the world.
   http://www.odci.gov/cia/publications/chiefs
This site is the official White House website.
   http://www.whitehouse.gov/
This site is the official website of 10 Downing Street, office of the British Prime Minister.
   http://www.open.gov.uk/
This site provides a biography and analysis of the political career of Napoleon Bonaparte.
   http://www.tarpley.net/fascism.htm
This site provides a biography and analysis of the political career of Adolf Hitler.
   http://despina.advanced.org/17120/data/bios/hitler/

Further Reference

Barber, James David. *The Presidential Character: Predicting Performance in the White House*, 4th ed. Englewood Cliffs, NJ: Prentice Hall, 1992.

Blondel, Jean, and Ferdinand Müller-Rommel, eds. *Cabinets in Western Europe*, 2nd ed. New York: St. Martin's, 1997.

Greenstein, Fred. *The Hidden Hand Presidency: Eisenhower as Leader*. New York: Basic Books, 1982.

Jones, Charles O. *The Presidency in a Separated System*. Washington, D.C.: Brookings Institution, 1994.

Kernell, Samuel. *Going Public: New Strategies of Presidential Leadership*, 3rd ed. Washington, D.C.: CQ Press, 1997.

Kutler, Stanely, ed. *Abuse of Power: The New Nixon Tapes*. New York: Simon & Schuster, 1997.

Laver, Michael, and Kenneth Shepsle, eds. *Making and Breaking Governments: Cabinets and Legislatures in Parliamentary Democracies*. New York: Cambridge University Press, 1996.

Linz, Juan J., and Arturo Valenzuela, eds. *The Failure of Presidential Democracy*. Baltimore, MD: Johns Hopkins University Press, 1994.

McDonald, Forrest. *The American Presidency: An Intellectual History*. Lawrence, KS: University Press of Kansas, 1994.

Nelson, Michael, ed. *The Evolving Presidency*. Washington, D.C.: CQ Press, 1998.

Neustadt, Richard E. *Presidential Power and the Modern Presidents: The Politics of Leadership from Roosevelt to Reagan*. New York: Free Press, 1991.

Schlesinger, Arthur, Jr. *The Imperial Presidency*. Boston, MA: Houghton Mifflin, 1973.

Administration and Bureaucracy

CHAPTER 16

The term **bureaucracy** has negative connotations: the inefficiency and delays citizens face in dealing with government. Actually, the great German sociologist Max Weber, who coined the term, disliked bureaucracy but saw no way to avoid it. Basically, a bureaucracy is any large-scale organization of appointed officials who implement laws and policies. Ideally, it operates under rules and procedures with a chain of command (or **hierarchy** of authority) and applies policy to particular situations. It enables government to operate with some rationality, uniformity, predictability, and supervision. No bureaucracy, no government.

Another definition of bureaucracy—a nicer name is "civil service"—is that it is the *permanent* government. Much of what we have studied might be called the "temporary government" of elected officials who come and go. The career civil servants stay, often spending their working lives with one government agency. They may take orders from the elected officials, but they also must follow the law and do things "by the book." They usually know a lot more about their specified areas than the new political appointee who has been placed above them. There is often friction between elected officials and career bureaucrats. The former sometimes want to redo the system with bold, new ideas; the bureaucrats, who have seen bold, new ideas come and go, move with caution. A bureaucracy, once set up, is inherently conservative, and trying to move it is one of the hardest tasks of politicians.

Almost any large organization will have a bureaucracy. In the middle ages, when Europe was composed of loose confederations of feudal powers, the Roman Catholic church had a complex and effective administrative system. Through

QUESTIONS TO CONSIDER

1. Must every large organization be bureaucratic?
2. At which level—federal, state, or local—do most American civil servants work?
3. How do agencies get "captured" or "colonized"?
4. Must communist countries be heavily bureaucratic?
5. Describe the higher ranks of the French bureaucracy.
6. How did Max Weber characterize bureaucracy?
7. Why is it hard for a government to control bureaucrats?
8. What was Djilas's theory of the "new class"?
9. How did smoking get on the U.S. political agenda?

KEY TERMS

bureaucracy The career civil service that staffs government executive agencies.

hierarchy Arrayed as on a ladder of command.

a hierarchy of carefully trained people who spent their life in the Church, authority flowed from the pope down to parish priest. Until the advent of strong monarchies, Church organization was the envy and model of **secular** rulers. Armies also have

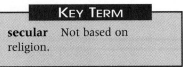

KEY TERM

secular   Not based on religion.

bureaucratic structures, based on the military chain of command and myriad regulations. Bureaucracy is pervasive in schools, hospitals, and large corporations, such as Exxon and General Motors. In the modern world, you can't escape bureaucracy.

The U.S. Federal Bureaucracy

Fewer than 15 percent of the civil servants in the United States are federal. Of our 22 million civil servants, some 15 million are employed by local governments, 4 million by state governments, and only 2.8 million (not counting military personnel) by the federal government. Remember, most government services—schools, police, and fire protection—are provided by local governments.

The Cabinet Departments

In the United States, the fourteen cabinet departments—employing between 85 and 90 percent of all federal civil servants—share a common anatomy, even though they differ in size and scope of operations. Each is headed by a secretary who is appointed by the president (with the consent of the Senate) and serves at the president's pleasure. The undersecretaries and assistant secretaries are also political appointees. This differs from most other systems, where officials up through the equivalent of our undersecretaries are members of the permanent civil service.

The basic function of the departments is to carry out legislative and executive policies. The Department of Agriculture, for example, enforces congressionally mandated farm-price supports. This is no simple matter, however, for the departments must determine how to interpret the intent of Congress. Often, when a controversial issue is involved, the only way Congress can muster a majority to pass the legislation is by couching it in the most general terms. Thus, the laws a department must enforce are often only broad guidelines, and the bureaucracy has latitude to establish specific working policy. Neither legislators nor executives can supervise everything a bureaucracy does.

Departments are subdivided into bureaus headed by career civil servants rather than political appointees. For example, the Bureau of Labor Statistics is part of the Department of Labor, and the Bureau of the Census is part of the Department of Commerce. Here, the day-to-day work of the departments is carried out, and bureau chiefs have a great deal of discretionary authority, even though they work under statutes and executive policy. The departments maintain local offices in each state and try to administer uniform policies across the nation.

Federal Agencies

Some independent agencies of the federal government, like the departments, are accountable to the president. Each is headed by a single administrator whom the president appoints and can remove. Sometimes created in response to a particular lobby, the agency performs a single, highly complex function that may be more political than administrative. The Environmental Protection Agency (EPA) was set up in response to growing public concern over pollution. The National Aeronautics and Space Administration (NASA) was organized to put Americans into space ahead of the Soviets.

Federal Corporations

Government-owned corporations are combinations of government agencies and private business enterprises that serve vital needs that private enterprise cannot meet. Although corporation heads are appointed by the president and, in many cases, confirmed by the Senate, they exercise autonomous power. They use their own judgment to handle and reinvest both **appropriated** funds and fees collected. The U.S. Postal Service, Export-Import Bank, Tennessee Valley Authority (TVA), and St. Lawrence Seaway Development Corporation are federal corporations. The latter two undertook massive public works that few private corporations could have financed. Similarly, no private corporation was willing to risk the post office's deficits. With its new autonomy and ability to change its fees and services, the U.S. Postal Service has become much more competitive and money-making. Federal corporations operate under congressional guidelines and, since few of them are profitable, they depend on appropriations, making them liable to congressional criticism.

Independent Regulatory Agencies

These agencies are charged with economic regulation of private businesses that directly affect the public welfare. They have **quasi-**judicial and quasi-legislative authority that derives from Congress. For example, Congress gives the Nuclear Regulatory Commission (NRC) the power to shut down unsafe nuclear power plants. Such decisions are enforceable in the courts and are not often overturned by the judiciary.

These agencies are often criticized. Ralph Nader and others charge that they are overly influenced by the very industries they should be controlling. Many commissioners are drawn from the ranks of private industry and, critics say, are more concerned with preserving vested interests than with protecting the public. The Federal Power Commission, for example, is accused of being staffed by representatives of industry rather than of consumers. There is some truth in this criticism, but agency employees need a technical understanding of the industries they regulate, and about the only way to get this expertise is to have worked in those industries. This is one way industries "capture" or "colonize" regulatory agencies.

Bureaucracies in Other Nations

Believe it or not, U.S. bureaucracy is relatively small and light compared to many other countries. Europe and Latin America, with their strong statist traditions (see p. 48), have much more bureaucracy and regulation than the United States.

Communist Countries

The Soviet Union was one of the world's most bureaucratic nations, and that was one of the causes of its collapse. Tied to the Communist party, the Soviet civil service was corrupt, inefficient, and unreformable. Although according to Communist dogma, a dictatorship of the proletariat had no need for a Western-style bureaucracy, immediately after the 1917 revolution the Soviets instituted strict bureaucratic management, and Stalin increased it with his Five-Year Plans in the 1930s.

Top Soviet bureaucrats were a privileged elite; their salaries and lifestyles were far superior to those of the average citizen. They got special shops, country houses, and Western clothes. To rise in the hierarchy, one had to be a party member, for the party interlocked with the bureaucracy. Soviet bureaucrats were generally university graduates, who in return for their free education had to work in a state agency for three years following graduation. After that, many of them stayed.

At the top of each ministry was a minister, who was a member of the Council of Ministers (roughly equivalent to a Western cabinet), the highest executive authority. It was made up of high-ranking party members, some of whom were also members of the Politburo. Trusted party members were placed strategically in subordinate positions to carry out policy the party had laid down. This made the Soviet bureaucracy extremely conservative, an obstacle no Soviet president has been able to overcome. Still guarding their perks, Russian bureaucrats are sabotaging Yeltsin's reforms.

France

In the seventeenth and eighteenth century, France dominated Europe, and most European countries patterned their bureaucracies on the French model. Most of Europe has code or Roman law (see Chapter 17) and centralized rule. After the French Revolution destroyed the monarchy, Napoleon restored central control of the bureaucracy and, by making it more rational and effective, increased its power. Napoleon, with the *intendants* of Richelieu as his model, created the **prefects** to carry out government policy at the local level.

Since then, education has been primary in the

KEY TERM
prefect Agent of French interior ministry who governs each French *département* (territorial subdivision).

appointment of French bureaucrats. Most top civil servants are graduates of one of the "Great Schools," such as the Ecole Polytechnique, an engineering school, or, since World War II, the Ecole Nationale d'Administration, which was specifically created to train government officials. The severe instability of the Third (1871–1940) and Fourth (1947–1958) Republics increased the bureaucracy's power because it had to run France with little legislative or executive guidance. In many cases, *directeurs* (roughly equivalent to American bureau chiefs), had to operate independently. The Fifth Republic brought greater stability and stronger ministerial control, but France is still heavily bureaucratic.

The American concept of decentralization has only recently come to France; Paris viewed local levels of government as administrative conveniences and still centrally controls the country's bureaucratic network. From the American viewpoint, centralization is often extreme. For example, at any given moment in the school day, all schoolchildren in a particular grade throughout France are likely to be engaged in the same activity. Local conditions, problems, or initiatives were secondary considerations in bureaucratic decisions. The Socialists, who swept to power in 1981, however, began the decentralization of France. A 1982 law reduced the powers of the prefects, and elected councils in the ninety-six *départements* and twenty-two regions got policy and taxation powers in education and economic development. Decentralization reversed five centuries of centralized French administration.

Germany

Prussia and its ruling class, the *Junkers*, put their stamp on German administration. Obedient, efficient, and hard-working, the aristocratic *Junkers* were a state nobility, dependent on Berlin, and controlling all its higher civil service positions. Frederick the Great of Prussia, who ruled from 1740 to 1786, had a passion for effective administration and established universities to train administrators. When Germany united in 1871 under Prussia's leadership, Prussian administrative styles permeated the new nation. Democracy was suspect among German administrators; loyalty to nation and emperor was all that counted. One of the reasons the short-lived Weimar Republic (1919–1933) failed was because the civil-servant class had only contempt for democracy. With the Third Reich, they eagerly flocked to Hitler.

The current German government has a strongly federal structure that limits Berlin's administrative powers. It is responsible for foreign affairs, collecting taxes, defense, transportation, the postal service, and some social insurance programs. Other domestic programs are administered by the *Länder*, much like U.S. states run most American programs. Today's German civil servants are committed to democracy. Generally trained in law—throughout Europe law is at the undergraduate level—German bureaucrats tend to bring with them the mentality of Roman law, that is, law neatly organized into fixed codes rather than the more flexible U.S. and British common law (see Chapter 17).

Great Britain

Britain, unlike France, has strong traditions of local self-government and dispersion of authority. This pattern of administration is an outgrowth of the Anglo-American emphasis on representative government, which encourages legislative control of administrative authorities. During the nineteenth century, the growth of British government at the local level also encouraged the dispersion of administrative authority; it was not until the twentieth century that the central government began to participate in local affairs.

Curiously, Great Britain was rather late in developing a modern bureaucracy. Until the Northcote-Trevelyan Report calling for major reform was issued in 1854, the bureaucracy was rife with corruption and nepotism. Positions in the bureaucracy (for instance, military commissions) were openly bought and sold. By 1870, however, a **merit civil service** based on competitive examinations had been established.

> ### KEY TERMS
>
> **merit civil service**   Civil service based on competitive exams rather than patronage.
>
> **apolitical**   Not interested in or participating in politics.

British ministers are accountable to Parliament for the conduct of their departments and, along with their cabinet colleagues, make departmental policy. However, real bureaucratic power is in the hands of the "permanent secretary" (a career administrator) and the career deputy secretaries, undersecretaries, and assistant secretaries who serve at lower ranks. Thus, even though the British and American bureaucracies share the same tradition of decentralized authority, control over the bureaucracy is tighter in Britain than in America. British bureaucrats pride themselves on being **apolitical**, so they faithfully carry out the ministry's policies whatever government is in power.

Characteristics of Bureaucracies

The first scholar to analyze bureaucracy was Max Weber (1864–1920). His classic study (see box on p. 292) provides the starting point for a current examination of bureaucracy.

At the turn of the century, Woodrow Wilson and Frank J. Goodnow made significant studies of the American administrative system. Bureaucracy in the United States, they noted, must work within the framework of a democratic society. But how can professional civil servants, who are not directly accountable to the electorate, be reconciled with the goals of democracy? Wilson and Goodnow set up a theoretical base that combined democracy and professional efficiency. They made a distinction between the political (policy-making) and the administrative (enforcement). To ensure democracy, they concluded that the elected political officials must always control the administrative officials and that every individual and agency understand this. Administrators, then, never initiate policy; they merely follow the laws and policies laid down by the political leaders.

Classic Works

WEBER'S CHARACTERISTICS OF BUREAUCRACIES

Weber's analysis of bureaucracy was based on the German bureaucratic model, but his principles can be applied worldwide. Weber's criteria for defining bureaucracy were as follows:

1. Administrative offices are organized hierarchically.
2. Each office has its own area of competence.
3. Civil servants are appointed, not elected, on the basis of technical qualifications as determined by diplomas or examinations.
4. Civil servants receive fixed salaries according to rank.
5. The job is a career and the sole employment of the civil servant.
6. The official does not own his or her office.
7. The official is subject to control and discipline.
8. Promotion is based on superiors' judgment.

Weber felt he was studying something relatively new. Some of the preceding characteristics could be found in classic China, but not all. Like the nation-state, bureaucracies started in Western Europe around the sixteenth century but were reaching their full powers—which Weber distrusted—only in the twentieth century.

Political scientists today feel that these distinctions are not closely applicable to modern government. Administrative officials, they note, often given only the broadest policy guidelines by Congress and the president, make policy decisions all the time. Many of these decisions are made on the basis of the administrators' expertise in their fields, which because of our highly specialized government, political leaders do not always have.

The overlapping of administrative and political functions is a result of the demands of modern government and not of the desire for power of bureaucrats. It is clear that the United States in the twenty-first century can no longer look to Weber or Wilson and Goodnow for an analysis of modern bureaucracy. Weber's bureaucracy served a highly stratified, authoritarian society—one in which the average citizen did not "talk back" to bureaucrats. America today is a far different place, and private citizens and legislators do not hesitate to criticize bureaucrats or demand that they explain their actions. Some investigations, however, can be carried to extremes, as the excesses of Senator Joseph McCarthy in the 1950s illustrate. McCarthy's almost fanatical crusade against alleged Communists in the federal government eliminated, among others, an entire generation of experts on China. Bureaucrats in sensitive political posts try to keep themselves attuned to prevailing public and congressional opinion. They do not—indeed, they cannot—function solely on the basis of precedent and paper rules and procedures.

Further, anyone who has had to deal with a bureaucracy can testify to the fact that it is not as impersonal, predictable, and precise as the Weberian ideal. Bureaucrats are psychological beings and seldom act in the sterile manner implied by Weber. In a bureaucracy, as in other organizations, friendship, improvisation, informality, and entrepreneurship in the decision-making process are common. In a word, bureaucracies are political.

Additionally, some political scientists have noted the tendency for government agencies to become interest groups themselves. Far from being neutral and passive administrators, bureaucrats are active participants in the formation of laws and policies. Elected and appointed executives are often entirely dependent on the data and ideas that career civil servants provide. Leaders, in effect, become followers. Civil servants frequently lobby legislators to get the programs they want. The danger here, some feel, is government of the bureaucrats, by the bureaucrats, and for the bureaucrats. It is startling to realize that no government, East or West, democratic or dictatorial, civilian or military, has managed fully to control its bureaucracy.

Bureaucracy in Modern Governments

Modern bureaucracies do administering, servicing, regulating, licensing, information-gathering, and "housekeeping" chores. All perform at least two of these basic functions, with some bureaus specializing and some carrying out multiple functions.

Administration

Most bureaus execute and enforce the laws enacted by the legislature and the policies promulgated by the executive. The United States, for example, channels federal funds to the states to pay for various welfare programs. The Department of Health and Human Services administers this policy by deciding how much federal money each state is entitled to and seeing to it that the money is used for its intended purpose. Britain provides free medical care to citizens; its National Health Service administers this policy by overseeing medical training, assigning patients to doctors, and running the hospitals. Administration is the implementation of public policy, and because it involves policy decisions, it also entails rule making. In conjunction with their administrative duties, departments often initiate campaigns to publicize their work and to educate the public about a program's benefits and purposes. In many countries there are programs of education on the ills of tobacco, traffic safety, fire prevention, and conservation of natural resources.

Patterns of administration vary from country to country. In China, for example, the party watches over the bureaucratic network. Virtually all Chinese officials are party members, and all offices have party people in them. What the party calls its control function keeps Chinese bureaucrats on their toes. If their unit doesn't run right or if they are egregiously crooked (and many are), they can be fired, demoted, or transferred to a remote area. This threat tends to make them extremely cautious and to go by the book. China's bureaucracy is huge, partly because it also runs state industries. If China goes all the way to a market economy, the number of Chinese administrators may shrink. Party control is probably indispensable for such a system. Note that the West does not have a comparable mechanism for supervising and checking its bureaucracies.

In Britain, executives and administrators oversee the day-to-day operations of their departments, and higher administrative officials draft proposed legislation as well as help their ministers answer questions from members of Parliament. Since Britain, like France, still has some **nationalized** industry, some steel plants, coal mines, railroads, and the telegraph and telephone are run by government-controlled corporations, which make policy decisions normally reserved to the private sector in the United States.

KEY TERM
nationalized   State-owned industry.

Services

Many government agencies are created to serve the general public or specific groups. The U.S. Weather Bureau is such a service agency, one vital to farmers. The U.S. Department of Agriculture conducts research in pest control, land management, and livestock improvement; dispenses surplus food to the poor; and provides public information about nutrition. In Britain, most health care is dispensed by the government. In Sweden and Germany, the government runs extensive job-finding services. And in China, the government provides free education at all levels for those who qualify.

Regulation

The regulatory functions of government are also designed to safeguard the general public's welfare. In the United States, the Securities and Exchange Commission (SEC), for example, protects investors by establishing guidelines for the registration of new issues and the buying and selling of stocks and bonds. Britain has had legislation since 1819 regulating working conditions in factories. The U.S. Department of Labor oversees elections in unions to make sure that they are conducted fairly; it can and does throw out crooked union bosses. In Germany, the enforcement of federal law by the *Land* governments is supervised by the Bundesrat (the upper house of the national legislature), and federal administrative courts are empowered to compel *Land* governments to enforce national law. In all instances, the regulation powers are backed by the potential of force. In the United States regulatory agencies can issue "cease and desist" orders. Although offenders may challenge these orders in court, most voluntarily choose to comply.

The Internal Revenue Service office in Andover, Massachusetts, is one of nine regional centers. It processes about $41 billion in taxes a year. (AP/Wide World Photos)

Licensing

Licensing is closely related to regulation. It enables governments to impose minimum standards and qualifications. For example, if you want to drive a car, practice medicine or law, sell real estate, teach in the public schools, or work as a barber, you must meet certain government standards. In the United States and other federal countries, these standards are usually set by the individual states. In countries such as France or Great Britain, the national government sets the standards and administers the tests.

Information Gathering

Information is needed to determine whether a law has been violated and to make policy decisions that are rational and based on factual evidence. For example, if a U.S. citizen complains that his or her civil rights have been violated, an investigation—usually by the Civil Rights Division of the Justice Department—has to be made before any action can be taken. The Environmental Protection Agency must know the exact state of air and water pollution before it can issue violations. The French government made an extensive study of the nation's energy needs and concluded that France needed nuclear energy.

Some agencies act only when there has been a complaint. Others, like the Food and Drug Administration (FDA), are constantly making investigations on their own initiative. The FDA does not allow a drug to go on the market until it is satisfied that the product is safe and effective. Sometimes the problem of invasion of privacy arises when organizations, such as the Federal Bureau of Investigation (FBI), investigate the activities of alleged subversives and question their friends, neighbors, and family members. The line between investigation necessary to protect the public interest and invasion of privacy is a fine one, and it is often difficult to tell where one leaves off and the other begins.

The Trouble with Bureaucracy

The world does not love bureaucracy. The very word has a pejorative connotation. In France and Italy, hatred of the clerk or official on the other side of the counter or desk has become part of the political culture. The United States, with its long-standing theories of minimal government and individual self-reliance, is pleased to hear every major candidate—from both parties—denounce the bureaucracy. One of the funniest experiences is to ride a commuter train or bus into Washington, D.C., and overhear career civil servants complain about "those damn bureaucrats." The paradox of the modern state is that bureaucratic administration is a necessity but is also often an impediment to the fulfillment of national goals.

Incoming U.S. administrations, particularly Republican, usually vow to bring business-type efficiency to public administration. They rarely make a dent in the problem and sometimes make things worse. "Efficiency" is much harder to apply in public affairs than in private industry. A businessperson can calculate profits and **productivity**; a civil servant doesn't make any profits and productivity is hard to measure. Government offices are sometimes overstaffed, but it is difficult to pick out which workers should be gotten rid of.

At its worst, bureaucracy can show signs of "Eichmannism," named after the Nazi official who organized the death trains for Europe's Jews and later calmly assured his Israeli judges that he was just doing his job. Nazi bureaucracy connotes treating people like things, a problem not limited to Germany. On the humorous side, bureaucracy can start to resemble Parkinson's Law: Work expands to fill the staff time available for it. Parkinson never called himself a humorist, and many who have worked in featherbedded, purposeless, paper-shuffling agencies agree that Parkinson's Law is accurate.

Bureaucracy and **corruption** are intertwined. Whenever there are rules to be carried out by public officials, there is a temptation to bend them for friends and benefactors. The more regulations, the more bureaucrats, and the more corruption. Only a few countries with a strong ethos of public service—New Zealand and Singapore, for example—have been able to maintain uncorrupt public administration. Most countries in the world are corrupt, some a little and some egregiously. Throughout the Third World, to be a public official means to take money on the side. Perhaps the most serious problem with bureaucracy, alluded to previously, occurs when it becomes interlocked with and sometimes replaces other branches of government.

KEY TERMS

productivity   The efficiency with which goods or services are produced.

corruption   Use of public office for private gain.

| Classic Works | DJILAS'S "NEW CLASS" |

Milovan Djilas (pronounced *Gee-lass*) was until 1954 a dedicated Communist and the right-hand man to Yugoslav Communist chief Tito. After World War II when the Yugoslav Communists took over the country, however, Djilas noticed that their earlier vision of a happy society of equals was fading. The Communists had eliminated capitalists as a class, he wrote, but they created a "new class" of bureaucrats, party officials, secret police, and army officers, who rigged the system to favor themselves.

Socialism brought no real improvement over capitalism, Djilas concluded; both were ruled by a social class out for its own interests. Bureaucrats had replaced capitalists. Additionally, he noted, communism brought with it tyranny over the mind and economic stupidity far worse than capitalism. For his candor, Djilas spent ten years in Yugoslav prisons.

Still, Djilas's book *The New Class*, published in 1957, became a classic analysis of why Communist parties can never lead societies into communism. Once the New Class is in power, it keeps things pretty much the way they are, with themselves at the top to grab extra helpings. Communism is bureaucracy to an extreme degree, and that is why it fails.

The Bureaucracy: Administrator or Policymaker?

The early theorists of bureaucracy (Weber, Wilson, and Goodnow) assumed that professional bureaucrats would never make public policy but merely execute the will of elected officials. And, indeed, nonpartisan administration was the original motivation behind merit civil services. However, as Guy S. Claire warned many decades ago, most Western nations have developed "administocracies" (an aristocracy of administrators), whose personnel are not publicly accountable but who nevertheless make policy. A return to the nineteenth-century spoils system is neither possible nor desirable, but the question of whether a democracy can afford to allow nonelected and nonresponsible administrators to make decisions that will affect the lives of the people must be considered. Here are some of the ways.

Adjudication Many regulatory agencies maintain administrative courts that operate much like regular courts and whose decisions are enforceable in the regular courts. Most U.S. states, for example, have administrative tribunals to **adjudicate** workers' compensation cases. All parties to such an action are entitled to legal counsel and may offer evidence. The FDA can order a drug off the market, and the SEC can ban trading in a particular stock. Some critics maintain that these tribunals' orders should be made by the regular courts. If a cosmetic is harmful, should not the courts—and not the FDA—make this decision? Proponents of the administrative

> **KEY TERM**
>
> **adjudication** Settling problems through courts of law.

courts answer by pointing out that the courts lack the expertise to judge techni-cal matters. Others feel that even though the law empowers agencies to "regulate in the public interest, convenience, or necessity," administrative courts gives administrators too much power, and unaccountable power at that.

Discretionary Implementation   When a statute is specific, enforcement is a relatively simple matter. However, this is not usually the case. For example, the U.S. Congress passed a law to clean up toxic dump sites. It enabled EPA to do whatever necessary to achieve this goal. The EPA had to set priorities, because every dump cannot be cleaned up at once, and each one entails different eco-logical, economic, and political problems. **Discretionary** implementation—deciding how to go about achieving the general goal—became the responsibility of the EPA. In effect, it is permitted to make law for society. No law can anticipate all circumstances, so administrators must have some leeway. Furthermore, administrators can always be overruled by pub-lic or legislative pressure or by executive edict.

KEY TERM
discretionary Ability of officials to decide questions on their own without adjudication or higher authority.

Rule Making   The rule-making authority of regulatory agencies is related to discretionary implementation. For example, higher rates for telephone use must be approved by the Public Service Commission (PSC).

Advisory Roles   The complexity of modern life has caused legislatures and executives to rely more and more heavily on the technical expertise of bureau-crats. Congress may decide that unsafe mines should be shut down, but only min-ing experts can determine exactly what conditions make a mine unsafe. Many laws require administrative interpretation. For example, Congress may outlaw deceptive advertising, but the determination of what *is* deceptive is made by the FTC. Lawmakers need the technical assistance of specialists, another way bureau-crats make policy.

Conflicts can arise, however. For example, Kennedy's Secretary of Defense Robert McNamara, a political appointee, was intent on cutting costs but ran into the angry opposition from generals, who claimed that they alone knew the tech-nical side of security needs. Similarly, in 1948, President Truman was under intense pressure by State Department experts not to recognize the new state of Israel. Truman ignored them with the remark, "There ain't many Arab voters in this country." Both McNamara and Truman realized that some decisions are inherently political and can be made only by a politically responsible official.

The bureaucracy's role of adviser is a feature of all modern industrial states. In France, laws and presidential decrees are drawn up and promulgated with the active assistance of the bureaucracy (particularly the Council of State), and career executives thus have the opportunity to shape policy. Bureaucrats play a large role in the framing of legislation in Germany. Since federal bureaucrats do not have to supervise field or branch offices, they can devote their energies to policy matters. In fact, they are often successful in convincing their political superiors to accept their way of thinking on issues.

Case Studies — BUREAUCRATS AND SMOKING

One of the best examples of bureaucratic rule making was the fight to force cigarette manufacturers to place health hazard warnings on their cigarette packages and to include them in advertisements. Congress would never have moved by itself because the tobacco industry is generous to its friends in Congress. Change came via a branch of the bureaucracy—public-health specialists and statisticians equipped with computers. In 1965 the Advisory Committee on Smoking and Health and the surgeon general (the nation's chief public health officer) presented solid data that heavy cigarette smoking increased lung cancer and shortened lifespans. The report disturbed the public, and public pressure on Congress increased. Since 1966 cigarette manufacturers have been required to print warnings on all packs.

Meanwhile, the tobacco industry tried, unsuccessfully, to discredit the surgeon general's report, and organizations such as the American Cancer Society were agitating for still firmer antitobacco legislation. In 1967 the FCC entered the crusade. Citing the fairness doctrine, it ordered all radio and television stations accepting cigarette commercials to make free time available for antismoking commercials. Soon the American Cancer Society was producing one-minute anti-smoking announcements.

In 1969 the FCC banned cigarette advertising on radio and television. And in 1971 President Nixon signed an FTC-sponsored bill requiring cigarette companies to print health warnings on all advertising copy as well as on every pack of cigarettes. Political scientist A. Lee Fritschler reached the following conclusion:

> The initiation and continuation of the cigarette controversy were possible because of both the political power and delegated authority possessed by bureaucratic agencies. Had the decision on cigarettes and health been left to Congress alone, it is safe to assume that the manufacturers would have triumphed, and no health warnings of any kind would have been required. The cigarette-labeling controversy is a clear example of agencies' power to influence and even formulate public policy.

Here was a vivid case of federal agencies openly lobbying for a particular policy and getting it.

What to Do with Bureaucracy?

Bureaucracy in the twentieth century has become big, powerful, rigid, unresponsive, and intrusive. Some contend it has taken on a life of its own, divorced from the needs of the citizens and governments that gave it birth. Can anything be done about this? As Joseph LaPalombara has observed, most of the ideas offered to cure bureaucracy entail *adding* more bureaucrats. Here are some suggested remedies.

Ombudsmen   As we discussed briefly in Chapter 14, the ombudsman is Sweden's contribution to the art of governance. Established by the 1809 Swedish constitution, the *Justitieombudsman* (literally, agent of justice) is named and paid by the parliament, not the executive. This is important, for no government agency can be its own ombudsman; that must come from outside. An official who says, "Bring all complaints to me. I'm my own ombudsman," doesn't understand the concept. Absolute independence is necessary for an ombudsman to work effectively. The ombudsman is a legislative-branch lawyer who intervenes on behalf of citizens treated wrongly by the bureaucracy. The ombudsman has subpoena power, and a reprimand to errant officials is usually enough to set things right. Denmark, Norway, Britain, and New Zealand have set up similar institutions.

Some have suggested the ombudsman concept for the United States. In a sense, we already have it: members of Congress, whose constituency work is much like that of ombudsmen. Furthermore, the United States is already overrun with lawyers, so no citizen has far to go to find one. Poor people can often obtain free legal assistance. Where the ombudsman idea works is in countries with a tradition of respect for law and a political and moral climate in which a simple reprimand is enough. The American context is not precisely as law-abiding.

Legislative Checks   The United States has other mechanisms to oversee the bureaucracy. Congress has the General Accounting Office (GAO), Congressional Research Service (CRS), and Congressional Budget Office (CBO). The GAO looks to see that federal funds are spent correctly and effectively; the CRS gives Congress the expertise needed to check on the executive-branch specialists; and the CBO, established in 1974, consolidates Congress's budget-making functions to reply to the White House's powerful Office of Management and Budget. In effect, what the United States has done is set up competing bureaucracies—one executive, the other legislative. This does not save money or reduce the number of bureaucrats; it does keep the executive side tied to the national purpose as represented on Capitol Hill.

Cutting   Americans dream of some golden yesteryear when there were no bureaucrats on their backs. Politicians often promise to cut the bureaucracy, but they rarely succeed. Cutting bureaucrats means cutting programs, and most citizens soon find their favorite programs getting the ax. They meant to cut other people's wasteful programs, not the necessary and prudent expenditures they benefit from. Once a welfare state has been built, it is terribly difficult to dismantle because so many people have a stake in its bounties. In the 1980s, the Reagan administration tried a different tack: Keep the programs on the books but fail to fund or staff them adequately. Many federal offices, especially those providing services the president and his supporters disliked, found themselves operating with reduce budgets and employees, unable to carry out their legislated mandates. At a time of massive federal budget deficits, Congress found it difficult to restore these cuts. In highly public areas such as education and environmental pollution, however, irate citizens and their interest groups demanded attention, and President Reagan had to back down partially. He did not, for example, abolish the Department of Education as he had promised during the 1980 campaign. Plans by Congressional Republicans to "save" Medicare (by cutting it) produced a similar outcry in the mid-1990s. The meat-ax approach to bureaucracy is tempting but hard to carry out in practice.

Decentralization   For highly centralized systems, as in France and Italy, decentralization offers some improvement. Decisions can be made closer to home, in consultation with the people they will affect. Decentralization can solve some problems but create others. It brings bureaucratic decision-making closer to the local level, but this can *increase* corruption and inefficiency. Without Paris or Rome looking over their shoulders, who knows what those bureaucrats in the provinces will do? For most of its history, the United States has had a decentralized education system. The result has been a great deal of freedom and local control but also extreme unevenness of quality and blatant racial segregation. Many Americans wish they could go back to strict local control, but they don't want to do without federal dollars. True decentralization means that localities have to raise their own taxes, something they dislike doing.

Decentralization may entail widely varying standards and problems of coordination. With Germany's strongly decentralized federal system, it took years to get the different *Länder* to agree on a program and standards to clear up the seriously polluted Rhine River. Each state saw its environmental responsibilities differently and didn't want its authority eroded. Further, decentralization does not mean reducing the number of bureaucrats, just placing them at different levels. As such, it may actually seem to put more bureaucrats on the people's backs, not fewer.

Politicizing the Bureaucracy   Most governments are proud that they have moved to a nonpolitical, neutral, professional bureaucracy. In the United States, we disdain the corrupt "spoils system" of the past century in which political bosses would place their people in choice jobs. But maybe we've gone too far with the career, neutral, detached bureaucrat. Perhaps it's time to reinject a certain amount of political control into the system. Political appointees bring fresh approaches, innovative plans, and a mandate from the people and elected officials for change. Bureaucrats live by routine and hate to rock the boat; they are not capable of changing their own system. Only outsiders, appointed from other walks of life for a few years, can do that.

The old U.S. urban machines, such as that of the late Mayor Daley in Chicago, were decried for their corruption, but they were generally responsive to citizens' needs and often worked better than the reform administrations that succeeded them. A new American president has some 3,000 appointive positions to fill, a very high number compared with the numbers in other countries. Some say this is too many, that we should use career civil servants to fill more of these slots. But it is this appointive power that gives a president what little leverage he or she has over the U.S. bureaucracy. Decrease it and the civil service will be less responsive.

The negative side to political appointments is the corruption that often comes with them. Because the political appointees are often from the very branches of industry their bureaus are supposed to be monitoring, they tend to see things the industry's way, to overlook irregularities, and sometimes to dispense favors to friends and party contributors. Almost all cases of corruption in U.S. government offices are wrongdoings of political appointees, not career civil servants. Career civil servants in the Federal Home Loan Bank Board in the 1980s, for example, tried early to signal irregularities with Lincoln Savings and Loan in California. Their politically appointed bosses and five senators, recipients of $1.3 million in campaign donations by Lincoln's owner, overrode the civil servants and delayed action against the firm. The Iran-contra fiasco occurred precisely because the White House insisted on bypassing State and Defense Department bureaucrats, who could have told them that the plan was illegal and unworkable. Political guidance of bureaucracy, yes; bypassing bureaucracy, no.

Bureaucracy and Society

For all our dislike of bureaucracy, we must remember that it was not visited on us from an alien planet. It was set up, funded, and given its duties by our elected representatives. To be sure, agencies sometimes take on lives of their own, but the initial reasons for them still apply. Do you think a lot of red tape is involved in getting a driver's license? Imagine a society where drivers weren't required to be licensed. Do you think bureaucrats interfere too much with private industry? What would happen if we rolled back our standards on foodstuffs, drugs, and product safety? Do equal-opportunity bureaucrats harm a white person's chances to get into law school or secure a good job by ensuring preference to minority candidates? It wasn't bureaucrats who set up these laws; it was Congress. Congress, to be sure, was vague and sloppy, leaving administrators too much lee-way in drawing up guidelines and then dropping the whole thing on the courts. But the bureaucrats themselves have only the smallest part of the blame.

We live in a complex society. We may try from time to time to make it sim-pler, to do away with what appear to be burdensome regulations and officious bureaucrats. But when we do, we discover anew that the regulations and civil servants were put there for a purpose. Whereas we may—indeed must—attempt to improve our rules and the agencies that implement them, we are unlikely to eliminate them unless we are prepared to return to a simpler age, a time without nuclear power, automobiles, telecommunications, or employment security. Until then, we are stuck with our unlovely bureaucrats, for in the final analysis, they are us.

Key Terms

adjudication (p. 297)	discretionary (p. 298)	productivity (p. 296)
apolitical (p. 291)	hierarchy (p. 286)	quasi- (p. 288)
appropriation (p. 288)	merit civil service (p. 291)	secular (p. 287)
bureaucracy (p. 286)	nationalized (p. 294)	
corruption (p. 296)	prefect (p. 289)	

Key Websites

The Tennessee Valley Authority website offers information about the agency—facts, vision, goals, press releases, and speeches by the chairman.
http://www.tva.gov/

The Ex-Im Bank, created in 1934, aids in financing and facilitating U.S. exports. The website gives information on bank loans and guarantees, eligible markets, and how to finance products and services overseas.
http://www.exim.gov/

The Securities and Exchange Commission is responsible for administering federal securities laws and protecting investors in securities markets.
http://www.sec.gov/

This is the IRS homepage.
http://www.irs.ustreas.gov/

Further Reference

Crozier, Michel. *The Bureaucratic Phenomenon*. Chicago, IL: University of Chicago Press, 1964.

Farazmand, Ali, ed. *Modern Systems of Government: Exploring the Role of Bureaucrats and Politicians*. Thousand Oaks, CA: Sage, 1997.

Fritschler, A. Lee. *Smoking and Politics: Policymaking and the Federal Bureaucracy*, 5th ed. Englewood Cliffs, NJ: Prentice Hall, 1995.

Fry, Brian R. *Mastering Public Administration: From Max Weber to Dwight Waldo*. Chatham, NJ: Chatham House, 1989.

Kerwin, Cornelius M. *Rulemaking: How Government Agencies Write Law and Make Policy*. Washington, D.C.: CQ Press, 1994.

Lindblom, Charles E. *The Policy-Making Process*, 3rd ed. Englewood Cliffs, NJ: Prentice Hall, 1992.

Ripley, Randall A., and Grace A. Franklin. *Congress, the Bureaucracy, and Public Policy*, 5th ed. Belmont, CA: Wadsworth, 1991.

Selden, Sally Coleman. *The Promise of Representative Bureaucracy: Diversity and Responsiveness in a Government Agency*. Armonk, NY: M. E. Sharpe, 1997.

West, William F. *Controlling the Bureaucracy: Institutional Constraints in Theory and Practice*. Armonk, NY: M. E. Sharpe, 1995.

Wilson, James Q. *Bureaucracy: What Government Agencies Do and Why They Do It*. New York: Basic Books, 1990.

Wood, Dan B., and Richard W. Waterman. *Bureaucratic Dynamics: The Role of Bureaucracy in a Democracy*. Boulder, CO: Westview Press, 1994.

Legal Systems and the Courts

Justice Oliver Wendell Holmes once remarked, "My freedom to swing my arm stops where the other man's nose begins." Freedom of action must have its limits if the freedom of all is to be preserved. But who decides what these limits are? Without a legal system, force alone would settle disputes. Even primitive societies use neutral third parties to settle disputes. Modern nations depend on laws and courts to maintain order. **Law** plays an especially big role in the U.S. system, as it fills in the gaps left by our limited government. Some say that Americans use law too much, expecting it to solve all manner of social, economic, and political problems.

Types of Law

We focus here on **positive law**, that which is written and compiled by humans over the centuries. Unlike natural law, positive law does use law books to discover right and wrong. Our complex society requires many types of law. There are five major branches of law.

1. Why is the U.S. political system so dependent on the courts?
2. Contrast natural and positive law.
3. What are the differences between common and code law?
4. Describe the U.S. court system.
5. How are European trials quite different from ours?
6. What does Germany have that resembles the U.S. Supreme Court?
7. How did an 1803 case give the Supreme Court vast powers?
8. In what major cases did the Warren Court make new law?
9. Have subsequent courts reversed Warren Court decisions?

law   That which must be obeyed under penalties.

positive law   That which is written by humans and accepted over time.

plaintiff   The person who complains in a law case.

Criminal Law

With fear of crime prominent, the criminal law system is the one we hear most about. Modern criminal law is largely statutory law and covers a specific category of wrongs that are considered social evils and threats to the community. Consequently, the state rather than the victim is the prosecutor (**plaintiff**). Offenses are usually divided into three categories. *Petty offenses*, such as traffic violations, are normally punished by a fine. Serious but not major offenses such as gambling and prostitution are *misdemeanors*, punishable by larger fines or short jail sentences. Major crimes, *felonies* such as rape, murder, robbery, and extortion are punished by imprisonment. In the United States, some criminal offenses such as kidnapping and interstate car theft are federal in nature; others, such as murder and theft, are mainly state concerns; and a few, such as bank robbery and drug trafficking, violate both state and federal laws.

> ### KEY TERMS
>
> **common law** "Judge-made law"; old decisions built up over the centuries.
> **civil law** Non-criminal disputes among individuals.
> **higher law** That which comes from God.
> **natural law** That which comes from nature and is understood by reasoning.

Civil Law

Many statutes govern civil rather than criminal matters. Marriage and divorce, inheritance, business deals, and bankruptcy are civil concerns. In most English-speaking countries, statutory law is supplemented by **common law**. **Civil law** provides redress for private plaintiffs who can show they have been injured. The decisions are usually in dollars, not in jail time. Private individuals, not the state, conduct most civil litigation.

Constitutional Law

Written constitutions are usually general documents. Subsequent legislation and court interpretation must fill in the details. An important role of U.S. courts, under our system of judicial review, is to make sure that statutory laws

---

Classic Works	THE ROOTS OF LAW

Terms such as **higher law** or **natural law** have appeared in philosophy since the beginning of civilization. Higher law grew out of a mingling of Stoic philosophy and the Judeo-Christian tradition; it was attributed to God or the Creator and was thus higher than laws made by humans. This concept is still around in the idea that people are "endowed by their Creator" with the rights to life, liberty, and the pursuit of happiness and the right to own property and enjoy the fruits of one's labor—rights that no just government can take away. Many argue that higher law takes precedence over laws enacted by humans, and some justify their defiance of ordinary laws by citing it. Mahatma Gandhi in India and Martin Luther King, Jr., in the United States claimed that their actions, which violated human-made laws, were moral because they conformed to higher law. Natural law, 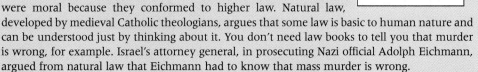 developed by medieval Catholic theologians, argues that some law is basic to human nature and can be understood just by thinking about it. You don't need law books to tell you that murder is wrong, for example. Israel's attorney general, in prosecuting Nazi official Adolph Eichmann, argued from natural law that Eichmann had to know that mass murder is wrong.

and administrative interpretations do not violate the spirit or meaning of the constitution.

In the United States the ultimate responsibility of interpreting the Constitution rests with the U.S. Supreme Court, and this changes with time. The cliché "The Constitution is what the Supreme Court says it is" is not unfounded. In 1896, for example, the Court ruled, in *Plessy v. Ferguson*, that state laws requiring racial segregation in public transportation did not necessarily violate the Fourteenth Amendment, which provides for equal protection under the laws, as long as the transportation facilities for whites and blacks were physically equal. In *Brown v. Board of Education of Topeka* (1954), the court reversed itself and ruled that separate public education facilities for whites and blacks are *inherently* unequal, even if physically alike. The Constitution didn't change, but society's conception of individual rights did. **Constitutional law** (indeed, law itself) is not static, but a living, growing institution.

Administrative Law

A relatively recent development, administrative law covers regulatory orders by government agencies. It develops when agencies interpret statutes, as they must. For example, federal statute prohibits "unfair or deceptive acts" in commerce. But what business practices are "unfair or deceptive"? The Federal Trade Commission must decide. As the agencies interpret the meaning of Congress's laws, they begin to build up a body of regulations and case law that guides the commission in its future decisions. These rulings may be appealed to the federal courts. The federal government now codifies administrative regulations, which are now quite large.

International Law

International law (IL) consists of international treaties and long-established customs recognized by most nations. It is an interesting body of law because it cannot be enforced in the same way as national law: It has no judges, courts, or police. IL, however, is generally observed, because it is in the interests of most countries to not break it. IL's key mechanisms are **reciprocity** and **consistency**. Countries generally like being treated nicely, so they must extend the courtesy to others. They also do not like being accused of applying different standards to various countries, so they try to keep their dealings consistent. Some IL is enforced by national courts. The U.S. Supreme Court has ruled that U.S. states have to observe international treaties. A U.S. business harmed abroad can seek redress in U.S. courts against the assets of the foreign firm that did the damage. We mostly study international public law, but international private law is a rapidly growing field as more and more businesses operate globally (see Chapter 21).

Primitive legal systems are oral and consist of customs and beliefs. Modern legal systems are written and largely codified, that is, systematically arranged. Putting laws in writing makes them more precise and uniform. Codification began in ancient times and has been a major feature in the development of civilization. The Ten Commandments and the Code of Hammurabi were early law codes, but the great

ancient code was **Roman law**. Its details, covering all aspects of social life and based on "right reason," were so universal, flexible, and logical that they are still in use in much of the world today. Roman law was incorporated by the Catholic Church in its **canon law**, and in the East by the Byzantine Emperor Justinian, whose celebrated Code of Justinian (*Corpus Juris Civilis*) of A.D. 533 is the foundation of most of Europe's modern legal systems. Modern European law is largely an amalgamation of Roman, feudal, and church law.

The Courts, the Bench, and the Bar

As legal systems developed, so did judicial systems, for it is these systems that handle the day-to-day administration of the law. The organization of a judicial system is always hierarchical, and different courts have specific jurisdictions; that is, they hear different kinds of cases and have authority in specific geographical areas.

The U.S. Court System

Our court system is unique, consisting of fifty-one judicial structures: the national system, comprising the federal courts, and fifty state systems. The federal system overlaps that of the states. The federal courts hear many cases in which the issue is one of state laws but the parties are residents of different states, the so-called "diversity jurisdiction." Also, of course, they hear cases concerning federal laws. Conversely, issues of federal law (constitutional or statutory) may arise in state courts. The Supreme Court of the United States can review the state court's judgment on a federal question.

The National Court Structure   The federal district court is at the base of the national court system. Ninety-four federal court districts employ over 500 judges and serve as trial courts in civil suits arising under federal law as well as criminal cases involving federal infractions. It also exercises the "diversity" jurisdiction. Most criminal cases, however, even those involving federal law, are tried in state courts.

Federal district court decisions can be appealed to a U.S. court of appeals. The thirteen courts of appeals, presided over by 132 judges, may also review the rulings of administrative tribunals and commissions, such as the Federal Trade

Key Concepts — COMMON LAW VERSUS CODE LAW

The English common law started with the customary usages of Germanic tribal law of the Angles and Saxons who took over England from the third to fifth centuries. This law stressed the rights of free and equal men and developed on the basis of **precedent** set by earlier judges; it is thus called "judge-made law." The Normans who conquered England decided the local, decentralized nature of this law hindered their governance of the country as a whole, so they set up central courts to systematize the local laws and produce a "common" law for all parts of their kingdom. They also added new features, such as trial by jury.

In administering justice, English judges and courts were forced to improvise. Most had a church education and were familiar with canon law. Accordingly, when royal law was inadequate, the judges applied canon law. If these were not applicable, they used their own common sense and the common practices of the English people. Over the centuries, a substantial body of common law developed—an amalgam of Roman law, Church law, and local English customs.

Common law has three distinctive features. First, it is *case law*; that is, it is based on individual legal decisions rather than on a comprehensive code of statutes. Second, common law was made by *judicial decision* and thus has great flexibility. Judges can easily reinterpret or modify previous rulings and principles to fit each case. Third, common law relies heavily on *stare decisis*, or precedent. Because no two cases are exactly alike, a judge can note points of difference to justify breaking precedent. In this way, common law retains a marvelous flexibility. With the rise of Parliament as a dominant institution in seventeenth-century England, statute law supplemented and then supplanted much of the common law. Today, when the two conflict, statute law always takes precedence.

Common law has declined in importance but still has considerable influence in England (but not Scotland), the United States, Canada, Australia, New Zealand, and a number of former British colonies. In many instances, statute law is the formal enactment of old common law provisions. Common law shaped the development of English society and politics and imparted distinctive political habits.

The legal systems of continental Europe (France, in particular) developed very differently. As French kings were overturning feudalism in favor of absolutism (see Chapter 3), Roman law was being revived by legal scholars to suit the changing conditions in Europe. Central governments were asserting themselves, and commerce growing, making obvious that some form of centralized justice was needed. French jurists saw the value of Roman law. It was universal, written, and worked so well for the ancient world. It was already known through canon law. Absolutist French kings found Roman law quite helpful in consolidating central authority.

Codifying the law was Napoleon's lasting contribution to French justice and, eventually, to much of the world. His *Code Napoléon* (1804), the first modern codification of European law, by-passed feudal laws and broke civil law away from religious influence. It preserved many of the gains of the French Revolution, such as elimination of torture and arbitrary arrest and imprisonment, as well as the guarantee of civil liberty and civil equality. Napoleon conquered most of Europe and brought the code with him; Europe's legal systems are still based on it. It is also in use in Louisiana, and European colonists carried it to Asia and Africa

---

COMMON LAW VERSUS CODE LAW (CONTINUED)

later in the nineteenth century. The centralization of French life even to this day is a reflection of its basic philosophy.

Today, most of the world lives under some form of Roman law as interpreted by the Code Napoleon. Most **code law** is detailed, precise (more so than the written laws in common-law countries), comprehensive, and understandable by laypersons. Judges are not expected to "make" law, merely to apply it. Precedent carries less weight. The judiciary is not independent of the executive as in the American system. Therefore, its powers of judicial review are quite limited—either shared with the legislative branch or assigned to a special constitutional court, which now most European countries have, a relatively new feature.

The differences between the common law and the Roman system are marked. The former is general and largely judge-made, and it relies on precedent and custom. The latter is specific and is largely the product of legislation. It is interesting to note that both systems developed to serve the needs of modernizing and centralizing monarchs—Henry I and II in England and Louis XIII and Napoleon in France. The two systems, however, are becoming more and more alike. As the volume of statute law increases in the English-speaking nations, the importance and relevance of common law decreases. More and more, the details of legislative enactment are being outlined by administrative agencies, whose regulations are now an integral part of the legal system. In both systems, the law is relatively uniform in its application, universal in its scope, and amenable to change.

Commission, the Federal Aviation Administration, and the Food and Drug Administration. Each court of appeals consists of three or more judges, depending on need, and arguments are heard by panels of three judges. These panels rarely question the facts of the case but consider only whether or not the law has been misinterpreted or misapplied. The court of appeals bases its majority-vote verdict on the **appeal** primarily on the **briefs** submitted by the attorneys for both parties; oral arguments are limited.

The pinnacle of the federal court system is the Supreme Court, consisting of one chief justice and eight associate justices. Its jurisdiction is almost entirely appellate, from lower federal or state supreme courts. For example, if a state supreme court declares a federal statute unconstitutional, it is almost certain that the Court will hear the case. Unlike a court of appeals, however, it is not obliged to hear every case and accepts for review only a few of the petitions that it receives. The Court will generally not hear a case unless it involves a substantial constitutional question, a treaty, or some significant point of federal law. Because the U.S. system is based on precedent, the Court's ruling *is* national law.

KEY TERMS

precedent   Legal decisions based on earlier decisions. (See p. 308.)

code law   Laws arranged in books, usually updated Roman law.

appeal   To take a case to a higher court.

brief   A written summary submitted by one side of a case containing the relevant facts, laws, and precedents.

The State Court System   Each of the fifty states has its own court systems, and they handle perhaps 90 percent of the nation's legal business. Most of their cases are civil, not criminal. Generally, state trial courts operate at the county level and have original jurisdiction in all civil and criminal cases. In rural areas, justices of the peace try minor matters. In urban areas, magistrate's or police courts do the same. These local courts operate without juries (serious cases go to state courts) and most of their penalties are fines or short jail terms.

Judges

Federal Judges   Federal judges are nominated by the president and are appointed with the advice and consent of the Senate. Federal judges hold their positions during "good behavior," which generally means that they serve for life unless impeached and convicted for criminal behavior. This is to free them from executive and political pressure.

Federal judges are invariably lawyers. Some owe their appointments to political favors, but they are usually well qualified. The attorney general will list eligible candidates; as vacancies occur, the president selects a few names from that list. The president typically considers the reputation-based ratings of prospective judges by the American Bar Association (ABA). The FBI inquires into the candidates' past and present activities. The Senate must approve all federal judges, a procedure that used to be routine but is now highly political. The opposition party accuses the president of trying to fill the **bench** with incompetent partisans and often tries to block confirmation. Under Clinton, many federal judgeships went unfilled because Senate Republicans rejected nominees as too liberal.

KEY TERM
bench   The office of judge.

Some presidents—President Eisenhower, for example—have argued that the federal judiciary should be nonpartisan, or at the very least bipartisan. Eisenhower appointed some Democrats to the federal bench (including Supreme Court Justice William J. Brennan) and made an effort to achieve a balance between judicial liberals and judicial conservatives. Most presidents, however, appoint judges of their own political party who share their judicial philosophy. President Johnson, for example, appointed Thurgood Marshall—a liberal who believed that the Court should take an active role in promoting social justice—to the Supreme Court. President Nixon, in contrast, appointed four justices whose general political philosophy was conservative and who believed that the Warren Court of the 1950s and 1960s went too far in protecting the rights of the individual, to the detriment of society as a whole. President Reagan followed the Nixon example with the appointment of a conservative who happened to be a woman, Sandra Day O'Connor, the first female on the Court.

State Judges   State judges are popularly elected or appointed, for terms ranging up to fourteen years. Both parties often nominate the same slate of judges, so the judicial elections have become largely nonpartisan affairs; only rarely do party fights for a judicial office take place. California justices are appointed but later have to be confirmed by voters. In a 1986 referendum, Californians ousted their state chief justice, Rose Bird, who had been totally opposed to the death penalty. Some observers believe that elected state judges run the risk of turning into crowd-pleasing politicians with shaky judicial skills. Others point out that appointed state judges can be the political pals of the governor.

Comparing Courts

What role should judges play? Should they act as umpires, passively watching the legal drama, confining themselves to ruling on disputed points of procedure? Or should they actively direct the trial, question witnesses, elicit evidence, and comment on the proceedings? The second pattern strikes Americans as strange and dangerous, because we have been raised in the common-law tradition of passive judges. Yet in code-law countries, judges are supposed to play just such an active role.

The Anglo-American Adversarial and Accusatorial Process   English and American courts are passive institutions—that is, they do not go looking for injustices to correct, and they do not apprehend lawbreakers. Instead, they wait until a law is challenged or a defendant is brought before them. The system operates on an **adversarial** and **accusatorial** basis. In the adversarial process, two sides (plaintiff and defendant) are vying for a favorable decision from an impartial court. Courts will not accept a case that does not involve a real conflict of interest; in other words, the plaintiff must demonstrate how and in what ways the defendant has caused damage. During the trial, the presiding judge acts as an umpire. Both parties present their evidence, call and cross-examine witnesses, and attempt to refute the other party's arguments. The judge rules on the evidence and testimony to be admitted, ensures that proper legal procedures are being followed, and rules on disputed points. After both sides have presented their cases, the judge rules on the basis of the facts and the relevant law. If a jury is hearing the case, the judge will instruct the jury members concerning the weight of the evidence and relevant laws. The judge makes an appropriate decision after the jury gives its verdict on the factual issues.

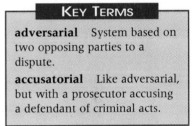

KEY TERMS

adversarial   System based on two opposing parties to a dispute.

accusatorial   Like adversarial, but with a prosecutor accusing a defendant of criminal acts.

In criminal cases, the police investigate and report to the public prosecutor, who must decide whether prosecution is warranted. The actual trial proceeds like a civil one, but the government is the plaintiff and the accused the defendant. Unless a jury has been waived, the jury determines the ultimate issue of guilt under instructions from the judge concerning the governing law.

The British Court System

The court system in operation in Britain today was established by the Judicature Act of 1873. For the most part, the system continues common-law traditions and is divided into civil and criminal branches.

Selection and Tenure of Judges   All British judges are appointed by the monarch on the advice of the prime minister, whose choices are based on recommendations of the lord chancellor, who presides over the House of Lords and is usually a cabinet member. To encourage independence, British judges are given lifetime tenure. By tradition, the English bench is above party politics and does not make policy—a tradition bolstered by the fact that there is no judicial review in Britain. Judicial review would be difficult in Britain because there is no written constitution. Whatever laws Parliament passes are automatically constitutional. The British judiciary—like most countries' judiciaries, a branch of the executive—is not supposed to be a coequal branch of government.

The Lawyer's Role   The United States and Britain share a common legal heritage, but there are important differences. One of the biggest distinctions is that in Britain the Crown—meaning the government—hires lawyers to prosecute crimes. There are no professional prosecutors like U.S. district attorneys. American lawyers may, if they wish, take on any type of legal work, in or out of the courtroom. In Britain, *solicitors* handle all legal matters except representing clients in court. That is reserved to a small number of lawyers called *barristers*, who are specialists in courtroom procedure.

The European Court System

Based heavily on the French system—the pattern for much of the world— European courts, unlike the English courts, are not divided into separate criminal and civil divisions. Instead, most European countries maintain separate systems of regular and administrative courts. European judges sit as a panel to rule on points of law and procedure, but at the conclusion of the trial they retire *with* a jury to consider the verdict and the sentence. Obviously, the lay jurors often go along with the superior—or at least professional—knowledge and wisdom of the judges. In some systems, such as the German, a judge either sits alone or with two "lay judges."

KEY TERM
investigating judge   In European legal systems, a judicial officer who both gathers evidence and issues indictments.

The Role of Judges in Adjudication: The Inquisitorial Process   In code law countries—that is, throughout most of Europe—judges play a more active role than in common-law countries. The prosecutor (French *procureur*, German *Staatsanwalt*) is an official who forwards evidence to an **investigating judge** (*juge d'instruction, Ermittlungsrichter*), a representative of the justice ministry who conducts a thorough inquiry (*enquête*), gathering evidence and statements. Without parallel in the Anglo-American system, the French or German investigating judge first makes a preliminary determination of guilt *before* sending the case to trial, something mind-boggling to Americans. In European criminal procedure, the decision to

indict is made not by a district attorney but by a judge, and the weight of evidence is not controlled by the adversaries (plaintiff and defendant) but by the court, which can take the initiative in acquiring needed evidence.

In the U.S. system, the accused is presumed innocent until proven guilty; in Europe the assumptions are nearly reversed. In an American or English court, the burden of proof is on the prosecution, and the defendant need not say one word in his or her defense; the prosecutor must prove guilt "beyond a reasonable doubt." In code-law countries, the accused bears the burden of having to prove that the investigating judge is wrong.

The Lawyer's Role   Unlike a British or American trial lawyer, the French *avocat* or German *Rechtsanwalt* does not question witnesses; the court does that. Instead, he or she tries to show logical or factual mistakes in the opposition's argument or case and sway the lay jury in the summation argument. For the most part, the role of the European lawyer is not as vital or creative as that of the American lawyer, for the court takes the initiative in discovering the facts of the case.

The Role of the Courts

Judicial review is more highly developed in the United States than in any other country, and Americans expect more of their courts than do other peoples. In no other country is the "courtroom drama" such a television staple. The reason: Few other countries have U.S.-style dramatic courtroom clashes.

Courts in other Western democracies may have structures that parallel the U.S. system, but they do not do as much. In Switzerland, for example, cases from the cantonal (state) courts come before the Federal Tribunal, which determines whether a cantonal law violates the Swiss constitution. However, the tribunal does not pass on the constitutionality of laws passed by the Swiss parliament. The German Constitutional Court reviews statutes to make sure they conform to the Basic Law (the German constitution). The court, located in Karlsruhe, was included in the Basic Law partly on American insistence after World War II; it was a new concept for Europe. It consists of sixteen judges, eight elected by each house of parliament, who serve for nonrenewable twelve-year terms. The court decides cases between states, protects civil liberties, and outlaws dangerous political parties. Its decisions have been important. In the 1950s it found that both neo-Nazi and Communist parties wanted to overthrow the constitutional order and declared them illegal. It found the 1974 abortion bill was in conflict with the strong right-to-life provisions of the Basic Law. Because the Constitutional Court operates with the more rigid code law, its decisions do not have the impact of U.S. Supreme Court decisions, which under the common law are literally the law of the land.

| Case Studies | LAW IN RUSSIA |

The Soviet legal structure has carried over into the post-Communist Russian legal system, because virtually all personnel were trained under the Communists. Now Russia is struggling to build "rule of law," including "bourgeois" concepts, such as property law and civil rights. In 1991 a Constitutional Court with fifteen justices was established, the first independent tribunal in Russian history. It can theoretically rule on the constitutionality of the moves made by the president and the State Duma. In practice, President Yeltsin gave himself so much power—including over selection of justices—that he was little bound by legal restraints. Crime is rampant in Russia. Newly rich *biznesmeny* hire *keelers* to remove anyone in their way, including members of parliament, journalists, and the competition. "The only lawyer around here is a Kalashnikov," despaired one Russian, referring to the assault rifle.

The basic concepts of Soviet law and the workings of the Soviet judicial process were quite different from those of the Western democracies, even though they were similar in strictly criminal—as opposed to political—matters. Soviet law started with Marx's idea that law serves the ruling class. Capitalists naturally have bourgeois laws designed to protect private property. Proletarians, theoretically in power in the Soviet Union, had socialist law to protect state property, the property of all society. After Stalin, monumental theft of state property became the norm for Soviet economic life and helped bring down the system. Almost nothing was said of private property, which scarcely existed. Another part of Soviet law dealt with sedition and subversion, areas of extremely minor importance in the West. Soviet citizens could receive harsh sentences to Siberia for "antistate activities" or "slandering the Soviet state."

Unpolitical cases were generally handled fairly under Soviet law. Prosecutors gathered evidence and brought cases to court but sometimes took into account mitigating social factors and asked for lighter sentences. Defense attorneys were permitted, but they merely advised their clients on legal points and did not challenge the prosecutor's evidence. There were no jury trials. All Soviet judges had to be Communist party members.

Some political cases never came to trial. Obedient Soviet psychiatrists used to diagnose dissidents as "sluggish schizophrenic" and put them in prisonlike hospitals with no trial. Nobel Prize-winning writer Alexander Solzhenitsyn was simply bundled onto a plane for Germany in 1974 with no trial. Likewise, dissident physicist Andrei Sakharov was banished to a remote city in 1980 to get him away from Western reporters. The Committee on State Security (KGB) was powerful and often acted independently of courts. The KGB was succeeded by the Federal Security Service (FSB in Russian) and, staffed by old KGB officials, continues the KGB's primary aim: to make sure those in power stay in power. In the midst of monumental murder and corruption, the FSB arrests few. Many observers fear that if rule of law is not established in Russia, democracy will die. The two are closely connected.

Case Studies — MARBURY V. MADISON

President John Adams, a Federalist, appointed William Marbury, a Washington, D.C., justice of the peace shortly before leaving office. For some unknown reason, however, Secretary of State John Marshall did not deliver the commission to Marbury. Marshall's successor, the Republican James Madison, refused to deliver the commission. Marbury brought suit in original jurisdiction before the Supreme Court, asking the Court to issue a writ of *mandamus* commanding Madison to deliver the commission. This presented the Court with something of a dilemma. If Chief Justice Marshall and the Supreme Court issued the writ, and Madison refused to deliver the commission, the prestige and authority of the Court would be dealt a severe blow. If, however, Marshall refused to issue the writ, he would in effect call into question the legitimacy of the hasty judicial appointments given to Federalists in the final days of the Adams administration. Marshall's solution was nothing short of brilliant, for it not only criticized Madison and Jefferson but also established explicitly the principle of judicial review. On the one hand, Marshall ruled that

Marbury was entitled to his commission and that Madison should have given it to him. On the other hand, however, he stated that the Supreme Court had no authority to issue a writ of *mandamus* in a case brought to it in original jurisdiction and that because Section 13 of the Judiciary Act of 1789 implied otherwise, that part of the act was unconstitutional. The decision infuriated President Jefferson, for he understood all too well how cleverly Marshall had escaped the trap and also asserted the authority of the Court. He realized that the precedent for judicial review had been laid and called it "both elitist and undemocratic."

The U.S. Supreme Court

The U.S. Supreme Court's power to review the constitutionality of federal legislative enactments is not mentioned specifically in the Constitution and has been vehemently challenged. Judicial review was first considered and debated at the Constitutional Convention of 1787. Delegates suggested that when in doubt, legislators might call on the judges for an opinion on a proposed law's constitutionality. James Madison stated that a "law violating a constitution established by the people themselves would be considered by the judges as null and void." However, this position was challenged by those who believed that such a power would give the Court a double check and compromise its neutrality. Others felt it would violate the separation of powers. Elbridge Gerry stated that it would make "statesmen of judges," a prophetic remark. At the close of the convention, judicial review had not been explicitly provided for.

Alexander Hamilton, however, argued in *The Federalist* No. 78 that only the courts could limit legislative authority. John Marshall (chief justice of the Supreme Court from 1801 to 1835) agreed with this position; in fact, he went on record in favor of it nearly fifteen years before *Marbury v. Madison* (1803), the landmark decision establishing judicial review. The doctrine has never been universally popular, however. Strong-willed presidents have resisted the authority of the Court. Thomas Jefferson, Andrew Jackson, Abraham Lincoln, and Franklin D. Roosevelt differed sharply with equally strong-willed judges.

From 1803 to 1857, the Supreme Court did not invalidate any act of Congress. In 1857, it threw out the Missouri Compromise of 1820, which had barred slavery in the old Northwest Territory. This touched off a political storm that was to make Abraham Lincoln president. In the twentieth century, the doctrine has been used extensively. The court itself, however, has always been divided on how it should be used. Judicial "activists," led by Hugo Black, William O. Douglas, and Earl Warren, have argued that the Supreme Court must be vigilant in its protection of the Bill of Rights. Advocates of judicial "restraint," such as Oliver Wendell Holmes, Felix Frankfurter, and Warren Burger, have argued that only Congress should make public policy and that unless a legislative act clearly violates the Constitution, the law should stand. The Warren Court (1953–1969), named after its chief justice, was markedly activist, issuing decisions in the areas of racial segregation, reapportionment, and rights of the accused that had substantial impacts on U.S. society. The courts that followed have been more cautious, reflecting the fact that most of its members were appointed by conservative Republicans.

The Supreme Court's Political Role

In this country, the Supreme Court's rulings often become political issues, rarely the case in other countries. When the Supreme Court of Franklin Roosevelt's day ruled that many New Deal laws were unconstitutional, FDR referred to the justices as "nine tired old men." Richard Nixon in the 1968 campaign charged that the Warren Court's liberal decisions had worsened crime and endangered society. The U.S. Supreme Court plays an important political role. Moreover, the appointment of just one new justice can change split decisions from five to four against to the same number for. It is important to know to what extent judges let their personal beliefs influence their decisions. Are their ideological views incompatible with the idea of the Court as an impartial dispenser of justice?

The Views of Judges

KEY TERM
WASP White, Anglo-Saxon, Protestant.

Justices may try to keep their personal beliefs out of decisions, but their outlook and background still influence them. Most Supreme Court justices are and have been **WASP** upper- or upper-middle-class males. Radical critics claim that such judges cannot identify with the needs of the poor or racially oppressed. The relatively recent arrival of blacks and women to the high bench have not necessarily overturned conservative tendencies, for black and women justices can be conservative in their own right. Many African-American lawyers were disappointed with Justice Clarence Thomas, the second black ever on the Court, who said he reached conservative conclusions by thinking for himself.

Other factors affect a judge's rulings. Southern jurists have usually been more conservative on racial matters, but one of the strongest champions of civil rights was Alabama's Hugo L. Black, who had been a member of the Ku Klux Klan in his youth. Similarly, eastern judges are often more responsive to the needs of large industry than judges from farm states. Occupational background may also affect decision making; for example, former corporation lawyers may be more sympathetic than others to the problems of business. Some justices, like Louis D. Brandeis (one of five Jewish justices) and Thurgood Marshall (the first black justice), were active in reform and civil rights causes and brought their liberalism to the bench. Others who have served on state courts believe that states' rights should be strengthened.

The two most important influences on voting, however, seem to be party affiliation and the justice's conception of the judicial role. Some studies indicate that Democratic justices are much more likely to support liberal stands than are Republican justices. Democrats tend to be judicial activists and to see the Supreme Court as a defender of oppressed minorities and economic groups. They are more likely to distrust state power and to favor an increase in federal authority, while also seeking to protect individual rights under the Fourteenth Amendment against state authority. Republicans usually favor judicial restraint, are more likely to uphold state authority within the federal system, and are less likely to accept the Bill of Rights as a blanket guarantee. There are, of course, exceptions. When President Eisenhower appointed California Governor Earl Warren in 1953, he thought he was picking a good Republican moderate as chief justice. Later, Eisenhower called the choice "the biggest damned-fool mistake I ever made."

Many justices see the Court's role as standing firm on certain constitutional principles, despite public opinion. Justice Jackson put it this way: "One's right to life, liberty and property, to free speech, a free press, freedom of worship and assembly, and other fundamental rights may not be submitted to vote; they depend upon the outcome of no election." But Supreme Court justices are influenced by changing public attitudes. In the 1936 election, after the Court had struck down several important laws designed to alleviate the Depression, President Roosevelt was given the greatest mandate in the nation's history. In 1937, he submitted legislation to expand the Supreme Court to fifteen members and encourage justices 70 or over to retire. The plan failed because many felt that Roosevelt was attacking the constitutional principle of an independent judiciary, but it did force the Court to look beyond its narrow world and accept change. Most legal scholars believe that the election of 1936 and the controversy over "court packing" led directly to the Court's becoming more restrained in dealing with New Deal legislation. As one jokester put it, "A switch in time saves nine."

Another influence is colleagues' opinions. Both Chief Justices John Marshall (1801–1835) and Earl Warren (1953–1969) were able to convert some of their colleagues to their judicial philosophies by force of personality as well as their judicial reasoning. In short, many factors—not all of them knowable—influence a given decision. Perhaps one factor overshadows all others, the fact that Supreme Court justices are appointed for life. They are independent and immune to congressional, White House, and private-interest pressures. This factor may change them, and in unpredictable ways. Liberals may turn into conservatives, activists into restrainers, and vice versa. The seriousness of their position and the knowledge that their votes may alter American life makes justices think deeply and sometimes change views. The office in considerable part makes its occupant.

The Political Impact of the Court

Our legal system poses a basic conflict. Justices are expected to be impartial, but the importance of the Court gives them political power. In the twentieth century this power is increasing. The **Warren Court** was as active as it was controversial, and in three key areas—civil rights, criminal rights, and legislative reapportionment—it substantially rewrote constitutional law. In the opinion of some, as ninety-six southern members of Congress put it, the Court overturned "the established law of the land" and implemented its "personal political and social philosophy."

Civil Rights   The Supreme Court's decision in *Brown v. Board of Education of Topeka* (1954) drastically changed American race relations. In a unanimous ruling, the Court accepted the sociological argument of Thurgood Marshall (then attorney for the NAACP) that segregated public school facilities were "inherently unequal" because they stigmatized black children and deprived them of the Fourteenth Amendment's guarantee of equal protection. A year later, in *Brown II* (1955), desegregation in the public schools was ordered to proceed "with all deliberate speed." Southern whites vowed massive resistance.

America's blacks, encouraged by this legal support, sought equal treatment in other areas. By 1963, passive resistance had given way to massive confrontation. In *Lombard v. Louisiana* (1963), the Warren Court supported the **sit-in**, ruling that blacks who had refused to leave a segregated lunch counter could not be prosecuted where it appeared that the state was involved in unequal treatment of the races. The Court relied on the Fourteenth Amendment that no state may deny any person the equal protection of the laws. The sit-in became a major weapon in the civil rights struggle. In 1964, Congress followed the Court's lead and passed the Civil Rights Act, which barred segregation in public accommodations such as hotels, motels, restaurants, and theaters. The Court led Congress.

KEY TERMS

Warren Court   The liberal, activist, U.S. Supreme Court under Chief Justice Earl Warren, 1953–1969.

sit-in   Tactic of overturning local laws by deliberately breaking them, as at segregated lunch counters.

indigent   Having no money.

Criminal Justice   The Warren Court's rulings in criminal justice were even more disturbing to many Americans. In *Mapp v. Ohio* (1961), the Court ruled that evidence police seized without a warrant was inadmissible in a state court. In 1963, in *Gideon v. Wainwright*, the Court held that **indigent** defendants must be provided with legal counsel. In *Escobedo v. Illinois* (1964), in a five-to-four decision, it ruled that a suspect could not be denied the right to have a lawyer during police questioning and that any confessions so obtained could not be used in court. One of the Court's most controversial rulings came in 1966 in *Miranda v.*

Arizona. The majority (five to four) ruled that as soon as a suspect is detained by the police, he or she must be told of the right to remain silent and to have a lawyer present during police questioning. Once again, the Court had upset local criminal procedures, and once again its ruling was unpopular.

Legislative Reapportionment   Equally important was the Warren Court's mandating of equal-population voting districts. Until 1962, state legislative districts had been gerrymandered notoriously, but the Supreme Court had maintained that only the states and Congress had the right to draw electoral boundaries. This meant that in many states rural districts were grossly overrepresented and cities underrepresented. In a series of decisions in 1962 and 1964, the Court found that unequal representation denied citizens their Fourteenth Amendment (equal protection) rights. The Court ordered that state legislatures apply the principle of "one person, one vote" in redrawing electoral lines.

Much of this angered people who felt they had been hurt: segregationists who didn't like to share schools or accommodations with blacks, police who felt hampered in dealing with suspects, and rural people who wanted a more-than-equal vote. There were billboards shouting "Impeach Earl Warren," and in 1968 Nixon ran as much against the Supreme Court as against Hubert Humphrey. The Warren Court overthrew **Jim Crow laws**, rewrote the rules for criminal procedure, and redrew legislative maps. With the possible exception of the Marshall Court, it was the most active, groundbreaking Court in U.S. history.

> **KEY TERM**
>
> **Jim Crow laws**   System of segregationist laws in the U.S. South.

The Post-Warren Courts   The Burger Court (1969–1986) and the current Rehnquist Court are sometimes characterized as conservative, an effort to roll back the Warren Court. Actually, their decisions are not so clear-cut. Overall, there has been a conservative drift, but an unpredictable one. The Burger Court in the 1978 *Bakke* case found that reserving quotas for black applicants to medical school violated equal protection for whites. The next year, however, in *Weber*, it found that quotas to help black workers attain skilled positions were constitutional. In criminal law, the Burger Court issued some hard-line decisions. In 1984 it added a "good faith exception" to the *Mapp* rule, which excluded wrongfully seized evidence. If the police, with a warrant to look for a particular piece of evidence, stumble on another, it may be used as evidence. This modified but did not overturn *Mapp*. In 1976, the Burger Court found that capital punishment was not necessarily "cruel and unusual" if the rules for applying it were fair.

The Rehnquist Court both pleased and alarmed conservatives. In 1988, in a move that stunned the Reagan administration, the Court upheld the constitutionality of independent federal prosecutors, something the White House said interfered with the powers of the executive branch. The 1989 *Webster* decision gave state legislatures the power to limit abortions. This was seen as a victory for pro-life forces, but in some states it energized pro-choice forces to block such laws. The Court also ruled that burning the American flag could not be outlawed; it is a form of free speech. This ruling brought a mass outcry and a new federal statute outlawing flag burning. In sum, the post-Warren Courts modified rather than repudiated the Warren Court.

One of the problems with evaluating the thrust of Court decisions is the definition of *conservative*. The term may be applied to the substance of decisions, such as giving minorities special treatment, or it may be applied to the maintenance of existing institutions. Often the two coincide, as when the Court says states can pass laws limiting abortion. That would be both conservative concerning substance and conservative concerning the powers of states. But sometimes the two can diverge, as when the Rehnquist Court unanimously overturned a $200,000 libel award for the Reverend Jerry Falwell. Some might call that a "liberal" ruling, but it really just upholds the First Amendment right to a free press. What the mass media and public opinion call "conservative" may be irrelevant to the Court, which is intent only on preserving constitutionality. "Liberal" and "conservative" are simplified labels used by the mass media and politicians; they are not used by the Supreme Court.

The U.S. federal courts are an integral part of the policymaking apparatus—not just mechanical interpreters of law. Judicial decisions influence and are influenced by politics. Groups whose welfare depends on the court's decisions will try to influence the court to adopt their point of view; and groups that do not succeed with the president or Congress hope that they will have better luck with the courts. Some have called the U.S. judicial system a back-up legislature or parliament of last resort, for it can take on issues the other branches are afraid to tackle. Without Supreme Court decisions leading the way, Congress would have not passed civil-rights bills and presidents would not have enforced them. Its autonomous and coequal judicial branch is one of America's great contributions to governance. Very slowly, this approach to judicial power is growing worldwide, contributing to rule of law and stable democracy.

Key Terms

accusatorial (p. 311)

adversarial (p. 311)

appeal (p. 309)

bench (p. 310)

brief (p. 309)

canon law (p. 307)

civil law (p. 305)

code law (p. 309)

common law (p. 305)

consistency (p. 306)

constitutional law (p. 306)

higher law (p. 305)

indict (p. 313)

indigent (p. 318)

investigating judge (p. 312)

Jim Crow laws (p. 319)

law (p. 304)

natural law (p. 305)

plaintiff (p. 304)

positive law (p. 304)

precedent (p. 309)

reciprocity (p. 306)

Roman law (p. 307)

sit-in (p. 318)

Warren Court (p. 318)

WASP (p. 316)

Key Websites

This Cornell University site, produced by the Legal Information Institute, features all Supreme Court opinions issued since May of 1990, plus over 580 of the most important historical decisions of the Court.
http://supct.law.cornell.edu/supct/

This is the Department of Justice website.
http://www.usdoj.gov/

The American Bar Association has a wealth of information and links to the various judicial systems in the United States.
http://www.abanet.org/

Court TV has an excellent site that gives the day-to-day developments in all sorts of legal matters, from local to federal to international.
http://www.courttv.com/

This site can help you find anything pertaining to the field of law.
http://www.findlaw.com/

Further Reference

Abraham, Henry J. *The Judicial Process: An Introductory Analysis of the Courts of the United States, England, and France*, 6th ed. New York: Oxford University Press, 1993.

Abramson, Jeffrey. *We the Jury: The Jury System and the Ideal of Democracy*. New York: Basic Books, 1994.

Baum, Lawrence. *The Supreme Court*, 6th ed. Washington, D.C.: CQ Press, 1997.

Brisbin, Richard A. *Justice Antonin Scalia and the Conservative Revival*. Baltimore, MD: Johns Hopkins University Press, 1997.

Carp, Robert A., and Ronald Stidham. *Judicial Process in America*, 4th ed. Washington, D.C.: CQ Press, 1998.

Carter, Lief H. *Reason in Law*, 5th ed. New York: Longman, 1998.

Dworkin, Ronald. *Freedom's Law: The Moral Reading of the American Constitution*. Cambridge, MA: Harvard University Press, 1996.

Farber, Daniel A., and Suzanna Sherry. *Beyond All Reason: The Radical Assault on Truth in American Law*. New York: Oxford University Press, 1997.

Hobson, Charles F. *The Great Chief Justice: John Marshall and the Rule of Law*. Lawrence, KS: University Press of Kansas, 1996.

Lazarus, Edward. *Closed Chambers: The First Eyewitness Account of the Epic Struggles Inside the Supreme Court*. New York: Times Books, 1998.

Schwartz, Bernard. *Decision: How the Supreme Court Decides Cases*. New York: Oxford University Press, 1996.

Simpson, A. W. Brian. *Leading Cases in the Common Law*. New York: Oxford University Press, 1995.

CHAPTER 18

Political Economy

Political economy is an old, changing, and flexible term. The classical economists of the late eighteenth and nineteenth centuries—Adam Smith, David Ricardo, John Stuart Mill, and Karl Marx—all wrote on what they called "the political economy." In doing this they were taking a leaf from Aristotle, who viewed government, society, and the economy as one thing. The old political economists also had a strong normative orientation, prescribing what government should do to promote prosperity. In the late nineteenth century, as economists became more scientific and numbers-based, they dropped "political" from the name of their discipline and shifted from "should" or "ought" prescription to empirical description and prediction.

More recently the term has revived, often with partisan overtones. Radicals use the term "political economy" instead of Marxism—which is a hard sell these days—to describe their criticisms of capitalism and the unfair distribution of wealth among and within nations. Conservatives use the term to try to get back to the original pure market system advocated by Adam Smith. We will avoid taking ideological sides and use the term to mean the interface between politics and the economy. And it is a very big interface.

Economics undergirds almost everything in politics. It is by promising prosperity that politicians get elected and by delivering it that they get reelected. Virtually all **public policy** choices have economic ramifications, and these are often sufficient to make or break the policy. A policy designed to protect the environment that causes a slowing down of industry and loss of

QUESTIONS TO CONSIDER

1. What policy choices do we now face that are not economic?
2. What was Keynes's solution to the Depression?
3. What started the U.S. inflationary spiral in the 1960s?
4. Are U.S. taxes too high? Compared to what?
5. What went right with the U.S. economy in the 1990s?
6. Why has income inequality grown in the United States?
7. How do entitlements differ from welfare?
8. How does ideology influence our views on poverty?
9. Which U.S. programs can realistically be cut?

KEY TERMS

political economy The influence of politics and the economy on each other; what government should and should not do in the economy.

public policy What a government tries to do; the choices government makes among alternatives.

jobs is probably not going to last very long. An energy policy aimed at squeezing fuel from oil shale or tar sands and delivering a barrel of petroleum at three times the cost of Saudi crude can continue only if the government is willing to subsidize it for, say, national security reasons.

With a growing economy, a country can afford to play around with new welfare measures, as the United States did in the booming 1960s. With a stagnant economy, an administration has to cut back on welfare expenditures and devise policies to spur the economy into greater production. Whatever the issue—environment, energy, welfare, you name it—it will be connected to the economy. Some of the worst policy choices are made when decision makers forget this elementary point. Accordingly, economic policy takes priority, and it overshadows all other policies. Every political scientist should be to some degree an economist. As candidate Bill Clinton constantly reminded himself during the 1992 campaign, "It's the economy, stupid!" And he was right; the economy matters most. Good times buoyed his popularity even as he was impeached. Low inflation and low unemployment made most Americans reasonably content with the Clinton presidency.

Government and the Economy

Nowadays, no one, not even a good conservative, expects the government to keep its hands off the economy. Everyone expects the government to induce economic prosperity, and if it doesn't, voters will punish the administration at the next election, as happened in 1992. President Bush had valid grounds for complaint; he was not to blame for the short, mild recession that preceded the election, but voters held him accountable. Earlier in the twentieth century this was not the case. Many European governments, as well as Washington, followed the "classic liberal" doctrines discussed in Chapter 6 and generally kept their hands off the economy. With the outbreak of the Great Depression in 1929, however, the hands-off policies tended to make things worse, and people began to demand government intervention.

A 1936 book by the English economist John Maynard Keynes helped chart the way. Keynes argued that the free market by itself may reach a balance of supply and demand only with unacceptably high unemployment. The solution, he suggested, was for government to increase "aggregate demand" by spending on public works and welfare. Some say the "Keynesian revolution" brought us out of the Depression. Others say Franklin D. Roosevelt's New Deal never fully applied Keynesianism; only the massive defense spending of World War II did that. Still others doubt that the New Deal achieved anything lasting except debt and inflation. But after World War II, government leaders all over the world, even those who disliked Keynes's theory, turned to Keynesian methods to correct their economies. As vice-president during the 1950s, Richard Nixon denounced Keynesian economics as a Democratic trick. In the White House in the 1970s, however, Nixon announced that he was "now a Keynesian" and could "fine-tune the economy." (He couldn't.)

What are some of our leading economic problems and government responses to them? Consider the approximate sequence of events the United States has gone through since the 1960s, and notice how the problems reoccur.

Inflation

Until 1965, the U.S. **inflation** rate was low, but it kicked up as President Johnson escalated the Vietnam war in 1965. War spending pumped some $140 billion (now worth more than four times that, after adjusting for inflation) into the U.S. economy but not a corresponding amount of goods and services to buy with it. Too many dollars chased too few goods, the classic definition of demand-pull inflation. The inflation engendered by the Vietnam war took on a life of its own and lasted into the 1980s. Johnson thought he could win in Vietnam quickly and cheaply, before the war had had much economic impact. He failed. Many economists say that he could have avoided the worst of the inflation if he had been willing to raise taxes at the start of the war.

Tax Hike

President Johnson was reluctant to ask for a tax increase to pay for the Vietnam war for two reasons. First, he had just gotten a tax cut through Congress in 1964; it would have been embarrassing to reverse course the following year. Second, he did not want to admit to the country that he had gotten it into a long and costly war. By the time Johnson and Congress had changed their minds and introduced a 10 percent tax surcharge in 1968, it was too late; inflation had taken firm hold. The moral is that if you must go to war, you should be sure to increase taxes simultaneously to mop up the increased government spending; if you don't there will be the devil to pay with inflation.

Balance of Payments

Starting in the late 1950s, the United States spent more abroad than it sold. With the war-induced prosperity of the 1960s, America sucked in growing imports without exporting enough to cover them. American industries invested heavily overseas, and American tourists spent freely. Large **balance-of-payments** deficits grew. The too-high value of the dollar in relation to foreign currencies meant it was cheaper to buy foreign goods but harder to sell ours in foreign markets. Japanese products especially took a large share of the U.S. market. American dollars flooded the world; they were too plentiful.

Gold Standard

In an effort to stem the outflow in 1971, President Nixon cut the link between the dollar and gold, a **fixed exchange rate** that had been in place since 1944. The Bretton Woods agreement—which fixed an ounce of gold at $35 and fixed other currencies in relation the the dollar—had been the basis of postwar recovery. But the inflation of U.S. dollars worldwide made our stock of gold way too cheap, so Nixon said no more gold and let the dollar "float" to a lower level in relation to other currencies. This **floating exchange rate** devalued the dollar by about one-fifth. The dollar went back up, however, and U.S. trade and payments deficits soared even higher.

Wage-Price Freeze

Nixon also froze wages and prices in 1971 to try to knock out the inflationary psychology that had taken hold. The 1971 wage-price freeze was popular at first, but then some began to complain that there was no corresponding freeze on profits, so that businesses were benefiting unduly. A bigger problem with wage-price freezes, however, is that when they are removed, pent-up inflationary pressures push inflation higher than ever. Many economists think Nixon's eighteen-month freeze just set the stage for even greater inflation. Some (mostly liberal) economists supported the idea of wage and price controls—called "incomes policy"—but now few economists of any stripe want to try them again.

Oil Shocks

International oil deals, like most international trade arrangements, are made with U.S. dollars. The dollar's loss in value meant that the oil exporters were getting less and less for their black gold. The price of oil in the 1960s was ridiculously low. As

The oil shortages of the 1970s made the United States aware of its dependence on imported oil. (Irene Springer)

a result of the 1973 Mideast war, the members of the Organization of Petroleum Exporting Countries (OPEC) were able to do what they had been itching to do: quadruple oil prices. In 1979, in response to the revolutionary turmoil in Iran, they increased prices again. Altogether during the 1970s, world oil prices soared from $2.50 to $34 a barrel. The impact on economies around the world was devastating.

Stagflation

KEY TERM
stagflation Strange combination of slow growth plus inflation in the U.S. economy in the 1970s.

During the 1970s a new word appeared—**stagflation**—to describe a new phenomenon, inflation with stagnant economic growth. Previously, economists had seen a connection between economic growth and inflation; as one went up, so did the other. In the 1970s, this connection was broken. Inflation hit double-digit levels (10 percent or higher), but the economy shrank and joblessness increased. Since 1973, the average American family has had a stagnant standard of living. The biggest single culprit is believed to be the massive increase in oil prices that affected every corner of the economy, from agriculture and transportation to manufacturing and construction. The United States was especially hard hit, for Americans had gotten used to cheap energy and had based their industry and lifestyle on it. The manyfold increase in petroleum prices produced inflation everywhere while simultaneously depressing the economy.

Interest Rates

President Jimmy Carter attempted to stimulate the economy, but this made inflation worse than ever; in 1980 it was 13.5 percent and probably cost him reelection. The members of the independent Federal Reserve Board, who are appointed by the president for four years and cannot be fired, took it upon themselves to stem inflation by means of "monetary policy," control of the growth of the U.S. money supply. The board (also known as the Fed) can force banks to raise or lower their interest rates on loans. High interest rates mean slower economic growth and a dampening of inflation. Economist Paul A. Volcker, appointed by Carter in 1979 and reappointed by Reagan in 1983, brought interest rates to record levels; at one point they were over 20 percent. It was painful medicine. Inflation did cool, but at the cost of the greatest rate of unemployment (over 10 percent) since the Depression. Americans became aware of how important the Fed is in our economic life. More recently, Fed chairman Alan Greenspan has kept a similar watchful eye on inflation and was celebrated as the architect of the prosperity of the 1990s.

Tax Cut

Again trying to stimulate the economy, President Reagan turned to an approach called "supply-side economics," which focuses on investment and production rather than on consumer demand, as Keynesian policy does. The inspiration of

Case Studies   HOW HIGH ARE U.S. TAXES?

Compared to other countries, U.S. taxes are not very high. The Organization for Cooperation and Development (the "rich countries' club") figured that in 1996 countries paid the following percentages of their GDPs in total taxes (including state and local):

Sweden	52
France	47
the Netherlands	45
Germany	39
Canada	38
Britain	36
Australia	32
Japan	29
United States	28

Americans complain mightily that their taxes are too high—they would complain if taxes were zero—but among the advanced industrialized countries, we are at the low end. Most Europeans, figuring they get a lot from the system, complain little about taxes. The question is how much and what programs are Americans willing to cut to bring taxes even lower? Defense? Social Security? Medicare? Besides, some of the "cuts" in federal programs are just tax **burdens shifted** to the state and local level.

supply-siders was the Kennedy idea that lowering tax rates stimulates economic growth and ultimately generates more tax revenue. Too-high taxes discourage effort and investment. Congress bought the idea and cut income taxes 25 percent over three years. Actually, this scarcely offset the "bracket creep" that American taxpayers had suffered as a result of inflation; their purchasing power had stayed the same, but they found themselves in ever-higher tax brackets. The Reagan tax cut did stimulate the economy, but it also helped produce another problem.

Budget Deficits

President Reagan presented Congress with budgets that featured both tax cuts and major increases in defense spending. He figured this would force Congress to cut domestic and welfare spending drastically. But Congress didn't cut much, and the U.S. federal budget reached record **deficits**—at one point under President Bush $295 billion. By issuing Treasury bills, the federal government borrowed the money, and this "crowded out" commercial borrowing and raised interest rates. Because interest rates were high, foreigners found the United States a good place to invest, so in effect much of the U.S. budget deficit was covered by foreign investment. The Reagan and Bush deficits acted like a gigantic vacuum cleaner that swept in both goods and capital from around the world.

Trade Deficits

America for several decades has consumed more than it produced and imported much more than it exported. The result is a gigantic foreign-trade deficit that makes the United States the world's greatest debtor nation. This in turn leads to the buying up of American assets by foreigners. Americans tend to blame foreigners for this, but it's really a nonproblem. If foreigners want to invest in America, it simply makes us more prosperous. Ultimately, foreign producers could stop accepting U.S. dollars as payment—they might want *euros* instead—but this would simply devalue the dollar and make U.S. products cheaper, something Europeans do not want. Some economists argue that the U.S. trade deficit is irrelevant because the U.S. economy is so strong foreign creditors know they will be repaid.

Budget Balancing

Clinton brought the federal budget deficit down to zero by 1998, even beating the call of Congressional Republicans to reach a balance between income and expenditures by 2002. Every year's deficit was added to the national **debt**—the sum total owed by the federal government, which now totals some $5.5 trillion—which is covered by government borrowing, provided Congress agrees to raise the debt ceiling. In a 1995 showdown with the White House, the Republicans under House Speaker Newt Gingrich (Republican of Georgia) refused to raise the debt limit, thus temporarily making the federal government broke and unable to pay its workers, who were sent home. The public was disgusted with both sides, and they compromised. The good news about a balanced federal budget is that the national debt automatically starts to gradually come down as U.S. bonds and treasury bills are paid off. The cuts involved in balancing the budget, however, were tough, and one of their chief targets was—and will continue to be—**entitlements**.

KEY TERMS

debt   The sum total of deficits over many years.

entitlement   U.S. federal expenditure mandated by law, such as Social Security and Medicare.

Who Is Entitled to What?

The federal budget is divided into two general categories, discretionary and mandatory. The former can be raised or lowered from year to year. Congress, for example, may decide to increase defense and cut highway spending. Mandatory spending cannot be so easily changed; it's what the federal budget is stuck with from previous statutory commitments. Mandatory spending in turn is divided into interest payments on the national debt (14 percent of the budget in 1998) and entitlements (47 percent in 1998); together they made up more than 60

Case Studies   THE VIRTUOUS CIRCLE

In the late 1990s, the U.S. economy was doing so well that some described it as a "virtuous circle" that other countries should learn from. Its interlocking components were as follows:

- Balanced federal budgets, which held down inflation and interest rates
- Low inflation, which increased investor and business confidence and held down wage demands and interest rates
- Low interest rates, which encouraged business expansion
- Modest taxes, which left plenty of money for spending and business expansion
- Slowly growing wages, which increased manufacturing
- Modest regulation, which encouraged the founding of new businesses and expansion of old ones
- Plentiful imports, which held down wage demands and inflation

As one element fed into another, the economy grew and generated enough taxes to balance the budget, which in turn fostered the positive factors. Could anything go wrong? Some economists feared that if the U.S. labor market got much tighter it would bid up wages and thus reignite inflation ("cost-push" inflation). Some noted that U.S. productivity had not increased much; workers were just putting in longer hours. Others worried that the stock market was a bubble that could burst. But most Americans just enjoyed their virtuous circle.

percent of the federal budget. Interest payments are totally untouchable; if they were cut, future offerings of bonds and treasury notes would lack credibility and customers. And entitlements are extremely difficult to cut because people are used to them and expect them as a right. They are payments to which one is automatically entitled by law: Turn sixty-five and you get Social Security and Medicare; earn an income below a specified level and you get Food Stamps and Medicaid. There is no annual cap on entitlement spending; it grows as more people are entitled. And grow it did; with the Great Society programs started under Johnson and greatly expanded under Nixon, entitlement spending doubled from 23 to 45 percent of the budget from 1963 to 1983. Now nearly half of American families receive some form of entitlement, averaging $10,000 per recipient family. For such reasons it is called "uncontrollable" spending.

Only a small fraction of federal payments is traditional "welfare" spending; more than 85 percent go to the middle and upper classes in the form of Social Security, Medicare, government retirement plans, and farm price supports. What goes to poor families includes Medicaid, food stamps, and Supplemental Security Income. With political realism in mind, what can be cut of the first category—middle-class entitlements? Some people argue that if we eliminated "welfare" spending we could cut taxes, but "welfare" is not the problem; entitlements are. Cuts in welfare spending save little and inflict hardship on society's most vulnerable

KEY TERMS

productivity The efficiency with which things are made.

bull market A stock market that keeps rising.

baby boom The big generation of Americans born from 1946 to 1964.

members, especially children. How did the U.S. welfare system come about?

In the mid-1960s, President Lyndon B. Johnson launched his War on Poverty, aimed at creating a Great Society by eliminating poverty. Johnson, who had long been Senate majority leader, got Congress to deliver almost everything he wanted. Then the Vietnam war, amid rising costs and acrimony, seemed to cut down the War on Poverty in its infancy. There wasn't enough money for the growing programs, and

Case Studies   THE GROWTH OF INEQUALITY

Late in the twentieth century, Americans' incomes grew less equal. The rich got a lot richer. The poor did not necessarily get poorer, but few climbed out of poverty. And the great American middle class, with largely stagnant incomes, shrank. Its lower members were shoved down into the working class. Those with a high-school education or less did poorly.

What had happened? Many economists believe that the industrial growth of other countries, especially East Asia and Mexico, limited the number and pay of American blue-collar manufacturing jobs. Globalization closed some U.S. factories. Unions—during the early 1950s some 40 percent of the U.S. workforce was unionized—declined to some 15 percent of the workforce, much of it concentrated in government employees' and teachers' unions. U.S. manufacturers learned to "outsource," to buy parts either from abroad or from cheaper, nonunion U.S. producers, a cause of many strikes. Because of these pressures, U.S. labor costs became rather moderate. By the 1990s, it was cheaper to manufacture many articles in the United States than in Japan and much cheaper than in Germany. (Germany has the world's highest labor costs, much higher than U.S. labor costs.) By holding down U.S. wages and boosting **productivity** through constant technological improvements and reorganization—including "downsizing"—the United States regained its economic luster.

The real winners in this were not average workers (or even mid-level managers) but top executives and investors. Chief executive officers were compensated extravagantly—many earn over $1 million a year—and shareholders saw the value of their stocks increase. Fueling the 1990s **bull market** was the conviction of the **baby boom** generation that Social Security was unreliable so they had to save for retirement, and stocks were the best way. With more and more people shoveling money into the stock market—about a third of U.S. families, a record high, were in the market, most through mutual funds—many investors did extremely well. The richest 5 percent Americans became very rich; the extra taxes they paid helped erase the federal budget deficit. Working-class Americans did not do so well, but most accepted their situations because they had jobs. Many, in fact, worked overtime or had second jobs to make ends meet. Unemployment was below 5 percent, the envy of the world (in Europe it was more than double that). The index of consumer confidence (see p. 221) was high. But an economic downturn and high unemployment could bring out political resentments.

Poverty in the United States: A homeless man—one of a growing number of poor—camps out under a bridge in New York.
(Michael Roskin)

Johnson became increasingly discredited. Many of the Great Society programs were substantially dismantled or left to die quietly on the vine. Some say the Great Society was never given a chance. The conservative conventional wisdom of the late 1970s and early 1980s held that the undertaking was

---

KEY TERM

welfare dependency
Getting stuck on welfare with no incentive to get off.

---

inherently impossible, a waste of money that often did more harm than good, locking recipients into **welfare dependency** and encouraging a subculture of drugs and crime. Some poverty specialists, however, say the Great Society programs generally did succeed and markedly lowered the incidence of poverty in the United States. Conservatives, they say, have exaggerated the inefficiency and misuses that accompany any welfare program and have understated the very real accomplishments.

The Costs of Welfare

Food Stamps   Begun as a modest trial program under Kennedy in 1961, the Food Stamp program was made nationwide under Johnson in 1964. From a few million dollars a year, it rose by 1995 to $27.5 billion a year. Over 10 percent of all U.S. households benefited, getting an average of less than $1,000 a year. One did not dine royally on food stamps; cost per meal per person was figured at about half a dollar. One-third of families headed by women received food stamps.

The Carter administration simplified the program in 1977 by eliminating the provision that recipients *buy* the stamps at a discount with their own money. This policy had meant that the absolutely destitute, people with no money at all, could get no food stamps. Congress changed the law to eliminate the cash payment, and the number of recipients expanded. Reagan, citing an apocryphal story of a young man who used food stamps to buy vodka, tightened eligibility requirements in an effort to eliminate fraud and misuse. The trouble was that some genuinely poor families were also bumped from the program, and hunger in America reappeared. Callous remarks by a White House official that he saw no proof of hunger flew in

---

Key Concepts   WHAT IS POVERTY?

Trying to define poverty can be tricky. What's "poor" currently might have been "comfortable" in previous eras. Ask your grandparents how they fared during the Depression. The U.S. Department of Labor came up with a formula in 1955 that has been used ever since, although it is obviously not a complete definition. They found that families spend about one-third of their incomes on food. The department therefore set the "poverty line" at three times an economy food budget, usually for nonfarm families of four. Using this definition, the percentage of Americans below the poverty line fell from 17.3 percent in 1965, when Johnson's War on Poverty started, to 11.7 percent in 1973, according to the Census Bureau. With the economic recession and budget tightening that started under Carter and expanded under Reagan, however, by 1983 the poverty rate was back up to 15.2 percent, the highest in eighteen years. (In 1998, it was 13 percent.) The black and Hispanic rates are much higher, and one-fifth of America's children are below the poverty line.

Conservatives point out that these figures do not tell the whole story, for the Labor Department's definition does not include *noncash* benefits transferred to the poor by government programs—food stamps, for example. Taking this factor into account raises some poor families above the poverty line. The poor, in other words, now have a certain cushion.

Further, before we conclude that the War on Poverty was either a success or a failure, we must look at the poverty rate in longer perspective. In 1950, some 30 percent of the U.S. population was classified as below the poverty line. Since then, the rate has dropped almost steadily, with one of the fastest decreases occurring between 1960 and 1965, *before* the War on Poverty programs were enacted. What explains this? The U.S. economy expanded from 1950 to 1965, especially during the early 1960s. Jobs were plentiful. It's hard to tell if the further drop in the poverty rate from 1965 to 1973 was the result of government programs or of an economy fueled by Vietnam war spending.

By the same token, when the poverty rate began to go up again in the mid-1970s, cutbacks in antipoverty spending were only partly to blame; also responsible were the recessions caused by the oil prices and high interest rates discussed earlier. Some blame the increase of poverty and homelessness on the transfer of much manufacturing to low-wage countries overseas, making many working-class Americans unemployed and pushing them down into the lower class. With the disappearance of modestly paying factory jobs they faced either low-paid service jobs ("flipping hamburgers") or unemployment and welfare. Antipoverty programs cannot offset massive unemployment caused by long-term trends in the U.S. economy. Most public-policy questions are based on the economy.

the face of widespread reports of a big increase in the number of homeless people eating at soup kitchens.

What should be done? The Food Stamp program has become bigger than expected, but outright fraud and waste have not been major factors. Recipients selling food stamps at 50¢ on the dollar to buy liquor and drugs probably account for only a few percent of the program. There are poor people in America. Should they be helped? Outright cash grants, considered for a time by Carter as a replacement for food stamps, could easily be misused. Direct delivery of surplus commodities, as was done on a small scale in the 1950s and episodically in the 1980s to get rid of government cheese stocks (the result of price supports for dairy farmers), was clumsy and spotty. One alternative to food stamps might be to borrow a tactic applied in many countries: subsidizing basic foodstuffs, such as bread and milk. However, subsidizing food basics, because it would benefit the nonpoor as well, would not necessarily cost less than food stamps. The Food Stamp program will probably continue with little change, for there is no clear, acceptable alternative.

The End of AFDC   A favorite target, especially of conservatives, was the "welfare mess," a name often applied to Aid to Families with Dependent Children (AFDC). The Republicans in charge of Capitol Hill voted in 1996 to end AFDC; President Clinton, himself not very pleased with the program, signed the measure, and AFDC folded in 1997 after sixty-two years. Fortunately, AFDC ended when the economy was good, and some people bumped out of welfare found jobs.

The original welfare program set up by the 1935 Social Security Act, Aid to Dependent Children (ADC, as it was then known) provided federal matching funds for state programs. For years, most states had either no ADC programs or only small ones. Starting in the 1960s, though, participation and costs grew to around $25 billion (partly state, partly federal) by 1993, going to 5 million families, most of them headed by single mothers. The average monthly family benefit was $373. The program was renamed AFDC in 1967, when Congress mandated work training for all adult recipients and gave dollar incentives. Day-care centers were to be provided. In practice, most of this aid went to single mothers for whom child care was unavailable. State efforts to make sure no man was around the house—if one was, the aid would be stopped—led to early-morning snooping. Conservatives pointed to AFDC as underwriting immorality and welfare dependency. Because many of the 14.5 million recipients were nonwhite, the issue became connected with the struggle for racial equality. Attacks against "welfare mothers" were sometimes veiled racism.

Undoubtedly, some welfare dependency was created. AFDC may also have encouraged a casual attitude toward bringing fatherless children into the world. But can we make it illegal for poor people to have babies? Should there be mandatory sterilization or abortion? Once a child is born, can we let it starve? Recognizing these problems, in 1973 Congress started WIC (Women, Infants, and Children) to improve the diet and give medical checkups to poor pregnant and

Key Concepts   POVERTY AND IDEOLOGY

The U.S. debate about poverty is passionately ideological. Conservatives say they want to curb antipoverty programs, and liberals generally defend them. The policy analyst must cast ideology aside and gather factual answers to questions such as the following:

Is the program we're talking about welfare or entitlement? The two categories overlap, but the essence of a welfare program is that it's "means tested," meaning recipients must demonstrate that they're poor according to certain criteria (typically, how much income and how many children). If the program is a pure entitlement, such as Social Security or Medicare, can it realistically be cut without incurring electoral wrath?

Do welfare programs have negative consequences? Here is the great conservative attack: Welfare programs offer incentives for unemployment, illegitimacy, and drug use. Can this be proved or disproved? New York City, with its extensive welfare programs, has a high incidence of poverty. But so does Mississippi, with its weak and underfunded welfare programs. As usual, causality is terribly difficult to prove. Would a massive, nationwide cessation of all welfare programs force the indolent to work? This raises the next question.

Is poverty an unfortunate circumstance or a character defect? Are people poor because they can't find work or because they don't want to work? In other words, are the poor really different from you and me? Do they embody a "culture of poverty" that instills a "radical improvidence," an indifference to providing for their families and futures? If poverty is a character defect, as most conservatives maintain, then there is little that can be done. If it is the product of unfortunate circumstances, as most liberals maintain, then programs that change those circumstances might get people out of poverty.

How much poverty is simply a lack of good jobs? Do the jobs available to poor people pay enough for them to raise their families? In most of America, people are willing to take jobs not much above minimum wage, even though a single mother earning that would fall below the poverty line. Good factory jobs are hard to find because many have been moved overseas to low-wage countries. Those who would drastically cut welfare should demonstrate there are sufficient jobs with adequate pay. But are poor people generally qualified for decent-paying jobs, or do they lack the skills?

Can we train people out of poverty? Job training and retraining have long been part of poverty-fighting programs. But do they work? Some who have completed job training still find few jobs. Can we take people with poor reading and math abilities and in a few months make them into skilled technicians? The deeper, underlying problem is the lack of proper education in grade schools, which creates an illiterate and innumerate workforce. But is the lack of proper education in America the fault of schools and teachers or families and attitudes? Liberals like to blame schools, conservatives families. Either way, how do you fix the U.S. education system?

What is the international context of domestic poverty? How much poverty is due to the export of American jobs to low-wage countries? Considering what Santa brought you last Christmas, how many of these gifts were made in Mexico, Indonesia, or Taiwan? While possibly lowering the cost of such items to consumers, overseas manufacturing has closed thousands of American factories. Is American poverty, then, in some degree the natural

---

result of an open world economy in which many countries have much lower labor costs? Should we close our borders to such commerce in order to boost domestic employment? If we did, many Americans would live a little less well—their shirts, rechargeable flashlights, and VCRs would cost more, so they would buy fewer of them—but other Americans would exit poverty through new factory jobs. Our trading partners in other lands would get very angry and retaliate by keeping out U.S. products, so other U.S. factories would close. On balance, then, would trade protectionism be worth it?

These are some of the questions we must ask. Simple ideological approaches, either liberal or conservative, often deal with consequences rather than causes. Where ideology reigns, reason has difficulty making its voice heard.

---

nursing mothers and their children. The results have been good, but WIC receives less than $5 billion a year and reaches only half of those eligible. WIC continued after the demise of AFDC.

Welfare programs did not vanish. They were transferred to the states, several of which introduced **workfare** programs that required recipients to either take jobs or training for jobs. Workfare, which had been tried for years, seldom works; it actually costs more than traditional welfare programs and places few poor people, many of whose skills and attitudes make them unemployable, into permanent jobs.

> **KEY TERM**
>
> **workfare**   Programs limiting the duration of welfare payments and requiring recipients to work or get job training.

Medicare and Medicaid   These are the two giants of entitlements; if taxes are to be cut, they will have to take some hits. Medicare and Medicaid, both enacted in 1965, serve different purposes. Medicare is a federally funded program for elderly people; Medicaid combines federal and state funds for poor people. Both grew so rapidly that even supporters had to admit that benefits had to be limited and eligibility requirements tightened. In 1998, Medicare for America's 37 million elderly alone cost $200 billion and will double and double again after baby boomers start to reach sixty-five in 2011. Who will pay for them? You will.

President Clinton arrived in Washington promising to revamp the nation's medical insurance programs. But a massive study chaired by his wife worked at cross-purposes: A new plan was to include all Americans—some 16 percent of Americans, mostly people working for themselves or in small firms, have no insurance—but it was also to hold down soaring costs. Congress rejected the complex and expensive proposals out of hand. In 1995 Congressional Republicans proposed to hold down Medicare growth (not cut it) and heard an outcry from older Americans, who read it as a cut in a program they had come to depend on. Anything that looks like a cut in medical care will face overwhelming resistance.

At least two factors induced exponential growth in medical assistance: more

Cut the federal government, say most citizens, but not programs that might help me, such as the Federal Emergency Management Agency (FEMA), here set up for one-stop disaster relief. (Michael Roskin)

people becoming eligible and soaring medical costs. Medicare is especially expensive, for everyone automatically qualifies on reaching age sixty-five, even rich people. The proportion of older people in American society is increasing steadily, and the elderly are by far the biggest consumers of medical care. On average, Americans consume most of their lifetime medical expenses in the last year of life.

Hospitals and doctors, once they are assured of payment, have no incentive to economize. When in doubt, they put the patient in the hospital—often at $1,000 a day—and order expensive tests with the latest multimillion-dollar machines. Some hospitals expanded into medical palaces, and some physicians got rich from Medicare and Medicaid. (Ironically, the powerful American Medical Association had for years lobbied against such "socialized medicine.") By 1998, medical costs consumed an amazing 14 percent of the U.S. gross domestic product, in part as a result of Medicare and Medicaid, which paid a good part of the nation's medical bills. Other countries paid less and had healthier populations.

Washington tried various ways of tightening up. Recipients were required to contribute more of the total payment to hold down overuse. Hospitals and doctors were monitored on costs and on how long they kept patients hospitalized. Hospices—nursing homes for the terminally ill—were made allowable under Medicare, as such care is cheaper than hospital care. Competitive bidding was begun in some states, and patients were assigned only to low-bid hospitals. Fees for each type of disorder were established, and overruns were not reimbursed. Recipients were encouraged to enter managed-care organizations (HMOs, whose efforts to cut costs generated fiery controversy). Every time the government tightens medical assistance patients, doctors, and hospitals complain bitterly, and they form a powerful lobby. Some hospitals turn away poor patients.

How Big Should Government Be?

Americans have the funniest ideas about where their tax dollars go. Many think most of the federal budget goes for welfare, which is not at all the case. Television exposés suggest it goes to food-stamp and Medicaid fraudsters, but this too is untrue. The bulk of federal spending goes not for welfare for the poor but for entitlements to the middle class; it is impossible to repeal or seriously cut most middle-class entitlement programs. Congressional Republicans suffered a drop in popularity when they proposed cutting Medicare; older Americans had come to regard it as something sacred. No one dares breathe a word about holding down Social Security. If you want to cut taxes, just what programs are you prepared to drop?

As noted earlier, the American welfare state is small compared to other countries. Should it get bigger? The American answer is to keep government small and to suspect and criticize expansion of government power. But we also recognize that we need government intervention in the economy, energy planning, environmental protection, and so on. We have trouble making up our minds how much government we want. Americans demand various forms of government intervention, but scarcely is the ink on new laws dry before we begin to criticize government bungling. Not understanding where Medicare comes from, one elderly American lady told an interviewer, "Don't let the government get its hands on Medicare!" Europeans and Canadians generally do not suffer from this kind of split personality; they mostly accept that government has a major role to play and do not complain much about their high taxes.

This reluctance to expand government's role may redound to America's long-term advantage. Government programs tend to expand, bureaucracy is inherently inefficient, and ending an entitlement program is all but impossible. Government programs become so sprawling and complex that officials don't even *know* what is in operation, much less how to control it. As political scientist Ira Sharkansky put it, "All modern states are welfare states, and all welfare states are incoherent." Accordingly, it is probably wise to act with caution in expanding government programs.

Key Terms

baby boom (p. 330)

balance of payments (p. 324)

bull market (p. 330)

burden shifting (p. 327)

debt (p. 328)

deficit (p. 327)

entitlement (p. 328)

fixed exchange rate (p. 324)

floating exchange rate (p. 325)

inflation (p. 324)

political economy (p. 322)

productivity (p. 330)

public policy (p. 322)

stagflation (p. 326)

welfare dependency (p. 331)

workfare (p. 335)

Key Websites

The Economist website is an authoritative source of information and opinion on international business and politics.
http://www.economist.com/

The IPENet maintains an extensive collection of electronically retrievable documents related to the global political economy.
http://csf.colorado.edu/ipe/ipeintro.html

This site has annotated links to U.S. economic numeric data, international economics, business and economics references, and business resources.
http://www.clark.net/pub/lschank/web/econ.html

The World Bank provides loans to middle-income countries and credit-worthy poorer countries.
http://www.worldbank.org/

IANWeb Resources has an International Political Economy website that maintains links to all sorts of resources and annotates these links with information drawn from the providers.
http://www.pitt.edu/~ian/resource/ipe.htm

Further Reference

Anderson, Martin C. *Welfare: The Political Economy of Welfare Reform in the United States*. Stanford, CA: Hoover Institution Press, 1978.

Blankenhorn, David. *Fatherless America*. New York: Basic Books, 1995.

Galbraith, John Kenneth. *A Journey Through Economic Time: A Firsthand View*. Boston, MA: Houghton Mifflin, 1994.

Gans, Herbert J. *The War Against the Poor: The Underclass and Anti-Poverty Policy*. New York: Basic Books, 1996.

Hibbs, Douglas A., Jr. *The American Political Economy: Macroeconomics and Electoral Politics in the United States*. Cambridge, MA: Harvard University Press, 1987.

Kaus, Mickey. *The End of Equality*. New York: Basic Books, 1995.

Krugman, Paul. *Peddling Prosperity*. New York: Norton, 1994.

Murray, Charles. *Losing Ground*, 10th anniversary ed. New York: Basic Books, 1995.

Payne, James L. *Overcoming Welfare: Expecting More from the Poor and from Ourselves*. New York: Basic Books, 1998.

Piven, Frances Fox, and Richard Cloward. *The Breaking of the American Social Compact*. New York: New Press, 1997.

Unger, Irwin. *The Best of Intentions: The Triumph and Failure of the Great Society Under Kennedy, Johnson and Nixon*. New York: Doubleday, 1996.

Wilson, William Julius. *When Work Disappears*. New York: Knopf, 1996.

Violence and Revolution

Political scientists—under the influence of the "systems" approach discussed in Chapter 2—often talked about systems and stability; some even depicted political systems as well-oiled machines that never broke down. But newspapers and television are filled with stories of violence and revolution, and in the late 1960s political scientists began criticizing the seemingly status-quo orientation of their discipline and directed their attention to breakdown and upheaval.

Sometimes scholars overlooked the tension and violence in their own backyards. With the black riots of 1965–1968, academics suddenly rediscovered violence in America. From viewing violence as abnormal, many came to suggest, along with black militant H. Rap Brown, that "violence is as American as cherry pie." By the same token, Europeans were shocked to learn, as the nationalities of ex-Yugoslavia slaughtered each other by the thousands, that they too were not immune from violence.

QUESTIONS TO CONSIDER

1. What causes political systems to break down?
2. What purposes can violence serve?
3. Which types of violence are most prevalent today?
4. How can modernization lead to unrest?
5. How can you tell if there has been a revolution?
6. Why are intellectuals prominent in revolutions?
7. What are Brinton's stages of revolution?
8. Do all revolutions end badly? Why?
9. Why is revolution no longer so fashionable?

System Breakdown

Political systems can and do break down. Indeed most countries have suffered or are suffering **system breakdown**, marked by major riots, civil wars, revolutionary movements, military **coups**, and authoritarian governments of varying degrees of harshness. Dictatorships are rarely the work of small bands of conspirators alone; they are the result of system collapse, which permits small but well-organized groups—usually the military—to take over. This is

KEY TERMS

system breakdown The malfunctioning or instability of a political system.

coup From French *coup d'état*, hit at the state; an extralegal takeover of government, usually by the military.

339

why it does little good to denounce a cruel military regime. It is true that some regimes commit acts of great evil; military regimes in Argentina, Chile, and Guatemala killed thousands on the slightest suspicion of leftism. But how is it that these military regimes came to power? Why does system breakdown recur repeatedly in such countries? These are the deeper questions that must be asked if we are to begin to understand these horror stories.

Underlying breakdown is the erosion of legitimacy, the feeling among citizens that the regime's rule is rightful and should be generally obeyed. Where legitimacy is high, governments need few police officers; where it is low, they need many. In England, for example, people are mostly law-abiding; police are few in number and very few carry firearms. But in Northern Ireland, until recently, terrorists killed with bombs and bullets, for a portion of the population saw the government as illegitimate. Here, the police are armed, and British troops, until recently, patrolled with automatic weapons and armored cars. The civil war in Northern Ireland cost some 3,600 lives.

One prominent reason for an erosion of legitimacy is the regime's loss of effectiveness in running the country. Uncontrollable inflation, blatant corruption, massive unemployment, or defeat in a war demonstrate that the government is ineffective.

Violence as a Symptom

Violence—riots, mass strikes, terrorist bombings, and political assassinations—by itself does not indicate that revolution is nigh. Indeed, the most common response to serious domestic unrest is not revolution at all but military takeover. Violence can be seen as symptomatic of the erosion of the government's effectiveness and legitimacy. Perhaps nothing major will come of the unrest; perhaps new leadership will calm and encourage the nation and begin to deal with the problems that caused the unrest, as Franklin D. Roosevelt did in the 1930s. But if the government is clumsy, if it tries to simply crush and silence discontent, it can make things worse. In 1932, the "Bonus Army" of World War I veterans seeking early payment of veterans' benefits to tide them through the mass unemployment of the Depression was dispersed by army troops under General Douglas MacArthur. Public revulsion at the veterans' rough treatment helped turn the country decisively against President Herbert Hoover in that fall's election.

Domestic violence is both deplorable and informative. It tells that not all is going well, that there are certain groups that, out of desperation or conviction, are willing to break the law in order to bring change. A government's first impulse when faced with domestic unrest is to crush it and blame a handful of "radicals and troublemakers." To be sure, there may well be instigators deliberately trying to provoke incidents, but the fact that people are willing to get involved should telegraph a message to the authorities that something is wrong. At the Democratic national convention in 1968, Chicago police went wild in attacking those who had come to protest the Vietnam war—as well as many who just happened to be in the wrong place at the wrong time. The convention ignored the protesters and nominated President Johnson's vice-president, Hubert Humphrey, who lost, largely because of his equivocal position on the war. The riot showed that the Democratic party had drifted out of touch with important elements of its constituency, which only four years earlier had voted for Johnson because he vowed to keep the country out of war. The Democrats should have been listening to instead of ignoring the protesters.

As much as we may deplore violence, we have to admit that in some cases it serves its purpose. The United States as a whole and Congress in particular paid little attention to the plight of inner-city blacks until a series of riots ripped U.S. cities in the late 1960s. The death and destruction were terrible, but there seemed to be no other way to get the media's, the public's, and the government's attention. The rioting in this case "worked"; that is, it brought a major—if not very successful—effort to improve America's decaying cities. When America "forgot" about its inner cities during the Reagan-Bush era, new rioting served as a powerful reminder.

The white minority government of South Africa used to announce with pride the capture or killing of black guerrillas. The South African security forces were proficient, but the fact that thousands of young black South Africans were willing to take up arms against the whites-only regime should have told the Pretoria government something. The ruling National party had imagined for decades that blacks (75 percent of the country's population) would simply keep their place (on 13 percent of the land). The whites-only government engaged in no dialogue with blacks; it expected them merely to obey. However, the growing violence in South Africa persuaded the government to begin a dialogue leading to the release of Nelson Mandela from prison, the political enfranchisement of the black majority and a government elected by all citizens.

Types of Violence

Not all violence is the same. Violence has been categorized in several ways. One of the best is that of political scientist Fred R. von der Mehden, who sees five general types of violence.

Primordial   Primordial violence grows out of conflicts among the basic communities—ethnic, national, or religious—into which people are born. Fighting between Armenians and Azerbaijanis in the ex-Soviet Union, Serbs and Muslims in ex-Yugoslavia, the multigroup war in Lebanon, and tribal war in Rwanda (which killed some 800,000 in the late 1990s) are examples of primordial violence. It is not necessarily confined to the developing areas of the world, though, for such antagonisms appear in Quebec, the Basque country of Spain, and Northern Ireland, where there was something akin to a tribal feud between Protestants and Catholics.

Separatist   Separatist violence, which is sometimes an outgrowth of primordial conflict, aims at independence for the group in question. The Ibos tried to break away from Nigeria with their new state of Biafra in the late 1960s, but they were defeated in a long and costly war. The Bengalis, on the other hand, did succeed in breaking away from Pakistan with their new state of Bangladesh in 1971. Croatia and Slovenia fought successfully to separate from Yugoslavia in 1991. Elsewhere in Europe, the Basques, Bretons, and Corsicans have given rise to separatist movements.

Revolutionary   Revolutionary violence is aimed at overthrowing or replacing an existing regime. The Sandinistas' ouster of Somoza in Nicaragua in 1979, the fall of the shah of Iran that same year, and the independence of the former Portuguese colonies of Angola and Mozambique in 1975 are examples of successful revolutionary violence. Until recently, Central America and southern Africa were scenes of continuing revolutionary violence. Von der Mehden includes under this category "counterrevolutionary" violence, the efforts of more conservative groups to counteract revolutionary attempts—for instance, the murders carried out by Salvadoran rightists. The attempts to crush liberalizing movements in Hungary in 1956, Czechoslovakia in 1968, and Poland in 1970 and 1980 would also come under this heading, with the ironic twist that here the Communists were the counterrevolutionary force. The distinctive form of terror of our day, the car bomb, is usually a tool of revolutionary violence.

Coups   Coups are usually counterrevolutionary in intent, aimed at heading off a feared revolutionary takeover. Coups are almost always military, although the military usually has connections with and support from key civilian groups, as in the Brazilian coup of 1964. Most coups don't involve much violence, at least initially. Army tanks surround the presidential palace, forcing the president's resignation and usually exile, and a general takes over as president. Some coups are virtually bloodless. When the military still senses leftist opposition, though, it sometimes goes insane with legalized murder. The Chilean military killed at least 3,000 people following the 1973 coup. Some 10,000 Argentines "disappeared" following the military takeover of 1976. Since the 1954 coup, the military in little Guatemala has murdered some 200,000 of their fellow citizens on suspicion of opposing the regime. In Latin America, the counterrevolutionary terror that follows some coups is far bloodier than anything the revolutionaries have done. Once a country has had one coup, chances are it will have another. Some countries get stuck in **praetorianism** and take decades to return to civilian rule. In part, coups occur because the conventional institutions of government—parties, parliaments, and executives—are terribly weak, leaving the military with the choice of either taking over or facing growing chaos.

Issues   Some violence doesn't fit into any of these categories. Violence oriented to particular issues is a catchall category and generally less deadly than the other kinds. The protests against the Vietnam war, student strikes at American and French universities in the late 1960s, riots triggered by the police beating of black citizens, and anger over economic problems are examples of issue-oriented violence. Amid worsening unemployment and rapidly rising prices, lower-class Brazilians sometimes invade and loot supermarkets. French farmers stop and burn trucks of Spanish produce, which they perceive as undercutting their livelihood. In 1976, black students in South Africa's Soweto township protested against having to learn Afrikaans in school; police shot down several hundred of them. Rightwing U.S. militias oppose what they deem the intrusive powers of federal law-enforcement agencies. There may be a fine line between issue-oriented violence and revolutionary violence, for if the issue is serious enough and the police repression brutal enough, protests over an issue can turn into a revolutionary tide.

All these categories—and others one might think of—are apt to be arbitrary. Some situations fit more than one category. Some start in one category and escalate into another. No country, even a highly developed one, is totally immune to some kind of violence.

Change as a Cause of Violence

Many writers find the underlying cause of domestic unrest in the changes societies go through as they modernize. Purely traditional societies with long-established patterns of authority and simple but workable economies are relatively untroubled by violence. People live as their ancestors lived and do not expect much. Likewise, modern, advanced societies with rational types of authority and productive economies have relatively minor types of violence. It is at the in-between stage, when modernization is stirring and upsetting traditional societies, that violence is most likely. The modernizing societies have left one world, that of traditional stability, but have not yet arrived at the new world of modern stability. Everything is changing in such societies—the economy, religious attitudes, lifestyle, and the political system—leaving people worried, confused, and ripe for violent actions.

Economic change can be the most unsettling. The curious thing about economic change is that improvement can be as dangerous as impoverishment. The great French social scientist Alexis de Tocqueville observed in the nineteenth century that "though the reign of Louis XVI was the most prosperous period of the monarchy, this very prosperity hastened the outbreak of the Revolution of 1789." Why should this be? There are several reasons. When people are permanently poor and beaten down, they have no hope for the future; they are miserable but quiet. When things improve, people start imagining a better future; their aspirations are awakened. No longer content with their lot, they want improvement fast, faster than even a growing economy can deliver. Worse, during times of prosperity, some people get richer faster than others, arousing jealousy. Certain groups feel bypassed by the economic changes and turn especially bitter; the Marxists call this "class antagonisms." Revolutionary feeling, however, typically does not arise among the poor but among what Crane Brinton called the "not unprosperous people who feel restraint, cramp, annoyance" at a government that impedes their right to even faster progress.

This is an extremely delicate time in the life of a nation.
Rebellion and revolution can break out. The underlying problem, as Ted Robert Gurr has emphasized, is not poverty itself
but **relative deprivation**. The very poor seldom revolt;
they're too busy feeding their families. But once people have
a full belly they start looking around and notice that some
people are living much better than they. This sense of relative
deprivation may spur them to anger, violence, and occasionally revolution. Gurr's
findings, it is interesting to note, are consonant with those of Tocqueville and

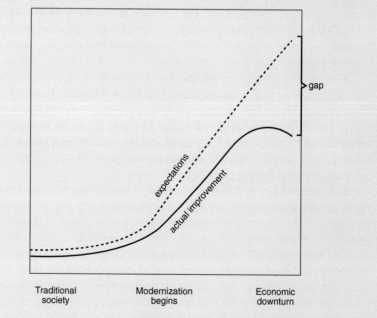

Key Concepts   RISING EXPECTATIONS

One way of looking at what economic growth does to a society is to represent it graphi-
cally. In the figure below, the solid line represents actual economic change in a modern-iz-
ing society—generally upward. The broken line represents people's expectations. In a still-
traditional society—at the figure's left—both actual performance
and expectations are low. As growth takes hold, however, expectations start rising faster than actual improvement. Then may come a
situation that produces a downturn in the economy—bad harvests,
a drop in the price of the leading export commodity, or too much
foreign indebtedness—and expectations are frustrated. A big gap
suddenly opens between what people want and what they can get.
In the words of Daniel Lerner, the "want:get ratio" becomes
unhinged, producing a "revolution of rising frustrations."

gap

expectations

actual improvement

Traditional   Modernization   Economic
society   begins   downturn

Brinton: Revolutions come when things are generally getting better, not when they're getting worse.

Other economic change can spur unrest. Anthropologist Eric R. Wolf has argued that the shift from simple subsistence farming to cash crops dependent on markets, landlords, and bankers impoverishes many peasants and turns them from quietude to revolution. It was precisely the economic modernization of agriculture in Mexico, Russia, China, Vietnam, Algeria, and Cuba that paved the way for successful peasant-based revolutions in those countries, according to Wolf. Economic change is, to be sure, not the only pressure on a modernizing society.

The political system may be out of date as well, based on inherited position with no opportunity for mass participation. As the economy improves, educational levels rise. People become more aware of abstract ideas such as "freedom" and "democracy." Especially among **intellectuals**, the educated elite, there is growing fury at the despotism that rules the land. Peasants may hate the system for squeezing them economically, but the urban intellectuals will hate it for suppressing rights and freedoms. It is the confluence of these two forces, argues Samuel P. Huntington—the "numbers" of the peasants and the "brains" of the intellectuals—that makes revolutions.

> ### KEY TERMS
>
> **intellectual** An educated person who thinks deeply about things.
>
> **revolution** Sudden replacement of an old system by a new one.

Revolutions

A **revolution** is a quick, dramatic system change. Change here means throwing out the old system along with its elites. A small or moderate change that essentially leaves the system intact may be reform, but it is not revolution. Some regimes, to quiet mass discontent, claim they are going through a revolution, but the changes may be largely cosmetic. One test of whether a real revolution has occurred is to see if it has swept out old elites. If they are still in power, there has been no revolution. In a radical revolution, the new elite gets rid of the old one by guillotine, firing squad, and exile. Revolution is not necessarily bloody, however. In 1989, most of the East European countries underwent a dramatic system change without bloodshed. (Romania was the bloody exception.) South Africa negotiated a revolution in the early 1990s.

Frustration is one thing; revolution is something else. People may be unhappy over one thing or another—peasants over crop prices, intellectuals over lack of freedom, businesspeople over corruption, and so on. But if there is no organization to focus their discontents, probably not much will happen. Unrest and discontent by themselves will not bring down a regime; for that to happen, organization is absolutely essential. In a study of Brazilian political attitudes, Peter McDonough and Antonio Lopez Pina found "a substantial amount of unchanneled dissatisfaction with the authoritarian regime," but it was "free-floating" resentment not especially directed against the military-run government. They suggest that "in the absence of organizational alternatives, resistance is most likely to take the form of apathy and indifference."

The previous factors we have considered may point to violence—rioting and strikes—but without organization they will not produce a revolution. Who provides the organization? For this we turn to the role of intellectuals.

Intellectuals and Revolution

> **KEY TERM**
>
> **utopia**   An imagined and idealized perfect system.

Intellectuals are nearly everywhere, discontent with the existing state of affairs because they are highly educated and acquainted with a wide variety of ideas, some of them **utopian**. Preachers, teachers, lawyers, journalists, and others who deal with ideas often have a professional stake in criticizing the system. If everything were fine, there wouldn't be much to talk or write about. Intellectuals, although often among the better-off, are seldom wealthy. They may resent people who are richer but not as smart—businesspeople and government officials.

Such factors predispose some intellectuals—but by no means all or even a majority—to develop what James Billington called a "revolutionary faith" that the current system can be replaced with something much better. According to Billington, revolution begins, first and foremost, with this "fire in the minds of men." Common folk, ordinary workers and peasants, are seldom interested in the intellectuals' abstract ideologies (see Chapter 6); they want improved material conditions. It is the intellectuals' idealistic convictions, however, that provide revolutionary movements with the cement that holds them together, the goals they aim for, and a leadership stratum.

It is an interesting fact that most twentieth-century revolutionary movements have been founded and led by educated people. Lenin, son of a provincial education official, was a brilliant law graduate. Mao Zedong helped found the Chinese Communist party while a library assistant at the Beijing National University. Fidel Castro and most of his original guerrilla fighters were law-school graduates. One of them, however—the famous Che Guevara, who was killed in 1967 while trying to foment revolution in Bolivia—was a medical doctor. The leader of Peru's Shining Path guerrillas was a university professor. The leaders of Iran's revolution against the shah were either religious or academically trained intellectuals.

The Stages of Revolution

In a classic book published in 1938, *The Anatomy of Revolution*, Harvard historian Crane Brinton developed a theory that all revolutions pass through similar stages, rather like a human body passing through the stages of an illness. In the English revolution of the 1640s, the American Revolution of 1776, the French Revolution of 1789, and the Russian Revolution of 1917, Brinton found the following rough uniformities.

The Old Regime Decays   Administration breaks down and taxes rise. People no longer believe in the government; in fact, the government doesn't believe in itself. The intellectuals transfer their allegiance from the regime to a proposed idealized system. All this is happening while the economy is generally on the upgrade, but this provokes discontent and jealousy.

The First Stage of Revolution   Committees, networks, cells, or conspiracies form, dedicated to overthrowing the old regime. People refuse to pay taxes. A political impasse arises that cannot be solved because the lines are too deeply drawn. The government calls in troops, which backfires because the troops desert and the people are further enraged. The initial seizure of power is easy, for the old regime has just about put itself out of business. Popular exultation breaks out.

At First, the Moderates Take Over   People who opposed the old regime but were still connected with it by dint of background or training assume command. They initiate moderate, middle-of-the-road reforms. These changes are not enough for the extremists among the revolutionaries; they accuse the moderates of being cowardly and of trying to compromise with the forces of the old regime. The moderates are "nice guys" and are not ruthless enough to crush the radicals, who exist side-by-side with the moderates in a sort of parallel government.

The Extremists Take Over   More ruthless and better organized than the moderates, knowing exactly what they want, the extremists overthrow the moderates and drive the revolution to a frenzied high point. Everything old is thrown out. People are required to be "good" according to the canons of the new, idealistic society the extremists try to instigate. "Bad" people are punished in a reign of terror. Even revolutionary comrades who are deemed to have strayed from the true path are executed: "The revolution devours its children." The entire society appears to go mad in what Brinton likened to a high fever during an illness.

A "Thermidor" Ends the Reign of Terror   Eventually the society can take no more. People come to a breaking point, at which they long to settle down, get the economy working again, and enjoy some personal security and pleasure. They've had enough of revolution. Even the extremists get tired of it. Then comes a **Thermidor**—so named after the French revolutionary month during which the extremist Robespierre was guillotined—which Brinton described as a convalescence after a fever. Often a dictator, who ends up resembling the tyrants of the old regime, takes over to restore order, and most people don't mind.

> **KEY TERM**
>
> **Thermidor**   Summer month of the French revolutionary calendar used by Brinton to mark the end of revolutionary extremism.

Case Studies	REVOLUTIONARY POLITICAL WARFARE IN VIETNAM

Many people speak of "guerrilla warfare," but this is a misnomer and a redundancy, for *guerrilla* is simply Spanish for "little war," what Spaniards practiced against Napoleon. It is not the use of ambush and punji stakes that should interest us but the accompanying political action. The two, when combined, equal revolutionary political warfare, which Bernard Fall described as the struggle "to establish a competitive system of control over the population." Fall, an expert on Vietnam who died when he stepped on a land mine there in 1967, emphasized *administration* as the crux of revolutionary warfare. "When a country is being subverted it is not being outfought; it is being outadministered. Subversion is literally administration with a minus sign in front."

In studies Fall conducted, both under the French in North Vietnam during the early 1950s and under the Americans in South Vietnam during the early 1960s, he discovered that the Communists were collecting taxes throughout most of the country under the very noses of the regimes they were overthrowing. The occupying power, whether French or American, deceived itself through its ability to drive through a village in an armored convoy; this does not indicate administrative control, which may be in the hands of the insurgents. The emphasis on military hardware is a big mistake, argued Fall, for it detracts from the human element.

The Vietnamese insurgents were able to outadminister the regime for several reasons. In the first place, they were able to identify closely with the population, something the French and Americans could never do. Indeed, the fact that the anti-Communist side in both Vietnam wars was connected with white foreigners gave the kiss of death to the effort. There was no political package the French or Americans might assemble that could be sold to the locals. Even the Saigon rulers had trouble identifying their own countrymen. The Diem and subsequent Saigon governments were run by Central and North Vietnamese Catholics who were at a considerable psychological distance from the largely Buddhist South Vietnamese. The Saigon officials were urban dwellers who disdained assignments in the provinces and working with the peasants. This was precisely the Communists' strong point.

Terror, to be sure, plays a role in revolutionary political warfare. The Vietcong murdered many Saigon officials and government-appointed village headmen. The villagers were not uniformly horrified at such terror, however, because it was selective and targeted at people who were outsiders anyway. To many peasants, the Vietcong executions seemed like extralegal punishment for collaborators. When the Americans made whole villages disappear, that was terror. There's nothing selective about napalm.

While the insurgent is patiently building a network to supplant the regime, the occupier or government is impatiently trying to substitute firepower for legitimacy. The killing of civilians produces more sympathizers and recruits for the guerrillas. The government's overreliance on firepower erodes its tenuous moral claims to leadership of the nation. Fall urged the following:

> What America should want to prove in Vietnam is that the Free World is "better," *not* that it can kill people more efficiently. If we would induce 100,000 Viet Cong to surrender to

---

REVOLUTIONARY POLITICAL WARFARE IN VIETNAM (CONTINUED)

our side because our offers of social reform are better than those of the other side's, *that* would be victory. Hence, even a total military or technological defeat of the Viet Cong is going to be a partial defeat of our own purposes—a defeat of ourselves, by ourselves, as it were.

Some critics wonder if the American people and leadership ever understood what we were up against in Vietnam. We fought a military war while our opponents fought a political war, and in the end the political mattered more than the military. Said one American officer as he surveyed the smoking ruins of a village, "Unfortunately, we had to destroy the village in order to save it."

After the Revolution

Revolutions show a persistent tendency to overthrow one form of tyranny only to replace it with another. In little more than a decade, the French kings had been replaced by Napoleon, who crowned himself emperor and supervised a police state far more thorough than anything the kings had had at their disposal. The partial despotism of the tsars was replaced by the perfect despotism of Stalin. Russian life was freer and economic growth faster at the turn of the twentieth century under the inefficient tsarist system than it has been at any time in Russia since. Fidel Castro threw out the crooked Batista regime, and Cuban freedom and economic growth declined abruptly.

What good are revolutions? One is tempted to despair with Simon Bolivar, the liberator of South America, who said, "He who aids a revolution plows the sea." In general, revolutions end badly. (As soon as you can accept that statement, you have become to some degree a conservative.)

But what about the United States? Don't we call our 1776–1781 struggle with Britain the Revolutionary War? Some say it wasn't really a revolution, for it was not an effort to remake American society. Indeed, some of its greatest leaders were wealthy and prominent figures in colonial society. They wanted simply to get rid of British rule but keep their elite positions. The American struggle was more a war of independence than a revolution, some argue, and extremists never seized control. Others point out that there was a great deal of revolutionary violence, directed especially at America's Tories, colonials who remained pro-British. Some 100,000 fled in fear to lands the Crown gave them in Canada.

The late, great Hannah Arendt also believed the American struggle was indeed a revolution, perhaps the only complete revolution that has ever been carried out, for it alone ended with a new foundation of liberty instead of the tyranny of other revolutions. According to Arendt, the fortunate thing for the American revolutionaries is that they did not have to wrestle with the difficult "social question" that obsessed the French revolutionaries. America was prosperous, and wealth was distributed rather equally. The American struggle didn't become sidetracked by the poverty problem, so it could focus on establishing a just and durable constitution with balanced powers and political freedom. It was the genius—or, in part, luck—of the American Revolution that it was a purely *political* and not a social matter. America needed no guillotine, for there was no aristocratic class to behead. It

Case Studies   THE IRANIAN REVOLUTIONARY CYCLE

The Iranian revolution closely followed Brinton's pattern. The Iranian economy boomed, especially following the quadrupling of oil prices in 1973–1974, but economic growth was uneven. Some people became very rich very fast, provoking jealousy. Corruption and inflation soared. Many educated Iranians came to oppose the shah's dictatorship; students especially hated the **shah** for his repression of freedoms. Networks of conspirators formed, rallying around the figure of exiled **Ayatollah** Khomeini and using mosques as their meeting places. By 1978 there was extensive rioting, but the use of troops to quell the rioting simply enraged more Iranians. Troops began to desert. Always disdainful of democracy and mass participation in politics, the shah had relied on his dreaded SAVAK secret police, but even they could no longer contain the revolution. In January 1979, the shah left and Khomeini returned to Iran.

Before he left, the shah named a moderate revolutionary, Bakhtiar, to head the government. But the very fact of being chosen by the shah ruined Bakhtiar, and the newly returned Ayatollah, who instantly became the de facto power in Iran, replaced him with Bazargan, another moderate, but one never connected with the shah. Bazargan's government didn't count for much, though, because real power resided with Khomeini's Revolutionary Council. In November 1979, radical Islamic students, angered over the shah's admission into the United States, seized the U.S. Embassy and began the famous "hostage crisis" that lasted over a year. Bazargan, realizing he was powerless, resigned.

The Iranian Muslim extremists, totally devoted to Khomeini, took over and a bloodbath ensued. Firing squads worked overtime to eliminate suspected "bad" people, including fellow revolutionaries who had deviated. Tens of thousands of young Iranians, promised instant admission to heaven, threw their lives away in repelling Iraqi invaders. Strict Islamic standards of morality were enforced—no alcohol or drugs, veils for women, and suppression of non-Islamic religions. After the elderly Khomeini died in 1989, the Iranian revolution gradually calmed and stabilized. There was not one single event to mark a Thermidor, but in 1997 a relative liberal, Mohammed Khatami, won the presidency in a landslide with promises of greater freedom and economic improvement. Still constrained by militant fundamentalists, he made cautious noises about improving ties with the United States, something most Iranians now want. It was almost as if thousands of Iranians had read and acted on Brinton.

needed no demagogues of the Robespierre stripe because there was no rabble to arouse. The French Revolution, deeply involved in correcting social injustice, became a bloody mess that ended in dictatorship. In Arendt's terms, it wasn't a really successful revolution because it didn't end with the constituting of liberty, as the American Revolution did.

In France, the French Revolution is still controversial more than two centuries after it occurred. Few celebrate it uncritically, and many French conservatives hate it. Most French people are proud of its original idealistic impulses—liberty, equality, fraternity—but many admit that it went wrong, that it turned to bloodshed and dictatorship. The big question here is whether this was an accident—the Revolution fell into the hands of extremists and fanatics—or whether there was something built into the revolutionary process that made breakdown inevitable. Most serious scholars now argue for the inevitability thesis.

In Russia, this question is asked about the 1917 Bolshevik Revolution. Lenin, an intelligent and sophisticated man, died in 1924. Had he lived, would communism have taken a more humane and less brutal path? Stalin, in the view of some diehard socialists, was the culprit who betrayed the revolution by turning it into his personal dictatorship. More recent scholarship has shown that Lenin was totally ruthless and willing to exterminate all opposition; there was nothing moderate or humane about him. Most Russians are now willing to admit that Lenin was wrong from the start.

The Waning of Revolution

Since World War II, the globe has experienced a tide of revolutions, but now the tide is waning. Revolution, popular in the 1960s, developed a bad reputation in the 1970s. By the 1980s, many radical countries were trying to back out of their revolutionary systems. There were no positive examples of a revolution that had worked out well. The Soviet Union and China, earlier the model for many revolutionaries, admitted they were in economic difficulty and tried to change to a more open, market system. The Communist lands of Eastern Europe simply walked away from communism. Then communism collapsed in the Soviet Union itself. In Africa, the revolutionary Communist lands of Angola, Mozambique, and Ethiopia liberalized their systems and begged for aid from the capitalist West.

The worst example of revolutionary horror was Cambodia. In the late 1970s, the Khmer Rouge (Red Cambodia) murdered an estimated 1.7 million of their fellow citizens. The nonfiction movie about this bloodbath, *The Killing Fields*, shocked the world. Vietnam, united by the Communists in 1975 after its fierce war with the United States, turned itself into one of the poorest countries in the world. Tens of thousands of Vietnamese "boat people" risked the open sea and Thai pirates to leave their starving land. Sadly, few countries wanted them. In 1995, Vietnam and the United States established diplomatic relations, and the Vietnamese economy turned to the world market. In Cuba, Fidel Castro continues to proclaim his regime revolutionary, but most Cubans have long since tired of the shortages and restrictions. In Nicaragua, a free election in 1990 voted out the revolutionary Sandinistas who still sought a socialist system and replaced them with a democratic coalition.

There are few major revolutionary movements struggling to overthrow regimes they alleged kept their lands in poverty and injustice. In Peru, the *Sendero Luminso* and *Tupac Amaru*, made up of radical students, wage guerrilla warfare and terrorism. They follow the revolutionary teachings of Mao Zedong that had been abandoned in China. In the Philippines, the Communist-led New Peoples Army, growing out of the terrible poverty of a society dominated by rich plantation owners, controls considerable areas of the countryside and ambushes army patrols. These movements are motivated by great passion and a burning sense of injustice.

Notice the difference between countries where revolution has triumphed and where it is still being fought. The former is characterized by disillusionment and bitterness; many people would like to get rid of the revolutionary regime. The latter movements are still idealistic and convinced they will bring a better social system. Revolutions are based on the belief that by seizing state power, a truly committed regime can redo society, making it just, fair, and prosperous. This feeling grows in societies that are unjust and miserable. But

"Albanians are revolutionary heroes" is the message of this mural facing Tirana's main square. The mural tries to foster the feeling that Albanian history is a steady march to communism. (Michael Roskin)

after seizing power, the revolutionary regime discovers it's a lot harder to make an economy work than they thought. For decades they blame capitalist holdouts and imperialist saboteurs. To control these alleged plotters, they give themselves draconian police powers to virtually stamp out private industry and criticism.

But things don't get better; they get worse. Farmers won't plant unless they get a decent price for their crops. Workers won't work without something to buy. Reluctant to admit they are mistaken after having killed so many people, the revolutionary regime locks itself into power through police controls. After some time of hardship and poor growth, a new generation may come to power and admit that the system needs to loosen up. Embarrassment may be a factor here. Comparing themselves with capitalist neighbors, the revolutionary country sees itself falling behind. The Chinese could note with regret that on China's rim—in Singapore, Hong Kong, and Taiwan—Chinese were prosperous, but not in China. Under Deng Xiaoping, China turned (incompletely) to capitalist industry and foreign investment. The great revolution had failed.

It takes large-scale revolutionary experiences to demonstrate that revolutions end badly. The revolutionary promise is golden; the revolutionary results are mud. If you don't see it, you don't believe it. With several revolutionary experiences to ponder, many would-be revolutionaries turned away from revolution. This helps explain why the 1980s was a conservative decade: It could look back and survey the results of the 1960s. By the 1990s, hardly anyone wanted a revolution.

The crux of revolutionary thinking is the feeling that it is possible to remake society. Without that, few would bother to make revolutions. With the discovery that remaking society leads to terrible difficulties and poor results, the revolutionary dream dies. Does this mean that we will not see another major wave of revolutions? Not necessarily. There is plenty of injustice in the world, and this brings rage. Rage, as Hannah Arendt pointed out, leads to revolution.

What can be done to head off revolutions? The answer is simple but difficult to carry out: reforms to end the injustices that revolutions feed on. Land reform in Peru and the Philippines and elected parliaments in Persian Gulf lands could dampen or even end revolutionary movements in these countries. But landowners are not about to give up their holdings, and they are politically powerful. The rulers around the Persian Gulf fear the loss of their wealth and power if they democratize. In practice, reforms are hard to apply because there is strong resistance from the conservative class in power that has much to lose.

In South Vietnam, for example, the United States repeatedly urged the Saigon regime to carry out sweeping land reform to win the peasants away from the Communist guerrillas. But landowners, many of whom collected exorbitant rents from tenant farmers, blocked land-reform bills. If they had given up their land, they might have saved their country; instead, they lost both. The message is to institute reforms before revolutionary feeling is implanted, to head off the problem before it becomes dangerous.

Case Studies   ANTI-COMMUNIST REVOLUTIONS

One of the more interesting phenomena of our day has been the revolution *against* communism. Communist regimes long claimed for themselves the title "revolutionary" and denounced as "reactionary" anyone against them. But if, as we argued, revolution means a sweeping system change, especially the ouster of the ruling elite, people who overthrow Communist regimes are also revolutionaries.

The impulse to revolution in Communist systems is the same as in other systems: injustice and poverty. Promised a socialist utopia for generations, workers tired of the failure to deliver. Actually, Soviets generally enjoyed rising living standards, but their expectations, fanned by the party propaganda line, rose faster. A really explosive element was jealousy. Soviets were aware that the privileged party elite enjoyed special apartments, food shops, medical care, and vacation cottages. They were also aware that much of the consumer economy ran on the basis of corruption. Desirable products never made it to the store shelf; they were sold through the back door for big profits. The same feelings that smoldered in non-Communist countries smoldered in Communist countries.

As in earlier revolutions, the most dangerous time in the life of a Communist regime was when it tried to reform itself. Reform in Communist countries was as difficult as in non-Communist countries, for Communist elites also had a lot to lose in terms of power and privilege. In their system, the Communist party elite became the conservatives who didn't want things to change and were in a position to block reforms. When things got so bad that reform had to come, it was too late. Things were bad in the Soviet Union under Brezhnev, but mass unrest didn't burst out until Gorbachev instituted major reforms. By admitting that things were wrong, he gave the green light to restive workers and nationalities to demand more than any had dared mention a few years earlier. By asking for support and patience, Gorbachev also showed he was running scared, a further incitement to revolution. By letting in more Western media, he showed the Soviets how well Americans and West Europeans lived. Soon the pressure for massive change became explosive.

Halfway reform does not suffice and often makes things worse. The Communist regimes of Eastern Europe tried to calm their angry people by promising reform and bringing in fresh, new leadership. But most East European citizens were not fooled; they recognized that the reforms would basically leave defective systems intact and that the new leaders were simply party bigshots intent on keeping the Communist party in power. In Czechoslovakia in 1989, for example, the rapidly growing Civic Forum movement hooted down a new cabinet that the frightened Communist regime presented. The "new" cabinet, still dominated by Communists, looked pretty much like the old one. After massive street protest, Civic Forum obtained a cabinet of non-Communists, some of whom had been in jail only two weeks earlier. This was what Czech President Vaclav Havel called the "velvet revolution." When an unpopular regime begins by offering "reforms," it may end by putting itself out of business.

Faced with this prospect, some regimes attempt to crush mass demands with military force. An example is the bloody 1989 crackdown in China. Hundreds of protesting students were gunned down in Beijing's Tiananmen Square because an elderly party elite feared what they called a "counterrevolutionary revolt." Deng Xiaoping had attempted halfway

---

ANTI-COMMUNIST REVOLUTIONS (CONTINUED)

reform only to find that it would not stay halfway. Halfway reform of a corrupt dictatorship is impossible because as soon as you let people criticize it, they demand to replace it. Give them a free-speech inch and they want a democratic mile. That, of course, would mean ouster of the Communist elite, which then fights tenaciously for its power and privileges. But by digging in their heels and refusing to institute major reform, the party elite just builds up a head of steam for a later and greater explosion. They can crush political opponents, but they can't produce the economic growth necessary to feed and house their people, who just get angrier. Ironically, Communist countries in the late twentieth century indeed led the way to revolution.

The secret police headquarters in Moscow was, until 1991, presided over by this statue of the KGB's founder, Felix Dzerdzinsky. Three months after this photo was taken, a mob tore down the statue. (Michael Roskin)

Key Terms

Ayatollah (p. 350)

coup (p. 339)

intellectual (p. 345)

praetorianism (p. 342)

relative deprivation (p. 344)

revolution (p. 345)

shah (p. 350)

system breakdown (p. 339)

Thermidor (p. 347)

utopia (p. 346)

Key Websites

National Security Institute's website provides links regarding terrorism, including legislation to combat terrorism, facts on terrorism attacks, and commentary on how to prevent terrorism.
http://nsi.org/Terrorism.html

The History Place website has a complete, concise history of the American Revolution, links to the Declaration of Independence and the Constitution, and biographies of key figures, including George Washington, John Paul Jones, and Marquis de Lafayette.
http://www.historyplace.com/unitedstates/revolution/index.html

This site details South Africa's history, with a detailed section on its apartheid period.
http://www.southafrica.net/government/history/default.html

This website examines the concept of genocide and its origins.
http://web.inter.nl.net/users/Paul.Treanor/genocide.html

Further Reference

Andrain, Charles F., and David E. Apter. *Political Protest and Social Change: Analyzing Politics*. New York: New York University, 1995.

Bell-Fialkoff, Andrew. *Ethnic Cleansing*. New York: St. Martin's, 1996.

Colburn, Forrest D. *The Vogue of Revolution in Poor Countries*. Princeton, NJ: Princeton University Press, 1994.

Defonzo, James. *Revolutions and Revolutionary Movements*. Boulder, CO: Westview Press, 1991.

Diamond, Larry, and Marc F. Plattner, eds. *Nationalism, Ethnic Conflict, and Democracy*. Baltimore, MD: Johns Hopkins University Press, 1994.

Greene, Thomas H. *Comparative Revolutionary Movements: Search for Theory and Justice*, 3rd ed. Englewood Cliffs, NJ: Prentice Hall, 1990.

Huntington, Samuel P. *Political Order in Changing Societies*. New Haven, CT: Yale University Press, 1968.

Linz, Juan J., and Alfred Stepan, eds. *The Breakdown of Democratic Regimes*. Baltimore, MD: Johns Hopkins University Press, 1978.

Marks, Thomas A. *Maoist Insurgency Since Vietnam*. Portland, OR: F. Cass, 1996.

Sederberg, Peter C. *Fires Within: Political Violence and Revolutionary Change*. New York: HarperCollins, 1994.

Snow, Donald M. *Distant Thunder: Patterns of Conflict in the Developing World*, 2nd ed. Armonk, NY: M. E. Sharpe, 1997.

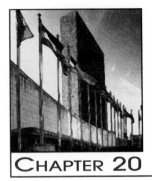

CHAPTER 20

International Relations

International politics is quite a bit different from the domestic politics we have been studying, because there is no sovereign power over nations to get them to obey laws and preserve peace. Compared to **domestic politics**, international politics is wilder and more complex. Sovereignty, as considered in Chapter 1, means being boss on your own turf, the last legal word within a country. The concept grew up in the sixteenth century, when absolutist monarchs were strengthening their positions and sought legal justification for it. Sovereignty is the dominant force within a country. Criminals, rebels, and breakaway elements are, in theory, controlled or crushed by the sovereign, who now, of course, is no longer a king or queen but the national government. Sovereignty also means that foreign powers have no business intruding into your country's affairs; their reach—again in theory—stops at your borders.

So much for theory. In practice, nothing is so clear-cut. Just because a nation is legally sovereign does not necessarily mean it really controls its own turf. Witness poor Bosnia in the 1990s: its territory occupied by outside forces (Serbian, Croatian, and international peacekeepers), its weak government propped up by friendly forces (the United States, Britain, France, Italy, and the United Nations), barely able to stop the violence among its ethnic armies. It was a real stretch to call Bosnia "sovereign." The opposite of Bosnia's fragmentation was Western

QUESTIONS TO CONSIDER

1. How do domestic and international politics differ?
2. Why does "power" loom so large in international relations?
3. What are the several types of national interest?
4. Which theory of war do you think is most satisfactory?
5. Are democracy and peace related? How?
6. Is there any effective way to prevent war?
7. What was the Cold War? Why did it begin and end?
8. What is the crux of deterrence? Does it work?
9. What is Paul Kennedy's theory of "imperial over-stretch"?
10. Which supranational organizations do the most good?

KEY TERMS

international politics
Interactions among states.

domestic politics
Interactions within states.

Europe's coming together in what earlier had been known as the Common Market but is now the European Union (EU). Its members had agreed to give up some of their sovereignty in order to form an economic and political union, which, if fully implemented, will mean a transfer of sovereignty from individual member to the EU headquarters in Brussels. Sovereignty is not a simple yes or no but a question of degree.

Further, the idea that sovereignty precludes outside intervention doesn't hold up. Small, poor countries are routinely dominated and influenced by large, rich countries. Afghanistan could scarcely be said to be sovereign under Soviet occupation, nor could the small countries of Central America under the watchful eye of the United States. Some Canadians claim U.S. economic and cultural penetration is so great that they are losing some of their sovereignty. What meaning had sovereignty in Somalia?

Still, the term sovereignty has some utility. Where established, national sovereignty does indeed bring internal peace, and most countries can claim to have done this..By and large, countries still do what they want to do. When France resumed nuclear testing in the South Pacific in 1995, there was nothing Australia and New Zealand could do to stop it, although they protested strongly. That was sovereignty in action. When the United States urged the economic isolation of Iran, most of the world ignored the call and made trade and oil deals with Tehran. Congress passed laws threatening legal trouble for foreign firms that did business with Cuba and Libya, but other governments pointed out that the U.S. Congress cannot pass laws for other countries; they ignored the U.S. prohibitions and traded with whom they pleased. President Clinton, aware that "extraterritorial laws" merely irritate other countries, refrained from enforcing them. No president could do otherwise. Congress, in its efforts to please domestic constituencies, often neglects the sovereignty factor.

Within a sovereign entity there is—or at least there is supposed to be—law. If you have a grievance against someone, you don't take the law into your own hands. You take the person to court. In international relations, nearly the opposite applies: Taking the law into your own hands—by the threat or use of military force—is quite normal. Often there is no other recourse.

This important difference between domestic and international politics sometimes exasperates skilled practitioners of one when they enter the realm of the other. President Johnson was a master of domestic politics; whatever he wanted from Congress he got. But he couldn't make skinny little Ho Chi Minh back down, for Ho was boss on *his* own turf. What worked domestically for Johnson—deals, threats, persuasion—flopped internationally. Some suggest that it was Nixon's use of the "dirty tricks" of international politics in domestic politics that brought about the Watergate scandal and his resignation. Nixon was a clever statesman; he simultaneously improved ties with the Soviet Union and China. But his deviousness and penchant for secrecy served him ill in dealing with a delicate domestic problem. International politics is not just domestic politics on a grander scale.

Power and National Interest

Lacking the sovereignty that prevails in most domestic situations, international relations depend a lot on power. Hans Morgenthau held that **international power** is the basic element of international politics and that idealists ignore it at their peril. Without sufficient power, a country cannot survive, let alone prevail, in a tumultuous world. One should bear in mind that power is not the same as force. Force is the specific application of military might; power is a country's more general ability to get its way. Power includes military, economic, political, and psychological factors. Power is tricky to calculate. Whole departments of the CIA spend millions trying to figure out how much power various countries have. Some elements of power—such as a country's geography, natural resources, population, and economy—are tangible or calculable. Some of the most important factors, however—such as a country's military capability, the quality of its political system, and its psychological determination—cannot be learned until it is involved in a war. The war then provides—at a terrible price—the answer about which side had more power.

In this situation, countries generally pursue their **national interest**. This makes international politics inherently selfish; nations rarely behave like saints. Countries may practice generosity and altruism, but often with an eye to enhancing their international power and prestige. The world did little to staunch the horrible bloodletting in Rwanda and the Congo in the 1990s; close to a million were butchered, far more than in Bosnia. Rwanda was out of the way and had no strategic or economic value. Only France sent some peacekeeping forces, because France wishes to portray itself as the dominant and protecting power of Central Africa, where it has strong economic ties.

It's sometimes hard to anticipate how another country will define its national interest. They see things through different eyes. Hungary in the 1990s was very cooperative with the West and eager to join NATO. In 1994, however, when the United States and France proposed air strikes to curb Serbian artillery atrocities in Bosnia, Hungary stopped the U.S. use of its territory for observation flights. An American looking at this refusal is puzzled: "But don't they want to be on our team?" A Hungarian looking at the refusal says, "We'll have to live with the Serbs for centuries; that border is a vital, permanent interest for us. Some 400,000 ethnic Hungarians live under Serbian control in Voivodina as virtual hostages. The Americans offer no guarantees of protection, but they expect us to join them in an act of war. Sorry, not a good deal." (The flights were quickly restored as the crisis passed.)

The diplomat's work is in finding and developing complementary interests so that two or more countries can work together. (Better diplomatic spadework would have signaled in advance the difference between Hungarian and U.S. interests in 1994.) Often countries have some interests that are complementary and others that are conflicting, as when NATO members cooperate to block the

Soviet threat but clash over who will lead the alliance. The French-U.S. relationship can be described in this way. Where interests totally conflict, of course, there can be no cooperation. Here it is the diplomat's duty to say so and find ways to minimize the damage. Do not despair in this situation; national interests can shift, and today's adversary may be tomorrow's ally.

Defining the national interest in any given situation may be difficult. Intelligent, well-informed people may come up with totally opposite definitions of the national interest. Hawks in the 1960s, for example, claimed a Communist

---

Key Concepts — TYPES OF NATIONAL INTEREST

National interests may be divided into the following four types:

1. vital versus secondary
2. temporary versus permanent
3. specific versus general
4. complementary versus conflicting

A vital interest is one that potentially threatens the life of your nation, such as Soviet missiles in Cuba. When a country perceives a threat to its vital interests, it often goes to war. A secondary interest is usually more distant and less urgent. The United States, for example, has an interest in an open world oil supply, with no nation restricting or controlling it. Nations are more inclined to negotiate and compromise over their secondary interests, although military action may become necessary, as against Iraq in 1991.

When nations have some important goals in common, their interests are "complementary." Many nations saw their national interests as complementary during the Gulf War. Several Arab countries sided with the West. Complementary interests are what make alliances. When interests conflict, as in French trade deals with Iran, countries pull apart.

A temporary interest is one of fixed duration, as in U.S. support for Iraq during its 1980s war with Iran. U.S. diplomacy had trouble understanding that as soon as that war was over, their complementary interests receded. A permanent interest lasts over centuries, as in the U.S. interest in keeping hostile powers out of the Western hemisphere.

A specific interest focuses on a single problem, such as Japanese trade barriers to U.S. goods. A general interest might be universal respect for human rights.

Two countries, even allies, seldom have identical national interests. The best one can hope for is that their interests will be complementary. The United States and Albania, for instance, may have a common interest in opposing Serbian crushing of ethnic Albanians in Kosovo, but the U.S. interest is a general, temporary, and secondary one concerning human rights and regional stability. The Albanian interest is a specific, permanent, and possibly vital one of forming a Greater Albania that would include Kosovo and possibly parts of Macedonia. Our interests may run parallel for a time, but we must never mistake Albanian interests for U.S. interests.

victory in Southeast Asia would destabilize the United States' strategic, econom-ic, and political interests. Others claimed Vietnam was a distant swamp of no importance to us. In 1999, Americans quarreled over whether Kosovo was a U.S. national interest or a foolish attempt to stop people who were intent on fighting each other. How can you tell when a genuine national interest is at stake?

Feasibility is linked to national interest; power is the connecting link. An infea-sible strategy—where your power is insufficient to carry out your designs—is inherently a bad strategy. If the type of power is wrong for the setting (for exam-ple, helicopters and artillery to counter Vietnamese or Afghan nationalism; air power to stop a three-sided civil war), you are undertaking an infeasible strategy.

The Role of Elites

Nowhere are elites (see Chapter 5) more important than in international rela-tions. The foreign policy of a country is inherently an elite game, however much we may dislike it. In a democracy the masses may influence foreign policy—as angry Americans did over the Vietnam War—but only long after the basic deci-sions have been made, usually in secrecy. Some suggest that foreign-policy deci-sions, even in democratic nations, are made by not much more than a dozen peo-ple. Notice how even in the United States, presidents and a few advisors make foreign policy—including the Vietnam War—and then announce it to the American people and Congress, which usually goes along with the executive ini-tiative. Later, of course, the American people and Congress may get angry over the executive decision.

Many argue that foreign policy must be decided by a handful because things move too fast in the modern age to allow for extensive popular and even con-gressional debate. A delay of a few weeks can be fatal. Furthermore, few citizens understand or even care about distant threats and problems. How many Americans pay attention to Iraq's efforts to build weapons of mass destruction? Or the global impact of loans to Indonesia from the International Monetary Fund? What the experts often lack, on the other hand, is the common sense of average citizens, who may have pretty clear ideas whether their sons should fight and die far from our shores. Pundits sometimes call these two perspectives "inside the beltway" (that loops around Washington) and "outside the beltway" (the rest of America). Too often the former engages in discussions only with other "inside" people and ignores average Americans. If foreign pol-icy stayed attuned only to the interests of most Americans, however, it would tend to isolationism, so a certain amount of agenda-setting and leadership by the White House is required.

Conventional usage often neglects the fact of elite leadership in foreign policy, as when we say "the Iranians" or "the Russians" are up to such and such. Only a minute fraction of 1 percent of Iranians or

Key Concepts   WHY WAR?

Much has been written on why there is war. Most thinkers agree that war has many causes, not just one. Very broadly, though, theories on the cause of war are divided into two general camps, the micro and the macro—the little, close-up picture as opposed to the big, panoramic picture.

Micro Theories

Micro theories are rooted largely in biology and psychology. They might attempt to explain war as the result of genetic human aggressiveness. Millions of years of evolution have made people fighters—to obtain food, defend their families, and guard their territory. In this, humans are no different from many animals. Most anthropologists reject such biological determinism, arguing that primitive peoples exhibit a wide variety of behavior—some are aggressive and some aren't—that can be explained only by culture, learned behavior. Writers with a psychological orientation explore the personalities of leaders, what made them that way, and how they obtained their hold over the masses and brought them to war.

Biological and psychological theories offer some insights but fall far short of explaining wars. If humans are naturally aggressive, why aren't all nations constantly at war? How is it that countries can fight a long series of wars—the Russian-Turkish struggle around the Black Sea or the Arab-Israeli wars—under different leaders who surely must have been psychologically distinct? Biological and psychological approaches may offer insights into some of the *underlying* causes of war but not the immediate causes. There is a certain human aggressiveness, but under what circumstances does it come out? For this we turn to macro theories.

Macro Theories

Macro theories are rooted largely in history and political science. They concentrate chiefly on the power and ambitions of states. States, not individuals, are the key actors. Where they can, states expand, as in the Germans' medieval push to the east, the Americans' "manifest destiny," the growth of the British empire, and the Soviets' takeover of Eastern Europe and Afghanistan. Only countervailing power may stop the drive to expand. One country, fearing the growth of a neighbor, will strengthen its defenses or form alliances to offset the neighbor's power. Much international behavior can be explained by the aphorisms *Si vis pacem para bellum* ("If you want peace, prepare for war") and "The enemy of my enemy is my friend." Political leaders have an almost automatic feel for national interest and power and move to enhance them. Does the pursuit of power lead to war or peace? Again, there are two broad theories.

Balance of Power   The oldest and most commonly held theory is that peace results when several states, improving their national power and forming alliances, balance one another. Would-be expansionists are blocked. According to balance-of-power theorists, the great periods of relative peace—between the Peace of Westphalia in 1648 and the wars that grew out of the French Revolution (1792–1814), and again from 1815 to the start of World War I in 1914—have been times when the European powers balanced each other. When the balances broke down, there was war. Fighting in Bosnia calmed only after power there

WHY WAR? (CONTINUED)

roughly balanced. When the Serbs were ahead, they had no motive to settle; when they were on the defensive, they decided to stop the fighting. Many thinkers consider the Cold War a big and durable balance-of-power system that explains why there was relative peace—at least no World War III—for more than four decades.

Hierarchy of Power   Other analysts have rejected the balance-of-power theory. First, because calculations of power are so problematic, it is impossible to know when power balances. Second, the periods of peace, some writers note, occurred when power was out of balance, when states were ranked hierarchically in terms of power. Then every nation knew where it stood on sort of a ladder or relative power. It is in times of transition, when the power hierarchy is blurred, that countries are tempted to go to war. After a big war with a definitive outcome, there is peace because then relative power is clearly known. If this theory is correct, then trying to achieve an accurate balance of power is precisely the wrong thing to do; it will lead to war because the participating states will think they have a good chance to win.

Misperception

Weaving micro and macro approaches together, some thinkers have focused on "image" or "perception" as the key to war. Both psychological and power approaches have something to contribute, but they are incomplete. It's not the real situation (which is hard to know) but what leaders perceive it to be that makes them decide for war or peace. They often misperceive, seeing hostility and development of superior weaponry in another country, which sees itself as acting defensively and as just trying to catch up in weaponry. John F. Kennedy portrayed the Soviets as enjoying a "missile gap" over us; he greatly increased U.S. missile-manufacturing efforts. It turned out that the Soviets were actually behind us, and they perceived the American effort as a threat that they had to match. The misperceptions led to the 1962 Cuban missile crisis, the closest we came to World War III. India startled the world when it tested nuclear weapons in 1998, claiming it needed them to offset combined Chinese-Pakistani power. Pakistan, however, saw this as an aggressive move and countered it with nuclear tests of its own. Both sides were trapped in their own insecurities. As Henry Kissinger brilliantly put it, "Absolute security for one power means absolute insecurity for all others."

In misperception or image theory, the psychological and real worlds bounce against each other in the minds of political leaders. They think they are acting defensively, but their picture of the situation may be distorted. In our time, it is interesting to note, no country ever calls its actions anything but defensive. The Americans in Vietnam saw themselves as defending the free world; the Russians in Chechnya saw themselves as defending their country. In its own eyes, a nation is never aggressive. A country, under the guidance of its leaders, its ideology, and its mass media, may work itself into such a state of fear that even its most aggressive moves are rationalized as defensive. Under rabidly nationalistic leadership, most Germans and Japanese in World War II saw themselves as defending their countries against hostile powers. Serbian dictator Slobodan Milošević played the Serbian nationalist card and got most Serbs to believe they were surrounded by evil enemies. Once convinced that they are being attacked, normally peaceful people will commit all manner of atrocities.

Russians are involved in foreign policy, so it is wrong to impute volition or responsibility to all of them. Iranians, for example, are tremendously hospitable to visiting Americans; the anti-U.S. views of some Iranian leaders are not widely shared. As in the United States, most Iranians and Russians don't care or are powerless to influence decisions made at the top. A more precise usage, favored by diplomats, is to name the nation's capital, "Tehran" or "Moscow," as a shorthand way of saying the top decision-makers in those two lands. Sometimes, of course, the two coincide, as when India's 1998 nuclear tests were applauded by most Indians.

Keeping Peace

Whatever its causes, what can be done to prevent or at least limit war? Many proposals have been advanced; none has really worked.

World Government

The real culprit, many thinkers claim, is sovereignty itself. The solution is to have states give up at least some of their sovereignty—the ability to decide to go to war—to an international entity that would prevent war much as an individual

---

Key Concepts   DEMOCRACY AND PEACE

Many scholars claim that no two democracies have ever gone to war with each other. This may not be absolutely true—the U.S. Civil War and Peru-Equador border squabbles may be exceptions—but it is an overwhelming tendency. Can you name any other cases where two democracies have fought each other? Argentina against Britain over the Falklands in 1982? But Argentina was then a military dictatorship. India against Pakistan seems a likely candidate, but Pakistan is often under military-backed rule and not a stable democracy.

Why, logically, should there be this happy coincidence between democracy and peace? Recalling our discussion in Chapter 5, democracy renders leaders accountable to the citizenry at large. When leaders know they are accountable and may be voted out of office, they tend to be cautious and to follow Friedrich's famous "rule of anticipated reactions" (see p. 113). They think, "If I take the country to war, how will voters react? Hmm, I guess I better not."
When President Johnson ignored such caution in Vietnam—because he thought voters would hold it against him if the Communists won—he suffered a dramatic fall in his popularity and could not stand for a second term. Dictators have no such inhibitions and may be inclined to reckless misadventures, as when Brezhnev invaded Afghanistan in 1979 or Saddam Hussein invaded Kuwait in 1990. The cause of peace was served by the spread of democracy in the late twentieth century.

country keeps the peace within its borders. But what country would give up its sovereignty? Would the United States place its future in the hands of the other 184 members of the UN General Assembly who might vote to share its wealth with poor countries? Did Serbia heed a UN call to give Bosnia its independence? Without the teeth of sovereignty, the United Nations, or any organization like it, becomes a debating society, useful as a place for diplomatic contact but little more.

Collective Security

The United Nations' predecessor, the League of Nations, tried to implement an idea that had been around for some time: **collective security**. Members of the League (which did not include the United States) pledged to join immediately in economic and military action against any aggressor state. If Japan, for example, invaded China, every other power would break trade relations and send forces to defend China. Aggressors, faced with the forces of the rest of the world, would not practice aggression. It was a great idea on paper, but it didn't work in practice. When Japan took Manchuria from China in 1931, the League merely sent a commission to study the situation. Japan claimed the Chinese started it (a lie), and the other powers saw no point in getting involved in a distant conflict where none of their interests was involved. Aggression went unpunished because the League had no mechanism to make the other countries respond. The same happened when Italy invaded Ethiopia in 1935. Japan, Italy, and Germany withdrew from the League to practice aggression on a larger scale, and the League collapsed with World War II.

> ### KEY TERMS
>
> **collective security** An agreement among all nations to automatically counter an aggressor.
>
> **functionalism** Theory that cooperation in specialized areas will encourage overall cooperation among nations.

Functionalism

Another idea related to world organizations is to have countries cooperate first in specialized or **functional** areas so that they will see that they can accomplish more by cooperation than by conflict. Gradually they will work up to a stable peace as a result of being increasingly able to trust each other. Functional cooperation will produce a "spillover" effect. Dozens of UN-related agencies now promote international cooperation in disease control, food production, weather forecasting, civil aviation, and nuclear energy. Even hostile countries are sometimes able to sit together to solve a mutual problem in specialized areas. But there is no spillover; they remain hostile. Sometimes the functional organization becomes a scene of conflict, as when the Third Word group expelled Israel and South Africa from the UN Educational, Scientific, and Cultural Organization (UNESCO) and the United States quit UNESCO over alleged Soviet dominance. Even the seemingly generous offers of the UN-related International Monetary Fund (IMF) to bail out distressed economies generates controversy, as the recipient country often claims that economic reforms mandated by the IMF are interfering with its sovereignty. The functionalist approach has brought some help in world problems but has not touched the biggest problem, war.

Third-Party Assistance

One way to settle a dispute is to have **third party assistance**—a party not involved in the conflict mediates between the contending parties to try to find a middle ground. Third parties carry messages back and forth, clarify the issues, and suggest compromises, as the UN's Ralph Bunche did between Arabs and Israelis in 1949, President Carter did with Begin and Sadat at Camp David in 1978, and Richard Holbrooke did at Dayton over Bosnia in 1995. Third parties can help calm a tense situation and find compromise solutions, but the contenders have to *want* to find a solution. If not, third-party help is futile.

Diplomacy

KEY TERMS
third-party assistance A party not involved in a dispute helping to settle it.
peacekeeping Outside military forces stabilizing a cease-fire agreement.
UNPROFOR UN Protective Force; ineffective peacekeeping effort in Bosnia in the early 1990s.

The oldest approach to preserving peace is through diplomatic contact, with envoys sent from one head of state to another. A good diplomat knows all of the foregoing power factors and the interests of the countries involved and has some suggestions for reaching a compromise that leaves both parties at least partly satisfied. This is crucial: There must be a willingness to compromise. This is often very difficult, however, because countries often define their vital, non-negotiable interests grandly and are unwilling to cut them down to compromisable size. If successful, diplomats draw up treaties—contracts between nations—which must be ratified and, one hopes, observed. If one country feels a treaty harms it, there is nothing to stop it from opting out. Countries enter into and observe treaties because it suits them. Some observers say the United States and Soviet Union, both relative newcomers to the world of great-power politics, were unskilled at diplomacy, too unwilling to compromise. The climate of mistrust between them was one of the hallmarks of the Cold War.

Peacekeeping

Related to diplomacy is the idea of using third-party military forces to support a cease-fire or truce to end fighting. Such forces, wearing the blue berets of the UN, helped calm and stabilize truce lines between Israel and its Arab neighbors and between Greeks and Turks on Cyprus. Such forces cannot "enforce peace" by stopping a conflict that is still in progress. The only way to do that would be to take sides in the war, and that would be the opposite of **peacekeeping**. It was therefore inherently unrealistic to expect **UNPROFOR** (the UN Protective

Force) to separate and calm the warring parties in Bosnia. UNPROFOR, given an impossible mission, covered itself with shame. The **IFOR** (Implementation Force) that took over from UNPROFOR was different and successful, because it came after the three sides—Bosnia, Croatia, and Serbia—agreed to a U.S.-brokered peace in Dayton. IFOR was also equipped and instructed to fight and win if attacked; these robust **rules of engagement** no doubt dissuaded some rambunctious elements, something UNPROFOR was unable to do. Some propose the IFOR model for future peacekeeping, but it must be borne in mind that such actions work only if a peace agreement has been reached beforehand.

> ### KEY TERMS
>
> **IFOR** Implementation Force; effective, NATO-sponsored peacekeeping effort in Bosnia following the 1995 Dayton Accords.
>
> **rules of engagement** Specifies when peacekeeping forces can shoot back.
>
> **Cold War** Roughly 1946–1989; period of armed tension and mistrust between U.S. and Soviet camps.
>
> **Truman Doctrine** Truman's 1947 call to oppose expansion of communism.

The Cold War

Starting in 1946 or 1947, the **Cold War** was both a cause and a result of profound mistrust between the Soviet Union and the United States. Each perceived the other side as a hostile aggressor. The Cold War started shortly after and as a direct consequence of World War II. Stalin's Red Army had fought the Nazis back through Eastern Europe, and Stalin was not about to give up what his country had lost over 20 million lives for. Stalin turned Eastern Europe into a protective barrier for the Soviet Union by setting up obedient Communist governments in each land and stationing Soviet troops in Central Europe. This state of affairs lasted until the Berlin Wall fell in 1989, which many accept as marking the end of the Cold War, for by that point most of the East-West tension was gone. The collapse of the Soviet Union at the end of 1991 confirmed that the Cold War was over.

During the height of the Cold War the West, led by the United States, viewed Stalin's takeovers of Eastern Europe with great alarm. Stalin looked like another Hitler, a dictator bent on world conquest, and the United States took steps to stop it. In the spring of 1947, Washington came up with three connected policies—the Truman Doctrine, the Marshall Plan, and containment—that formed the basis of U.S. foreign policy for decades.

The Truman Doctrine

President Harry S Truman asked a joint session of Congress for military aid to prevent the Communist takeover of Greece and Turkey, then under Soviet pressure. The United States should come to the aid of "free peoples" anywhere in the world. This, the **Truman Doctrine**, was a repudiation of traditional American attitudes of isolationism and, some say, contained the seeds of a globalism that eventually wrecked itself in Vietnam.

The Marshall Plan

At Harvard's 1947 commencement, Secretary of State George C. Marshall proposed the **Marshall Plan**, a multibillion-dollar U.S. aid package to lift up wartorn Europe and prevent its takeover either by local Communists or by the Red Army. The aid started flowing in 1948 and put Western Europe back on its feet.

Containment

Also in 1947, a State Department official, George F. Kennan, was drafting an influential memo that was soon published in the journal *Foreign Affairs* under the byline "X" (to conceal his identity). Republished many times since, "The Sources of Soviet Conduct" spelled out the Kremlin's expansionistic tendencies and called for a "policy of firm and vigilant **containment**" of them. Wherever the Soviets tried to expand, we would stop them.

The Berlin Airlift (1948–1949), the formation of the North Atlantic Treaty Organization (1949), and the Korean War (1950–1953) deepened the Cold War and the U.S. containment policy. The two major U.S. parties competed over which of them could best stop communism. A "red scare," fostered by the accusations of Senator Joseph McCarthy (Republican, Wisconsin), persuaded most public figures to appear tough and hawkish; no one wished to be accused of being "soft on communism."

At the height of the Cold War, the world seemed divided into two camps, one led by Washington, the other by Moscow, with very little in between. The condition was called *bipolarity*, which we will explore further in the next chapter. Some see a bipolar system as essentially stable and comforting: You know where you stand. Others argue that it was a dangerous system, for it induced a "zero-sum" mentality (whatever I win, you lose), which pushed the superpowers into dangerous positions in the Third World. Every place on earth seemed to be strategic and worth fighting for. The United States, for example, intervened in Iran, Guatemala, Indonesia, Lebanon, the Congo, the Dominican Republic, and elsewhere on the suspicion that if we did not secure these areas, the Soviets would. What is called the "contingent necessity argument" was often heard: If we don't take it, someone else will. In this way, Cold War fears drove both superpowers to extreme and ill-advised interventions, the Americans in Vietnam and the Soviets in Afghanistan.

> ### KEY TERMS
>
> **Marshall Plan** U.S. aid to uplift wartorn Western Europe.
>
> **containment** Kennan's 1947 call to block expansion of Soviet power.
>
> **escalation** Tendency of conflicts to enlarge and intensify.

Deterrence

At no time did the superpowers—the only two countries with global warmaking powers, the United States and the Soviet Union—fight each other directly. Both were afraid of **escalation**, possibly leading to World War III. If U.S. and Soviet forces started even a little battle somewhere, say, over Berlin, it would probably grow, engaging conventional forces all over Europe. Then one or both sides would use small tactical nuclear weapons. The other side would strike back with bigger nuclear weapons, and soon the superpowers would be raining nuclear missiles on each other's homeland. The fear of such escalation is the basis for **deterrence**; both sides are so afraid of the results that they deter each other from starting a major war.

> ### KEY TERMS
>
> **deterrence** Preventing an attack by threatening great harm to the attacker.
>
> **crisis stability** Persistence of deterrence standoff under stress.
>
> **INF** Intermediate-range Nuclear Forces; 1987 U.S.-Soviet treaty that eliminated this class of weapons.

The crux of deterrence is not just having enough nuclear warheads and missiles to deliver them but also making sure that enough of them could survive a *first strike* by the other side. Then you can hit back in a *second strike*. If you have credible second-strike capability, the other superpower will not attack you, for it knows that it will be horribly mutilated in retaliation. Deterrence is based on both sides understanding that they will suffer mutual assured destruction.

Did deterrence work? Sure, say its proponents; there was no nuclear war. Skeptics wonder, though, what could have happened in times of great stress, when mistrust is especially high and fingers are very close to nuclear triggers. Supporters argue that the deterrence system had **crisis stability**, the ability to withstand even a major U.S.-Soviet confrontation. They point to the Cuban missile crisis of 1962 as a close call. We learned decades later that there were indeed Soviet nuclear warheads in Cuba and that local commanders would likely have used them if attacked. We also learned decades later that Kennedy never intended to attack Cuba; he knew it could easily escalate into World War III. The missile crisis had a sobering effect on both superpowers, which soon began arms control talks to slow down and control the arms race. Perhaps the high point of arms control was the 1987 Intermediate-range Nuclear Forces (**INF**) treaty by which the Soviets eliminated 1,835 missiles with 3,000 warheads and the United States 850 missiles with one warhead each. Triumphantly, President Reagan left office as a man of peace. The fall of the Berlin Wall in late 1989 and the breakup of the Soviet Union in late 1991 ended the Cold War.

Beyond Sovereignty?

The end of the Cold War and of the most violent century in history brought into question the basic point of international politics, sovereignty—namely, is sovereignty slipping? Increasingly, the world community is acting in ways that infringe on the internal workings of sovereign states. For some decades the International Monetary Fund has been able to tell countries that wanted loans to stop their inflationary economic policies. The recipients of such advice often fumed that the IMF was infringing on their sovereignty, but if they wanted the loan, they took the advice. With the end of the Cold War, now even former Communist countries are going along with this sort of infringement on their sovereignty.

After a broad, U.S.-led coalition booted Iraq out of Kuwait in 1991, UN inspectors combed through Iraq looking for the capacity to build **weapons of mass destruction**. The Baghdad dictatorship screamed that Iraq's sovereignty was being infringed upon. Indeed it was, and most of the world was glad of it. Should the international community stand back while a tyrant develops the power to annihilate neighboring countries? By the same token, should the civilized world stand by while Somali warlords and bandits steal from the starving? Should the rest of Europe act as if Balkan massacres were none of its concern?

Key Concepts · THE SOVIET UNION AND "OVERSTRETCH"

We now realize that Soviet President Mikhail Gorbachev was willing to relinquish Eastern Europe and give up nuclear warheads because the Soviet economy was in terrible shape. He had to call off the Cold War because he was broke. The socialist economic system was defective and every decade fell farther behind the West's, especially in the crucial high-tech sectors. Soviet defense spending ate perhaps a quarter of the economy. The Soviets' far-flung empire cost billions in subsidies for Eastern Europe, Cuba, Vietnam, and several African countries.

The Soviet Union was going through what Yale historian Paul Kennedy called **imperial overstretch**. The crux of Kennedy's argument is economic, especially relative economic growth. Strong powers are constantly tempted to expand. They have the money and work force, and other areas seem ripe for domination. Their empires expand until they overexpand; then they decay. Gradually their economic base weakens, and their empires grow increasingly expensive to maintain and defend. Other powers, whose economies have not been drained by imperial expenses, grow faster and become richer and more powerful.

Kennedy's theory accounts for the rise and fall the **Habsburg** and British empires. The Habsburg dynasty of the sixteenth century united Spain, the Netherlands, and Austria and had shiploads of gold and silver pouring in from the New World. The wars it fought were only partly wars of religion—Catholic versus Protestant, in which the Hapsburgs were the leading Catholic power. They were also a Habsburg attempt to dominate Europe. The Hapsburgs overstretched themselves and went into bankruptcy and decline. Spain especially was economically ruined and stayed backward for centuries.

Britain, the world's first industrial country, used its sea power to construct an incredible empire, with holdings on every continent. But Britain's economic growth did not keep up with its imperial expenses. By the late nineteenth century, several powers, including Germany and the United States, had become economically more powerful. The two world wars finished off the British Empire. The theory also explained Soviet collapse beautifully—a military empire that the decaying Soviet economy could no longer afford. Empire is a wasting asset.

The world seems to be changing, willing to move beyond sovereignty and toward some kind of order. The trouble is, no one knows what kind of order. President Bush used the term *new world order* in building a coalition against Iraq, but he dropped the expression just as debate on it was starting. What to

> ### KEY TERM
> **supranational**   A governing body above individual nations (such as the UN).

do in the face of the disorder unleashed by the dissolution of Soviet power? Paradoxically, the world was more orderly during the Cold War, because the two superpowers controlled and restrained their respective allies and spheres of influence.

Few wanted the United States to play world cop, but most understood that if there was to be leadership, only America could provide it. Could **supranational** (above-national) entities be getting ready to take on some of the security responsibilities previously associated with individual nations' right of self-defense? If so, which entities?

The United Nations

The United Nations comes quickly to mind, and indeed, the UN has been functioning far better after the Cold War than during it. But it still has problems. As permanent members of the Security Council, Russia and China have the power to veto anything they don't like. Russia, for example, was reluctant to do anything against Serbia, long regarded as a Slavic little brother. The UN has sent many peacekeepers to observe truces, as in the Middle East and Balkans, but these few and lightly armed forces from small countries were in no position to enforce peace. The bloodthirsty Khmer Rouge in Cambodia repeatedly kidnapped UN peacekeepers, knowing they would do nothing. Without enforcement powers and fragmented into blocs, the UN remained largely a "talking shop."

The North Atlantic Treaty Organization

NATO is arguably the best defensive alliance ever devised. Poland, the Czech Republic, and Hungary were happy to join NATO, as it assured their security. Since 1949 NATO coordinated Western Europe and North America to act as a single defender under unified command in the event of Soviet attack. But now its very reason for being has come into question. Why not use NATO for something else? But the North Atlantic Treaty is extremely specific—that an attack on one member in Europe or North America be treated as an attack on all—and it has no validity anywhere else, not in the Middle East, the Balkans, or Africa. Anywhere else is called "out of area." NATO members can, to be sure, cooperate out of area, but it's on a purely voluntary basis, as they did in Bosnia with IFOR. What worked in Bosnia may not work elsewhere. Accordingly, NATO would not be a reliable force for keeping peace. Another, much broader European entity, the OSCE, has been suggested for such a purpose.

Organization on Security and Cooperation in Europe

OSCE grew out of the 1975 Helsinki Final Act that guaranteed borders and human rights in Europe. It helped to stabilize and eventually end the Cold War. Afterward, all European states, including the republics of the former Soviet Union and Yugoslavia, joined the OSCE, bringing total membership to fifty-two. The OSCE, however, is weak; it has no enforcement provisions or NATO-style command structure. It could take on such functions, but all or most members would have to agree. The ideal blend, some observers think, would be to combine the command structure of NATO with the broad membership of OSCE. This would still, however, cover only Europe.

There is no security organization that seriously covers Europe, let alone the entire world. Should there be one, or should the civilized world put together a series of ad hoc arrangements as the spirit moves it? Either way, the United States will have to take a leading role if anything is to be done effectively. If we don't lead, no one else will.

Key Terms

Cold War (p. 367)

collective security (p. 365)

containment (p. 368)

crisis stability (p. 369)

deterrence (p. 369)

domestic politics (p. 357)

escalation (p. 368)

functionalism (p. 365)

Habsburg (p. 370)

IFOR (p. 367)

imperial overstretch (p. 370)

INF (p. 369)

international politics (p. 357)

international power (p. 359)

macro theories (p. 361)

Marshall Plan (p. 368)

micro theories (p. 361)

national interest (p. 359)

peacekeeping (p. 366)

rules of engagement (p. 367)

supranational (p. 371)

third-party assistance (p. 366)

Truman Doctrine (p. 367)

UNPROFOR (p. 366)

weapons of mass destruction (p. 370)

Key Websites

This is the official web page for the United Nations. There is a wealth of information here, including information on International treaties, humanitarian affairs, and UN documents.

http://www.un.org/

BosniaLINK is the official Department of Defense information system about U.S. military activities in Operation JOINT GUARD, the NATO peacekeeping mission in Bosnia.
http://www.dtic.mil/bosnia/

This site—The Internet and the Bomb: A Research Guide to Policy and Information about Nuclear Weapons—covers everything from U.S. policy on nuclear weapons to weapons systems to nuclear arms treaties to peaceful uses for nuclear energy.
http://www.nrdc.org/nrdcpro/nuguide/guinx.html

The U.S. State Department's web page describes the duties and policies of the U.S. State Department, details its structure, and has links to many related topics.
http://www.state.gov/

The American Foreign Policy Council's goal is to provide information for those who make or influence state policy and to assist leaders in the former USSR and other parts of the world in market economies.
http://www.afpc.org/

Further Reference

Blainey, Geoffrey. *The Causes of War*, 3rd ed. New York: Free Press, 1988.

Brown, Seyom. *International Relations in a Changing Global System: Toward a Theory of World Polity*. Boulder, CO: Westview Press, 1992.

Dougherty, James E., and Robert L. Pfaltzgraff, Jr. *Contending Theories of International Relations: A Comprehensive Survey*, 3rd ed. New York: HarperCollins, 1990.

Ehrenreich, Barbara. *Blood Rites: Origins and History of the Passions of War*. New York: Metropolitan Books, 1997.

Gabriel, Jürg Martin. *Worldviews and Theories of International Relations*. New York: St. Martin's, 1994.

Ikenberry, G. John, ed. *American Foreign Policy: Theoretical Essays*, 2nd ed. New York: HarperCollins, 1996.

Jervis, Robert. *Perception and Misperception in International Politics*. Princeton, NJ: Princeton University Press, 1976.

Kennedy, Paul. *The Rise and Fall of the Great Powers: Economic Change and Military Conflict from 1500 to 2000*. New York: Random House, 1987.

Kissinger, Henry. *Diplomacy*. New York: Simon & Schuster, 1994.

Lukacs, John. *The End of the Twentieth Century and the End of the Modern Age*. New York: Ticknor & Fields, 1993.

Morgenthau, Hans J. *Politics Among Nations*, 6th ed. New York: Knopf, 1985.

CHAPTER 21

The Global System

With the 1990s, the world has clearly moved beyond the Cold War bipolar system. Moscow gave up Eastern Europe and no longer poses any invasion threat to Western Europe. Russia itself is terribly weak. Western Europe moves closer to unity in the European Union (EU) and new euro currency. Across the Pacific, Japan has become the third largest economy in the world. (Second place: Germany.) Other Asian lands also enjoy great economic growth, somewhat tarnished by financial irregularities. The United States in the late 1990s strengthens its position as the world's largest economy, but massive trade deficits also make us the world's biggest debtor. The United States does not have the economic dominance it once had to call the tune and get compliance from allies in Europe and Asia.

Added together, observers agree that these changes produce a new **international system**, but they do not agree on what kind

QUESTIONS TO CONSIDER

1. Is the world too messy to constitute an international system?
2. How did balance of power work? Why did it stop working?
3. Was the Cold War bipolar system stable?
4. What kind of global system seems to be emerging?
5. What forces could bring globalization to an end?
6. What is Huntington's clash-of-civilizations theory?
7. Is there a U.S. consensus on our foreign policy?
8. Can a case be made for U.S. noninterventionism?

of system. Because of this, political leaders cannot devise a rational, coherent foreign policy for the United States. Phrases like "new world order" or "enlargement of democracy" do not resonate. The 1996 presidential election was conducted with scarcely a mention of world affairs or foreign policy. In the absence of a clear threat, most Americans simply do not care.

KEY TERM

international system The pattern in which countries interact.

Historical Systems

International systems have many components (countries or groups of countries) that interact with each other (by means of trade, alliances, hostilities, diplomacy, and so on). These systems change over time, with the rise of new

Key Concepts — INTERNATIONAL SYSTEMS AND MODELS

An international system is what's out there in the real world, whether we are able to perceive it correctly or not. A "model" is what we construct from data and our own imaginations in the hope that it matches the real-world system. The better the model's fit with the real world—and it will never be perfect—the more we will be able to anticipate the unfolding of events and possible dangers and disruptions. Notice that we are not looking for a "perfect" system, for we are not in charge of anything and are not able to "design" a system. Systems come into being from natural causes rooted in power, economics, and history. The best we can do is find a model that explains a good deal of the real working system. It will never explain everything.

A model is in effect a theory of how the world works. We construct them because without a model widely shared by our decision-makers that approximates the real world, we will engage in mistaken and possibly self-destructive moves. If our foreign-policy elite settles on one model of the international system and it is a good fit with reality, they will generally make wise decisions, which both aid the United States and contribute to world peace. If they embrace a model that doesn't fit reality, they may lead us into catastrophes. It would be like trying to play an unplayable game. Underlying assumptions—unfortunately, many of them unexamined—are the basis for a sound foreign policy. Or, as some thinkers have long understood: "There is nothing so practical as theory."

powers, technologies, economies, and alliances. Looking back over a more than a century, scholars believe there have been at least three international systems, each operating with different numbers of major players and with a different logic. The models constructed at the time to explicate these systems were never fully accurate; most understated their economic components.

The Nineteenth-Century Balance of Power System

Relative peace prevailed after the fall of Napoleon and agreement among the major European powers to not try for supremacy. Instead, they agreed to carve up the globe into great empires. This agreement decayed after the rise of two new major players, unified Germany in 1871 and rapidly modernizing Japan after the Meiji Restoration of 1868. **Balance of power** requires flexible, shifting alliances, but by the beginning of the twentieth century, Europe was arrayed into two rigid, hostile blocs. The game had changed. The start of World War I in 1914 did not necessarily prove that balance of power does not work; it showed that the balance had already broken down.

> ### KEY TERM
> **balance of power** A system in which major nations form and reform alliances to protect themselves.

The Interwar System

In World Wars I and II, the European powers destroyed themselves. Between the two wars, Britain and France, drained by the first conflict, refrained from trying to balance Germany's resurgent power under Hitler. The United States and Soviet Union stood aside. The Axis dictatorships—Germany, Italy, and Japan—sensing passivity, expanded to take what they could. The interwar system was inherently unstable, what E. H. Carr called "the twenty years' crisis." After World War II, the European powers were so weakened that they had to give up their empires, and they became dominated and in some cases occupied by two new giant empires, the United States and the Soviet Union.

The Bipolar Cold War System

After World War II, the world seemed to be generally divided between the two superpowers into what Stalin called *sotslager* and *kaplager*, the socialist camp and the capitalist camp, what we called Communism and the Free World. Most of the small- and medium-sized powers found themselves in alliance with a super-power, the United States or the Soviet Union, some voluntary, some coerced. Some neutrals aligned with neither camp. A "zero-sum" mentality dangerously exaggerated the importance of peripheral countries such as Cuba and Laos. The **bipolar** system contained the seeds of its own decay. The superpowers' arms

KEY TERM
bipolar   A system of two large, hostile blocs, each led by a superpower, as in the Cold War.

race grew increasingly expensive and drained both economically. Third World nationalism burned both the Americans (in Vietnam) and the Soviets (in Afghanistan). The Soviet bloc split; China moved out of it in the 1960s. Seeing his economy fall behind, Gorbachev attempted reform but merely succeeded in collapsing the regime. Central Europe turned westward as the Warsaw Pact dissolved.

The Cold War bipolar system could have blown up in nuclear war over a miscalculation, such as over Cuba in 1962. Said President Kennedy as that crisis eased: "We were lucky." Some argue that it was a rather stable system, "the long peace." Many Americans liked the Cold War system because they knew where they stood and what kind of foreign policy they had to pursue: to stop the spread of communism. Kennan's famous "containment" doctrine lasted four decades with only nuanced change.

What System Is Emerging?

Now things are not nearly so clear. Several new, emerging systems have been suggested, but so far none has established itself as the accepted paradigm. We therefore discuss the following as models, as imagined possibilities, rather than as real-world systems. We do not yet know which of these, if any, will fit the real world, so all are tentative. As one wag put it, "The model's not for marrying."

A Unipolar Model

Just as the Cold War was ending, the 1991 Persian Gulf War seemed to show the United States in command, able to rally and lead much of the world against aggression. President Bush called it a "new world order," and some envisaged an emerging **unipolar** system, with the United States as the single remaining superpower. The Clinton administration's short-lived "enlargement of democracy" supposed such a unipolar system. But unipolarity failed to emerge and probably could not. Two basic ingredients were lacking: The United States did not wish to lead, and the rest of the world did not wish to follow. The Gulf War happened under special circumstances—a threat to the flow of the world's main source of petroleum—that most countries agreed had to be dealt with. Other situations—Bosnia, the Middle East, Rwanda—brought much bickering and no agreement among the powers. Washington tried to lead in isolating Iran, but many of our allies said the policy was counterproductive and sought business ties with Iran. U.S. armed forces were cut, and Washington hung back from using them in any risky situations. The death of nineteen U.S. soldiers in Somalia, for example, persuaded Washington to withdraw all troops. Washington hesitated for years, while some 200,000 Bosnians were being killed, before sending peacekeeping forces. This was hardly the behavior of a "superpower."

A Hub-and-Spokes Model

A variation on the unipolar system is one in which the United States is the biggest economic and military power but not interested in dominating the world. Instead, numerous countries seek protection and stability by establishing strong U.S. ties. Europe, South Korea, Japan, Taiwan, the Persian Gulf monarchies, Turkey, and Israel want a U.S. security guarantee and U.S. forces in the area. Washington becomes the world hub and these security deals are the spokes.

A hub-and-spokes system has some weaknesses. The "spoke" relationships are essentially **bilateral** and not **multilateral**. Many look to Washington for help but are unwilling to shoulder burdens out of their own areas. Europe wants the Americans to defend Europe but are not interested in isolating Iraq and Iran or settling disputes in the China Seas. After a while, America gets tired of looking after all the spokes when the spokes won't help each other. And the big limiting factor is still America's interest in the outside world. Are the American people and Congress willing to pay money and send troops to preserve stability in far corners of the globe? For how long?

A Multipolar Model

Multipolar is the most commonly used word to describe the post-Cold War world, but the term is vague and covers several patterns; no one can be sure how

it will work or if it will last. Its main feature is the breakup of the old bipolar blocs into several blocs. Most prominent are the European Union and a Japanese-led Pacific Rim, both of which tend to ignore American leadership. The United States, Canada, and Mexico joined to form the North American Free Trade Agreement (NAFTA), which could spread southward and eventually link up with Mercosur, a free-trade area of the southern cone of South America to form a giant Free Trade Area of the Americas (FTAA). Other, small blocs dotted the globe. Instead of military confrontation, in a multipolar world economic growth becomes an obsession as countries and blocs strive to hold down unemployment, develop trade advantages, and move ahead technologically. Fear of falling behind motivates all the players.

The good news about such a system, if it indeed develops, is that the chances of major war are much reduced. The world relaxes as Russian and U.S. troops and nuclear weapons pull out of Europe. The zero-sum mentality and struggle for Third World clients recedes: What good are they? Cuba and Laos diminish in importance; no one wants to fight over them. The two powers reach important arms control agreements and reduce the warheads they have aimed at each other.

The bad news about such a system—already visible—is the murderous quality of the economic competition. Some players are more efficient than others. They develop huge trade and capital surpluses and start buying up the weaker players. There is a constant temptation to turn protectionist, to keep out foreign products and limit foreign business takeovers. Nasty accusations of trade protectionism already flow both ways across the Atlantic and the Pacific. What will happen cannot be foreseen. Much depends on the abilities of politicians to keep the blocs open to foreign trade. Should they close, trade wars could disrupt the global economy and plunge the world into a new Great Depression. We are sobered to remember that economic closure contributed to the coming of World War II.

A Stratified Model

A **stratified** model, which combines the features of unipolar and multipolar systems, may better fit the emerging reality. In a stratified system, the United States is still, relative to other nations, the premier military power, but it depends on other powers in undertaking important international moves. The United States has the best military technology, especially airlift capacity, to project its power around the world, but it can't do it alone. Other countries, with either moderate power-projection capabilities (Britain and France) or money (Japan and Saudi Arabia), form a "second tier" without which the United States cannot or will not intervene in world hot spots. When the top military power, the United States, can rally the second-tier powers, they can accomplish much, as in the 1991 Gulf War. But when Washington tried to rebuild the same alliance in 1997 to punish Iraq, only Britain offered support. The other former partners said no, and the enterprise evaporated.

A Zones-of-Chaos Model

Another stratified model has a top layer of rich, high-tech countries, Europe and North America. The second layer consists of middle-income industrializing lands, such as South Korea and Brazil. The third layer is a zone of chaos dominated by crime, warlords, and chronic instability. It is startling to realize that the world's biggest single industry is now crime, much of it connected to the flow of drugs from the poor countries to the rich countries.

The top-layer countries can devastate most military targets, but they can't control the chaos of the bottom-layer countries, whose guerrillas and drug cartels offer no good targets. Somalia, Colombia, and Bosnia are examples of chaos that the top-layer countries would like to avoid, but they may not be able to. Many of the world's natural resources—especially oil—are in these chaos zones, so the first layer is inevitably drawn into their difficulties. And the rich lands' appetite for illicit drugs means the bottom layer reaches into the top layer.

A Repolarized Model

In the late 1990s, Russia, China, and Iran showed occasional signs of drawing closer to each other, and some worried that they could form an anti-U.S. alliance. All three had grudges against the United States. Moscow resented America's triumph in the Cold War and worried that the eastward expansion of NATO was a threat to Russia's security. Beijing turned nationalistic and resentful of U.S. prodding on human rights. And Tehran still smoldered in anger over U.S. support for the shah and the U.S. presence in the Persian Gulf. Russian weapons, the Chinese economy, and Iranian oil could form a "triangle from hell," a sort of Cold War II with the world again polarized into two blocs.

This is not likely to ever happen, for there are more forces driving the three apart than pulling them together. All three know their economic future is in trade with the West, not with each other. Russians still have racist attitudes toward Asians and Muslims. Beijing is in no mood to bankroll a declining Russian economy. And Iran's future is in developing itself as the north-south transportation corridor by which the Central Asian states reach the sea. This makes Iran a competitor with Russia, which wants to continue to be Central Asia's outlet to the world. Still, a repolarized world is a possibility that we must guard against by making sure the three discontented countries don't get together. If an "angry bloc" came into being, it could have some of the features of both the interwar antibalance of power system and the Cold War bipolar system. It would consist of a bloc of angry countries, but at least some of the other major players (the United States) would not be passive but would try to "contain" them. A new containment system, however, would require a United States willing to intervene overseas plus the cooperation of other major players (West Europe, Japan). If they lapsed into passivity or tried to gain commercial advantage with the angry bloc, the system could slide into the dangerous situation of the interwar period, when passive major powers waited until too late to block expansionist powers.

A Globalized Model

Even before the Cold War ended, **globalization** began to emerge; many believe it is now a strong trend. (Some, such as economist Paul Krugman, argue that it is not, for a big majority of goods and services are still pro-

> **KEY TERM**
>
> **globalization** Free flow of commerce across borders, making the world one big market.

duced in the countries where they are consumed.) In a globalized system most countries become economic players in the world market, a largely capitalistic competition where goods, money, and ideas flow easily to wherever there are customers. The motto of a globalized system: Make money, not war. The few countries that don't want to play, such as Cuba and North Korea, live in isolation and poverty. After some years, most countries want to play. As such, the rules of a globalized system are self-enforcing: Play capitalism or stay poor.

Globalization can bring much good. With a largely free flow of trade, the world economy is growing as never before, especially in the Third World. Poor countries, some written off as basket cases, are stirring to life. More products, including previously expensive items, are produced in abundance and at low cost, enabling most of the world to enjoy VCRs and computers. Big, transnational corporations are proud to be able to design an item in one country, assemble it in a second country with components from a third, and market it in a fourth. For these corporations, borders are just nuisances that impede business efficiency. "Philosophers used to dream about one world," these corporations in effect say, "We are making it happen. We are more effective than the UN in promoting world peace and prosperity."

But there are many problems that may limit and even terminate a globalized system. The first problem: Is globalization a cause or a consequence of peace? Are the two intertwined? If so, what happens to one when the other is disrupted? Predictions that economic interdependency would prevent war (widely believed before World War I) have proved false. Prosperity does not necessarily bring peace. Indeed, newly affluent countries often demand respect, resources, and sometimes territory. As China got richer in the 1990s, for example, it defined its borders more grandly, reaching far out into the South and East China Seas, where there is undersea oil.

A second problem: Who are the key players in a globalized system: countries, blocs, or transnational corporations? Will the corporations become so rich and powerful that they challenge and override traditional nation-states and even trade blocs? A globalized system could be a paradise for giant corporations, who, if they don't like the costs, taxes, and restrictions of one place happily move to another continent. "Don't give us any grief," the corporations tell governments and workers, "or we'll move our plants to Indonesia." Countries and their workers naturally fight such behavior, and if they are successful will build barriers against the free flow of goods, capital, and jobs. Not everyone likes the transnational corporations.

A third problem: Economic growth is highly uneven, and some countries, especially landlocked countries with few resources, fall further behind. Eventually, they may turn into a "zone of chaos." In a globalized world, do the rich countries get richer at a faster rate, opening a bigger gap between the have and have-not countries? Or is the advantage to the poorer countries, which, thanks to their lower labor costs, may enjoy faster growth? Either way, there will be discontents.

A fourth problem: Will all play the globalization game by the rules? Most countries talk "privatization" and "free trade" but sometimes protect domestic industries and banks and erect trade barriers, undermining the basis of a globalized system. The financial meltdown of East Asia in 1997 revealed that many banks were unregulated and sometimes crooked; they extended loans recklessly until the bad debts were too big to hide. Their economies looked modern and global, but at their heart were informal networks of politicians, bankers, and businesspersons who did favors for each other. Some economists fear that someday such a meltdown might ripple out until it engulfs the world and triggers a new depression.

A fifth problem: As globalization spreads it tends to create resentments, especially in Muslim and other lands with proud and different cultural traditions, at the American and capitalist culture of a globalized system: "McWorld." These countries in effect say, "We'll become modern, but in our own way. Our culture is old and good, and we will not abandon it to imitate the Americans." The whole world does not wish to become America, as Huntington understands well with his "clash-of-civilizations" model. Taking all these problems together, we should not count on the stability or durability of a globalized system.

A Resource-Wars Model

If a globalized system falls apart, it may do so over the scramble for natural resources, especially petroleum. Already thinkers speak of "the geopolitics of oil." As East Asia, particularly China, industrializes its citizens produce and drive far more motor vehicles. Its peoples want to live like Americans, who consume energy prodigiously. Where will it come from? Will the world stay open to the free flow of natural resources, or will nations seek to gain advantage by exclusive deals with and control over the oil-producing areas? This is why questions of who owns the China Seas and who controls transportation corridors from the Persian Gulf and Central Asia loom larger and larger. We may have already had our first resource war, the 1991 Persian Gulf War.

A "Clash-of-Civilizations" Model

In 1993 Harvard political scientist Samuel Huntington advanced a controversial theory that the post-Cold War world would be dominated by clashes among eight

civilizations, each based heavily on religion: Western (with European and North American branches), Slavic/Orthodox, Islamic, Hindu, Sinic (China and its offshoots), Japanese (unique to one country), Latin American, and African. Some of these civilizations get along with each other tolerably well (Western and Latin American), but Islamic civilization clashes with most of its neighbors. "Islam has bloody borders," wrote Huntington. Countries home to two or more civilizations Huntington calls "cleft" countries. Bosnia, home to three civilizations (Western, Slavic/Orthodox, and Islamic) was thus a natural candidate for civil war. Countries with a Westernized elite but traditional masses, such as Mexico and Turkey, Huntington calls "torn" countries; they are torn between become Western and staying in their old civilization.

Clearly, much of the real world matches Huntington's civilizational theory. Religion is reviving as potent political force, as we see in Iran, India, and Israel. Many of the world's worst conflicts are where Islam meets other civilizations (Bosnia, Kosovo, Chechnya, Israel). The Catholic countries of Central Europe (Poland, Czech Republic, Hungary) adopt to markets and democracy much quicker than the Orthodox lands further east and south (such as Russia, Serbia, and Bulgaria). Likewise, the European Union considers the application of Central European countries to join, but not Turkey. Japan and China quarrel over minute islands.

But much does not fit. Huntington's theory cannot explain massive fighting within a given civilization (the horrifying massacres of Rwandans) or the cross-civilizational links based on security (Western-Islamic alliances) or commerce (Western oil interests in the Persian Gulf and Caspian areas). Most of Huntington's civilizations contain serious splits and hostilities. Europe and the United States, supposedly one civilization, are often at odds. Vietnam, whose history is essentially a long fight against China, still fears it. Islam may have bloody borders, but money sometimes heals the wounds. Cash trumps culture.

A Proliferation Model

What would happen if many countries had nuclear weapons? For some decades only five major powers openly had nukes—the United States, Britain, France, the Soviet Union, and China—and these were precisely the five permanent members of the UN Security Council. The 1968 Nuclear Nonproliferation Treaty (NPT) tried to block the further **proliferation** of nukes, but several countries quietly built nuclear weapons. The way they saw it, only nukes confer security and prestige. If you have nuclear weapons, you are treated with respect. With such reasoning, Israel, South Africa, India, and Pakistan quietly developed their own nuclear bombs. (South Africa dismantled its few warheads, figuring they did no good.) India denied it had nukes but in 1998 dramatically tested them, and most Indians were proud of it; now no one would push India around. This type of reasoning is infectious. Now Pakistan had to test its nuclear devices, which had long been under development. Iran and North Korea, isolated and fearful, worked to build their own nukes.

Where will it stop? The more countries that possess nuclear weapons, the greater the chance they will be used. Eventually, some argue, an unstable character like Saddam Hussein of Iraq will acquire nukes—and Iraq's secret nuclear program was more advanced than we thought—and use them in a fit of anger. Or will the deterrence stalemate discussed in Chapter 20 prevail, forcing even unstable dictators to behave cautiously? Paradoxically, there is a greater chance of nuclear war after the Cold War than during it. A world with ever-growing numbers nuclear powers, including those with active grudges, will be a dangerous world. It may limit the amount of international cooperation or leadership anyone can exercise. Some countries might hunker behind their nuclear barriers rather than seek peace and trade.

One can construct other international models that might, to greater or lesser degrees, match reality. Some could be combinations of the above; others could not. One valid model might combine multipolar economic blocs with the passivity of the interwar system. One could not combine a globalized system with a clash-of-civilizations system, as Huntington emphasizes. We must be also aware that one system can decay into another. A failed globalized system might fragment into hostile trade blocs, which in turn could engage in resource wars, which could turn nuclear in certain circumstances.

Historical systems are of some help in constructing a new model. Notice how many of the possible models have an **isolationism** component of only limited U.S. interest and leadership. This suggests something of the interwar system, in which the democracies, who should have led, stayed passive until almost too late. This may be undesirable, but we cannot simply talk Americans out of a post-Cold War tendency to minimize foreign affairs. Impolite student behavior over threatened U.S. military action in the Gulf helped reacquaint Team ABC (Albright, Berger, Cohen) with the domestic factor in foreign policy.

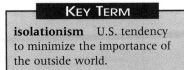

KEY TERM

isolationism   U.S. tendency to minimize the importance of the outside world.

Foreign Policy: Involved or Isolated?

Unfortunately, in the absence of an agreed-upon model that explains the workings of the real-world system, we are left floundering. Neither Republicans nor Democrats, legislators or executives have a clue. Some attempt to carry on as if the Cold War had never ended. Critics of NATO's eastward expansion accused its proponents of still acting under Cold War assumptions. The end of the Cold War reawoke an old question that had been asleep during the long period of tension

Key Concepts
THE IMPORTANCE OF ECONOMICS

One common thread among most of the models of an emerging international system is economics. In place of military might and alliances, economics now looms large in almost everyone's thinking, the biggest single factor in structuring the globe. The globalization model comes right out and says it, but most of the other models have substantial, even key, economic components (exception: Huntington). Economics, of course, was always important in the international system, but many refuse to recognize its impact until too late. The big flaw in the Cold War bipolar model was that it all but left out economics, the very factor that doomed the Soviet Union. Adherents of bipolarity went on and on about containment, nukes, and falling dominoes, and could not comprehend—much less predict—the collapse of Soviet power, largely because it had fallen behind economically (exception: Kennan). In the words of Harvard economist Jeffrey Sachs, "Markets won."

But will markets stay the winner? Free-market thinking is based on the profound insights of Adam Smith, discussed on pp. 94–95. Compared to controlled economies, markets are flexible, innovative, and ever-changing. But historically countries have shown a strong tendency to control, regulate, or own their industries. Overall, perhaps the most free-market economy is that of the United States, but it too has numerous government subsidies, tax breaks, and regulations. The European pattern has been to construct large and expensive welfare states whose controls and taxes work against starting new enterprises. The East Asian pattern has been for the state to guide and subsidize what are deemed key industries, aimed at rapid growth and dominance of certain markets. Many say Adam Smith's ideas on a free economy are great, but few totally practice them.

In recent years controlled economies got a jolt from British Prime Minister Margaret Thatcher's radical attack on the welfare state and her promotion of capitalism. "Thatcherism" spread to many countries, leading to cuts in public spending and freer markets. Some countries—in large part because domestic interest groups strongly objected—resisted the encroachments of free markets; they tended to hide behind **tariffs** or **quotas**. And a few countries simply prohibit certain foreign imports; Japan, for example, for decades allowed no imported rice. In every case, domestic interest groups—Brazilian machinery producers, French car makers, Japanese rice farmers—have sufficient clout to diminish the inflow of foreign goods.

Keeping world trade open by cutting tariff and other barriers is the task of the World Trade Organization (WTO), a branch of the United Nations with some powers of judicial settlement of disputes. Its predecessor before 1995, the General Agreement on Tariffs and Trade (GATT) did the same thing, but without enforcement powers. GATT and WTO have done much good. Tariffs are at an all-time low, and most goods flow unhindered over the globe, but now nontariff barriers increasingly irritate international economic relations, many of them concerning nonindustrial products. Several countries (including Canada and France) limit U.S. movies and television shows, arguing that they replace local productions and endanger cultural and national identities. Some countries (including Japan and China) keep out U.S. banks and insurance companies, arguing that such vital areas belong under national control. We argue that if television and banking are what we do best, our products should flow wherever there are customers. Keeping world trade open

THE IMPORTANCE OF ECONOMICS (CONTINUED)

is a neverending task, for new industries are always developing, and countries continually come up with excuses to keep out the new foreign products.

Should the WTO falter in its task and the world go back to self-enclosed, protected markets, the results would likely be catastrophic. We have only to remember the effects of the very high Hawley-Smoot tariff, which the United States introduced in 1930 to protect U.S. farmers and manufacturers from foreign competition as the Great Depression began. Our trading partners retaliated, locking out U.S. goods, and this made the Depression deeper and longer and worldwide. This U.S. tariff was thus one of the factors contributing to World War II. Much of the lifespan and impact of whatever global system is emerging depends on keeping world trade open.

with the Soviet Union: Should the United States defend its interests on the near or far side of the oceans? For most of America's history, it was assumed that we should generally stay on our own shores, that little overseas really concerned us. For the most part, Americans are natural-born isolationists. With Pearl Harbor in 1941, however, isolationism was rejected in favor of massive involvement in world affairs, first in winning World War II and then in waging the Cold War. Isolationism was not an option. Suddenly, as the Berlin Wall opened in 1989 and the Soviet Union dissolved in 1991, it became an option.

Under the budgetary squeeze discussed in Chapter 18, the size of U.S. armed forces shrank to half or less what it had been during the Cold War. There was no clear mission for them. Presidents Bush and Clinton both articulated idealistic new uses for U.S. forces overseas. Bush sent peacekeeping forces into chaotic Somalia, where the government had collapsed and people were starving as local warlords robbed everything. The mission, a partial success in getting food to the hungry, continued under Clinton, but a shootout in the streets of Mogadishu with the warriors of an ambitious strongman left eighteen U.S. soldiers dead. The body of an American helicopter pilot being dragged through the streets was shown on television. Americans quickly lost their idealism, and Clinton withdrew U.S. forces.

In 1993, with Haiti in the hands of a brutal dictatorship and desperate Haitians fleeing in rickety boats to Florida, President Clinton was faced with a decision on using U.S. forces. Much of the country, including the White House and Congress, hesitated. The image of guerrilla warfare in tropical jungles, with us since Vietnam, was not far under the surface. Senator Robert Dole (Republican of Kansas) was against U.S. military intervention. The arrogance of Haiti's dictator and arrival of thousands of Haitians in Florida finally forced Clinton to intervene. Although many

KEY TERMS

tariff   A tax on an import. (See p. 384.)

quota   A numerical limit on an import. (See p. 384.)

Americans were skeptical, the 1994 intervention went well. In almost textbook fashion, U.S. forces first disarmed and then deposed the dictatorship with scarcely a shot fired. Democracy has a tough time in a country as poor as Haiti, but at least we gave democracy a chance.

At this same time, massacres in Bosnia horrified American television viewers, but few wanted any direct U.S. intervention. Many swore it would turn into another Vietnam; besides, it was none of our business. Finally, in 1995 the U.S. mediated a peace agreement among the warring parties in Dayton, Ohio, and then contributed 20,000 U.S. troops to a 60,000-troop NATO peacekeeping force, IFOR (Implementation Force). Clinton made the decision even though U.S. public opinion was two to one against sending troops, and Congress nearly blocked the move. Again, the operation went well, and the United States showed it could and would take a leadership role in the world. The follow-on Stabilization Force (SFOR) was smaller but also effective. Bosnia demonstrated that at low cost and no battle casualties the United States could lead in stabilizing a dangerous part of the world. But Congress was still discontent and demanded a clear deadline for the withdrawal of all American forces.

The old question thus remained: Should the United States send forces overseas? Even when no direct U.S. national interests were involved? If the United States turns its back on horror and aggression overseas, the emerging international system will resemble the unstable and chaotic interwar system, a system in which the democracies held back from involvement until they were plunged into World War II. U.S. foreign policy tends to swing between extremes of interventionism and isolationism. Can we find a stable and moderate middle ground?

Many scholars think not; they have advanced views that U.S. foreign policy tends to swing like a pendulum between extremes of overinvolvement and underinvolvement. Stanley Hoffmann discerned "the two *tempi* of America's foreign relations," alternating "from phases of withdrawal (or, when complete withdrawal impossible, priority to domestic concerns) to phases of dynamic, almost messianic romping on the world stage." Hans Morgenthau saw U.S. policy moving "back and forth between extremes of indiscriminate isolationism and an equally indiscriminate internationalism or globalism." Getting more specific, historian Dexter Perkins divided American foreign relations in cycles of "relatively pacific feeling," followed by "rising bellicosity and war," followed by "postwar nationalism," and then back to "relatively pacific feeling." If Perkins is right, in which phase of the cycle are we now? Most thinkers would pick postwar nationalism, our sense of triumph after the Cold War.

Has the United States slid into a kind of isolationism? We have to be careful how we define that term, as it may connote rigidity and ignorance. We may prefer the term **noninterventionism**, an unwillingness to use U.S. forces overseas. It is more precise than trade, communications, tourism, or student semesters abroad. Post-Cold War, we have generally

---

KEY TERM

noninterventionism A policy of not sending troops abroad.

Classic Works | Cycles of U.S. Foreign Policy

A behaviorally inclined political scientist, Frank L. Klingberg, using such indicators as naval expenditures, annexations, armed expeditions, diplomatic pressures, and attention paid to foreign matters in presidential speeches and party platforms, discovered alternating phases of "introversion" (averaging twenty-one years) and "extroversion" (averaging twenty-seven years). Klingberg added: "If America's fourth phase of extroversion (which began around 1940) should last as long as the previous extrovert phases, it would not end into well into the 1960s." Writing about 1950 and making no reference to Vietnam, Klingberg virtually predicted the impact of the Vietnam War, for it was precisely in the late 1960s (1940 plus 27 years) that the U.S. public and Congress tired of the Vietnam War and intervention in general, an amazingly accurate prediction.

avoided using U.S. forces abroad or do so only with great caution, ever mindful of the risk of casualties. This suggests the United States at this time is not ready to assume a world leadership role. In the new world, the United States has been called "the reluctant sheriff." Should the United States intervene overseas to stop horrors that do not directly affect U.S. national interests? Do we have, in Stanley Hoffmann's words, "duties beyond borders"? The answers to such questions are the great challenge to your generation. You have the privilege of coming of age precisely as the world is undergoing system change. By your political participation and choices, you can help influence the pace and direction of change.

Key Terms

balance of power (p. 375)

bilateral (p. 377)

bipolar (p. 376)

civilization (p. 382)

globalization (p. 380)

international system (p. 374)

isolationism (p. 383)

multilateral (p. 377)

multipolar (p. 378)

noninterventionism (p. 386)

proliferation (p. 382)

quota (p. 385)

stratified (p. 378)

tariff (p. 385)

unipolar (p. 377)

Key Websites

This website covers World Government issues, and has many links to related sites and topics.
http://www.bath.ac.uk/htsearch/

The Fourth Freedom Forum site explores options for the nonviolent resolution of international conflict through education, research, and public advocacy.
http://www.fourthfreedom.org/

This is the official website of the European Union (EU).
http://europa.eu.int/index.htm

AntePodium (AtP) is an electronic journal dedicated to scholarly research on the politico-strategic, politico-economic, and politico-cultural dimensions of world affairs.
http://www.vuw.ac.nz/atp/frmain08.html

The World Trade Organization (WTO) is the legal and institutional foundation of the multilateral trading system. It provides the principal contractual obligations determining how governments frame and implement domestic trade legislation and regulations, and it is the platform on which trade relations among countries evolve through collective debate, negotiation, and adjudication.
http://www.wto.org/

The International Monetary Fund (IMF) is a cooperative institution of 182 countries that consult with one another to maintain a stable system of buying and selling their currencies so that payments in foreign money can take place smoothly and without delay between countries. The IMF also lends money to members having trouble meeting financial obligations to other members, but only on condition that they undertake economic reforms to eliminate these difficulties.
http://www.imf.org/

The Commission on Global Governance—with documents, speeches, articles, and general information on UN reform—is one of the major contributors to the debate on the future of cooperation in the post-Cold War era.
http://www.cgg.ch/

Further Reference

Barber, Benjamin R. *Jihad vs. McWorld*. New York: Random House, 1995.

Brzezinski, Zbigniew. *The Grand Chessboard: American Primacy and Its Geostrategic Imperatives*. New York: HarperCollins, 1997.

Callahan, David. *Unwinnable Wars: American Power and Ethnic Conflict*. New York: Hill & Wang, 1998.

Clemens, Walter C., Jr. *Dynamics of International Relations: Conflict and Mutual Gain in an Age of Global Interdependence*. Lanham, MD: Rowman & Littlefield, 1998.

Cyr, Arthur I. *After the Cold War: American Foreign Policy, Europe, and Asia*. New York: New York University, 1997.

Greider, William. *One World, Ready or Not*. New York: Simon & Schuster, 1997.

Haass, Richard N. *The Reluctant Sheriff: The United States after the Cold War*. New York: Council on Foreign Relations, 1997.

Holbrooke, Richard. *To End a War: From Sarajevo to Dayton—and Beyond*. New York: Random House, 1998.

Huntington, Samuel P. *The Clash of Civilizations and the Remaking of World Order*. New York: Simon & Schuster, 1996.

Nordlinger, Eric A. *Isolationism Reconfigured: American Foreign Policy for a New Century*. Princeton, NJ: Princeton University Press, 1996.

Schaeffer, Robert K. *Understanding Globalization: The Social Consequences of Political, Economic, and Environmental Change*. Lanham, MD: Rowman & Littlefield, 1997.

Singer, Max, and Aaron Wildavsky. *The Real World Order: Zones of Peace/Zones of Turmoil*, rev. ed. Chatham, NJ: Chatham House, 1996.

Index